I Wouldn't Ever Change a Thing ∽ Cindy's Lament

Picture Tells a Story ∽ Mag[...]olin

You Wear It Well ∽ Farew[...]ixie

the Name of Rock and Roll ∽ Stone Cold Sober ∽

Fool for You ∽ The Killing of Georgie (Part I and II)

My Heart (The Final Acclaim) ∽ Born Loose ∽ You

y? ∽ Dirty Weekend ∽ Ain't Love a Bitch ∽ The

tive Female Wanted ∽ Blondes (Have More Fun) ∽

Passion ∽ Foolish Behaviour ∽ So Soon We Change

My Girl ∽ She Won't Dance with Me ∽ Somebody

rt Me) ∽ Tora, Tora, Tora (Out with the Boys) ∽

Give Up on a Dream ∽ Dancin' Alone ∽ Baby Jane

Am I Gonna Do (I'm So in Love with You) ∽ Ghetto

Infatuation ∽ Bad for You ∽ Heart Is on the Line

Heartache ∽ A Night Like This ∽ Who's Gonna

Vay ∽ Every Beat of My Heart ∽ Ten Days of Rain

Forever Young ∽ Dynamite ∽ Crazy About Her

∽ When a Man's in Love ∽ Go Out Dancing ∽

uck ∽ Muddy, Sam and Otis ∽ Delicious ∽ When

stal Boys ∽ Tonight I'm Yours ∽ Little Queenie ∽

∽ Three Button Hand Me Down ∽ Bad 'n' Ruin

Judy's Farm ∽ Love Lives Here ∽ That's All You

Banners ∽ My Fault ∽ If I'm on the Late Side ∽

th (Water Down the Drain) ∽ The Hangman's Knee

ROD | THE AUTOBIOGRAPHY

ROD | THE AUTOBIOGRAPHY

CROWN
ARCHETYPE
NEW YORK

ROD

STEWART

Copyright © 2012 by Rod Stewart

Published in the United States by Crown Archetype,
an imprint of the Crown Publishing Group,
a division of Random House, Inc., New York.
www.crownpublishing.com

Crown Archetype with colophon is a trademark of
Random House, Inc.

Library of Congress Cataloging-in-Publication Data
is available upon request.

ISBN   978-0-307-98730-3
eISBN 978-0-307-98731-0

Printed in the United States of America

Book design by Barbara Sturman
Photography inserts designed by Silver Square Studio; photography credits
    appear on page 381
Jacket design by Michael Nagin
Jacket photographs: (front, spine) Penny Lancaster; (back) courtesy of the
    author except Rod and Elton John: Richard Young/REXUSA;
    Rod in red jacket: WireImage

10 9 8 7 6 5 4 3 2 1

First Edition

ROD | THE AUTOBIOGRAPHY

INTRODUCTION

In which the high-flying hero of our story gets goosed.

We call it "doing a runner," and it's the best way on earth to beat the traffic after a show. At the end of the last encore, drenched with sweat, I make my final bow to the whooping, applauding crowd, then jog from the stage—and keep on jogging, into the wings, where someone drapes a towel around me as I pass. In the hall, the lights stay down and the crowd continues to call for a third encore. But I'm off down the fluorescent-lit backstage corridors, where the air is suddenly cool after the heat of the stage, and out through the service doors at the back of the arena, into a waiting car, the noise of the clapping and stamping receding behind me, until the clunk of the limo door seals it out completely and the car sweeps me away.

Away, on this one night in particular, in July 1995, to an airstrip near Gothenburg, and a waiting private plane. A change of clothes is ready for me in the limo and I wriggle into them as we drive. Behind me, 30,000 hollering Swedish fans. Ahead of me, a short flight to London, in the company of a few members of my team who were also primed to "do a runner" at the show's end. The *Spanner in the Works* tour kicked off in June and is scheduled to run until May the following year, but there is a window in the schedule and I'm heading home.

And this is always the moment, with my feet outstretched as the plane picks up speed and lifts off the runway, when I finally relax, allow the adrenaline of the previous two hours to settle, enjoy the prospect of a night in my own bed, and anticipate the meal that the cabin crew will soon prepare, the glass of cold white wine that will go with it, and the satisfaction at the end of a day's work.

Except that this time . . .

Thump!

"What the hell was that?"

We are hardly into our ascent when there is an almighty wallop on the left-hand side.

"Was that the wing?"

The plane banks sharply, then gradually levels.

"What's happening?"

Startled rigid in my seat, I look around the cabin at the faces of the people with me, seeking comfort. Next to me, my great mate Alan Sewell—solid, dependable Big Al, a secondhand car dealer by trade and a gentleman of ample proportions, often mistaken for a bodyguard at my side—has turned white and is about to begin shaking like jelly.

Opposite, Annie Challis, part of my manager's team, gives me a reassuring look and says, "I'm certain it's nothing, darling." But that reassuring look seems to be costing her some effort, which kind of removes the reassurance from it.

Meanwhile, near Annie sits my beloved and all-knowing manager,

Arnold Stiefel, engrossed in the latest issue of *Architectural Digest*. As he continues to turn the pages, Arnold alone seems unperturbed, although I notice he is sniffing the air rather quizzically. Seconds later he blithely declares, "It smells just like Thanksgiving."

It's true. A strangely wholesome smell of roasting fowl has begun to pervade the cabin. Odd time to start heating up my meal, surely.

No time to worry about that. The pilot speaks to us from the deck. We're going back to the airport. He sounds relaxed enough. But they always do, don't they? That's what they're paid for.

The minutes that follow, in which the plane haltingly turns and readies itself to descend, hang heavily. Big Al continues to tremble. Annie continues to look unreassuringly reassuring. Arnold has discarded both his magazine and his confident demeanor and is intensely studying the in-case-of-emergency laminated card, as if in preparation.

Now, in a flood of cold fear, I begin to wonder: Is this it? Is this where my number finally comes up? True, my life has been a full one—more spectacular and privileged and colorful than I would have dared even dream, with adventures and wealth and love beyond my share—but even so, is this how it all ends: in the arms of Big Al, in a field in Sweden?

Through the window of the plunging plane, I notice that the runway has been covered in foam and the perimeter of the airfield is alive with the blinking lights of emergency vehicles.

But I somehow keep it together. I rein it in and remain calm and in control. If it must be, then so it must be. "It's all right," I say, in a quiet voice. Then, slightly louder, "It's all right." Then in a kind of half-shout, "It's all right!" Then, finally, in a shrill and rising scream, "It's all right!"

t was all right. A bird strike, apparently. One unlucky member of a passing flock of geese, sucked into the engine. The bird was ruined, and so, too, was the engine. Good thing the plane had another one and was able to land. It wouldn't have been the first time in my long and distinguished career that I had handed the tabloids a gift-wrapped headline: "Rod Cooks His Goose."

And luck within luck. After we had driven back to the hotel where the band were staying, and joined them in the bar for several stiff drinks and some dramatic reenactments of the incident, I learned that, only the previous day, our pilot had attended a refresher course on controlling a plane in the event of an engine loss.

Kind of sums up my life, really. An awful lot of the way, it's been a long, luxury aircraft ride. But just occasionally the plane flies into a goose.

And somehow, every time it does, I get lucky and live to tell the tale.

CHAPTER 1

*In which our hero is born, just over six years of global conflict ending
shortly thereafter; and in which he goes to school and develops,
peculiarly enough, an intense loathing for singing in public.*

Obviously I was a mistake. Definitely some kind of oversight
in the family-planning department. An "unforced error,"
they might call it in tennis. Otherwise, explain why Bob
and Elsie Stewart, at forty-two and thirty-nine, with four children to
feed, the youngest of them already ten, would suddenly take it into
their heads to produce another baby. Furthermore, explain why they
would do this *in the middle of the Second World War.*

Hence, eventually, the family joke: "Roddy was Dad's slipup. But,
as Dad's slipups go, a fairly lucrative one."

I can't say I was ever made to feel like a mistake, though. On the
contrary, despite my late arrival (or perhaps because of it) I seemed
to be welcomed very warmly—by the six members of my immediate family, at any rate. Less so by Hitler. My point of entry into the

world, on the evening of January 10, 1945, was a small bedroom on the top floor of a terraced house on the Archway Road in north London whose windows had been blown out so many times by the aftershock of exploding bombs from Germany that my dad had cut his losses and boarded them up.

The worst of the Blitz was almost over by then, and, indeed, the war in Europe would end altogether nearly four months later. But, with no regard for my best interests, the Germans had bombed London throughout my mum's pregnancy: first with V1 flying bombs, known cheerfully as "doodlebugs," and less cheerfully as "buzzbombs" on account of the noise they made before they killed you; and then, in the later stages of her term and in the first swaddled days of my life, with the even more vicious V2 rockets, launched across the Channel from the French coast.

Those bastards tended to leave a 25-foot-deep crater where your house used to be. You didn't want to be under a V2 when it landed—pregnant, swaddled, or otherwise.

There's a widely told story that, within an hour of my arrival, a rocket unceremoniously took out Highgate police station, a mere three-quarters of a mile away—slightly pooping the party atmosphere at my birth scene, while at the same time impressing on all of us, in a meaningful way, important and lasting lessons about fortune and the uncertainty of our lease upon this world, etc. It's a good little parable, but alas, completely untrue—just one of those legends, fables, and downright lies told in the name of publicity that we will have cause to unpick as this story goes along. Some weeks separated my birth and the bombing of the cop shop.

Life in London in those days was one long close shave, however, and many Londoners shared that "lucky to make it" feeling, not least if their house overlooked railway yards, as ours did, thereby inadvertently becoming a magnet for bombers with poor aim. While my mum was pregnant with me, the air raid siren would usually sound at around 1:30 A.M. and Mary, the eldest child at seventeen, would get my brother Bob, who was ten, and sister Peggy, nine, out of their beds and into their coats and lead them, each carrying their pillow, into the garden in the pitch black and down into the family Anderson shelter—six sheets of government-issue corrugated iron, formed into a shed and half sunk into the ground, with earth and sandbags thrown on top for extra blast-proofing. Then they would all crawl into the narrow metal bunk beds and try to sleep through the noise and the fear until morning. My brother Don, who was fifteen at this point, preferred to stay in the comfort of his bed in the house—unless something dropped close by and he felt the walls shake, at which point the appeal of a metal bunk in the garden would suddenly become irresistible.

Of course, thousands of other London families were out of harm's way—the children evacuated to the country, temporarily adopted by kindly rural folk in houses that were less likely to get a rocket through their ceilings. But my family had talked about it and decided that they couldn't bear to separate—neither the children from the parents, nor the parents from the children. The Stewart attitude was "If we go, we go together." We were very clanlike in that way. We still are.

Still, that didn't mean information necessarily flowed freely between the family members. It will tell you something about how little sex and its consequences were mentioned in those days that Don had no idea our mum was pregnant. He was slightly mystified by the amount of knitting his elder sister was doing (especially in the bomb shelter, where it passed the time). And if you had pressed him, he might have admitted that he was puzzled, too, that his mum seemed to be getting larger. Otherwise, the first thing he knew about it was that Wednesday evening, when he was asked if he wanted to go upstairs and see the new baby.

My sister Mary was in on it, though—excited about this baby as if it were her own, and coming home from work in an increasing hurry as the due date neared. Wednesday was her roller-skating night. "It won't come today," Mum told her. So off Mary went. But Mum must have been in labor already, because in the time it took Mary to get back, put her skates down, and run upstairs, she had acquired another brother, Roderick David Stewart. My sister was struck, not so much by the sight of me, in all my radiant, newborn glory, as by the sight of Mum, who looked shattered and as white as the sheets. It was at that point she realized what Mum had been through, and also why Mum had sent her out that night: to spare her the details.

Dad seemed to take these latest developments equably enough, though he must have wondered how he would cope. He was a Scotsman, from Leith, north of Edinburgh, with a spell in the merchant navy behind him, who had followed his brothers to London for work. He had met my mum, who was a Londoner, at a dance in Tufnell Park. When I came along, Dad was doing twelve-hour days as a plumber, returning home at seven in the evening, where he would peel off his boots and put his damp feet up by the fire, causing his slowly warming socks to give off the most shocking stink. Dad never drank. Someone had got him drunk once on a building site somewhere, and he had sworn it off there and then. But he smoked and he gambled (on the horses in particular), and a fifth child was unlikely to ease his occasional problems with cash flow. Our house at 507 Archway Road was rented from Grattage the landlord. Even now, for me, the name Grattage carries a cold wind of fear and loathing. "Here comes Grattage! Hide!"

Archway Road was a noisy, traffic-filled thoroughfare, dotted with small shops, in a mostly working-class area, with the far posher residences of Highgate away to the north. There was a trolleybus stop right outside our front door, and the wind forever blew discarded bus tickets into the gulley in front of our basement, to the irritation of my dad, who was constantly out there picking them up. Much later, after we had moved, the house was demolished so that the road could be widened, the local council finally achieving what Hitler had failed to pull off. But, while it stood, it was handsome enough—a pretty big house, actually, for a jobbing plumber's family. Three bedrooms on the top floor, two more on the floor below that, and on the ground floor, along with the kitchen and the bathroom, the tall-ceilinged dining room, which contained a baby grand piano that my mum and occasionally my brother Don played, and which once, years later, would provide me with a convenient shelter for some experimental fumbling with a member of the opposite sex.

Our house's other luxury item was a telephone—an almost unparalleled technological wonder in those days. It had a coin box attached to it, and you needed a threepenny bit to phone out. Hard to account for the mystery and awe that would descend whenever it rang, which wasn't often. Who could it be? Who could it *possibly* be? And who would answer it? That could take a while to sort out. Whoever was chosen had to use their best voice: "Mount View, six-one-five-seven." You had to talk posh on the telephone in the 1940s and 1950s. The telephone demanded that.

My dad needed the phone to organize the football club that he ran as a hobby: Highgate Redwing, a weekend club with a first team, a reserve side, and even a youth team for a while. My brothers Bob and Don played for them, and I would too, eventually, but while I was small I could only look up to these men who filled our house, and marvel at them. They were my first sporting heroes. The meeting point before games on a Saturday morning was our house, so there would be a couple of dozen footballers milling in the kitchen and the hall and spilling out onto the pavement. And, beforehand, for me, this excited anticipation: the guys were coming round. For a penny a shirt from club funds, my mum washed the kit* each week, heaving these muddy clothes into a giant boiler and stirring them all round. And afterwards a line of black-and-white shirts would hang, gleaming, the length of our garden. It was a heavenly sight to me.

---

* Uniforms

I remember family holidays at Ramsgate on the Kent coast—all of us Stewarts stuck on the beach in the freezing cold in the traditional British way—but not nearly as strongly as I recall the annual football club outings: two "charabancs," or buses, full of the players and their wives and kids, leaving the Archway Road at eight in the morning, my mother and sisters making dozens and dozens of sandwiches for the day out at Clacton-on-Sea. Just wonderful.

And similarly the football club parties. My dad would go down in the basement and shore up the dining-room floor from below with scaffolding and planks, and everyone would pour in for dancing and singing. I would be put to bed, but I would sneak down and sit under that baby grand piano, watching the feet and the kilted legs. My love of a singsong was born right there. Sometimes a conga line would leave the dining room, head down the steps, and set off up the road and back. It wasn't hard to understand the exuberance of these adults, when you realized what they had so recently been through. They were dancing off the war.

Mary and Peggy, my sisters, would take me to watch speedway at Harringay, which was hugely popular then. And Mum and Dad sometimes treated me to a trip to the cinema—the Rex, in East Finchley, where the stalls* took a big dip in the center: the front rows were higher than the rows in the middle, and the back rows were higher still. Maybe it was war damage. One day, when I was eight, my mum said, "We're going to see *Monsieur Hulot's Holiday*. This will be the funniest thing you've ever seen"—a big buildup to give a film. But she was absolutely right. It was slapstick, but so subtle in the way it went about it. We sat there in the Rex's battered stalls, and I had never laughed as hard as I laughed at Jacques Tati, haplessly creating havoc. Even today Ronnie Wood and I remain huge Tati fans.

Of course, the age gap between me and my siblings meant the

---

* The seats in front of the stage at the lowest level of a theater

family at home rapidly shrank on me. First Mary married Fred, a lorry driver for Wall's ice cream, so that was my guardian angel gone from the house. And then Peggy married Jim, a wonderful cockney greengrocer who had fought in the war at Monte Cassino—an unforgettable experience for him. Many years later, when I had made some money, Jim was part of one of our big family trips on a private plane to watch Scotland play football. Our journey took us down over Italy. Jim sat there, rolling himself a cigarette, as he liked to, and as he looked reflectively out the window at the ground below, he said, "I used to get paid fourteen bob a week to murder that lot."

Life would be so cruel to Peggy. She was a wonderful tennis player, a real outdoors person, but she was struck down by multiple sclerosis and in a wheelchair in her mid thirties. Multiple sclerosis meant my mother, too, would need a wheelchair eventually. Unfair.

The next to leave the Archway Road was Bob, who married Kim, and finally, when I was still only eleven, Don married and left home as well, at twenty-six. News of his imminent wedding to Pat reduced me to tears at his feet. I had cried just the same when he had left for national service—though mostly because I couldn't envisage this place he was destined for, Aldershot, nor how anybody would get there, let alone come back. This latest betrayal, though, seemed final. How could he desert me like this? Don took me to the West End and talked me round to the idea as best he could, with lemonade.

Yet, in truth, even when my brothers and sisters moved out, they didn't go far. They took apartments and houses a few doors away, or round the corner at worst: that Stewart clan thing again. I would come to value this proximity a few years later, when an interest in my appearance properly gripped me and I needed to borrow Mary's hairdryer or my sister-in-law Pat's hairspray. Very handy.

"Spoiled rotten" tends to be the family shorthand for my childhood. I object to that, on the grounds that materially there wasn't much around to spoil anyone with. "Somewhat indulged" might be a better expression. At the same time, I acknowledge that Mary never came home from work on a Friday without bringing me a toy—some little car or soldier—from Woolworths. Was that being "spoiled rotten"? Possibly.

I also concede this: my mum used to make a rabbit stew, and before my arrival the rabbit's heart—small, but considered a treat—was cut into four and shared between the children. Once I came along, the heart was given to me.

Dutiful but undistinguished at school, I failed the Eleven Plus exam to nobody's particular astonishment and was sent off in a gray flannel outfit and a black-and-white tie to William Grimshaw Secondary Modern—where, coincidentally, Ray and Dave Davies of the Kinks also went, at around the same time, although we only worked that out years later. I used to take the bus to North Finchley from outside the house, which was highly convenient. At the other end, though, there was a mile walk the length of Creighton Avenue, which was less agreeable. Still, I traveled light. Schoolboys seemed to then. These days, when my little lad Alastair goes off to school, he has bags and books and laptops and *stuff.* I seemed to go through my entire secondary school career armed with a solitary pencil. Less than that, actually: a solitary pencil stub, tucked into the top pocket of my blazer. It seemed to be all I needed.

I was diligent enough, and happy enough too, by and large. I was certainly worried about missing school, anxious about falling behind, so I was no big truant, and certainly no big troublemaker. Fights would always find me on the periphery, looking on—never involved. I made friends easily, but I wasn't one of those kids at the center of things in the playground, effortlessly attracting all the attention. And I definitely didn't think of myself as a showman. I would only develop that kind of confidence in myself later, through being in bands.

I showed some talent with a paintbrush—although it emerged in a routine test that I am color-blind (I have some problems distinguishing browns, blues, and purples). I got by in most things and did well in sport, becoming captain of the cricket team and captain of the football team. There was only one thing I really couldn't be getting on with, and that was, bizarrely enough, given my later path, music with Mr. Wainwright.

I had always known I was petrified of standing up in front of the class. In Mr. Wainwright's music room, I now discovered what I was even more petrified of: standing up in front of the class and singing. It wasn't shyness so much as a fear of being singled out and made to look ridiculous. Maybe it was all in my head, but I swear he used to pick me deliberately because of that. He would haul me up to sing a few lines of a song, with him on the piano at the front, and I would quail and quiver and grope miserably for the notes and feel more uncomfortable than I had ever felt, anywhere, in any circumstance.

It was for this reason that I developed the Fake Sick trick.

For the Fake Sick trick you will need: one Shipham's meat-paste pot, empty; a small quantity of mashed potato, scraped from the side of your school lunch plate; a small quantity of carrots, ditto; and some water. Instructions: While at the table in your school cafeteria, add the potato, carrots, and water to the paste pot. Mix thoroughly, using a knife or any other available utensil. Withdraw with the pot to the school playground and, in a quiet and preferably unobserved moment, sling the resulting goo onto the tarmac. Thereafter, summon the on-duty teacher with a cry of "Sir, I've been sick" (or similar), gesturing all the while to the splattered ground. Hey presto: you're off music for the afternoon and on your way home. Or, in my case, to the pictures.

It's probably fair to say, then, that the music bug hadn't significantly bitten at this point in my life. Don had taken me to see Bill Haley and the Comets at the Gaumont State Cinema on Kilburn High Road in 1954. Don liked Bill Haley and could sing "Everybody Razzle

Dazzle" probably better than Haley could. (Don really was the singer in the family, as they like to remind me.) I remember being up on the balcony with him and looking down at this heaving mass of jiving, rioting teddy boys in the stalls, and Haley and the band in their tartan jackets, prompting all this mayhem. The rhythm, the brightness of the clothes, and the reactions of the crowd—all affected me, and maybe a seed was sown. But it didn't make me a huge fan.

There was a slight glimmer of the performing bug, though, after my dad gave me a Spanish guitar, with a red tasseled cord for a strap, for my fifteenth birthday—completely crushing my hopes initially, because I had been holding out for a wooden Tri-ang model railway station. (The view from our windows of the Highgate marshaling yards and the line beyond, running steam trains from Euston up to Alexandra Palace, had long inspired my interest in model railways, which, to some people's completely unnecessary surprise, lives with me to this day.)

Who knows why my dad thought this guitar would be a good present for me? It's possible that it fell off the back of a lorry, or was offered to him on the cheap. But I swallowed my disappointment and messed around with it for a while. I took it to school, where other people also had cheap guitars. A bunch of us who had picked up the general idea would head into the playground at break time and attempt to commit this thing they called skiffle, the sound that was reviving the old American homemade "jug band" style of the early twentieth century, with its banjos and washboards and pots and pans. This was when Lonnie Donegan was starting to happen, and Don had Lonnie's "Cumberland Gap" on a Pye 78. We called ourselves the Kool Kats, which we fancied was a pretty clever name, and at our peak we had seven guitars and one bloke on tea-chest bass. Not your typical lineup, and a bit guitar-heavy, but we hammered away at "Rock Island Line"—the best Lonnie Donegan song, a real rattler, probably the first number I could sing all the way through, and almost bombproof when attacked by novices. That said, the Kool Kats' version might have sounded better if any of us had had the first clue how to tune a guitar. Alas, that deep musical mystery eluded all seven of us, so we just slapped the strings and hoped.

Fortunately, my dad knew a bloke with the knowledge, so I would set off to his place periodically, clutching my guitar, for a tune-up. Unfortunately, he lived about a mile and a half away, so by the time I had trekked home, the guitar was out of tune again. If there were traces of a future career in these early shamblings, they were hard to spot.

Secondary education's other principal gifts to me were two immense, highly formative, and entirely unrequited crushes: the first on Mrs. Plumber, who taught history and, more important from my point of view at the time, wore a pencil skirt which came to just below the knee; and the second, at thirteen, on Juliet Truss, who was two years above me, had long red hair and enormous breasts, and was utterly, utterly unobtainable, although this didn't stop me from going and standing uselessly outside her house, near the bus terminus at Muswell Hill. If she even noticed me at all, she never indicated as much. And if she had asked me what I was waiting for, I wouldn't have been able to tell her, because I didn't know either.

Near the end of my time at school, I was caught up in an unfortunate and deeply regrettable incident involving the release of an air-filled condom in the corridor. (Mindless and juvenile, clearly. But they really go, if you blow them up hard enough.) For this I was given the standard caning (which, I don't mind reporting, bloody hurt) and was temporarily stripped of my hard-won football and cricket badges. And soon after that, accompanied by no qualifications, and a still lightly throbbing backside, I left.

I was fifteen, the whole world lay before me, glittering with possibilities, and what I was going to do next was . . .

I hadn't got a clue.

CHAPTER 2

*In which the door to a career in professional football opens,
only to slam again about an hour later; and in which
sundry shockingly menial employments are undertaken,
culminating in a period of rebellious smelliness.*

There was, of course, professional football: the classic outlet
for the underqualified, unconnected working-class kid. But
here, again, our tale must diverge from some of the previously handed-down versions. According to these, I get snapped up at
the age of fifteen by Brentford Football Club in the English professional leagues, and sign a contract as an apprentice. All is then set for
me to break overnight into the first team, lead Brentford to new and
undreamed-of heights, reluctantly accept that I have taken the club
as far as any player on his own can, agree to a transfer to somewhere
bigger, such as Manchester United or Real Madrid, and eventually
change the face of world football everlastingly.

But, alas (one version of the story continues), I very quickly realize
that the duties of an apprentice at a professional football club include

such pain-in-the-arse chores as cleaning the first team's boots and sweeping out the changing rooms, work which strikes me as beneath my dignity and causes me to pack my bag and quit Brentford, and English football, with my chin held high, after about a fortnight.

I like this story. I may even have . . . helped it along a little, shall we say, from time to time, in moments of weakness, and in televised conversations with Michael Parkinson, among others. The truth is, though, I was never an apprentice footballer—at Brentford, or anywhere else. And I never turned my nose up at sweeping out Brentford's changing rooms, because Brentford never actually asked me to. I think I may have mentioned in an interview at some early stage that I wouldn't have fancied the boot-cleaning had the boot-cleaning come up (and I'm sure I genuinely wouldn't have fancied it), and the story took off from there. But let's be completely clear about it: I no more signed with Brentford than Gordon Ramsay played for Rangers. (He once said he did, but you will find the record books to be awfully silent on the matter.)

Not that I didn't show a talent for football—and enough for Brentford to be interested in me for at least a glimmering moment or two. Like a large number of boys of my age and generation, I was genetically programmed to devote huge amounts of time—nearly all of my time, in fact—to the project of kicking a tennis ball against a wall. My dad did not discourage me in this. Indeed, he coated my tennis ball with white emulsion so that I could carry on kicking it against a wall after dark, bashing it against the outside of the Wellington Inn, where on Saturday evenings he took my mother for their weekly night out. I would occasionally pause from kicking the tennis ball against the wall long enough to drink the lemonade and eat the crisps that had been brought out to me, and to look through the distorting bottle-glass of the pub window and see my mum inside with her gin and tonic on the table and her handbag on her lap, my dad beside her, not drinking.

I was physically slight but I could win the ball and move it around, so at school they started me out at center back and then moved me into midfield and the position known in those days as right half. (Not until I went to live in California and began playing weekly with the legendary Exiles did I make the transition to my natural position, right back. I have a reputation for sitting tight, defensively, in an old-fashioned kind of way, but it's howlingly unfair. The statistics will show that, in some thirty-five years of competitive action since then, I have crossed the halfway line at least once.)

I also prematurely knew glory in the men's game at the mere age of eleven, in an incident which for some reason goes largely unmentioned in the game's history books, but to the momentousness of which we will try and do justice here. I was hanging around on a Saturday morning, as usual, near the pitches* where the Highgate Redwing sides were playing, when the reserve team realized they were a man short. There followed a scene which will be immediately familiar to anyone who has ever read a boys' football comic: a huddled conversation between adults, at the end of which all eyes turn in unison to the pale kid standing on his own on the sideline, looking hopeful. And if someone didn't actually say to me at this point, "You'd better get changed, son—looks like you've made the team," then they ought to have done.

The kit, of course, was too big. The fabled black-and-white striped shirt came down to my knees, creating the perfect illusion that I was wearing a dress. Just to increase my uncertainty, I was aware of my brother Don, who was due to play for the Redwing first team on an adjacent pitch, protectively having a quiet word with the opposition players before the match, telling them to "go easy on the kid, for Christ's sake."

And what happens? Fourteen minutes in, I only go and score with a 25-yard volley that screams into the top corner past the goalkeeper's

---

* Fields

vainly stretching fingers. Oh, all right, then—with a tap-in from about two feet out which it would probably have taken more skill than I possessed to miss. But anyway, there's a very grown-up roar of delight from my adult teammates that I can still summon into my head now, and the news spreads to the parallel pitch where my brothers are playing, and there's a grown-up roar there, too. "'Ere, Don—the lad's only gone and scored!" And I was probably prouder in that moment than I had ever been—proud enough to rescreen the action on a loop in the cinema of my imagination for, seriously, weeks afterwards.

Later I played for a weekend team my own age—Finchley Under-15s—in a shirt that fit me, and it was while there that I was summoned to Brentford for closer examination. Brentford F.C. had been a bit of a force in the English First Division in the 1930s, but by 1960, when I turned up, they were well into a long and largely undistinguished phase of toing and froing between the game's third and fourth professional levels. Nevertheless, news of this honor made the sports pages of the local paper, the *Finchley Express,* and carrying, clearly, the hopes of all Finchley on my fairly narrow shoulders, off I went to the far west of London.

My trial took place at Brentford's ground on a warm summer evening, and we played a game of five-a-side across the middle of a pitch while a couple of blokes in tracksuits watched from the sidelines. Did I do OK? I can't recall. But I can't have set the place alight, because they never called back. Yet again, the phone in the hall at 507 Archway Road failed to ring. And that was the end of my career in professional football.

Brentford's loss. What have they won since?

It would have suited my dad, though, had it worked out differently. He was a really good footballer himself. He had turned out for a team in London called the Vagabonds and, during his wartime duties, for an Air Raid Patrol side. He was gentle at home—the one who put an arm round me and cuddled me far more than my mum did—but on a football pitch he was a stout, tough-tackling, gritty Scotsman. I once saw him play an entire match on a wet pitch in his shoes; he had come without his boots, but he wouldn't let the team down.

Then there was the famous Battle of Highgate Woods: just a normal Saturday morning game for Highgate Redwing, but something sparked on the pitch and the most almighty fight broke out. I would have been eight at the time. I was on the sideline, cutting up the oranges for half-time on the big black wooden box that held the medical kit. And when I looked up it was like a medieval war had broken out: blokes, including my two brothers, were knocking lumps out of each other. I ran over to my dad and clung on to the back of his legs in terror as he squared up to this guy and they started shouting in each other's face. It was then that I realized exactly how seriously my family took football.

In one of my favorite photographs of me and my dad together, we're on a square of grass in Glasgow, kicking a ball about before going to see Scotland play England at Hampden Park in an international match in 1974. (Final score, for anyone tuning in late: Scotland 2, England 0.) In that picture, the fact that he is sixty-nine and wearing a suit doesn't seem to stop him shaping up to the ball like a twenty-two-year-old.

My dad unashamedly put football first, or as close to first as he could get it within the terms of a lasting marriage. My mum once slung his football boots in the fire because he ended up spending Christmas in hospital after breaking his leg in a match in which she had asked him not to play. On the morning of my sister Peggy's wedding, my dad and brothers didn't see why they shouldn't attend the scheduled Highgate Redwing fixture. Unfortunately, it was a cup game and it went into extra time, so they were late for the wedding. My mum exploded, and for a while it looked as though Dad's boots would be going on the fire again, but this time with Dad still in them. My mum used to say: "Bloody football has brought more trouble on this household than two world wars." It was only a small exaggeration.

I can only imagine that my dad had a lot invested in my Brentford trial—more than I did, in truth. I suspect that he allowed himself to believe the big time was about to beckon me. And when it didn't, and the phone stayed silent, I also suspect it crushed him far harder than it crushed me. Don and Bob were both good players, but neither had made it professionally. I was Dad's last shot at football greatness.

Still, he got over it. Later on, he managed to feed the press the story that I had failed in professional football as the result of an ingrown toenail, caused by a tight pair of winkle-pickers. And they lapped it up.

As for me, I loved football; my dad and brothers had ensured that. They took me to my first England v. Scotland international at Wembley in 1959, the game in which the England legend Billy Wright earned his hundredth cap, and I wondered at first why my family were all cheering for Scotland, until the penny dropped. We went home miserable: the English won, 1–0. The events of that day, my dad's passion, and the pictures of Scottish footballers on my brother Bob's bedroom wall alerted me to my Scottish heritage and started me on the long and winding (and expensive) road I'm still on as a Scotland and Celtic fan. But play the game for a living? That wasn't something I really thought about. It wasn't burning a hole in my chest in the way that music very soon, and quite suddenly, would be.

So, instead of football, wallpaper. My dad found me a full-time job working as a screen-printer for the Shand Kydd wallpaper company at Kentish Town. It paid well—enough that I could give half my weekly wage to my parents for my keep (why don't my own children do this?) and still become the proud owner of a post office savings account. (Note: I was smart with money from the very start.) Remember, though, that I was color-blind. That's always going to limit your possibilities in the wallpaper industry. If you are color-blind, one of the things you can't be is an aircraft pilot. One of the other things you can't be is a wallpaper designer.

So Shand Kydd laid me off, and I got a job putting picture frames together, in a little side business belonging to a bloke who ran an undertaker's in North Finchley. Again, short-lived. There was a day or two helping out an electrician at a house in Richmond, bent double, feeding wire into conduits. And there were a couple of Saturdays up at Highgate Cemetery, earning a few quid by measuring out plots and marking them off with string. You learn a lot about yourself, doing physical work. And what I learned about myself was that I didn't like doing physical work.

Incidentally, it was from these few hours of casual labor at the cemetery that the popular myth arose (one I happily rode along with) that I was once a gravedigger. It's a delicious, mysterious piece of backstory, but again we must move to strike it from the record. I was no more a gravedigger than Gordon Ramsay was a gravedigger who played for Rangers.

And so it went on, through my teens, with me sliding from one brief and unsatisfactory job to another, and still living in the parental home—which was soon to stop being 507 Archway Road and to become a two-bedroom flat above a sweetshop and newsagent farther up the road, where a sign would say "JR Stewart, Confectioners." This place had been run seemingly forever by an eccentric old girl who did all the newspaper deliveries herself and stomped around the streets with her feet wrapped in cloth. It had been famous among the locals for its pokiness, musty smell, and the solitary chocolate bar with a faded wrapper that constituted its window display. When the old girl died, my dad, approaching retirement and fancying something less grueling than plumbing, took it over. The business was never going to make his fortune, although things did at least start well. Clearing out the stacks of old newspapers which the previous tenant seemed to have owned in place of furniture, my dad was delighted to discover banknotes carefully stored between the pages—the old girl's savings, hidden away.

The pros and cons of living above your parents' newsagent? On the plus side: instant access, at any hour of the day, to a Cadbury's Flake. On the negative side: a more than averagely high likelihood of being forced to do a newspaper route. In those periods when I was un- employed, my dad couldn't see why I shouldn't help him out. I would get shaken awake at six in the morning—not something which has ever gone down well with a teenager—and stumble blearily into the shop to sort papers into routes with the other paperboys, who were, without exception, nine- or ten-year-old kids and (also without ex- ception) cheeky sods. Here was humiliation more extreme than any- thing reality television has yet dreamed of.

Still, freed at last from school uniform, and with a bit of money coming in, I had begun to take an interest in clothes. In this, I very much caught the mood of the times. While I was a kid, shops had really only seemed to offer "menswear" and "boyswear"; and boyswear was menswear, only smaller. Now, after the 1950s, and the rise of teen- agers, like me, with a bit of spare cash in their pockets, clothes for young adults were their own separate boom area, and London in par- ticular was rapidly ascending to the height of fashionability.

It was a great time to be young and fancying yourself as a bit dap- per. On the Seven Sisters Road you could pick up good stuff cheap: a bolero jacket with a little belt in the back; drainpipe trousers with a buttoned slit up the side—I loved the buttons—and winkle-picker shoes, made out of compressed cardboard, leather being in short supply after the war and unaffordably expensive. Not great, cardboard shoes. Wet weather inevitably added an unwanted white salt-mark across the tops, and accidental immersion in a puddle would effectively convert your shoes into spats—but in a bad way. Six months in, you would be shoving in further bits of cardboard to block the holes in the soles and prevent your socks from filling up with rain.

It wasn't until 1963, when I was eighteen, that I had enough money set aside to splash out on a deeply longed-for pair of leather Chelsea boots from Anello & Davide in Covent Garden. I was proudly wearing these, thinking that I looked rather special, when I stepped into a coffee bar in Muswell Hill, only to find another bloke wearing an identical pair. His name was Ewan Dawson, and we bonded over our boots. We became firm friends and fellow adventurers for many years thereafter.

So, clothes had begun to seem exciting, and so had sex—although, as at Brentford, I was very much a trialist at this point. A girl had allowed me to touch one of her breasts outside the Odeon cinema in Finchley—a fantastic breakthrough. Only one breast, mind. If I had touched both, we would have had to get married. Later, a different girl let me touch the promised land, a reward which brought me enormous pride and a refusal to wash the honored hand for several days. And after that, with a third girl, I made the enormous tactical error of going to second base straightaway, without going via first, and was sternly reprimanded: "Tits first, please!"

Hard, though, to be a budding Lothario when you live with your parents in a two-bedroom flat above a sweetshop. Neither this, nor the perfectly neat and respectable council house around the corner on Kenwood Road that my mum and dad were moved into when JR Stewart Confectioners was demolished to widen the Archway Road, seemed to me likely to impress women in the way I imagined women needed to be impressed. So I would invite a girl "back to my place," but then stay on the train an extra couple of stops to East Finchley and walk with her along Bishops Avenue, which is broad and lined with grand detached houses with tarmac driveways. I would pick a mansion with some cars on its driveway and bring us both to a sudden halt on the pavement, pretending to be dismayed because my dad had "businesspeople over," so we "couldn't possibly go in." Then we'd turn around and walk back, and, if I was lucky, the girl would have been impressed enough by my landed status to put her hand in my trousers at the Tube station. I swear to you, this ploy worked many more times than you would perhaps imagine.

At sixteen, I'm at home most nights apart from football training on a Wednesday, staying in and saving money and energy for the weekend, when it's off to the pubs of the West End—to the Duke of York on Rathbone Street, the Porcupine in Leicester Square. Or perhaps one of my old schoolmates—Kenneth Pearson, Clive Amore, Kevin Cronnin, Brian Boreham, all, just like me, with burgeoning interests in music and clothes and girls—might know about a party in Earls Court, in which case you would jump on the Underground and head over there with a big tin of cider under your arm and listen for the noise in the street.

And then one time someone mentions the Beaulieu Jazz Festival— a weekend of music and drinking outdoors on the grounds of a stately home in the middle of the New Forest in Hampshire. Beaulieu was in its sixth year in 1961 and was really leading the way for the music festival culture that would explode later in the decade. And hadn't there been a bit of a riot at the end of it the previous year? Didn't the traditional jazz fans and the modern jazz fans end up having a bit of an alcohol-fueled punch-up? Who wouldn't want to see some of that? None of my group of pals is particularly into jazz at this time, modern or traditional, but that's not the point. The point is, it's a scene. Bit pricey, obviously, but that needn't be a problem because apparently there's this beautiful pub, the Montagu Arms, beside a tidal river, across from the festival site. The word is that you can drink in the pub until the water level drops, at which point it's possible to wade across and climb into the festival through the sewage pipe without paying for a ticket. You won't smell too great afterwards, but you'll be in for nothing.

So I go along, and it works out extremely well. We stay in the pub until the water level is right, and then set out to investigate our proposed access point. It turns out that the pipe is an overflow, rather than strictly a sewage pipe, which is obviously good news. We'll get wet around the ankles and a bit muddy, but nothing worse. The pipe is about four feet in diameter, so quite an easy crawl, and although there's a metal grille at its far end, blocking the top half of the pipe, which we have to duck under, that's the only difficult bit, and then we're inside.

And here in 1961, on a secluded patch of grass, some hours after emerging safely from an overflow, and to the muffled strains of trad jazz, possibly supplied by the Chris Barber Jazz Band, or maybe by the Clyde Valley Stompers, or even by good old Acker Bilk, the legendary clarinetist, I lose my by then not remotely prized virginity to an older (and larger) woman who has come on to me very strongly in the beer tent. How much older, I can't tell you exactly—but old enough that she was highly disappointed by the blink-and-you'll-miss-it brevity of the experience. (Elements of this encounter, much altered and enhanced, later filtered into the song "Maggie May.")

It was good to pass such a key personal milestone, of course, although, as a life-changing, direction-altering experience, I can't say that short moment in the grass really matched what happened to me in 1962, which is when I got to hear Bob Dylan's first album. Now that really *did* move the earth.

Other recordings had made an impact on me: the exuberance and show business of the Al Jolson 78s that my mum used to put on and which I adored; Eddie Cochran's "C'mon, Everybody" from 1958 (some of my first efforts at singing publicly were blatant attempts to sound like Cochran on that song); or, on the radio at Shand Kydd wallpapers, the honey-and-grit sound of Sam Cooke singing "You Send Me," which would later become a huge part of what I aspired to as a singer.

But nothing had altered the air around me like that Dylan album. I would play it over and over on the family radiogram, the dial of which promised, but never delivered, stations in impossibly exotic places such as Moscow and Kabul. But in this case, and to my young ears, as that record spun inside its wooden tomb, something in the timbre of the voice and the mystery of the lyrics genuinely seemed to be coming from far away. It sounded like America to me. It summed up what I thought America was like. Dylan sang "Talkin' New York," and it made me want to run away there. Not to upset my parents— I loved my parents—but just to experience this world of possibility that seemed to be there in the music, the vastness and openness of America. It didn't just broaden my horizon, this record: it drew my horizon. No other album has worked on me this way since.

I wanted to be able to sing these songs and I wanted to be able to play them—to inhabit them entirely. I had £10 saved up and I borrowed another £30 off my brother Bob to buy a proper steel-strung acoustic guitar—a Zenith, from a music shop called Ivor Marants in the West End. Unlike my first guitar, it had the useful ability to hold its tuning—and, hallelujah, I now had the ability to tune it. I also had a capo to clip across the strings, which seemed to me the height of musical sophistication. And from somewhere else I got hold of a harmonica and a frame to go around my neck, so that I could do the Dylan thing in full. (It was at least a year before someone pointed out to me that you can suck, as well as blow, on a harmonica—and, furthermore, that it's a combination of sucking and blowing that releases the instrument's uniquely expressive potential. Until then, I had only blown, thereby mostly producing the noise of a chicken being strangled over and over again. But hey—it's a learning process.)

Some days my dad would need to head off down to Islington to order stock and leave me to mind the newspaper shop. And as soon as he was gone, I would put up the "Closed" sign and sit in the tiny backyard, next to the outside khazi*, trying to master Dylan songs on the guitar—tough for me, because my guitar-playing wasn't up to much, but I was finding I could get my voice around them well enough. This procedure would absorb me for hours, until I'd suddenly realize that Dad was due back, put the guitar down, and quickly fling open the shop again. Dad would say, "Blimey, you haven't taken much today." And I would say, "It's been really quiet. Hardly anyone in."

And thus, with a head full of Dylan, and a heart full of vague teenage rebelliousness, I entered a highly stylized beatnik phase. Its crucial opening gambit? Extreme hair growth. All these years on, it's hard to impress upon people exactly how shocking long hair was in Britain in 1962. In a country that was still very unified and uniform, it seemed like the abandonment of all social values, an act of almost grotesque rebellion, a deeply offensive affront to everything that was right and proper. When I worked at the picture framers in North Finchley, three or four of the guys had properly thick, shoulder-length locks, and when I walked up the street with them, the stir they caused would make my skin prickle. People would literally cross the road. There was nothing threatening or aggressive about these guys; they just had long hair. Long hair was enough.

So I let my hair grow. It seemed like the way forward. I thought long hair looked great, and I thought the reaction long hair got was even greater. And then I stopped washing that hair, for added straggliness. In fact, I stopped washing everything else, too. Smelliness was an important part of being a beatnik, as I understood it, in the version of beatnik culture which had filtered across to us in tantalizing glimpses from America. You weren't a proper beatnik if you didn't whiff. So I

---

* Toilet

gave up baths and washing my clothes—my prescribed beatnik outfit of jeans, roll-neck sweater, and leather waistcoat. My parents hated this development, and my sisters and my brother Don were appalled—worried mostly about the strain I was causing Mum and Dad. Mary took me aside once and scolded me because she thought I was taking years off Mum and Dad's lives. Only my brother Bob was easy about it, but he had a bit of the rebel in him and had been through a major teddy-boy stage, earning himself many confrontations with my dad. Bob probably knew these things come and go in stages.

I also became intently, if superficially, political. You name it, I'd ban it. "What are you rebelling against?" "What have you got?" That kind of attitude. I started buying the *Daily Worker,* the extreme socialist newspaper, just to annoy other people who weren't extreme socialists. At lunchtime, at places where I worked, I would take it out and open it up noisily, giving the pages a decent rustle, and then sit there behind it. I didn't have the first clue what I was reading about, but I thought it produced the right effect.

Of course, this was one of protest's golden periods. In October 1962, we had to sweat our way through the Cuban Missile Crisis—Khrushchev and Kennedy going head-to-head for a fortnight, with Britain playing piggy in the middle, and the war to end all wars about to break out over our heads. That said, my mates and I had it worked out. As the situation deepened, we packed rucksacks with clothes and tins of baked beans and set off, hitchhiking, in the direction of Scotland. We figured that if we headed as far north as we possibly could, with as many baked beans as we could possibly carry, we could still come out of this OK. Which might have been a touch naïve. In any case, we only got as far as Luton and then we turned back.

Equally earnestly, I took part in a couple of Aldermaston marches, in which members of the Campaign for Nuclear Disarmament and other antinuclear protestors walked in thousands between the controversial government nuclear research center at Aldermaston and

Trafalgar Square in central London, fifty miles away. Well, I say "earnestly." These marches were kind of like rolling music festivals, with bands and buskers along the way, and could involve a couple of overnight stops. Sympathetic schools beside the route would throw open their gymnasiums, or you might be able to unroll your sleeping bag in a village hall. Now, I definitely had a social conscience. I didn't approve of nuclear bombs any more than the marcher next to me. When I shouted "Polaris—out!" along with everyone else, I meant it. But at the same time, young people? Overnighting? In sleeping bags? I would be lying if I didn't admit that as an Aldermaston weekend approached, one of the thoughts at the forefront of my mind was "I might get my leg over here."

Of course, in practice, sex between two people in sleeping bags is never easy, and the lights in those school halls were only ever dimmed, rather than extinguished, so the sheer number of people around you made extremes of intimacy difficult. But a lot of highly enjoyable fumbling took place.

I took my guitar on those marches—strapped to my back, along with my black roll-bag with the big, homemade CND patch I had drawn for it. It was just what you did, if you had a guitar: you carried it along, and then, almost whenever you were stationary, you sat down and busked, picking away at the scraps of American folk that you knew—the Dylan stuff, some Ramblin' Jack Elliott, some Woody Guthrie—and you heard other people playing, and added stuff from their repertoires to your own. Those marches were really the beginning, for me, of performing, of taking what I had learned in the backyard when I should have been minding the shop, and making it public. Similarly, on weekends, I started going to Brighton on the south coast of England—the cool destination for "beats" and wannabe "beats"—catching the train down from Victoria Station with my pals, and sitting on the beach in my duffel coat, with my guitar, being very beatnik. And people would say, "Rod, play 'San Francisco

Bay Blues,'" or "Rod, do that Dylan one," or "Rod, give us 'Cocaine Blues,'" and when that happened, perched on the stones with a small audience gathered around me, I began to realize I had a voice that people would listen to.

In the summer of 1962, a couple of us made a halfhearted effort to see the world in what we took to be the required bohemian manner. It was my first time abroad. In fact I had never been much farther afield from London than Brighton. I borrowed some money, took the ferry to France, and hitchhiked to Paris, thumbing a lift down Route Nationale 1. There I busked outside the café Les Deux Magots, gave them "You're No Good," "It Takes a Worried Man to Sing a Worried Song," and "Rock Island Line" over and over again, earned a handful of francs, bought myself some French bread, camped out under a bridge by the Seine quite near the Eiffel Tower, and came home. A second hitchhiking trip, a while later, took me south to Spain, where I slept rough in a group of traveling Brits under the cantilevered stands around Camp Nou, Barcelona's football ground. For that we were scooped up by the police and dumped on the British consul, who arranged to fly us home in mild disgrace—my first time on an airplane.

I cost my parents some anxiety in this period, I belatedly realized. A lot of the time they didn't know where I was, which worried them. The hair and the smell worried them too, as did my general lack of direction.

But I was only expressing myself—and not very convincingly, as it happened. At Shoreham, near Brighton, there was a proper beatnik crew who hung out on a houseboat and eventually made the national news by fighting a battle with the police who came to evict them, using hosepipes. The law pitched up and, basically, washed them off. Until then, though, the aspiration for the likes of me and Kenneth, Clive, Kevin, Brian, and our little group of London interlopers was acceptance by this beatnik elite. I think I only got onto that boat once—and I can still remember the smell. By the proper hard core,

I was regarded as a bit of a weekend beatnik, a weekend raver, not quite the real deal. I remember going to Brighton once for three days in succession and thinking, "This is it. I've cracked it—I'm here on a Monday morning, loitering about on the beach." Still no hard-core acceptance, though. And fair enough. I was, after all, a rebel with a post office savings account—the beatnik who went back to his mum's.

Back in London I hung out, unbeknown to my parents, with some beatnik squatters at a large, deserted guesthouse up in Highgate, near Jack Straw's Castle, a pub now closed. One night we took it into our heads to cook up some baked beans over an open flame and ended up setting fire to the roof. Cue the arrival of the fire brigade and also of a policeman, P. C. Brown, who—fortunately or unfortunately, it could have gone either way—knew my dad, and dragged me home.

"I've got your Roddy here," he said. "He just set light to a roof." My reward was a wallop around the head—the only one my father ever dealt me. There and then, my mum took my jeans, my roll-neck sweater, and my leather waistcoat, and, as she had done with my dad's football boots, burned them.

It was like the click of a switch. Overnight I smartened myself up and became a mod—or, at least, insofar as the London "mod" scene was interested in sharp fashion and dressing smartly I became a mod. Other aspects of that burgeoning branch of youth subculture—the interest in ska music, the use of mopeds—passed me by. But I was with them on the value of a neatly pressed shirt and a decent pair of shoes, and I went from being as smelly a human being as there ever was in the civilized world to being this guy you couldn't get out of the bathroom.

And that's when the hair started. But the hair deserves its own chapter.

DIGRESSION

In which our hero, sparing no detail, discusses his hair.

IT's WHAT I HAVE in common with the Queen: both of us
have had more or less the same hairstyle for the last forty-five
years. Well, if you find something that works for you . . .

For Her Majesty: the carefully organized shampoo and set.
For me: the tousled mop of spikes—equally carefully organized,
I should add. You think this hair of mine just happens? Wrong.
It takes work.

But before there was the blond and spiky look, there was
the bouffant. Or, as we called it, "the bouff"—as in "Mind
the bouff, mate" or "Oi! Get off me bouff." (One was very
protective of one's bouff.)

The bouffant was my first major hair development after
I dropped the beatnik thing and cleaned myself up. When I
had gone to Paris and busked, I had seen these French guys
with huge, upwards-pointing dos with curtains of hair at the
front. I thought they looked great. Now I decided to create
my own version. It was all in the back-combing and the blow-
drying. The back-combing wasn't going to be a problem, but
the blow-drying was complicated by the fact that my parents'
house entirely lacked a hairdryer. A television, yes—we were
a proper family in that respect—but a hairdryer, no. Hairdryers
were a relatively rare commodity in the early 1960s. If you
wanted to dry your hair, you simply stuck it in front of the
fire, or even (and this isn't particularly recommended in the
manuals) put it near and sometimes inside the oven, and sort
of baked it dry.

But you can't bake a bouff. Or not a good one, anyway. Fortunately, my sister *did* have a hairdryer. Even more fortunately, she was living just up the road. So I would hop out of the bath, dry, dress, and leg it round to Mary's while my hair was still wet. And because I had a lot of hair to work with, the bouffant that I was able to create by back-combing and blow-drying was, quite simply, enormous. It was beehive-scale: a bouffant you could bounce coins off. It made Dusty Springfield look like a rank amateur.

Of course, the problem was not getting the hair to stand up; it was getting it to remain standing. Male grooming products? Forget it. The DIY answer to the problem was to mix a spoonful of sugar into a small quantity of water and apply that to the hair just prior to the blow-drying phase. The heat from the hairdryer would then cause the sugar to set and (if you were lucky) your bouff would solidify with it.

This was the perfect solution, in terms of hold. But it had its downside in the long term. When you woke up in the morning, it was as though someone had attacked you in the night with a stick of candy floss. And, even fortified with sugar, you were still prey to the elements—especially if, like me, you were using London Underground trains to get to your chosen destination in the evenings. Down in the Tube, the network of tunnels and the comings and goings of the trains create their own series of backdrafts. The imminent arrival of your train is often signaled by a serious and prolonged blast of air along the platform. Picture me if you will, then, carefully dressed and styled for the night, accompanied by my mates, and standing down in Archway Station as the train thunders in—and all of us cowering into the wall, with our arms up over our heads, trying to protect our bouffs from getting toppled by the wind.

The bouffant stayed with me and then evolved into the

spiked top during the Jeff Beck Group days. I developed this
look in tandem with Ronnie Wood, who was also in that band
and had the same kind of hair, although his is a bit thicker
than mine. Ronnie and I used to do each other's barnet* in
that period—in hotel rooms or at each other's parents' house.
And we didn't go in for some amateur, pudding-bowl setup,
either. We had this method of pulling the hair down between
thumb and forefinger and chopping at it with the scissors—very
professional. And we'd stop all the time to check it in the mirror.
We'd take ages doing it, ages, to get it right for each other. What
a wonderful bond that is between two men. Most blokes would
have been sabotaging each other's hair. "Yeah, that looks all
right, leave it." Not us.

The idea with the top bit was to look as though you had just
rolled out of bed after a night of enviable debauchery—though,
again, the look wasn't casually achieved. An awful lot of work
went into looking that disheveled. In particular, there was a
lot of hanging upside down at the drying stage—or, at least,
hanging forward from the hips and letting gravity play its part.
This was the technique taught me by a female hairdresser in
Chicago in 1968 while I was on tour with Jeff Beck. She told me
that bending forward and blowing through from the nape of the
neck downwards gives the hair a lot of body and makes use of
the natural oils far more efficiently and to far greater effect than
back-combing. I said, "Fantastic, I'll try it." And then I basically
had an exploding head for the next four decades.

It's not true that my hair hasn't changed at all through all
those years, though. There have been some breakout moments,
some experimental phases, some variations on the basic theme.
For example, I went red a couple of times. Once was in the

---

* Cockney rhyming slang: barnet = Barnet Fair = hair

mid-1970s, when I was in a relationship with the actress Britt
Ekland. We both did it—just for the shock value, really, because
it wasn't what people expected from two famously blond people.
Did it shock anyone? I can't remember. I think it got a few looks,
which was probably the point. And then we went back to being
blond.

In London in the 1980s, I used to go to Denny, a mad
hairdresser at Sweeney Todd's on Beauchamp Place. I loved
that shop. I made sure I got in at about six in the evening,
when it was starting to get quiet. And then we'd send out for
pints and shorts from the pub opposite and all proceed to get
bombed out of our minds. A haircut in those circumstances
would take about five hours. But it would be the most
convivial haircut you ever had.

Denny, too, persuaded me to go red for a while, towards
the end of the decade, going shorter with the hair this time and
teaming it with a beard: kind of like an Action Man soldier doll
with henna. Looked all right, I thought. My problem with facial
hair is that I can only grow it around the mouth and chin and
not on the cheeks. (Before anyone raises any questions about
machismo, permit me to mention the name of someone else who
has this issue: Muhammad Ali.) Again, the red was a brief phase,
and then I went back to blond. If you're sensible, you always
come back to what works best.

The blond aspect started to come in when I moved to
California in 1975 and my hair naturally turned that way in
the sun. I then began to accentuate the effect artificially—
from the softer shades all the way up to the full-blown near-
white peroxide with dark roots of the 1980s. Right now it's a
combination of three colors, mixed together by a girl who comes
to the house to do it.

And the length of the hair has also varied somewhat. It

probably grew to its record length in the early 1970s, when I was with the Faces. The top was still chopped into spikes but the back got down to shoulder-blade level—which was, of course, a highly popular male approach at the time. If you were doing it properly, and ensured the hair was clean enough and sufficiently blow-dried, it would bounce slightly around the ears as you walked. This was the desired effect, anyway.

The spikes provided something you could pull at with your fingers—very handy during television interviews. There's some footage on YouTube of an interview I did with Russell Harty on British television in 1973 in which I appear to devote at least as much energy to reorganizing my hair as I do to answering his questions. I also appear to be holding a glass of rum and Coke, and, to judge from the state of my eyes, have had several similar glasses behind the scenes. Excellent rock 'n' roll behavior— though, of course, founded on the sheer terror of live television as much as anything else.

The hair has shortened considerably at the back since then, but I've not had it above collar length since childhood. Above collar length would just seem wrong to me. The idea of exposing the back of my neck . . . no, that would run counter to nature. And the spikes have stayed. Their length has gone up and down a bit, according to my mood, the times, the state of the economy, etc. But the basic principle has remained the same. At Steven Carey's salon, my hairdresser in Mayfair, I have written on the wall, below the mirror, the length above which my hair must not go: "6 cm." In Los Angeles my hairdresser uses a six-centimeter measuring stick.

These days there is no sugar involved in the creation of my hairstyle. I may use a spot of product (I get sent all sorts; my general feeling is that they are all pretty much the same thing). And there is no back-combing either. I still employ the upside-down drying method—although, after years of spiking, it now seems to grow in that direction in any case. Even if I wanted to try another style, the hair wouldn't let me.

My hair is also a very efficient warning system. Ronnie Wood and I have this in common: if our hair doesn't want to stand up, after all the tricks, all the product, and drying it upside down, then we know we're sick and it's time for us to take to our beds. Our hair is our barometer.

Do I still spend a lot of time thinking about and working on my hair? Yes. Am I aware of having good hair days and bad hair days? Definitely. Am I more than averagely relieved to have been unaffected by typical male-pattern baldness? You bet. (Had it set in, I would have gone for a weave, like Elton.) Do I consider myself blessed that the barnet hasn't gone gray beyond a few easily colored-in bits at the sides? Indeed I do. (I must be in the right profession, seeing how President Obama has gone gray overnight, along with Kenny Dalglish.) Does any of this interest in my own hair border on narcissism? Well, say so if you must.

But it's understandable, surely. The hair is part of the job. It's my signature: a convenient shorthand for me and what I do, and, if you will, a logo for the business. Even now it would be possible to go into any barber's in Britain, plonk yourself down in the chair, and ask for "a Rod," and without further explanation the barber would know what you are talking about.

It announces my presence, and my availability for work, as effectively as the light on the top of a taxicab. If I want to go unnoticed, a baseball cap or a trilby or any kind of hair-concealing hat will do it, pretty much every time.

The cover of my *Out of Order* album from 1988 is a photo-graph of the top of my head. No face visible: just hair. The cover for the *Storyteller* box set that came out in 1989—and similarly the posters advertising the residency that I took on at Caesars Palace in Las Vegas in 2011—shows a drawing of the back of my head.

And forgive me, but I take a little bit of pride in that—in being someone who can be recognized by his hair alone, seen from the back, or even from directly above. That means your hairstyle is working for you, doesn't it? That means the hours with the hairdryer have paid off. That's doing hair properly.

CHAPTER 3

Events most grave.

n 1962, at the age of seventeen, I met a girl called Susannah Boffey at a party in London. She was extremely pretty, of medium height, with brown hair, well spoken, well educated, thoroughly middle-class—altogether out of my league. Yet I charmed her and made her laugh and she was my first serious girlfriend. And within a year, to the profound shock of both of us, she was pregnant.

It must have happened in Brighton. Although I had put my beat-nik phase aside and smartened up, those weekend trips to the beach with mates and a guitar continued, and Sue was part of them—with me, cuddled up in British Rail train carriages, arm in arm along the promenade. In late March and early April, all of us used to sleep on Saturday nights under the arches beneath the road along the seafront. Or we might use the beach in front of the area called Black Rock, beside the wall of the art deco lido. If the police moved us on, which frequently happened, we would pick up our things and find a spot under Brighton Pier instead. And in one of those locations—and certainly not in a bed—the baby was conceived.

It was bewildering. We were eighteen, blithely having fun, being teenaged, riding trains out of London for kicks, unused to weighing consequences. Nothing about our lives was formed or settled. Neither of us had regular jobs or money, although Sue's background was more affluent than mine. I remember the disbelief I felt on the evening she told me—assuming that she was joking and then realizing from the expression on her face that she wasn't. And I remember the disbelief being replaced with fear—fears, too immense and vague to process at once, about what this would mean for our lives, but also fear, very sharply, of my parents and their certain reaction. They would be scandalized. I had got a girl pregnant, out of wedlock. In their eyes, I would be visiting shame upon the whole family. No distress I had ever caused them would be comparable with that.

So I kept the whole story from them. I told myself I was protecting them from something they didn't need to know—although, of course, I was protecting myself from them at the same time. The only member of the family in whom I confided about Sue's pregnancy at the time was my brother Bob. I was in tears when I told him. He was angry with me for my carelessness, but sympathetic too. He was my brother, in other words. He went to see Sue and told her that if he could be of any help to her, he would be. Sue told him, "I'll manage."

Our friends weren't scandalized. They rallied around us in their own ways. The lads—being the lads—proposed having a whip-round* for an abortion but abandoned the idea when they realized they wouldn't be able to raise the required fee. Remember that abortion was illegal in Britain until the Abortion Act of 1967—four years

---

* Taking up a collection

later—and Sue never had any intention of terminating the pregnancy, and I never suggested to her that she should. Her chosen course was to have the child and then give it up for adoption. At first, during the pregnancy, we carried on seeing each other and trying to behave as we were before: two young lovers, boyfriend and girlfriend, enjoying the freedom of London in the early 1960s. But obviously things between us were permanently altered. After four months we separated. An incident on Brighton Beach, not long before we split up, indicates how fractious the relationship had become.

Sue was just beginning to show. I was sitting, as ever, with the guitar, and people around me were saying, "Sing that Dylan one, Roddy." Perhaps I was ignoring Sue, not giving her the attention she deserved while in such a delicate state, because suddenly there was a clunk and a crack and the instrument jumped in my hands. It seemed she had picked a large stone off the beach and heaved it through my guitar. I can only assume that she was trying to get my attention, which she most certainly did.

The scene nearly became very ugly. One of the lads started to grab hold of Sue, forgetting she was pregnant, but everyone shouted at him to calm down. Meanwhile, in silent horror, I stood there examining the damage to my guitar—my prized Zenith steel-strung guitar, which now had an ugly split across its body. (I still, incidentally, have that broken guitar at home.) It wasn't long after that, as the summer ended, that we parted.

The next thing I remember about all this is that it's November, and I am being woken at midnight, in the bedroom above my dad's newspaper shop, by a woman shouting my name up at the window. I push back the curtain and see two of Sue's friends on the pavement down below. I open the window and look out blearily, and they say, "You'd better get down the hospital. Sue's having the baby."

I throw on some clothes and slip out as quietly as I can, so as not to disturb my sleeping and still entirely unaware parents. I go down to Whittington Hospital in Highgate and wait, walking up and down in the corridors, until I am told that the baby is born, that it's a girl, and that the mother is well. But I don't see the baby. I want to see her, but at the same time I don't want to because I am afraid of what I might feel.

I sign the adoption papers. And then I walk out into the cold street and go home, assuming that this passage of my life is closed and expecting never to hear anything more.

CHAPTER 4

In which our hero has a fortuitous and life-changing encounter in a railway station, is almost asphyxiated in the back of a van, and conducts his first experiment with tartan trousers.

owe so much to Long John Baldry. He discovered me—on a bench in a railway station, as the perfectly accurate story goes—and he turned me into a singer and a performer, but that's really only the beginning of it. I loved him while he lived and was distraught when he died. I carry his picture in my wallet and, I've got to tell you, there is not a day goes by that I don't think of the guy.

The station in question was at Twickenham, out to the west of London, which was somewhere I ended up a lot in the period between 1962 and 1963, when I was going to clubs, watching bands, wondering if I fit in—though I felt pretty confident that I did—but also *where* I fit in, which I had yet to work out.

Over in Richmond, down the way from Twickenham and placed conveniently opposite the railway station, was the Crawdaddy

Club—nothing more than the back room of a pub, but a sensational place to be when it was packed with people jumping around and going nuts. It was where I saw, and loved, the Yardbirds. They had a guitarist called Eric Clapton, who didn't seem too shoddy. The Crawdaddy had to close eventually because it got a bit too rowdy, but everyone simply shifted over to the Richmond Athletic Club, where there was no stage and the audience could get right in a band's face. Incredible atmosphere.

But the legendary Eel Pie Island Hotel was the big hangout for me—an ancient, damp ballroom stuck out on a lump of land in the middle of the Thames and reached by a rickety wooden footbridge. The place was used for ballroom dancing in the 1920s and 1930s and was then a jazz venue until the early 1960s, when it started booking the newly emerging rhythm and blues bands. At the end of the bridge, two old dears in fur coats would be waiting to take your thrupenny toll.

Inside the club, a bar ran the length of one wall—and never ran out of glasses, which was strange given that the sport at the end of the night was lobbing your beer mug into the river. Debate continues to rage over whether the dance floor was sprung, or simply rotten on one side. Either way, when people danced on the left, people on the right would bounce up and down whether they wanted to or not.

The bands' dressing room, meanwhile, was a strange kind of hutch, or doll's house, suspended above the stage, with little curtained windows through which the performers could look down on the audience. The stage was accessed via a narrow staircase in the corner. Many were the singers who attempted a dramatic entrance down those steps and finished on their arse in the audience.

The ruler of this unique kingdom was a shrewd bloke called Arthur Chisnall. As I discovered when I started to play there, Arthur paid the bands in one-pound notes and fivers—never anything bigger. At the end of the night, he'd thumb out the money and you'd leave with a stack of notes too big for your pocket.

But at first I went there as a paying customer—riding the Tube down to Waterloo and changing to the overground train for Twickenham. That was a pretty lengthy journey to make from Archway, where I lived. And it could be even longer going back if, tired and a little the worse for wear, as one frequently was, I fell asleep, skipped through Archway, and woke up with a jolt at the end of the line in High Barnet. Still, it was worth the effort. When you dressed up in your finery and carefully arranged your hair and set off for Eel Pie Island, you had the palm-tingling sense that you were heading somewhere truly exotic. Membership cards for the club were done up to look like mock passports—marked "Eelpiland"—just to make the message absolutely clear: the place was its own country. And that country was densely populated with music nuts, art students, and pretty girls in short dresses. As George Melly once said, "You could see sex rising from Eel Pie Island like steam from a kettle." It was a fantastically exciting destination, and the place where I really began to understand the power of rhythm and blues, when it's done right.

I was eighteen and going out with Sue Boffey. Sue had a friend called Chrissie, who one night wanted us to go and see her boyfriend's band, over in Richmond. This boyfriend was some kind of singer, evidently. Sue and I agreed to go.

Chrissie's surname was Shrimpton, her boyfriend was called Mick Jagger, and his group was called the Rolling Stones. I wonder what became of them. The night we saw them, they were sat on stools, wearing cardigans, playing blues covers and one or two numbers of their own. The singer could certainly hold a room's attention. Long John would later describe Jagger as "a medieval rendering of a hobgoblin," which pretty much summed it up. I didn't meet Mick on that occasion, but I remember thinking the band was great, while also having this nagging feeling inside: "I could do this." In fact, I may even have been bold enough to think, "My voice is better than that." I could draw a few people around me with a guitar on a beach; why couldn't I take it up a level and enthrall an audience from a stage?

But who with? I had hung about a bit with the members of a group from round my way called the Raiders, who knew that I could sing. But that hadn't worked out particularly well. The band got an audition with Joe Meek, the record producer, and invited me along to do vocals at the session. Meek was an intimidating bloke in a suit and tie who sported a rather magnificent rock 'n' roll quiff and had a studio in a three-story apartment above a leather goods shop on the Holloway Road. We trudged up the stairs, set up in the sound room, and played for a few minutes—I can't remember what. But I can remember that, at the end of the number, Meek came through from the control room, looked me directly in the eye, and blew a long raspberry. I got my coat. I guess that was my first official review. The band became a solely instrumental group after that. Not an especially auspicious start.

I got a kinder break eventually with a band called Jimmy Powell and the Five Dimensions. Powell was a blues singer from Birmingham, built like a boxer, a tough old fucker who had become a bit of a player on the gig circuit through the fact that he could do a really accurate Ray Charles impression. How did I land up playing with Powell? It was all about who you knew. The aforementioned Raiders turned into the Moontrekkers, and the Moontrekkers' guitarist went on to play with the Five Dimensions, and he in turn mentioned me to Jimmy Powell. And that, clearly, was how you got yourself a gig.

Well, sort of a gig. If I stood around for long enough, looking hopeful, I would be invited up onstage to play harmonica on a couple of numbers at the Ken Colyer Club in the basement of a building on Great Newport Street, just off the Charing Cross Road in central London. Colyer was a thirty-four-year-old jazz trumpeter who had come back from a stint in the merchant navy with wide experiences of American, and particularly New Orleans–style, jazz, and had become a pioneering performer and promoter of jazz in London. Lonnie Donegan, who made the skiffle records that fascinated me at school, was a guitarist in Ken Colyer's Jazzmen for a while. Originally a place for traditional jazz, the Ken Colyer Club was now hosting the emerging wave of rhythm and blues acts, which is how Jimmy Powell and the Five Dimensions came to be there, and I would stand there at the side of the stage and give it some huffing and puffing in G, while the audience looked on, nodding appreciatively, or possibly asking themselves, "Why the hell doesn't someone teach this bloke to suck as well as blow?"

My other principal job was to entertain the band in traffic jams by throwing open the back door of the Dormobile we drove around in, and rolling out onto the road. Never fails to get a laugh.

However, after a short while, my role got bigger when Jimmy asked me if I could sing backing vocals on Ray Charles's "What'd I Say," which was the band's showcase number. Obviously, this seemed like a major promotion, so I was very happy to accept—only to get given the elbow almost immediately.

Now, why do you suppose that happened? Was it because my backing vocals were truly appalling—so bad that they could not possibly be heard in public again? Hmmm. Or was it because Powell suddenly realized I could sing and didn't fancy having competition in the band from some young guy with smart clothes and a nice haircut at the side of the stage?

I couldn't possibly comment. You be the judge. All I know is, I was out . . .

. . . only to be gathered in again, not long after, by Long John Baldry. To say that Long John stood out on the music scene in those days is to put it mildly. He was six feet, seven inches tall, for one thing, a singer with a huge, rich voice, fair-haired and almost shockingly handsome. He had charisma to spare, and was an almighty presence on a stage. He was twenty-three when I met him—just five years older than me, but decades more worldly. He was well spoken and always immaculately dressed, a great proponent of the silver sharkskin, three-button suit, worn with high-heeled boots—Carnaby Street fashion, you might have said, except he wouldn't get his stuff from Carnaby Street, but from a backstreet Greek tailor who could do it cheaper. He had a duffel coat, I remember, when that was a truly exotic item to be wearing, but he mostly specialized in suits—the high style inherited from the American blues musicians that Long John loved, with their superb three-pieces and shined shoes and carefully selected socks. You sang about poverty, and you may actually have been poor, but you never dressed like less than a million dollars: that was the deal.

John was a grammar school* boy from Middlesex, just outside London, and seriously intelligent. In fact, his parents used to say his decision to spend his life in music was "a terrible waste of a wonderful brain." He had an approach to music that was almost scholarly—and he had the cool records, the American pressings, seemingly before anyone else. It was John who turned me on to a lot of blues music, moving me on from my earlier, folk interests. I remember being in his flat on Goodge Street once, before we went off somewhere for a gig, and asking him if I could borrow his copy of Muddy Waters's *At Newport 1960*—the one with the cover shot of Muddy standing on the stairs in a fantastically cool white tie. John said, "I'm afraid not. I've only just got it back from Keith Relf of the Yardbirds, and Mick and Keith want it next." The Stones wanted to make copies of it on their reel-to-reels. Everyone wanted to hear this stuff. It was as though Long John was the lending library.

He was also a prodigious drinker of vodka and a big fan of what he called "madness," which was basically his code word for stupid behavior in the name of fun. He was also gay, which (and this is an indication of how unworldly I was) it took me some time to work out.

---

* State-funded high school that selected pupils based on academic ability

Looking back now to the very first days of us being in a band together, it was beyond coincidence how many times I would turn up at his flat to wait for the van to collect us for a gig, and find John just out of the shower, only wearing a towel, or sometimes completely naked. And this didn't even register with me, in my naïveté, as a signal. In football changing rooms, men walk around naked all the time. It seemed totally normal to me, and I was completely unfazed, let alone driven to interpret his motives.

I even ended up sharing a bed with him one night—on tour with the band, in some crappy hotel in Bolton where there weren't enough rooms to go round—and was none the wiser. Only when I went down for breakfast the next morning and some of the other band members sniggered and made remarks such as "Are you sure your trousers are on the right way round?" did the penny belatedly begin to drop—that Long John was, as people said in those days, "one of them pooftahs."

Then again (and how incredible and barbaric this seems now), it was actually illegal to be gay in Britain in 1964, and would remain so until 1967, so it would be understandable if this were not something you necessarily wanted to go around advertising or even confiding to people. I'm sure things must have occurred, but I don't even remember Long John picking up anyone out of the crowd when we gigged. In later life, he would openly have boyfriends. In those early days, however, he carefully kept them hidden—and therefore had to put up with the usual stuff from aunts, asking him when he was "going to find a nice girl and settle down" and also from his mum, who apparently once expressed to John her concerns about him hanging out with me, on the grounds that she found me "a bit poofy."

Long John was steeped in music. He had hung out at the Ealing Jazz Club—a damp basement where they had to hang a sheet over the ceiling above the stage to stop the condensation dripping down on the musicians—and became a part of the Blues Incorporated collective, with Alexis Korner and Cyril Davies, who took Muddy Waters as their model and declared themselves "the first white electric blues group in the world." Then, when Korner decided to turn Blues Incorporated into a progressive jazz band, Long John went off to sing with Davies in the Cyril Davies R&B All Stars, which favored the Chicago blues that John liked most.

Davies was a balding, burly bloke with a suitcase full of harmonicas who could play a real storm, having had less difficulty than me getting his head around the whole blow/suck business. Unfortunately, his health abruptly became unsound and then rapidly deteriorated, and in January 1964, after a period of illness, he died—of heart inflammation, people said at the time, although it seems that what he actually had was leukemia. He was only thirty-one.

Long John decided to mark Davies's passing with a tribute performance by the All Stars at Eel Pie Island: a wake in the form of a gig. I went to that show, although I remember very little about it. History relates, though, that also in the audience that night was Ian McLagan, later the keyboard player with the Faces, and that the support act was a band called Jeff Beck and the Tridents. But that's how tight it all seemed to be in those days: at any time, almost everyone who would later matter would be standing around in the same place. One unfortunate gas explosion under the wrong club on the wrong night, and three-quarters of the history of British rock music would have been taken out in one go.

Anyway, I do recall what happened after the show, which is that I went and sat on the platform at Twickenham Station, waiting for the Waterloo train. And, to pass the time, I took my harmonica out of the pocket of my overcoat and started to play. And what I played was the riff from Howlin' Wolf's "Smokestack Lightnin'," a blues number that I knew roughly how to blow my way through.

In the version of the story that Long John would later tell, his ears pricked up at the sound of a beautiful wailing blues carried on the wintry night air through the desolate station. Lovely. But that can't be right, given the state of my harmonica playing. So maybe he was drunk. Or maybe I was drunk, and playing better than I ever had. Either way, he approached me, all wrapped up against the cold—a bundle of rags, as he described me, with a big nose sticking out of it—and introduced himself.

The train came, we traveled back into central London, we talked about how he was taking on the Cyril Davies R&B All Stars in Davies's absence, and by the time we reached Waterloo he had asked me if I wanted to join the band as backing vocalist. He was proposing renaming the band Long John Baldry and the Hoochie Coochie Men. And what he was also proposing was paying me £35 per week.

Now, at this moment, if I'd still been playing the harmonica, I probably would have swallowed it. Thirty-five quid a week! Twenty a week was a thousand a year, and people with serious jobs were getting £1,000 per year in those days. And he was offering me £35 . . . to sing backing vocals?

How did he even know I could sing? Maybe he had seen me get up with Jimmy Powell. Maybe someone had told him something. Or maybe he just fancied me (though he certainly didn't say as much). It all seemed peculiarly magical and easy—like something out of a film. One moment you're at a loose end, waiting for a train; the next you're being offered drop-dead terms as a professional musician.

So, did I leap at it? No. I did what any good boy of nineteen would have done: I told him I would have to ask my mum first.

I guess, somewhere in my mind, I was already envisaging how this encounter might translate into conversation at home the next day. "I met this good-looking man on a train last night and he said he's going to pay me to drive around the country with him." Knowing my mum, she would have a number of things to say about that, and "Off you go, then, son—and be sure and have a wild old time" wouldn't necessarily be the first of them.

But it was here that Long John played an absolute blinder. He said he perfectly understood—he, too, was still living with his mother at this time—and that he would come round and talk to my mum himself.

And, typically, he was as good as his word. Long John might have been a big name on the British live blues circuit, but my parents, of course, didn't know him from Adam. Yet through the door of my dad's sweetshop comes this clean, beautifully turned out, well-spoken man, the perfect parent-calming device, bringing (the clinching touch) a bunch of flowers. My mother had a lot of questions: Would I be going outside London? What time would I be back?

"Don't you worry, Mrs. Stewart. I'll look after your Roddy."

All my mum's motherly fears of show-business debauchery and on-the-road seediness melted like butter in a pan.

"Well, all right, John. You're a gentleman."

And, just like that, I had a job in a band.

There wasn't time to rehearse. My brother Don took me into the West End and treated me to a white shirt with a high collar and a tie, and off I went. We had a show pretty much straightaway at the Twisted Wheel in Manchester. On the way up in the van with the rest of the group Long John said I'd need a song. The idea was that I would come on with the band, sing a number, and then introduce Long John. I said I could do "The Night Time Is the Right Time" by Ray Charles. "Can you play that?" I asked the band in general. There were arched eyebrows, as if I'd just asked, "Is water wet, or the Pope a Catholic?"

The gig was an all-nighter, which meant I would have to sing twice. A crowd would come in for the evening session, and we'd do a set. Then that crowd would be cleared out and the club would let the all-night crowd in, and we would play again.

The evening session nears, there's a big audience in, and I'm a bit of a mess. Underconfident. Also shaking quite a lot. And feeling pretty sick. Sick to the pit of my stomach. Noticing my condition, Cliff Barton, the band's bass player—a brilliant guy—quietly presses something into my hand and utters something along the lines of the classic doctor's expression: "Take this, you'll feel better."

I find I am holding a small black pill.

"What is it?" I say.

It is, apparently, a "black bomber." I have heard of them, but I've never taken one, or anything like it.

"It will just help you along slightly," Cliff assures me. "A bit like having a cup of coffee."

Genuinely alarmed, I tell Cliff, "But I don't drink coffee."

But Cliff is adamant—and, again, somewhat doctorlike. "Trust me," he says.

I trust him. I swallow the black bomber in a slug of brown ale. For a short while, absolutely nothing happens. Then, very suddenly, absolutely everything happens. I feel as though someone has plugged my forefinger into the mains. Amphetamine courses through my system. My eyes widen until they are the size of dinner plates. And doubtless my hair would have stood up on my head as high as Dusty Springfield's, had I not already carefully back-combed it into that position.

When I take the stage, I am more awake than I have ever been in my entire life. I feel like my feet are about six inches off the ground. The band drops into "The Night Time Is the Right Time," and I go at it like an attack dog seeing off a burglar. We haven't rehearsed, remember, so the number is held together by signals between us, and potentially endless. Bad idea. I want another verse, another chorus. I am barking at the band, "Again! Keep the jam going!" The band are looking at each other in a state of mystification. I have no idea what it sounds like. I only know that it feels absolutely fucking brilliant. The crowd certainly seems enthusiastic—or at least for the first six minutes. After that, it's possible that their attention wanes slightly. But I wouldn't really know. Eventually, after what may have been the longest version of "The Night Time" in performing history, the band manages to batter the song to an ending and I bring on Long John so that the show proper can begin. An "upper"? An "over-the-topper," more like.

I'm wired for the rest of the night. They have to chisel me off the stage.

I don't think I slept for about four days.

My first gig.

Others quickly followed. The band was busy. I could see why the pay was handsome: Long John's reputation as a singer went ahead of us, and we were earning big money—out several nights of the week, up and down the country, playing the clubs, doing the universities. At the peak of it, we'd be booked for seven nights a week and sometimes playing as many as three shows per night on the weekends.

Our transport was an old, bright yellow moving van, for which Long John had paid £40. It was driven by a bloke called Mad Harry, who had flown Lancaster bombers in the RAF in the Second World War and had never really come down. He had the dashboard done out like the cockpit of a plane, with altimeters and clocks and dials and redundant bits of aircraft memorabilia, and he wore a uniform of goggles, a leather jacket, and a silk scarf. Mad Harry's other duty was to announce the band onstage each night, and to milk the audience for their appreciation at the end. For this he changed into a tailcoat with his service medals pinned to its front.

The band would be sat around in the back of the van, on four knackered old sofas which were grouped around a paraffin stove, tied down to the floor with ropes to prevent it upending when the van turned corners. The stove kept us warm. It also filled our throats and eyes with oil fumes. I'm not sure "health and safety" would have been impressed. And God knows what would have become of us all in the event of a crash. Any collision at speed would have converted the van into a rocket.

The sense of danger was increased by Mad Harry's driving style, which owed a lot to the accelerator and not much to the brake pedal. For Harry, speed was everything. He drove at all times as though hammering a plane along a runway. Long John—a nervous passenger at the best of times—would permanently be thumping on the dashboard and shouting, "For the love of God, man, slow down!"

Mad Harry had a special trick for the last stages of the trek to Eel Pie Island, which was to take the final corner at speed and nearly put the van over the side of the road into the Thames. It was his signature move—his barrel roll, if you like. Long John eventually got tired of being scared and started taking the train to gigs whenever he could. Ian Armitt, the pianist—Scots boy, fabulous player—bought himself a car, specifically because he thought it would increase his chances of staying alive. I probably would have done the same, but I was still saving up.

Of course, it was pretty punishing for the van, too. It eventually decided it had had enough on the way to a gig at Newcastle University, when it ground to a halt and would go no further. We turned up for that show in the back of a tow truck.

Still, by then, the mock Lancaster bomber had carried us the length and breadth of Great Britain. It had taken us to Stoke-on-Trent, to a club called the Place, where the audience went nuts, punching the air in delight—to the confusion of Long John, who, misinterpreting the gesture, thought he was witnessing some kind of Nazi gathering and halted the band in order to announce, "We'll have none of that fascist bullshit here!" It killed the gig stone dead.

And it had taken us to Dundee, where a performance at the university was the setting for my first experiment with tartan clothing onstage. Long John had suggested we go into the city and buy some Scots-themed trousers and waistcoats. He thought this would be a winning gesture with the crowd, which we knew could be tough to please. In the event, the audience took one look at this tall English guy and his mate with the big nose and the Dusty Springfield hairdo, both of them wearing tartan to try and ingratiate themselves, and decided they were having none of it. Beer cans rained down on the stage. It would be a few years before I tried that again.

In some places, of course, I didn't need to be wearing tartan to attract hecklers. Sometimes the hair was enough. Every now and again you'd get some wag who would ask loudly, between numbers, "Are you a boy or a girl?" I had my stock answer ready: "Come up here and I'll show you." Not that witty, maybe. But effective.

Mind you, it was John himself who nicknamed me "Phyllis." Hence the graffiti, by unknown hand, which appeared on the wall at Eel Pie Island, and in which "Long John Baldry and the Hoochie Coochie Men" had been amended to become "Ada Baldry and the Hoochie Coochie Ladies featuring Phyllis Stewart." This was the price you paid for taking care of your hair in 1964.

At the Manor House in London, where we had a residency for a while, the stage was made of planks and crates, none of it nailed down. Over the course of a show, cracks would open up, into which entire members of the group and their instruments would disappear. Either that or the drummer would disappear off the back of the stage and there would be a short pause while he dusted himself down and the drums were reassembled. I saw Zoot Money at that venue once. Little sharkskin jackets and skinny ties—what a band they were. And could they drink.

My trouble was holding it. One night onstage at Eel Pie Island I was taken short by the urge to empty my bladder, and because the toilets were a fair old hike out to the back of the club, I elected to dash upstairs into the doll's house dressing room and relieve myself into an empty beer glass instead. This would have been a more sanitary procedure if I hadn't stood the glass on the floor and then accidentally kicked it over in my haste to return. The liquid soaked its way through the floorboards and later reappeared in the form of a succession of warm drips directly onto Long John's head and shoulders.

Lesson of this story: never build a dressing room directly over a stage. I had to give Long John the money to get his suit dry-cleaned.

My solo repertoire had begun to expand. As well as "The Night Time Is the Right Time," I started being trusted with Muddy Waters's "Tiger in Your Tank" and with John Lee Hooker's "Dimple." Did I think of myself as a blues singer? Not really. I was a folkie at heart. But I have always thought I could turn my voice to most things, and I gave these numbers what I had. No more "black bombers" necessary, by the way. I would have a bottle of Newcastle Brown and, alongside it, a scotch and orange juice—a remarkable combination, probably as bad for the teeth as for the liver—and that would last me all night. If it was a London gig, at the Marquee, say, I would leave home in the early evening, holding on to my hair, and walk up to Archway Station, stopping in at the Woodman pub, and have my brown ale and scotch and orange there. Then back on the Tube at the end of the night, still slightly pissed and pleased with myself.

My presence in the band seemed to be bringing a new contingent into the Hoochie Coochie Men audience—namely figures from the mod scene, who liked a bit of R&B sung by someone in a tailored suit with well-controlled hair. Reflecting this, the billing in some places would be altered to become "Long John Baldry and the Hoochie Coochie Men, featuring Rod 'The Mod' Stewart." Long John started introducing me that way from the stage: "Ladies and whatever you've got with you—here he is . . . Rod 'The Mod' Stewart!"

And, even as that was happening, I was learning one of the great truths of human chemistry: girls quite like a singer. Indeed, it was clear that, having seen a person sing, girls would happily approach that person directly, open a conversation with him, and seek to spend some time in his company. This turned out to be the magic bestowed by singing: pulling power. It was exceptionally good news. My great trick at these times was to head to a venue's bar awhile before I was due onstage, and get into conversation with an attractive girl, without telling her I was part of the evening's entertainment. Then, when Mad Harry got up and introduced the band, I would be able to say to the girl, "Excuse me—got a show to do," and set off through the audience to the stage. This rarely failed to be an impressive surprise, and when you rejoined the girl after the show, you were usually made.

In March 1964 we got to support Sonny Boy Williamson, the American blues singer and harmonica player and one of the great originators, in a gig to open the Marquee Club at its new premises on Wardour Street, Soho—a huge deal for me, because I was such a fan. Williamson, who was to die of a heart attack only a year later, aged fifty-three, was in an immaculate two-tone suit and seemed almost impossibly charismatic—the real deal.

No alcohol license at the Marquee at that time, by the way: Coke and coffee only. This was the venue where, one night, a member of the audience at a Hoochie Coochie Men gig had the temerity to stand near the front reading a newspaper—intending to convey, I suppose, his contempt for our faux-American R&B stylings. Long John dealt with him most efficiently. He stepped down off the stage and, using a cigarette lighter, set fire to the paper.

We played a gig with Little Walter, too, another of the formative American bluesmen and still the only person to be inducted into the Rock and Roll Hall of Fame exclusively for services to harmonica playing. He was a little frightening, to be honest, and may have had one or two problems with anger management. At any rate, he asked me backstage to find him some girls and then, when I looked doubtful about it, threatened to pull a knife on me. I spent the rest of the night carefully avoiding him. Great harmonica player, though, obviously.

There is only one stormy patch that I recall in this whole period, and we ran into it in Portsmouth, on the south coast of England. The

Beatles had invited Long John to make a guest appearance on one of their television specials—not the sort of invitation you were likely to decline, claiming that your hair needed washing—and he had remained in London for the filming, promising to join us in Portsmouth later, in time for a gig at the Rendezvous Club.

Come showtime, though, there was no sign of him and we were obliged to take the stage by the angry club owner, with me filling in. I'd only really got three numbers to offer, and I drew them out for as long as I could, but I was struggling and the audience was getting restless. There was the occasional cry of "We want Long John" and "Fuck off, you big queer." A couple of numbers in, Long John finally entered through the audience and, in my anger at having been hung out to dry, I made the mistake of greeting him from the stage, with something along the lines of the traditional "About fucking time." Long John climbed on the stage, completed the show, and then, backstage afterwards, very calmly fired me—causing me, I don't mind admitting, to burst into tears. I didn't think firing was something that happened to people in bands. I thought it was only something that happened in the real world of work.

My banishment lasted a week and I was readmitted, with no lasting rift, fortunately. In June, Long John, who had a solo record deal with United Artists, asked me to sing backing vocals on a version of "Up Above My Head," the Sister Rosetta Tharpe gospel song, for the B side of his single "You'll Be Mine." The resulting recording will not go down as one of my more relaxed performances. In fact, it has all the classic hallmarks of a novice in the studio—bursting to impress and oversinging like a maniac. The song is a "call and response" number, but in this case the response is louder than the call. It sounds like I'm trying to get the upper hand in a shouting match—and mostly succeeding.

My first released recording.

But what an eye-opener this period was altogether—and what an apprenticeship. When I first climbed into the back of that van with the Hoochie Coochie Men and breathed my first lungful of the paraffin smoke, I was a total musical novice. I could barely get my head around a simple twelve-bar blues at that point. Yet here I was onstage with proper, highly accomplished, much older musicians like Cliff Barton, Ian Armitt, and the guitarist Geoff Bradford, a brilliant jazz player who could also switch effortlessly into blues. Some of these guys were in their thirties and forties. They had all come up through the trad jazz scene and they were properly schooled, hugely experienced, road-tested, tight as a nut. When Geoff Bradford played John Lee Hooker it was perfect. When they did "Hoochie Coochie Man," which John sang, or "Got My Mojo Working," which was the finale, it sounded like the record—it sounded like Muddy's band. For a singer's first band to be this good—it was almost unfair. And also not a little scary, because I knew how good they were.

And then, arching over it all, there was the influence of Long John, which was unquantifiable as far as I was concerned. He led the way for me, partly by example, partly by direct instruction—everything from basic stagecraft to the delivery of a vocal. He told me to make sure that I stood at the microphone with my feet apart, and never with my feet together, which gave you no presence or authority. He showed me how to inhabit a song—to take it over, make it your own. He showed me how to talk to an audience, how to engage with people from a stage, how to forge a connection with a roomful of people that you mostly can't see. Here were lessons that would inform what I did for the rest of my career and will continue to do so for as long as I stand up in front of people with a microphone in my hand.

Mind you, not all of his wisdom was entirely trustworthy. He once advised me that giving oral sex to women would eventually ruin my voice and that I should desist from the practice immediately, if I valued my career. It was one of the rare occasions when I felt able to ignore him.

Those were golden days, though. I thought: "This is it. This is as good as it gets. Wonderful. Doing what I want: singing three or four songs a night, having a drink, looking at the birds, maybe pulling one of the birds, and then going home."

One of the questions my mum asked me when I went home and told her about Long John's job offer was, inevitably, "Is there a future in it?" And I'm sure I bluffed and blathered and came up with something to the effect of "Yes." The truth is, though, I didn't know. I certainly hoped so. But whatever happened, I thought, I've probably got a job here for nine months, and if that happens, I'll have enough to buy an MG Midget sports car, which was about £430 at the time. And if I could own an MG Midget—well, happy days.

But it wasn't just me. Everyone thought what was going on in the music business in the early 1960s was a sudden bright flash in the sky which was destined to fade and fall just as fast as it rose. We thought that the Beatles would have "Love Me Do," and that would be it. We felt the same about the Stones with "It's All Over Now." We didn't think this music that was sweeping across Britain, and carrying us with it, was going to last. We thought it was a fad—a big crush that everyone would get over eventually. And so, when you joined a band, you weren't thinking about the future, or your so-called career path. It was all new, so there was no context or preexisting pattern to enable you to think of it that way. You were in it because you loved it now, this minute, and anything else that happened along the way was a bonus.

CHAPTER 5

In which management is appointed, a single is recorded which inexplicably fails to set the airwaves alight, and we hear tell of an early brush with Gary Glitter.

John Rowlands and Geoff Wright first saw me sing with the Hoochie Coochie Men at the Marquee Club in London in April 1964. They must have thought I was all right, because they came up afterwards and asked if they could manage me.

At my age (I was nineteen at this point), and so early on in my life as a singer, just to be approached by people offering something as sophisticated as "management" was pretty entertaining. At the same time, I was smart enough to know that these are famously shark-infested waters—and that, classically, this is the moment in the story when the emerging singer naïvely, and possibly even drunkenly, signs everything away without realizing he has done so, thereby eventually buying some bloke in a suit a big house in Barbados and condemning himself to a life of poverty and expensive court cases.

But Rowlands and Wright clearly weren't sharks. Or they kept their teeth very well hidden if they were. I rather liked the cut of their jibs. Neither of them seemed exactly hip. Rowlands looked like John Major, the future British prime minister. Wright resembled David Attenborough. He would later say that he found it slightly embarrassing to walk next to me in public, on account of the hair and the clothes. Is that an asset in a manager? Probably not.

But Rowlands had been the "Ovaltine Man" in television commercials, and there's not a lot of people who can say that. He would later build a PR firm around the careers of Tom Jones and Engelbert Humperdinck. Wright had worked with Tommy Steele, Val Doonican, and Des O'Connor (big names, whatever else you want to say about them), and had also looked after the interests of Associated London Scripts, which was the company formed by Spike Milligan, Eric Sykes, Frankie Howerd, Ray Galton, and Alan Simpson—among the funniest writers in English comedy. These were pretty good calling cards to be able to set down.

So I told them I would be happy to have a look at a contract and they, in due course, drew one up and gave it to me. This, again, is a potentially vulnerable moment for the green artist. It's a classic Catch-22, in fact. What you really need is a manager to advise you on whether or not you should sign a contract with your manager. But, of course, you can't ask your manager because you don't have one.

Anyway, I didn't sign it there and then. I took it home and showed it to my brother Don, who understands numbers, and we both looked at it pretty carefully, and I sat on it, all in all, for about a fortnight, which had the useful effect of increasing Rowlands's and Wright's keenness. I've heard stuff said about the shrewd, businesslike mind that I've allegedly been able to call upon during my career, and up to a point there's some truth in that. But let's not exaggerate the case. Mostly what it comes down to, it seems to me, is not being taken entirely for a mug. So I returned to Rowlands and Wright with the contract and told them that I was happy with it, so long as we could insert a clause confirming that they couldn't have a percentage of anything I earned from singing with Long John and the band. (That arrangement pre-dated them, after all, so why should they get a piece of it?)

The document duly adjusted to our mutual satisfaction, there followed a celebratory champagne dinner in the Barrie Room at the Kensington Palace Hotel, by the end of which I had fallen asleep at the table, facedown in my plate. Exhaustion, I would claim, rather than the champagne, although it's possible that the champagne played a part.

My new managers now went about trying to get me a record deal. They needed a demo recording for that, so they booked some time in a pretty basic studio on Poland Street in Soho, got Ian Armitt and Cliff Barton along from the Hoochie Coochie Men, and we recorded seven songs in the space of about four hours: Oscar Brown, Jr., and Nat Adderley's "Work Song"; Jimmy Reed's "Ain't That Lovin' You Baby" and "Bright Lights Big City"; two Big Bill Broonzy numbers, "Moppers Blues" and "Keep Your Hands off Her"; Willie Dixon's "Don't You Tell Nobody"; and Howlin' Wolf's "Just Like I Treat You." It was rough and ready, but it was serviceable and probably as good as a demo needed to be.

Some of the feedback from record labels was that my voice was too rough for big commercial success. There's a bit of gravel in it, and people at the time seemed to be looking for something smooth. I think EMI, specifically, declined me on those grounds. There was also ap-parently anxiety in some quarters about whether I was conventionally pretty enough to make it as a solo singer. Ruthless old business, isn't it? Essentially, as far as some executives at the time seemed to think, I was offering gravel and a big nose to a marketplace that wanted smooth and pretty.

Yet with these recordings (and with no attempt to hide my nose), Rowlands and Wright managed to convince Mike Vernon at Decca

Records to release a single by me. Decca at that point was the home of the Rolling Stones, last seen (by me) sitting on stools in Richmond, wearing cardigans, but now apparently getting screamed at all over the place. It seemed a decent enough place to start.

However, have there been more professional recording sessions than the one that resulted in my first single? I think we may end up agreeing that there have.

The Decca Studios were in Broadhurst Gardens in West Hampstead, and on the morning of September 3, 1964, I report to reception, clutching (I'm not kidding) a small packet of cheese sandwiches made for me that morning by my mum.

"Rod Stewart," I say, casually enough. "I've got a booking."

Which I have—but, as the receptionist discovers, after a few confused moments of flipping through the diary, the booking is for September 10, a week later. My mistake. I return home, along with my packed lunch.

The following Thursday morning, I'm woken at home some time after eleven by my mum. Apparently, Geoff Wright is on the phone, wondering where I am. Well, actually, in bed is where I am, and slightly the worse for wear after a Hoochie Coochie Men gig the previous night. But I get downstairs to the phone and Geoff reminds me where I ought to be, which is Broadhurst Gardens. The band is in the studio, everyone's waiting: no singer.

"Jump in a taxi," says Geoff.

"I can't," I say. "It'll cost a fortune."

"I'll pay at this end," says Geoff. (Do you see what I did there?)

So I sit in a cab for half an hour or so, while my head slowly clears, and eventually walk into the studio at around midday, two hours into the appointed session, to find an atmosphere of thinly disguised impatience.

The tension doesn't substantially ease when I then suggest abandoning the proposed songs—which, to be perfectly frank, I haven't really bothered to learn. (Unlike the band, for whom these songs have been carefully arranged in advance.) The problem is, the material consists of new songs that Decca have put forward, from their catalogue of possible future hits, and they sound a bit poppy, a bit light, and (not to put too fine a point on it) a bit crap to me, and nowhere near the sort of earthier, bluesier stuff that I would automatically have in mind for myself.

"So, what are you suggesting we *do* record?" asks Geoff, with a smile so thin-lipped that it isn't really a smile at all—more a sort of grimace. Studio time, remember, is slipping by at however many pounds per minute, and all these assembled musicians are on Musicians' Union rates.

My idea, in fact, is that we should record this Sonny Boy Williamson track, which I can imagine getting my voice around.

"OK," says Geoff, tentatively. "So where's the music?"

Good question. Hadn't really thought about that.

But here's a brainwave: Why don't I just pop out to a local record store and buy a copy of the record? We can play it into the studio, and everyone can pick it up.

Geoff runs this idea past the band, who seem more or less amenable but are probably ready by this point to do anything likely to bring this amateur hour to an end.

"OK, then," says Geoff. "Off you go and get it."

One small problem: Could I borrow a couple of quid? (Do you see what I did there? Again?)

So I buy the record, with Geoff's money, and it gets piped through speakers from the control room into the studio, and the band busks along with it until they've got it down right. The bassist in particular, I'm driven to observe, seems to know what he's doing. He's called John Paul Jones and he will later have a certain amount of success in a beat combo called Led Zeppelin. Pretty quickly we have an acceptable version of the song "Good Morning, Little Schoolgirl." For the B side we knock out Big Bill Broonzy's "I'm Gonna Move to the Outskirts of Town," a number we all know anyway. And there it is.

My first single.

I'm not sure how the people at Decca must have felt when this recording was first played back to them. They were banking on getting a piece of chart-ready pop to throw onto the airwaves, and instead they got a fairly raw version of an old blues standard with a slightly saucy (in fact, downright lecherous) lyric. Still, however upset they were, it didn't stop them releasing it, just over a month later, on October 16, 1964.

Pretty thrilling for me, obviously, to see the navy-blue Decca label printed up with my name on it. Equally thrilling for the press, I'm sure, to receive their copies of the record along with a press release in the form of a Q&A, bringing them up to speed on my "Real Name" (Roderick David Stewart), a revelation of the thing I was "Not Very Fond Of" (I put "Scotland," amazingly enough—must have been the aftermath of that Dundee experience in tartan with Long John), and my "Dislikes" ("Plonkers"*—I'll stand by that).

Note, though, my "Ambition": "To sing with the Count Basie Orchestra." Even then I seem to have been taking the broader view.

This package may not have been enough to inspire coverage in the national press, but it did tweak my local paper, the ever-loyal *Hampstead & Highgate Express,* to print an interview with me. In the accompanying photograph I am in the Wellington Inn, on the Archway Road, with a glass of bitter to hand, and wearing a tartan scarf, a pair of trousers in a rather fetching blue-and-white stripe, and a pair of high-heeled boots. I told the paper's readers, "I'll stay on the bandwagon as long as it's there," and added, "Sure, I'm in it for the money."

---

* Stupid people

This bravado was clearly the cue for the single to die a swift and brutal death. Which it most certainly did, although not before either the Decca promotions department or Rowlands and Wright had managed to blag me a slot on *Ready Steady Go!*, ITV's hip and happening Friday-night pop music show.

That was, potentially, a pretty big break. In a Britain which had only just acquired a third television channel, *Ready Steady Go!* had immense powers of communication. You could be sure that virtually the entire record-buying public would be tuned in. "The weekend starts here" was the show's opening statement. If you played it right, your record sales started here, too.

So off I go to Rediffusion Studios in Kingsway. Nervous? Obviously, although I have done my best to take the edge off those nerves by stopping at a pub on the way to fortify myself with scotch and orange juice. The producers decide that I should appear alone, on a primitive gantry, with an electric guitar slung around my neck—despite the fact that the guitar you hear on the record is an acoustic, and despite the fact that it wasn't played by me in any case. But that's show business.

I have brought with me a bag containing a faintly beatnik-looking black round-neck sweater, and some altogether more voguish gray hipster trousers and a webbing belt—a good look, I feel able to tell myself, as I examine the effect of this outfit in the dressing-room mirror. At the appointed hour, I am led from the greenroom to my position on the set, where there is a brief but agonizing wait until the floor manager gets the word through his headphones and waves me on. At which point, as I step forward, I catch one foot behind the other and literally stumble into the nation's sight.

Terrible. The next three minutes pass in a blur of mortification, during which I can only comfort myself that I didn't fall flat on my face, which would have been far worse.

At the end, I take the customary bow before the generously

applauding studio audience, and then, as I return to the upright position, bring my hand up to steady the hair, which, heavy with lacquer, was always in danger of coming to grief during the bow recovery phase.

Incidentally, warming up the audience in the studio that night: Paul Raven, whom you—and, for that matter, the relevant authorities—will know better as Paul Gadd, aka Gary Glitter. Paul/Gary and I would bump into each other a fair bit in the early 1970s, when he was stomping around in shiny suits and having huge hits, and when neither I nor anyone I knew would have predicted a future for him in a Vietnamese jail. In fact, he seemed like a perfectly nice bloke. I particularly remember a party in Windsor when he fell in the swimming pool and became separated from his wig, which floated away like some sort of upturned duck. But now I'm getting ahead of myself.

After the recording at Rediffusion, I go to a pub in Soho to have a few drinks and to bask in the sensation of being "that person who was just on the telly"—an enjoyable if slightly deluded state, in which it becomes impossible for you to think that there is anyone in the room who *doesn't know*. Or anyone in Britain, in fact. And a bloke that I've seen around a fair bit but never spoken to comes over. He has back-combed hair a bit like mine and he has a big nose a lot like mine, and there is an immediate sense of kinship.

> HIM: Hello, face.
> ME: Hello, face.

(In those days you were a "face" if you were a fashionable type or a "mover" on the scene.) And then we fall to talking, and I tell him where I've just been and about my stumble onto the set of *Ready Steady Go!*, and we have a bloody good laugh about it and order another round of drinks. And that is the start of my still-firm friendship with Ronnie Wood.

It was, by some stretch, the most lasting thing to come out of that night. Boldly defying the odds, my big solo TV appearance did not send "Good Morning, Little Schoolgirl" crashing into the charts. Converting the single into a hit proved beyond the powers even of *Ready Steady Go!* It didn't exactly help that the Yardbirds released a version of the same song at exactly the same time.

Mind you, the Yardbirds' version only got to number forty-nine in the British chart. And, as the old sporting saying goes, first is first, forty-ninth is nowhere.

Blame the song choice. Whose idea was that anyway?

DIGRESSION

❧

*In which our hero owns up to a habit most
shocking and time-consuming.*

IN DECEMBER 2010, I reached a major career milestone.
I appeared on the cover of *Model Railroader* magazine for the
second time. Getting on the front of *Rolling Stone* had nothing
on this.

In 2007, when *Model Railroader* first ran a feature on the
layout that I am building on the top floor of my house in Los
Angeles, the reaction I got was extraordinary. People were
coming up to me all over the place and saying, "Well done, Rod.
I've been a closet model railroader for years and now there's a
rock star doing it who's not afraid to admit it."

Well, my pleasure. You could also mention Roger Daltrey,
with whom I exchange e-mail about his British layout, and Jools
Holland, who shares pictures with me every now and again, and
wanted a building of mine for his own model. Frank Sinatra, Jr.,
too, is one of us.

But so are thousands upon thousands of other people, and I'm
unashamed about being a model railroader—if a little guarded,
like most of us are, about the typical reactions you get, the stupid
"Chuff Chuff Rod" headlines and so on. As long as people don't
call it a "train set." I have a diploma from the National Model
Railroad Association of America declaring me to be a "Master
Model Railroader." Forgive me for saying so, but you don't get
one of those for making a "train set."

In any case, it's not really about the trains. They don't

especially interest me. I'm not a trainspotter and I can't recognize different classes of locomotive, or anything like that. What interests me is the modeling of the city and the landscape around the railway tracks, trying to get that right and make it look real. For me, the trains are just the way into the heart of it, which is the modeling.

What Dad bought me when I was seven—now that *was* a train set, a tiny circle of Tri-ang track and an electric train. I still played with it after the electrics packed up, pushing the train around the track by hand. Going into my teens, I started building my first proper layout on a board, six feet by four feet, which seemed huge at the time. But then my dad bought me a guitar, and railways got dropped for a while.

They stayed dropped until my dad retired and my parents moved out of the Archway Road newsagent's and into a neat little council house a couple of streets away at 24 Kenwood Road in 1966. I built a layout right around my bedroom, at the level of the windowsill, on a board about two feet wide, with a hinged lift-out section in the doorway—a pretty complex piece of engineering, even though the room was tiny. I constructed a papier-mâché hillside for it, with a tunnel running through. My bed was squeezed in under the baseboard. Mum always had to crouch when she came in to give me a cup of tea in the morning.

Ronnie Wood stayed over at Kenwood Road one night— this must have been around the time the Jeff Beck Group was getting going, in 1967. Mum came in with the morning tea and Woody sat straight up—"Oh, thank you, Mrs. Stewart"—and smacked his head on the underside of the boarding, an incident he has never let me forget. And one warm evening I lost an entire train and its carriages when it derailed and dropped out the open window, smashing to bits on the concrete below.

But you will know about that incident already: it went down famously in history as the Great Rail Disaster of Kenwood Road.

Music intervened once again when my solo career and the Faces were taking off, and the hobby was dropped until 1971 when I bought Cranbourne Court, near Windsor, where I knocked two bedrooms through into one. That was a fairly serious layout: I got the baseboards in, got the track laid and the wiring done.

But that track had to be abandoned when I moved to America in 1975. At Carolwood Drive, Beverly Hills, when I was living with my first wife, Alana, I used to fiddle about, making buildings from kits, but I had no layout to put them on. The current layout was only made possible when I built the house I now live in, in Beverly Park, in 1993, while I was married to Rachel Hunter. Malcolm, my personal assistant at that time, who used to be a roadie for Strider but came over to work for the Faces, was also a model train guy, and he helped me to lay the tracks.

It's in the attic of the house, in a room fifty feet long and twenty-one feet wide, with a workshop across the corridor. It's based on an American city in the transitional period between steam and diesel; diesel is just being phased in. So it's about 1945, the end of the war. Plain roofs are the giveaway: there are no air-conditioning units or ducts, except on some of the big factories, which had started to incorporate cooling systems by then. There's a city scene, which could be any major American city in that period, with skyscrapers, some of which are five feet tall, and then an industrial area, with factories and an oil refinery, and then the train lines head out across the countryside. The layout is properly stage-lit to convey late afternoon sunshine and there's a sound system for ambient noise. It's about two-thirds completed, so it should keep me going for a while. Nick Barone, who runs the Allied Model Trains store in LA, comes in and helps with things I can't do myself—electrics are not my strong point—and the bridge over the river is modeled on the Brooklyn Bridge and was made for me by a friend who builds architectural models. But otherwise the buildings and the street scenes and the hand-painted figures have been assembled by me.

I'm fascinated by the buildings, and in particular the aging process, the weathering. I take a lot of photographs of buildings for reference, especially when I'm in places like Chicago or Kansas City, the great railroad towns. Even seemingly simple things, like the way rust lies on a piece of corrugated iron, can be incredibly tricky to replicate. The only way you do it is by looking at photographs and getting your paints right and your pastels and your inks. It's like being an architect: you put buildings on there sometimes, and they look wrong and have to come out. But I've got an eye for where they should be, and the scale of them.

The buildings I make are from kits, or adapted from kits. Three padded flight cases travel with me on the road, with paints and tools and whichever model I happen to be working on. I make the big structures in pieces and then put them together when I get home. Those cases go all over the world. When we schedule the hotels for the tours, we request a suitable clear table and a bright light, and from Jakarta to Saskatoon, many a quiet and otherwise vacant afternoon has been whiled away with modeling.

When I'm at home, I regard a day as wasted if I haven't spent at least a little time working on the layout. My wife, Penny, likes it because it keeps me upstairs and out of the way for a while. But it's pretty addictive—and totally absorbing. The world disappears while I'm doing it.

So there is no wearing of peaked caps, waving of flags, or blowing of whistles. Furthermore, anyone found in the vicinity of the layout making train noises will find themselves forcibly ejected without further question.

My daughter Ruby was on her own in that upstairs room not long ago, and she said she found herself thinking, "If I didn't know my dad, I would say the person responsible for this was a psychopath."

Well, it's a point of view. I prefer to remember what my dad used to tell me. He always said, "To be properly contented, son, a man needs three things: a job, a sport, and a hobby."

So, in my case . . .

Job: singer.

Sport: football.

Hobby: model railroading.

Loud and proud.

CHAPTER 6

In which our hero continues vainly to ply his nascent trade in sundry popular and not-so-popular beat combos, learns an important lesson about loyalty and French holidays, and plays the London Palladium in front of his aunt Edna.

So, my first single flopped. And on top of that my band broke up. And a happy Christmas to you, too.

Long John Baldry and the Hoochie Coochie Men came off the road in October 1964. I was nineteen and had been on board for the best part of ten months. The bookings had dried up a bit and then it reached the point where Long John was veering dangerously close to bankruptcy by keeping us all on those rather lovable wages. He reckoned he owed £3,000 eventually—a steep old sum at 1960s prices. So that was it. I was gutted. I loved going out to sing with that band. In terms of pay, colleagues, working conditions, and opportunities, I couldn't have had a better apprenticeship. Also, I hadn't yet saved up enough to buy a car, which was the broader point of the project.

But such was the live circuit back then. Your novelty quickly exhausted itself. You found a band, and you worked it as hard as you could until the work ran out. And then you found another one. (And, if you were lucky, bought a car.)

Or, better still, your managers found you another job. Rowlands and Wright, who weren't keen on my being unemployed for long, sent me to try out as the front man with a band called Ad Lib, and when that didn't really work, they put me together with a group from Southampton called the Soul Agents. They were a four-piece: a great organ player called Don Shinn; Tony Goode, who was the guitarist; Dave Glover on bass; and Roger Pope, who played drums and would much later tour the world in Elton John's band. The Soul Agents eventually had a couple of singles out on the Pye label, but while I was with them, as I recall, we mostly played R&B covers: Rufus Thomas's "Walking the Dog," Tommy Tucker's "Hi-Heel Sneakers."

For getting about the place, the band had a fully functioning Commer van with a conventional, factory-fitted heater rather than the Hoochie Coochie Men's recklessly imported, oil-fired deathtrap, so I guess that was a step up. At the same time, while I was with the Soul Agents we had a weekly residency at the Marquee for a couple of months and were only paid £15 a night, which was quite a comedown after the £35 per week that Long John had been paying me in the Hoochie Coochie Men. The Soul Agents did get booked to support Buddy Guy, the Chicago blues guitarist. In March 1965 we drove up to Manchester to the Twisted Wheel and opened the midnight session, and then I went off and the rest of the band stayed on the stage as Guy's backing band. Quite good fun, but as good as it got.

The truth is, at this point, being a band's sole front man wasn't something I felt completely comfortable about. In the Hoochie Coochie Men I had been second string to Long John, and I think I was happier being slightly sheltered that way—getting to have my moments of attention, but not having to carry the entire show. It's possible that I still had some shyness to shake off as a performer. It would certainly be several years before I felt ready to deal with being a front man.

After six months with the Soul Agents, I went back to sitting around at home and vaguely bothering my parents by being indolent on a semiprofessional basis. And then, in the summer of 1965, another vacancy opened for me, and once again the provider of the opportunity was Long John.

At the Twisted Wheel in Manchester, Long John had become enthused about working with a twenty-five-year-old organist called Brian Auger and his group, the Brian Auger Trinity. Auger's manager was Giorgio Gomelsky, who was one of the pivotal figures in British pop music—a big bloke on the scene, and a big bloke literally, with a tubby stomach, a lot of presence, and a throaty Eastern European accent. He had persuaded the Marquee to stage a weekly blues night in a period when there was outright hostility to the idea among the trad jazz purists. Then he started the Crawdaddy Club at the Station Hotel in Richmond and gave the Rolling Stones their first break as the house band. When they moved on, he brought in the Yardbirds as a replacement, and they were no slouches either. People inevitably thought of Gomelsky as someone who knew his onions.

The plan that Gomelsky cooked up with Auger and Long John was to create a kind of revue show, or a record label package, but all in one act—a one-stop shop, if you like, for all your live R&B and soul music needs. Long John proposed me—his protégé, as he referred to me—as part of the bundle. Gomelsky thought the band should also have a female singer, and he put forward Julie Driscoll, an eighteen-year-old who, at that point, wasn't doing much more than opening the Yardbirds' fan mail in Gomelsky's office but whom he knew to have a great, clean, and powerful voice and an interest in Motown records.

The idea was that Auger would come on with the band—Ricky Brown on bass and Micky Waller, who was to become a long-standing compadre of mine, on drums—and do a few Jimmy Smith numbers and some stuff of his own. Then he'd introduce Julie, who would sing a couple of Motown songs. And then Julie would bring me on and I would do some Sam Cooke and some Wilson Pickett. Sam Cooke was truly coming through as the real deal for me in this period. The albums of his that had the most influence on me were *Night Beat* (1963) and the two live albums, *Live at the Harlem Square Club* (1963) and *Sam Cooke at the Copa* (1964). I had them at the time, and I still listen to them now—such simple songs, written around such simple chord sequences. And just the beauty of his voice. I always fancied myself as sounding like him, and now, within this revue format, I had the scope to try to do so. And in trying to sound like him and also like Otis Redding, and David Ruffin from the Temptations, I eventually arrived at my own style.

So I would do my thing, and then I would bring on Long John, and Julie and I would sing backing for him on his blues set. The name of the band was Steampacket—a type of river boat, obviously, but also a reference to the "package" idea and an allusion to the term "a steamer," popular in the day, as in "he's a proper steamer, that one," and used to mean someone who was really throwing themselves into it, partywise.

Looking back, this was pretty obviously a dangerously combustible premise. Three lead singers and a thrusting organist who also sang—that's an awful lot of ego for one small touring van to contain, and an awful lot of ego to try and wedge onto the stages of some fairly poky provincial blues clubs. And so it would prove, eventually. Yet the band lasted a year—working hard, playing five nights a week and commanding £500 for a show in some places, which was as much as the Small Faces were getting in those days, and they'd had hit records. And we were a really good unit. Auger was a storming organ player, Brown and Waller were dead tight, and the sound of me and Julie singing backing for Long John could lift the hairs on your arms when we got it right. And we looked great—dressed to the nines, a complete fashion parade: me in a broad pinstriped blazer over a dark polo neck with cream trousers; Julie in a twinset over a stripy top; and John in a light-colored suit with double-breasted jacket and skinny lapels and a tie with a tiny knot. John was rarely without a tie.

I was fascinated by Julie: bobbed hair, kohl-rimmed eyes, great dress sense. She would later, along with Brian Auger, have a hit with "This Wheel's on Fire" and become something of a 1960s icon. She loved Nina Simone and Martha and the Vandellas, and she was learning French and would often study her textbooks in the van. We had a few stolen minutes of passion in a field near the Richmond Athletics Club, but nothing more than that. In fact, I ended up going out with Julie's best friend, Jenny Rylands, who was also exceptionally pretty, with long blond hair and what seemed to me at the time a fabulously exotic interest in using makeup to create a "sun-bronzed" look. Jenny had a flat in Notting Hill, and we spent afternoons there, drinking tea and eating toast and listening to the Otis Redding album *Otis Blue* over and over again. She occasionally mentioned an artist friend of hers called David Hockney. I wonder what became of him.

I, of course, was still living with my parents, but Long John would generously lend me his flat on Goodge Street for assignations. I also owed it to Long John for expanding my social horizons in those days. Long John knew Lionel Bart, who wrote the musical *Oliver!*, and he took me one night to a swish party at Bart's house in Chelsea, which was full of theatrical furniture—thrones and props of all kinds—and where the great and good of London's theater scene stood drinking champagne and eating from trays of canapés, while, visible for everyone's entertainment through a large two-way mirror, people periodically hopped onto a bed in the room next door and had sex. Tucking into a sausage roll while watching an unknown couple have it off struck my wide-eyed nineteen-year-old self as the height of sixties sophistication.

Anyway, Steampacket's biggest show came right at the start of the band's life. In August 1964, Gomelsky got us booked to open for the Rolling Stones and the Walker Brothers on a short British tour, including the London Palladium—a grand and iconic theater venue, of course, and a different league from the usual damp basements and sticky-floored student dance halls. Even more than lip synching on a gantry on *Ready Steady Go!*, singing at the London Palladium seemed to suggest seriousness, which is presumably why this gig attracted members of my family—specifically my brothers Don and Bob, my sister Mary and her husband, and my aunt Edna—to come and see me perform for the first time.

I couldn't get any free tickets, so they had to pay for themselves— which put them right up high, way out of sight at the back of the balcony. This may have been to my advantage: if you're a self-conscious performer, in the sensitive, early stages of your public career, catching your aunt Edna's eye mid-show could potentially ruin you. The Palladium was otherwise mostly stuffed with screaming girls and wired boys—there for the Stones and the Walker Brothers, obviously, although they screamed and leaped around for Steampacket, too. It was my first proper taste of fan hysteria. At one point, to the alarm of the Stewart family party, the balcony began to bounce as if it might detach itself at any time and drop in on the stalls. My brother-in-law Fred had soon had enough and went downstairs to wait in the foyer. Mary, loyally, stuck it out and maintains that that night she had the very first glimmer that something might become of me in this line of work.

Not with Steampacket, though. At one stage the opportunity came up to tour America with Eric Burdon and the Animals, but John turned it down. I was pretty disappointed about that: I was bursting to see America because it was the home of so much in music that I loved. "My American public isn't ready for me," John joked, but it was sheer terror and cowardice, so far as I could make out. So instead we just plowed on around the university circuit, in what rapidly came to feel like a diminishing circle. The problem was, no matter how hot we were as an act—and we could be blisteringly hot—in the end we were always a covers band, an imitation of something better. Inevitably, frustration set in. It's often said that a band is like a family, and that may well be true, depending how often your family is tired and drunk. What's definitely the case is that if you sit in a small van with the same people for long enough, and drive up and down enough motorways late enough at night, tensions will eventually emerge. Micky Waller was in love with Julie. Julie was always in love with someone, but never, alas, with Micky Waller. Ricky Brown had just got married and grumbled loudly if he ever had to travel any farther than an hour up the road.

I, meanwhile, seemed to have created a small pot of lightly bubbling resentment by not responding with particular enthusiasm to the task of humping the band's gear in and out of venues. When we arrived at a venue, for example, it was sort of understood that you would pick up a piece of equipment as you left the van. However, I would often be in such a hurry to get to a mirror to sort out my barnet that I would accidentally omit to grab an amplifier or a speaker cab along the way. I would say now, in my defense, that this was not untypical singers' behavior. Singers reason that they need nothing more cumbersome than a microphone and a microphone stand in order to go about their business, and rarely consider that they were put on this earth to hump someone else's organ, as it were. However, my perfectly standard behavior in this regard seems to have infuriated everyone in Steampacket, and especially Auger.

But then Auger was almost permanently in a snit because pretty much the entire running of the band had fallen to him—including being the driver. There were two vans, one for the gear and one for the musicians, but only Auger and the roadie had driving licenses, so Auger ended up providing the band with a taxi service. He lived out west in Richmond, and on gig days he would have to drive across to Vauxhall, in south London, to pick up Julie, then come north over the river to collect Long John and then head up to Archway for me. And at the end of the night, perhaps frazzled by the combination of a gig and a long drive back from, say, Stockport, he had to repeat the whole pan-metropolitan process in reverse. It was probably adding about an hour and a half to the length of his working day. Auger was also responsible for collecting the money from the club managers after the shows and for seeing that everyone got paid. Essentially, then, he was acting as organist cum chauffeur cum tour manager. It's amazing that nobody asked him if he would mind cleaning their windows at the same time.

As for Julie, she was the junior member of the band and, of course, the sole woman present, and she had to fight her corner—which she did with some style. There was a certain amount of rivalry between us over material and who was going to sing what. I knew that she wanted to have "In the Midnight Hour," but so did I, and I hogged it. We did manage to share Mary Wells's "My Guy," which we sang as a duet, and generally a perfectly amicable peace reigned. However, in the dressing room before a show at the Klooks Kleek Club in West Hampstead one night, in a fit of I don't know what, I said something unpardonably rude to her about her legs. Quite rightly incensed, Julie did a lot of shouting and an equal amount of flailing and a pint glass got lobbed in my direction—breaking on the floor, as it happened, rather than on me, although I would have deserved it. And then, with the tension between us still crackling, we went out onstage and sang perhaps the least sincere version of "My Guy" ever witnessed. Ah, show business.

It all finally boiled to an end in the summer of 1966 when the band was offered a tempting four-week residency at a club called La Papagayo in St. Tropez. Auger must have been over the moon at the prospect. Not only was he not going to have to drop off anyone in Vauxhall for a whole month, but he was finally going to get a holiday. And in the south of France, to boot. I think Long John really fancied the idea as well. The composers Leslie Bricusse and Lionel Bart were going to be in the area at the same time, and John was no doubt envisaging a month of yacht-borne jollity.

A meeting was held, at which neither I nor my management was present. I don't know what my management's excuse was, but I think I may have skipped it. Big tactical error there, for it emerged in the course of this meeting that the only thing that wasn't tempting about the St. Tropez deal was the pay, which was tiny. In fact, it was hardly worth going at the rate being offered.

I like to imagine a silence falling around the table at this point in the meeting, and a certain amount of tapping of pencils occurring as everyone wrestles with their consciences and the images in their minds of the clear blue Mediterranean Sea in the gorgeous sunlight. And then someone (I bet it was Auger, although frankly it could have been any of them) says, "You know, there is a way that we could make this work . . . but it would involve leaving a member of the band behind."

And then everyone else pipes up and says, "Oh, no, no, that's unthinkable. No, no, we couldn't possibly do that . . . could we?"

Guess which member they chose.

Bastards.

Sold me up the river for a few hours on a sun bed. Still, they got their comeuppance. By all accounts the St. Tropez residency was a disaster. Long John became distracted by the availability of cheap, good-quality French wine and was not always, shall we say, in a position to give of his best. In fact, sometimes he went AWOL altogether. When they came back, Steampacket were no more.

I, meanwhile, like a spurned lover jumping into the next available bed, signed straight up with a band called Shotgun Express, with the organist Peter Bardens and Beryl Marsden, a gutsy singer from Liverpool. More cover versions, more revue-style staging, and one wince-inducing set of publicity shots in which Shotgun Express posed with (guess what?) shotguns. It was Steampacket all over again, except that, lacking an authority figure like Auger, there was an added element of organizational chaos—band members forgetting to turn up, or going to the wrong club on the wrong night, or being so late that club owners docked half the fee, that kind of thing. I don't have especially happy memories of those months—and, incredibly, there were at least eight of them, going through to February 1967. Was I going to be stuck doing "Knock on Wood" for eternity?

By the way, the drummer in Shotgun Express was Mick Fleetwood and the guitarist was Peter Green. I think it's safe to say that their later band, Fleetwood Mac, worked out better for them.

During this period I also found time to record not just one but two further solo singles that nobody wanted to listen to. This time the label was Columbia Records, Decca having somehow decided they could afford to pass on their contractual option of a second recording from me after the "Good Morning, Little Schoolgirl" adventure. So, my second solo single, emerging to a very muted fanfare in November 1965, was "The Day Will Come," a number picked for me by the record company—like a slightly watered-down version of Barry McGuire's "Eve of Destruction," which had just been a hit, with a thumping beat and a big 1960s orchestral setting. On the B side was a ballad called "Why Does It Go On?" Now, there's a title which was a hostage to fortune, if ever there was one.

Then, in the spring of 1966, Columbia tried again, this time with a recording of the dance-floor number "Shake." I went more for the grab-you-by-the-neck, force-you-up-against-the-wall Otis Redding version of the vocal than the gentler Sam Cooke take on it, but either way I might as well have dropped it down a mine shaft for all the impression it made on the record-buying public.

Still, amid these prolonged fumblings, it was becoming pretty apparent to me what the missing ingredient was: original material. Turning out a pitch-perfect Wilson Pickett cover on a wet night in Derby was one thing. If I was going to get anywhere, I was going to need to write some songs.

CHAPTER 7

In which our hero meets a guitarist of no small renown, accidentally invents heavy rock, tours America for the first time, and declines the opportunity to have his penis commemorated in statue form.

The Cromwellian was, as the big sign attached to the iron railings outside informed you, a "Cocktail Bar & Discotheque," located in a classic white nineteenth-century terrace on Cromwell Road in London. In the mid-1960s it was among the most "in" hangouts for musicians and one of the places where Swinging London went to swing—or, more specifically, to eat, drink, and dance, as well as gamble in the small casino on the top floor. It was where, in 1966, down in the basement, I watched a recently flown-in guitarist called Jimi Hendrix—or Jimmy, as we were then allowed to call him. (No string-chewing or guitar-burning in his act at that stage, but already, clearly, one hell of a player and set to scare the life out of anyone in England who played a guitar.) And it was where, in

January 1967, in the slightly bleary early hours, I had my first formal encounter with someone else who was no slouch on the guitar: Jeff Beck.

The conversation opened roughly as follows:

> ME: Are you a taxi driver?
> HIM: No, I'm a guitarist. Are you a bouncer?
> ME: No, I'm a singer.

Of course, we knew each other by sight. Jeff had seen me sing with Steampacket and liked my voice. And I would have to have spent the 1960s locked in somebody's garage not to know who Jeff was. He had been in the Yardbirds and was spoken of in awe among musicians as a hot guitarist—hotter than Clapton, many felt, including me. But the Yardbirds had brought in Jimmy Page, who could play guitar a bit himself, and after the inevitable tensions between Page and Beck—two virtuosos fighting for space—and a fair bit of glaring at each other across a smoldering stage, Jeff had decided to leave. Now he was looking to form a group of his own and he wondered if I wanted to talk about it. We arranged to meet the following afternoon in quieter and more sober circumstances at the Imperial War Museum. In retrospect it was a fairly appropriate location, given some of the battles that would later ensue.

I've heard it said that I hated Jeff Beck, but that wasn't true at any stage in the two and a half years we were in a band together, nor since. Clearly, though, there were phases when the two of us struggled to enjoy each other's company, and certainly to relax with one another. The Jeff Beck I met at the Cromwellian was a serious, slightly self-conscious, sometimes rather abrupt figure. He could be aloof—but then he was already a star when I met him, so maybe that's understandable. The band we were about to form, though ostensibly his band, would cast us as twin front men, so there was always the scope for skirmishes between us. But we certainly respected each other. I respected him for his playing, and he respected me for my voice, and we knew that when the two of us got together and it worked, we could produce music that was pretty extraordinary.

All that, though, lay ahead as we walked around the museum that afternoon, among the siege engines and examples of early blunderbusses, and Jeff set out these visionary ideas he had about creating a new kind of rock group, pushing it all in another direction, away from pop—Chicago blues but harder and heavier. "Grungy, Motown rock" was another expression he had for it—white rock with a black soul feel to it. The job as vocalist was mine, if I fancied it. Being intrigued by the prospect—and also jobless—I very much did.

First of all, though, Jeff had a solo single to record. His manager, Mickie Most, a wheeler-dealer who was never known to spurn a commercial opportunity and clearly had his own notion of where Jeff's musical future lay, had found him a song called "Hi Ho Silver Lining." Most once told Jeff, "All that wangy-yangy Hendrix stuff is history." Because Most was one of the day's more powerful music business forces, he could say that kind of thing to Jeff without getting thumped. Anyway, "Hi Ho Silver Lining" was at the opposite end of the spectrum from wangy-yangy: a thumpingly obvious pop song, with stupid lyrics and a big idiotic stomp-along chorus—almost the exact opposite of everything that Jeff was interested in. He hated it, and so did I. It has some of the most diabolical and cheesy lyrics you are ever likely to come across.

And, of course, on its release in March 1967, it proved to be a monster hit, just as Most knew it would be—not so much in terms of getting into the singles chart, where it only reached number fourteen, but in terms of seeping into the culture forever afterwards. For the next forty years it would be virtually enshrined in British law that "Hi Ho Silver Lining" had to be played at all student dances, village

ft: This could be a photo of any of my kids when they were the same age. Clacton, circa 1950.
ght: The Stewarts on holiday minus the sun. You will note my father wearing a tweed jacket,
eater, shirt and tie on the beach in June. Bless the British.

he family gathered except for brother Bob and his wife, Charlotte, who were probably round
e corner up to no good! Please observe a collection of thin ankles. From left to right: my
other Don; Don's wife, Pat; my sister Peggy (who sadly passed away too soon); my mum, Elsie;
; my dad, Bob; my sister Mary; Mary's husband, Fred.

Archway Road, 1945. The place of my birth.

Me and Dad going into a fifty-fifty. Thanks for the tartan pride, Dad.

My mate Kevin
Cronnin, Sue Boffey
(Sarah's mother), and
me, posing before
boarding a third-class
carriage to Brighton.
Nice hair all round.
Circa early sixties.

I love this picture of me
and my two brothers
turning out for Highgate
Redwing. Please note
my attention to fashion:
short shorts—Italian
style—and a Beatles
haircut. The other two
couldn't give a damn.

My pals Kevin Cronnin (left), Clive Amore (right), and me proudly displaying our harmonica. My bouffant appears to have collapsed entirely. Duke of York pub, London, circa mid-sixties.

My old pal Ewan Dawson and me outside my parents' council house, posing with someone else's ca

l Pie Island, where I made one of my first appearances, and where an unfortunate incident
curred with a beer mug.

e Dimensions, looking full of promise.

Left: My hero Long John Baldry. There's not a day goes by when I don't think of him. I owe John everything. *Right:* Onstage with Long John at the Marquee Club, 1964.

My first TV appearance on *Ready Steady Go!*, before which I deemed it necessary to spend all afternoon in the pub, gathering Dutch courage. My eyes are a dead giveaway. You can't stop me now! *Inset:* Shotgun Express: Beryl Marsden, Peter Bardens, and myself.

e, Ronnie Wood, Micky Waller, and Jeff Beck. It was a great honor to play alongside such an nazing guitarist, although Jeff looks like he wants to kill the photographer. Micky looks like a rarian. Don't even mention the stupid hat.

ny Newman on drums, with the rest of the Jeff Beck Group in the background, at rehearsals.

Attempting to reach a high note, which was unavailable.

hops, weddings, and bar mitzvahs on pain of arrest, and also to be sung at football grounds. For Jeff, who, more than anyone I knew, genuinely couldn't have given a toss about commercial success, releasing that song was like shooting the world's biggest albatross. It was, as he used to say, as though someone had hung a pink toilet seat around his neck for the rest of his life.

He had done his best to get out of singing it. Jeff took me along to the recording session, which Most was producing, and suggested to Most that, as I was the singer in the new band that Jeff was getting together, and as I had a more characterful voice than he did, maybe it would be a good idea if I recorded the lead vocal on "Hi Ho Silver Lining." But Most, who I don't think ever quite liked the cut of my jib, wasn't having any of that and I ended up singing backing vocals on the chorus while Jeff did the lead. The same thing happened with the next single Jeff recorded, "Tallyman"—a Graham Gouldman song, and again more commercial than anything Jeff would have chosen for himself. Jeff thought I should sing it, and again Most said no and gave the vocal to Jeff. I thought Jeff maybe could have stood up to him, but he seemed in thrall to Most and this was something we argued about.

Against this backdrop of commercial indecision, the Jeff Beck Group came into being. Jeff's first idea was to invite Jet Harris, once of the Shadows, to play bass, and Viv Prince, formerly of the Pretty Things, to be the drummer. This was an ambitious plan—or, you might even say, raving mad. Harris looked great—he had a big peroxide hairdo—but he was still in recovery from a terrible car accident and was known to be having some struggles with alcohol. Prince's drumming style, meanwhile, made Keith Moon look conservative. Jeff had spoken of wanting to find "a hooligan" to be the drummer, and Prince certainly fit the description—perhaps a little too closely, though. After about half an hour of flailing away at a twelve-bar blues in a rented room above the Prince of Wales pub on Warren Street, Jeff decided that neither of those players had the feel he was looking for and promptly disinvited them.

I think it may have been me who suggested bringing in my mate of more than two years, Ronnie Wood, who started off as the guitarist but then switched to bass, having thieved one from a West End instrument shop for the purpose. (Apparently he went back and paid for it as soon as he could afford to, bless him.) Woody was a good player but he was also an incredibly easy person to have around, and it's possible I sensed his charm might come in handy in a band shaped by Jeff's volatility. Jeff, however, was an exacting employer and was constantly changing the band. Even Woody found himself handed his P45* on at least two occasions that I can remember, for sundry musical misdemeanors in the workplace. And Jeff went through drummers at an alarming rate. For a while the job was Micky Waller's, my old pal from Steampacket, and for another, relatively stable phase the job was Aynsley Dunbar's, but you never really knew, from show to show, who would be sitting behind you when you turned round.

Is Jeff the main basis for the character of Nigel Tufnel, the guitarist in the spoof documentary *This Is Spinal Tap*? I can't say for sure, beyond noting that Jeff, too, has an extensive guitar collection which no one is allowed to touch or even look at. But the writers must surely have got the idea of the ever-changing drummer from the Jeff Beck Group.

The band's first gig, at Finsbury Astoria in London on March 3, 1967, gave no indication that the Jeff Beck Group would ever amount to much. Indeed, it was pretty much your textbook example of a 24-carat disaster. We had been booked, far too soon, onto a package tour, supporting the Small Faces and Roy Orbison, both of whom had had big hits by this time and could pull a sizable audience. One number into our badly underrehearsed show, some unseen hand pulled out

---

* Employment severance form

a plug backstage and silenced us. An act of mercy, probably, although Beck (in a way that was very Jeff) always suspected sabotage by the Small Faces, and in particular Ian McLagan, the keyboard player, because it was exactly the kind of thing he would have taken enormous delight in doing. Mac claims he wasn't even in the venue at the time. Whatever, the power outage caused the stage manager to drop the curtain—much to the surprise of Ronnie Wood, who was standing directly underneath it at the time and was almost killed by about half a ton of falling velvet (because, let me tell you, in those days a curtain was a curtain). It was while we were backstage, getting the power restored, that I noticed I had spent the entire opening number with my fly undone.

We went out again, this time with my trousers on properly, but it didn't get any less shambolic and, as a review in *Melody Maker* rather gently put it, we "created a very poor impression." The audience was there to see Orbison and the Small Faces, and our false start pretty effectively killed off any interest they may have mustered. Jeff's response—as so often in a moment of doubt—was to sack the drummer, Roger Cook, which was a bit of a shame because his dad had bought him a new kit especially for the occasion. Jeff's second response was to pull the band off the tour and stick us all back in a rehearsal room until we could make a noise that was publicly acceptable. He also began inviting me and Ronnie to his flat in Surrey for long listening sessions, where, doing our best to ignore Jeff's big, old, smelly Afghan hound called Pudding, we would spend hours just listening to music for inspiration and courage—anything from original electric bluesmen like Jimmy Reed through to Motown pop acts like the Four Tops. The idea of finding an outlet in which I could combine my love of Muddy Waters with my love of soul vocalists like Sam Cooke and Otis Redding and Levi Stubbs was inspiring to me and seemed genuinely innovative.

In due course we emerged again, reemboldened, and set off round

Britain to the usual haunts. We were guaranteed to attract a high level of public interest by the presence of Jeff—though that interest was quite often initially suspicious of me. Jeff had his fans, guitar worshippers who would come to the shows to stand and study his fingers, and they were highly protective of Jeff and given to wondering why he was hanging out with this relatively unknown high-voiced singer. Fair play to Jeff, though: he stood up for me. Confronted in an interview with the suggestion that I was "too camp" to be working with a serious rock guitarist, Beck issued the following resounding denial: "He's not camp. Campish, maybe."

For me, though, this was a massive learning curve. By contrast with the tight, instrumentally dense club bands I had played with so far, there was so much air in this group; a lot of room for me as a singer, space in which I could spread my wings. And there was a guitar player who would listen to me—and I'd listen to him and we would bounce off each other, which was what made it special. It was call and response between voice and guitar; none of it was worked out in advance, just done by feel. Jeff never once played over me; he always sensed when I was going to come in, sensed when I was going to extend a vocal a little bit, knew when to step back and get out of the way, and then come in blasting. And I can't think of another band that was doing that kind of thing at the time. It felt like something new and tremendously exciting.

However, it was obvious that, in order to progress, this band needed some distinctive, original material—and not just "Hi Ho Silver Lining," which, being Jeff's big hit, we were obliged to play, though we took to distancing ourselves from it by performing it with silly hand gestures, dumb smiles and overenthusiastic vocals. (Woody and I were especially lackadaisical about it. Sabotage, you might call it.) Without original material, we would surely be doomed to burn out fast (which is exactly what happened). The right kind of music for this band was hard to find, though. There was nobody out there writing made-to-fit material for a rock guitar virtuoso teamed up with a would-be soul singer. Jeff wasn't creative in the writing area. Woody and I, drawn on by the lure of cracking the code and coming up with a massive hit, had started to compose a few things together, mostly at his mum's tiny council house in Orpington, in the sitting room in front of the electric fire. (Money was tight: we were allowed to switch on one bar only.) But the songs Woody and I came up with in those early times tended to owe more to simple folk music than to futuristic heavy blues.

Our creative partnership got off to an inauspicious start. The first time we tried songwriting, Ronnie and I simply sat there one afternoon, with the fire on, each of us with a pad of yellow foolscap paper and a pencil, and waited. For some reason it didn't occur to us to get a guitar out. We just sat and hoped for words. An hour later: nothing. Not a syllable. Ronnie opened a bottle of wine, and over the next hour we gradually drained it. Still nothing. Blank sheets in front of us. After about two and a half hours, Ronnie's mum came in and found us both lying on our backs on the carpet in silence, next to an empty bottle, still waiting for inspiration to come. "Well," she said, "you two aren't going to be much of a threat to the Beatles, are you?"

Hence, when the Jeff Beck Group album *Truth* came out, in the summer of 1968, it was basically a record of cover versions: Willie Dixon's "You Shook Me," Howlin' Wolf's "I Ain't Superstitious"— even Jerome Kern's "Ol' Man River," which was my very cheeky suggestion and on the recording of which Keith Moon bashed timpani. Otherwise, we took old blues songs—Buddy Guy's "Let Me Love You Baby," B. B. King's "Gambler's Blues"—twisted them around, musically and lyrically, made them our own, and credited them to "Jeffrey Rod."

Virtually the whole thing was recorded at Abbey Road in two two-day sessions in May 1968. You didn't hang about in those days. You went in at eleven in the morning and worked through to midnight. It was the first LP-length collection of songs that I had been involved in. I still rate that record really highly. There's some great singing and playing on it, and it had an influence on a lot of stuff that came shortly after—particularly if you listen to Led Zeppelin. John Bonham and Jimmy Page came to see us play all the time in those early days, when they were getting the New Yardbirds together. They were trying to do the same thing that we were doing—and they managed it, and then some. Jeff retains a grudge, I think, because they took the nucleus of what we had and made it more commercial. The Jeff Beck Group could in due course have been Led Zeppelin, frankly, except for the crucial detail that they were a step ahead of us in coming up with original material.

At the time, though, I merely noted that *Truth* was credited, simply, to "Jeff Beck," with no mention of the "Group"—for which I cursed Mickie Most, rather than Jeff. It felt odd to be the singer in a band and not even be pictured anywhere on the sleeve, but that was the situation and I just had to try and be grown up about it.

In June 1968, we climbed aboard a BOAC plane at Heathrow and set off to tour America. At last: the promised land. Beck had been there numerous times by then, and as the star of the show was casually ensconced in luxury in the first-class cabin. But it was all new to me and Woody as we squeezed into economy and taxied creakily down the runway in the direction, finally, of the country that we had read about and talked about and thought about and dreamed about since childhood. Plus there was a trolley! And it served drinks! Free drinks! An awful lot of cheering and shouting ensued. We thought life couldn't get much better.

No one ever forgets their first view of Manhattan, rising into the sky ahead of them, nor their first drive up its concrete canyons. Woody and I were in ecstasy—possibly even silenced momentarily, gawping at the scale of it all. In terms of architectural grandeur, it didn't have much in common with Orpington.

We had been planning all along that, as soon as we had checked into the hotel, which was at around lunchtime, we would make a pilgrimage to the Apollo Theater in Harlem: the home of the musicians we had worshipped for so long from so far away. We were pretty naïve about it. We didn't even think it might be a dangerous place for a couple of unaccompanied white boys to go. One taxi driver ran his eye up and down us, in our Swinging London finery, with our combed-up hair and highly visible jet lag, and flatly refused to take us. But another drove us up there, and probably *because* of the way we looked—because we were unmistakably musicians or performers of some kind—nobody was bothered about us. In fact, we felt welcome. We walked under the marquee that spread the width of the pavement, paid our entrance fees, and saw an afternoon session, with Martha and the Vandellas on the top of the bill, after which we left in a state of enchantment.

If you had told me, in our returning taxicab that afternoon, that one day I would be back at the Apollo to sing on a bill that included Wilson Pickett, the Four Tops, Diana Ross, Smokey Robinson, and, indeed, Martha Reeves, I would have laughed so hard I would have paid the fare. Yet it came to pass—in 1985, for the "Motown Returns to the Apollo" show, where I took the opportunity to kneel in adulation at the feet of James Brown. I was a very proud man that night, as I am sure you will understand.

The day after my and Woody's adventure on 125th Street, we played our opening show: the first of a four-night stint at the Fillmore East, on Second Avenue in the East Village. The promoter Bill Graham had recently converted this old theater into a 2,700-capacity rock venue, an East Coast counterpart to the Fillmore that he was already running in San Francisco. We were due to go on after a band called Buzzy Linhart's Seventh Sons. Backstage, Jeff began to explain an idea he'd had about joining the first two numbers together to give the show a more theatrical opening, but I wasn't really listening to him because my attention had been drawn by an awful noise seeping through the dressing-room wall, as if cattle were being horribly tortured in an adjacent room. They weren't, though. It was the sound of Buzzy Linhart and every single one of his Seventh Sons getting the mother and father of all boo-offs from 2,700 unimpressed New Yorkers.

This didn't do much to settle my nerves, which were already badly jangled by a number of factors, including the size of the venue (so much larger than the 200- to 800-capacity clubs we had been playing in Britain) and the worrying thought that I was about to perform, for the first time, in a country in which people were allowed to own guns.

Most worrying of all, though, was the fact that, within the context of the whole "grungy Motown rock" idea, I was, essentially, a white guy trying to sing like a black guy, and I was fairly sure, this being America, and specifically the Lower East Side of New York, that when the curtain went back the audience would be revealed to contain some genuine black guys who might have some quite strong opinions about that kind of thing. (I was wrong on this count: the audience was almost completely made up of white, long-haired hippies.)

So I sang the first lines of "I Ain't Superstitious" from a semi-crouching position behind the amps at the back of the stage. I wasn't entirely hiding, you understand. I was just trying to look like I was busy doing something important and technical: changing a fuse, maybe, or fixing a plug. When the first verse passed off without (a) a stage invasion by aggrieved blues purists, wanting their money and their music back, and (b) noticeable gunfire, I found the courage to stand up and come forward into the lights.

Whereupon we proceeded to blow the place apart. Absolutely destroyed it. Hammered them with colossal versions of "Rock Me, Baby" and "You Shook Me." The theater went nuts. I looked across the stalls at one point and it was a churning sea of tossed hair, as far as the eye could see. I had never witnessed a reaction like it. I had certainly never been part of a band that generated a reaction like it. Encore after encore.

And the reviews—my dear! *The New York Times* said, "They were standing and cheering for a new British pop group last night at the Fillmore East," and reported that "the British group upstaged, for one listener at least, the featured performers, the Grateful Dead of San Francisco."

The review further noted, "The group's principal format is the interaction of Mr. Beck's wild and visionary guitar against the hoarse and insistent shouting of Rod Stewart."

Not sure about the "shouting" there, but go on.

"Their dialogues were lean and laconic, the verbal Ping-Pong of a musical Pinter play."

How about that? Mind you, the Pinter allusion was slightly lost on me at the time. I thought he played right back for West Ham.

It was some gig, though. Blowing away the Grateful Dead in New York was an unimaginably good result, away from home. Even the grouchy old *New Musical Express*, back in England, was impressed, especially by me and Jeff. "The only possible description of their two-fold dynamite," the writer said, "would be to suggest it's like watching the brilliance of Jim Morrison teamed with Eric Clapton."

Backstage afterwards, a happy delegation from EMI Records came up to me in the greenroom.

"Jeff!" one of them said. "Fucking great show, man! And great guitar player you've got there."

Jeff looked on thunderously. For a moment, I thought he was going to deck him.

Leaving aside the odd mix-up over who was who, America totally got the Jeff Beck Group. Audiences completely understood it—more quickly and more enthusiastically than people in Britain. We ended up touring America five times in total, staying out for two months, playing theaters and eventually massive festivals, which were the new burgeoning format for live rock. At an outdoor gig in the Poconos, we found ourselves on a bill with Jimi Hendrix, and Woody and Jeff joined him onstage for a jam. I, however, sat in the bus and sulked. It took a lot to get me to join in on a jam session. I never quite knew what I was meant to do. How's a singer supposed to jam? Scat? I have never been comfortable with it.

Mind you, one jam session that I did stick around for took place onstage at the Singer Bowl Music Festival in July 1969. The Singer Bowl was an open-air venue near Shea Stadium, in the borough of Queens. On the bill that time were Led Zeppelin, and while we were in the middle of a number called "Rice Pudding," a perhaps over-refreshed John Bonham, Led Zep's drummer, ambled onto the stage, grabbed hold of some drumsticks, and joined in. The next minute, I look around and there's people piling onto the stage from all corners: Jimmy Page; Robert Plant; Glenn Cornick, the bassist from Jethro Tull; Ric Lee, the drummer from Ten Years After; and Carmine Appice, the drummer from Vanilla Fudge, who were due on after us. So suddenly we've got four drummers, two guitarists, two bassists, and two vocalists and we're playing a version of "Jailhouse Rock" that only ends when Bonham performs a striptease, thereby earning himself an arrest for indecent exposure. Heady days.

The other thing I remember about that Singer Bowl show was that the Edwin Hawkins Singers were on the bill. They were the gospel group that had the big late-1960s hit with "Oh Happy Day!" Woody and I thought we would go up beside the stage and have a listen to them. The choir seemed to be about sixty people strong. There were probably only about twenty of them before they had the hit, but now there were sixty. And as Woody and I looked across from the side we noticed that two of the guys in the back row, on the podium, weren't singing at all but were in the middle of a card game. We wondered whether we should inform Edwin Hawkins that he was carrying passengers, but somehow the opportunity never arose.

The second Jeff Beck Group album, *Beck-Ola* (you'll need to be aware of the jukebox company Rock-Ola to get the pun), had been released the month before. It was recorded over a positively leisurely six days this time, but it still found us lagging behind the contemporary way of things by supplementing our own new material with covers (not one but two Elvis Presley hits, for heaven's sake: "All Shook Up" and the aforementioned "Jailhouse Rock"). Woody and I, along with Jeff, came up with a song called "Spanish Boots" for which I wrote the lyrics—a load of old nonsense about monasteries and tapestries and putting your boots on. I cringe to think of it now. I mostly remember the sessions for a series of confrontations between Mickie Most, who was producing it, and an increasingly moody and reluctant Jeff.

Still, even this slightly disappointing follow-up made number fifteen on the *Billboard* album chart. Yet somehow, despite the constant touring and the record-making, money remained extremely scarce. The band members were badly treated by Beck's management: Most and Peter Grant, who would later manage Led Zeppelin, and this accountant they had called Derek Nibb, which is a superb name for a pen pusher, now I come to think of it. Ronnie and I would go up to Nibb's office in London to get our wages and arrive at ten in the morning, and he would sometimes keep us sitting around and waiting until the afternoon before he paid us—just for the fun of it, as far as I could make out. The pair of us were always plotting dark acts of vengeance on Nibb and his office, but we never got round to them.

Jeff was the star, so when we were in New York he stayed at the Waldorf-Astoria on posh Park Avenue, while Woody and I would be installed a little way across town in the much cheaper Gorham Hotel. But that was OK. It was a rock 'n' roll haunt at the time and you would always run into bands there: Cream, Sly and the Family Stone, Ten Years After. Janis Joplin, who was by no means a shy or retiring kind of woman, was always chasing Ronnie and me around the place, trying to shag one or the other of us, though without success. We were terrified of her and would hide behind the potted plant in the lobby until she had gone past.

Six years later, in 1974, when we were on tour with the Faces, Ronnie and I went back to the Gorham for a visit. We were staying in more gracious circumstances at the Plaza by that time, but we thought we would pop in and have a look at the old place. And, just for a laugh, Ronnie asked at the desk if there was any mail for us. And then we stood there sniggering while the receptionist dutifully went away . . . and came back with a postcard, sent to me at the hotel six years earlier by my girlfriend of all those years ago, Sarah Troupe. Extraordinary.

The American girls that I met on those first trips to America—the ones who came to the shows and then hung about with us backstage afterwards—struck me as more friendly, more open, and more up for a laugh than girls in England, but not necessarily more promiscuous. They needed to be charmed and persuaded, though an English accent seemed to help. The problem was, the budgets for those Beck tours often only allowed for a twin room for Ronnie and me, which could have been restrictive, from the point of view of entertaining female company. But we were ingenious enough not to let it become so. We created a modicum of privacy for each other by building a wall between the two beds out of suitcases and any conveniently loose hotel furniture, such as dressing tables, chairs, or wardrobes, converting the room into an ad hoc suite, or subdivided sex parlor.

But then, in the dark, behind the screen, going about our fumbly business, the schoolboy gene would kick in and Woody would make a ridiculous noise, and I would make an even more ridiculous noise, and then an escalating "ridiculous noise" war would break out, culminating, frequently, in one or the other of us knocking down the barrier and burying the adjacent couple in a mound of luggage and chair legs. The extent to which our companions for the night found this as amusing as we did tended, I suppose, to vary. Frankly, in retrospect, to be a groupie attached to me or Woody on those nights, you would have needed the patience of a saint. Very often we got more pleasure out of each other than we did out of the girls.

Another game we liked to organize was entitled "Wood & Stewart Operations," for the purposes of which our shared room became a surgery and we became doctors, complete with toy stethoscopes and white gowns, ready to offer girls an examination and possibly even an operation. Many girls ran a mile in the other direction at this suggestion. Many, however, didn't.

Still, the availability of sexual companionship in America didn't seem to stop us yearning for our girlfriends in England, the aforementioned Sarah Troupe and Krissy Findlay, who later became Woody's first wife. Sarah and Krissy happened to be sharing a flat off the Fulham Road in London. Woody and I would split desperate, operator-timed, three-minute transatlantic phone calls—one of us mournfully sending our love and pleading our homesickness while the other sat by, counting off the minute and a half before grabbing the handset for their turn. The most cunning ruse of all, however, was to pull a girl who was prepared to take you home, perhaps to her parents' house, and then, in a quiet moment, to avail yourself of the telephonic apparatus for a call to the girlfriend back in London at no cost to you personally. Devious? Perhaps. But it's important to keep in touch.

In California, Woody and I had our encounter—it was almost statutory by this time—with the fabled Plaster Casters, Cynthia Albritton and her assistants, friends of Frank Zappa who had taken it upon themselves to preserve the fellated penises of rock stars in plaster of Paris. As I recall, the approach was very businesslike. They came to our hotel, bringing with them, in a bag, autographed samples of previously cast appendages, which they solemnly put out on a table for inspection: plaster phalluses of Jimi Hendrix and Eric Burdon were the two authenticated samples offered for our approval, as I recall. And then the girls offered to ready us for casting, should we wish to be thus commemorated. Obviously it would have been a pleasure and an honor. However, Woody and I took a look at the rather challengingly splendid specimens on the table before us, considered for a moment the slightly more modest scale of our own endowments, and said, "Hmm. Nah, I don't think so, thank you."

From my and Woody's point of view, these adventures were very bonding and it's not difficult to see how, as our friendship grew, and our catalogue of shared larks expanded, Jeff would have come to feel alienated by us, or excluded from our mini-gang, and possibly even slightly threatened by it. The division would sometimes be visible, even as we performed. On one side of the stage there would be Jeff, going about his serious, guitar-playing business, in jeans and an un-fussy shirt; on the other there would be Woody and me, a bundle of crushed velvet and bell bottoms, big crosses round our necks, pratting about.

Jeff, for his part, was a perfectionist. If he felt you hadn't been quite "on it" in a gig, he would have no hesitation about raising it with you afterwards in a confrontational postmortem. Of course, these headmasterly scoldings only had the effect, again, of bringing out the schoolboy in me and Woody, and reinforcing our anarchic alliance.

As I've said, Jeff was no "bread head." Money didn't concern him in the slightest. It was all about the music, as far as he was concerned. That's what his mind was full of and that's what he was determined to get right. Which is, of course, a highly admirable approach to take. But it made him a hopeless group leader. He appeared unconcerned about how the band's financial affairs were being run and about stay-ing on top of things on behalf of his musicians. On tour in America, for instance, daily allowances often weren't forthcoming from the tour manager. Woody and I were so hungry in New York on one oc-casion that we nipped into a deli and stole ourselves some food. I don't think Jeff should have allowed a situation like that to develop, but he didn't seem to believe it was any of his business. I never felt he was going to put an arm around someone and check that they were all right. Sometimes he would hop in his limo and leave me and Woody to call a taxi. He was in his own world.

Other people had to step in and look after us. Jimi Hendrix's girl-friend often took pity on Woody and me, in our hours of penury, and took us out for lunches and dinners. Indeed, her largesse extended to taking us both to bed one evening, lying between us and rummaging around in our underpants for a while, although I think consciousness of Hendrix's famously generous endowment in the trouser area, as revealed to us by the Plaster Casters, may have slightly spoiled the pleasure in it for both of us.

In 1969, with things getting ever more fractious and beginning to spiral downwards, Jeff kicked Woody out of the band because he felt he was complaining too much, which in turn had the effect of stretching my patience with the whole project. There was no fun in it without Woody. That said, a guy called Doug Blake came in to play bass, and had what was, in retrospect, an important influence on me. Not only did Blake take to the stage, no matter how hot it was, in a frock coat and a pair of fingerless mittens, he also had a trick of flipping his bass guitar in the air and catching it again, which would in turn prompt me, slightly competitively (not wanting to be upstaged by the bassist, of all people), to throw my microphone into the air and catch it—a tiny lob the first few times, and then higher and higher as confidence grew. It was the beginning of a whole new phase for my stage act: the opening of a whole new repertoire of movements.

Our last American tour was a short jaunt up the East Coast in the summer of 1969, taking in the Fillmore East, where it had all begun, Maryland, and the Newport Jazz Festival, with the intention to end the trip at some outdoor event or other in upstate New York in August. On the eve of that last show the band was billeted in a hotel at JFK Airport, the plan being to hop over to the event and back and fly out to London on the same night. But then the call came through. The gig wouldn't be happening. Jeff had already flown out on the 5:30

flight that afternoon. Apparently he had got wind from somewhere of a rumor, which turned out to be false, that his missus was having an affair with the gardener, so he was quite keen to go home.

The name of that festival we didn't play: Woodstock.

Ah, well. Seen one outdoor festival, you've seen them all.

n 1983, I bumped into Jeff in Los Angeles when he was doing some shows with Eric Clapton and Jimmy Page, and without any particular agenda really, and almost just for the hell of it, we went into a studio for a day to see what would happen. At Jeff's suggestion, we recorded a version of Curtis Mayfield's "People Get Ready," the vocal on which came out rather nicely, if I may say so myself, and we had a minor hit with it as a single.

I then asked Jeff to play a solo on the track "Infatuation" for my *Camouflage* album, which came out in 1984. And on the back of that, we asked Jeff to come out on tour with us. The idea was that he would appear in the middle of the set and play an instrumental while I took a breather offstage and put my hair back in place. And then I would come back on and we would do "Rock My Plimsoul" and "I Ain't Superstitious" from the Beck Group days, and then Jeff would stay on for "Infatuation," "People Get Ready," and a couple of others. The problem with this, from the outset, was that it all too obviously cast Jeff in a supporting role, which he was pretty much guaranteed to hate, however handsomely remunerated. The tour was set for seventy dates over four months. Behind the scenes, a lot of people were muttering and saying, "This is doomed—he won't last two shows." But they were all wrong. He lasted three. And then he left, saying something about how the audience was all housewives, which was a little bit rude of the old scamp.

Some fifteen years later, in 2009, with little or no contact in the interim, I got a call saying that Jeff was doing a show at the El Rey Theater in Los Angeles and that he would love me to come down and maybe sing something. I went along to the soundcheck and we ran through "People Get Ready." And then, that night, he started the song and I stepped out and sang it, and it was really fucking great, and by the end Jeff, bless him, was in tears and we gave each other a big old hug.

And afterwards, because it had felt good, we talked about trying to do a blues album together—a contemporary blues album. We talked about a few songs and even went through a few keys to set them in. And then Jeff went away and made some demos, and I didn't like any of them. And I went away and made some demos, and Jeff didn't like any of those. All this was happening while I was preparing to sign a new record deal with Universal, who were less than enthusiastic about the idea of a contemporary blues album and wanted me to commit instead to a country album, a Christmas album, and an album of new songs. Jeff felt he'd wasted his time. We haven't spoken since. I sent him an e-mail saying, "Let's go back to the drawing board. Keep the faith." But I heard nothing back. I sent him another e-mail at Christmas in 2011, wishing him and his family well. Again, nothing. It seems when Jeff gets the hump, he gets the hump. Maybe we're too headstrong now to work together, in any case. Which is a shame because there's nothing like it—Beck's guitar and my voice.

However, I'm glad we didn't play Woodstock. Woodstock made quite a few people's reputations, but at the same time it rather set them in stone. It was hard to slip away from your image as "an act that appeared at Woodstock."

And that would have been the worst moment for me to get typecast, because things had just started opening up interestingly. After a Jeff Beck Group show in Los Angeles, in the lobby of the Hyatt International Hotel, Lou Reizner, the head of Mercury Records for

Europe, had approached me. And Reizner had said, "Hey, Jeff, fucking great show, man."

Actually he didn't. But he did ask me if I would be interested in signing a deal for a solo album. I said I would. My asking price? £1,300—the cost of a brand-new, yellow, twin-seater Marcos sports car.

DIGRESSION

Another digression, in which our hero recounts his love of the automobile, recalls some of his adventures behind the wheel, and remembers the time he helped someone steal his own Porsche.

THE TRUTH ABOUT ME and cars is that, mechanically speaking, I don't really know one end from the other. They keep asking me to go on *Top Gear,* but I'm worried they're going to start talking to me about camshafts and drivetrains and using words like "torque," at which point I'd be lost.

I've always loved cars, though: driving them, the look of them, the messages they send, the way they make you feel. And there were very few points in the formative years of my career when the desire to own a particular car wasn't a major motivating factor. Sometimes it was *the* motivating factor. That was the ethos I grew up with: work hard, save up, buy the car you want. So I did.

As I've already mentioned, the whole time I was with Long John in the Hoochie Coochie Men, I was saving for an MG Midget—the first car I really had my heart set on. This was 1964, when I was nineteen. Price new: £430. I was stashing cash away in a box in the kitchen when I came home from gigs, and I had got up to £360, tantalizingly close to the target, when I got the box down from the top of the cupboard one day and found it was empty. It turned out my dad had used the money to settle a bill from the tax man. Inevitably I was pretty upset and angry about it. He could have asked. At the same time, I could see that it was somewhat irrelevant for me to be saving for a car while my dad was struggling to pay important bills. At least I had proved to Dad that I could earn some useful money. He had been through a period of wondering if I ever would.

So the MG Midget plan went to the wall, and it wasn't until 1967, when I was with the Jeff Beck Group, that I felt flush enough to get my first car: a secondhand Mini Traveller with the old basket-weave-type paneling on the side and sliding rear windows. This was much to the relief of Pete Saunders, one of Jeff's roadies, who had the job of driving me and the similarly car-free Ronnie Wood all over London, and was growing tired of it. If Pete wasn't available after gigs, a tactic of Ronnie's and mine was to find girls in the audience who would give us a lift home. But mostly the taxi duties fell to Pete, who was so keen to be shorn of them that when I told him I hadn't yet passed the driving test (I had only had lessons up to that point), he volunteered to take it for me.

In the days before photographic licenses, this was a fairly simple deception to pull off. So, one morning, Pete set off to the test center, signed in as Mr. Roderick Stewart of Highgate, and took my test. And I passed, I'm pleased to say. To this day I have never taken a driving test in Britain. (Note to the authorities: I took a driving test in California upon my emigration to America in 1975, which in turn qualifies me to drive in Britain. I'm completely legal now, is what I'm saying.)

So I bought the Mini, and Pete was happy, and so was I—extremely happy. There's nothing like the feeling of owning your first car. It spells freedom. For me, in the ranks of the great breakthroughs of growing up, car ownership is right at the top. Forget drinking and shagging. They're great, but driving makes everything available. So now I could head down to Marble Arch and pick up Sarah Troupe from her rather fancy apartment and take her out for the evening. And, later, drive home drunk.

(Shocking to relate, but we did an awful lot of drunk driving in those days—and, worse still, thought almost nothing of it. Inconceivable now.)

I used to look after that Mini so well. I put black paint on its tires and attached a little GB sticker to the back to cover up a small patch of rust. And I wired two enormous speakers to the radio and stood them on the backseat, where they remained perfectly happily until you put your foot on the brake and the whole lot slid onto the floor, forcing you to reach around and stuff them back again. Today's children would be baffled, but getting audible music of any kind into a car in the 1960s and early 1970s was a Herculean struggle: a constant battle with portable cassette players that wouldn't play loudly enough and tape machines that jumped and skipped and chewed your music to pieces when you went over bumps. A nightmare.

Of course, I realized in due course that, even with big speakers on its backseat, a Mini Traveller wasn't exactly a four-wheel babe magnet. So I took a big step up with my next car and bought, circa 1968, a white Triumph Spitfire: a proper twin-seat sports car, with fake mag alloy wheels, go-faster stripes down the side, and a GT oil sticker on the back. I trimmed it out inside by taking a manky old fox-fur coat and cutting it up to fit across the transmission hump and sticking squares of fur on the floor for mats. Beautiful. It was like sitting inside a taxidermist's workshop.

Woody had an old Lotus at this time, and we thought we were the business, driving around together. If I had a girl with me, I would pull the choke out at traffic lights, flood the engine a bit, then bung the choke back in when the lights changed and leave everyone standing. Mind you, one time I tried to do this I revved the car so hard that one of the fake alloys sprang off and rolled away into the gutter. There are very few things as humiliating as having to get out at the lights, pick up your fake mag alloy, and put it in the back of the car.

Me and my mate Ewan Dawson, who shared my love of cars and their effects, worked out pretty quickly that there was no point driving to the pub in a car like a Triumph Spitfire if you were going to park it round the corner where nobody could see you get out of it. That entirely defeated the object. There was one pub down the Bayswater Road where the quality of the female clientele was exceptionally high, and Ewan and I would drive round and round the neighboring streets for as long as it took until someone moved off so that we could park right outside. Some nights we started at six and didn't get parked until eight thirty. But it was worth it, because then we could make a proper show of getting out, going into the pub, coming outside again with a pint, and drinking it leaning against the car. Terrible poseurs, yes. But these things were important. And why else would you own a Triumph Spitfire?

My next car was a Marcos, bought in 1969—and now I really was beginning to get into the big time. On tour with the Jeff Beck Group I carried the brochure for that car all over America, looking at it every night, longing for it. And so I fixed my solo deal with Mercury Records at the price of a new one: £1,300. It was a kit car, essentially, though I bought mine ready-made, not having the remotest inclination to fool around with spanners.

I chose yellow with a white stripe up the middle: Jack the Lad colors. This was a car that you really had to lie down in—a proper shoulder-blades-to-the-tarmac kind of sports car. And shagging inside it would have been an absolute impossibility. Indeed, even preliminary groping was fraught with complexity on account of the height of the transmission hump between the two seats. It didn't really go very fast—I think it had a 1600cc Ford Cortina engine in it, which wasn't likely to blow your hair off. And mine had a leaky sunroof, so water would drip onto my suit when it rained. But it did look the bollocks—absolutely eye-catching.

I traded it in for another Marcos eventually: a 2500 Ford V6, in silver gray. They were all the rage in those days. Andy Fairweather Low, the singer with Amen Corner, had a purple one, as I recall. And then, in an epochal moment, around the spring of 1971, with the Faces doing well, and money coming in from my first solo albums, I splurged on my first Lamborghini: a Miura S, with big air intakes on the hood and huge bug-eyed headlamps, and switches overhead, like in the cockpit of a plane. It was the beginning of a long and expensive love affair with the brand.

This Miura was a considerable investment: £6,500. Be aware that my first house, which I had just bought, in Muswell Hill, had only cost me £5,000. So, for a while there, my car was worth more than my house. And there was no off-road parking, so I had to leave it on the street. Small wonder I couldn't sleep at night. If there was so much as a bump in the night I'd be up and at the window, checking the car. I kept it covered in plastic and even went so far as to put little red plastic cones around it, so that no one could park too close and put a dink in it.

Don't bother to ask me how it handled in the wet. I never took it out if it was raining. It was far too expensive for that.

The Miura had only been launched in 1966, so it was a pretty prestigious car to have with a bit of a lad inside. However, it gave me more problems than every other vehicle I had owned combined. You needed leg muscles of steel to get the clutch down, and it was constantly overheating. When Ewan and I planned trips, we had to factor in time for sitting at the side of the road, waiting for the engine to cool down. I loved the attention, though. And I loved the feeling that owning the car gave me: *This is what I worked for, this is mine.*

Soon after this I acquired a white Rolls-Royce, just for the heck of it. It was while driving this car down Tavistock Hill one Sunday evening in 1971 that I heard on the radio that "Maggie May" had gone to number one. At which point I turned around and went all the way back to my mum and dad's house, 24 Kenwood Road, and gave them both a big hug to celebrate. Note how, before "Maggie May" even, I had the money for a Roller and a Lambo. It shows you how much I saved up.

In the mid-1970s, when I had moved into my first really big house, in Windsor, I bought the Lamborghini Espada, which was a four-seater and had an eight-track cartridge player, and there were two or three further Miuras after that. Jeff Beck would always sneer at my Lambos and Ferraris. His taste was for hot rods, which he would build and rebuild himself, in proper grease-monkey style. I always found them rather ugly, though, with those stupid wheels on the back, and the fat exhaust pipes and lightning stripes. Give me a Lambo any day.

When I moved to America in 1975, I thought about buying a Corvette but ended up getting a Shelby Cobra. Now, that was a maniac's car. I couldn't keep it on the road. I had to put big bags of sand in the trunk to stop it sliding into buildings.

I was rather relieved to go back to Lamborghini with the Countach, a big, slabby, angular thing with scissor doors that lifted up and then out. I had a couple of those to keep me going through the mid- to late 1980s, and drove them like a fair old idiot.

Astonishingly, though, I've only had a couple of proper accidents, both in Los Angeles. The first took place in a gray Lamborghini Miura on Sunset Boulevard in the early hours of one morning in 1982. Alana was in the car. We were, as I recall, stoned out of our tiny minds. Somewhere near the point where Tower Records used to be, somebody cut me off in a pickup truck. The Lambo basically slid right under it, back as far as its roof, so that the view out my windscreen was entirely filled by the underside of this truck.

The driver of the pickup got out and I began to panic slightly because he was enormous—a mountain of a man with a long, bushy beard, like one of the guys from ZZ Top. Maybe he *was* one of the guys from ZZ Top. Anyway, whoever he was— joy of joys—I realized he was stoned. And he said, "I think we'd both better get out of here quick, don't you?" I said, "You're absolutely right, my friend. See you later." So we extracted our cars and went our separate ways. Extraordinarily, the Lambo had suffered only minor denting.

The second accident occurred when, driving like a madman through the hills, I took a Lambo up an embankment and got stuck under the wire around a tennis court. That's a very Beverly Hills kind of accident. I had to reverse the car, and there was this terrible teeth-edge noise as the wire left a perfect trail of scratches down the hood.

Incredibly, I've only been carjacked once. This, too, was on Sunset Boulevard, in April 1982. I part owned an empty building that was going to be turned into a restaurant—although the project never came together—and in the meantime I was using the place as a lockup for storage. I drove down there at ten one morning in a black Porsche Turbo Carrera. With me was Kimberly, my eldest child, who was then only two.

I parked outside, let us both in, and, leaving the front door to the building ajar, set off down the corridor to the room where my stuff was. As I stood unlocking that second door, the front door was pushed open and a figure came in. He was just a silhouette, because of the sunlight behind him, but I could see he was pointing a gun. When he got closer, I noticed he was sweating and shaking. He was saying, "Gimme the keys, gimme the keys. Back up against the wall and gimme the keys."

So, obviously, I waited until he was near enough and then, using a signature kung fu move taught to me by the masters in Peking in 1972 . . .

Oh, all right. I handed him the keys immediately, and also my wallet, saying, in as light a tone of voice as I could muster while thinking of the safety of my precious two-year-old daughter, "Here you go, mate, no problem here, we're backing up, take the keys and the wallet, you go and have a good time." And he grabbed the stuff out of my hand and ran back out the door.

Huge relief descended—although it suddenly occurred to me that it was terribly silent outside. No engine noise. No sound of a stolen Porsche driving off. A minute later, our friend with the gun returned.

"I can't start it."

Well, fair play: some of those Porsches are tricky if you don't know how. It's not just a key-in-the-ignition job. You have to depress the clutch and press the start button.

So out I went at gunpoint to help this man start my Porsche so he could steal it. This little part of the drama was witnessed by someone in a hairdresser's opposite, who called the police. They picked the guy up about eight hours later and found my Porsche about three months after that, stripped of absolutely everything.

The Porsche was a mild aberration, though. Mostly I've stuck with Italian cars, for the beauty of them. In 2002 I bought an Enzo Ferrari to use in England. I have always enjoyed the driving experience more in England than in America.

I especially love driving around London, where, incidentally, I can find almost any place you care to name, as long as I start from St. John's Wood. But I had to get rid of the Enzo. Drawing attention to yourself is one thing, but that car was ridiculous. Only four hundred of them were ever made, and every time you came back to it there would be a crowd gathered around it; you were forever having to clear frenzied car lovers out of the way just to get back into the driver's seat.

I was better off with the Ferrari Testarossa and the red Lamborghini Diablo, and in 2009 I bought myself a pale blue Murciélago—still in love with the marque, still drawn to the pleasures a smart car can bring. But I'm a very much calmer kind of driver these days, and I can remember exactly the moment when that calming down happened. It was on holiday in Spain with Penny in 2004, and I was hurtling us down a mountain in a Ferrari F50—showing off, frankly. As we took a blind corner, I was confronted by the nightmare scenario: a lorry coming the other way in the middle of the road. I somehow found a gap and we slipped through, just grazing the wing mirror. But it felt like a warning.

As you get older, you don't feel as precise with your driving as you once were. These days, if it's a tight spot, I have no qualms at all about getting out and leaving Penny to park it. She's better at that than I am. Altogether I don't drive as much as I used to, nor as fast. It dawned on me eventually: I've got a lot to lose. Too much to lose.

CHAPTER 8

In which our hero finally knuckles down and releases some rather fine recordings and then manfully weathers the consequent storm of praise and money. But not before a drummer has been rudely cast out on the street and a song called "Maggie May" has almost been thrown away for not being up to much.

The albums I made for Mercury Records between 1969 and 1974 were my coming-of-age. They represented the first occasions I took the talent I had and found a channel for it that felt absolutely right. They were the point at which I stopped mucking about and finally stood up as a singer, and also as a songwriter. And they're on sale in the foyer during the intermission, ladies and gentlemen, so do avail yourselves if you haven't already.

Within the record industry towards the end of 1969 there was still, I think, by and large, a sense that I had something to offer. At the same time, a few people started to have creeping doubts, and you could hardly blame them. I was twenty-four, going on twenty-five—and even Paul McCartney had said he would pack it in if he hadn't made it by the age of twenty. I had been knocking around for the best part of seven years. The Beatles had come and, for all intents and purposes, gone in that time. The Rolling Stones, whom I had peered at curiously in smoky pub backrooms and then supported at the London Palladium, had risen up and marched off in search of global domination. Every band I had been in had crumbled, for one reason or another. I had had singles out with major labels, sung on television in the biggest outlets of the day, and died a magnificent death with my boots on every time. Decca Records had recently declared that, although they liked my voice, they weren't sure that I was "current." With these various unsightly stains and pockmarks on my CV, there would have been justifiable skepticism about whether I would ever properly amount to anything. To this extent, I had to reckon, at the back of my mind, that the offer from Mercury Records to go into a studio and make an album of my own was a last shot at the big time. Screw this up and who knows? It would probably be cruise ships forever after.

However, I wasn't able to hurry into anything. Nine months passed between Lou Reizner signing me, in 1968, and me going into the studio to begin work, because I was still busy with the Jeff Beck Group. The first Mercury album was eventually recorded in a small window just before what would prove to be the band's final tour of America. And in I went, with the instruction to compile, sing, and produce an entire long-playing record. Incredible, really, that I would be entrusted with a project as broad as that. I was so naïve about the process, yet I seemed to go into it nervelessly, instinctively, which I guess you need to be naïve to do. I was still confident in my voice; confident that I knew not just how to sing a song but how to occupy it, make it my own. That confidence had grown through those years of singing with Long John's bands—with the Hoochie Coochie Men and Steampacket—and had crystallized in the Jeff Beck Group. I think I now understood that when I sang a song it didn't come out sounding like a copy of something that had come before. I was blessed with distinctiveness. The voice had its own character, and it was a character—as I knew from taking it onstage so much—that spoke directly to people. With that first album I was out, above all, to prove myself as a singer. As for the production of the record—well, we'd just have to see, wouldn't we? I had sat there while Mickie Most produced the Jeff Beck Group, seen him, during the recording of the *Beck-Ola* album, say vague things like "Can we try something with the bass?" and thought to myself, in a callow, twenty-something kind of way, "How hard is that job, really?"

Anyway, I wasn't going to be entirely alone. Lou Reizner was going to be along in a hand-holding role. Indeed, Reizner is credited as co-producer on my first two albums for the label. But I don't remember him doing all that much in terms of directing the music. He had a collection of classic Rolls-Royces and would casually turn up at the studio in one of them. He was one of the sweetest men on earth, but he wasn't exactly a roll-your-shirtsleeves-up type of producer. And he certainly didn't do much on the second album: for a fair amount of the time that we were in the studio, Reizner was over in America, attending his brother's wedding. But even on the first album my recollection is that he essentially sat to one side and simply supervised. Maybe if the whole thing had started going pear-shaped, he would have intervened. But it didn't, and as a result I think of both those albums as having been produced by me.

Handed the task of assembling a band of suitable musicians, I mostly got my mates in: Ronnie Wood, obviously, for bass and guitar, Ian McLagan from the Small Faces for piano and organ. Mac was a scruffy art student who had been on the scene since the early days of going to Eel Pie Island and was a handy player. And I brought in Micky Waller, who was in Steampacket and had briefly taken his turn in the revolving door for drummers in the Jeff Beck Group.

Micky was the only person I knew who could somehow hold down a regular job as a session drummer without ever seeming to be in possession of a drum kit. He would turn up at the studio with a fag in his hand, his dog (Zak, a boxer) and a tuning key, and nothing else. (It's Zak, incidentally, who can be heard barking on "Sweet Little Rock 'n' Roller" on the *Smiler* album.) Drums would have to be rustled up for him—begged off a band down the hall or borrowed from a local music shop. This was still happening two whole albums later, in 1971, when we recorded "Maggie May." On the afternoon that song was taped, we had managed to find Micky some drums, but no cymbals. All the cymbal crashes had to be overdubbed another day, when cymbals were finally available. Would Elvis have put up with that? I somehow doubt it.

But Micky was worth it. He was a great drummer, the sole licensed purveyor of the "Waller wallop," as it used to be called. He was also more than commonly vulnerable to a windup—and it's always good to have someone like that in on a session, for general mood-enhancing purposes in times of duress. One day I sent Micky into the sound room to record a tambourine part, and then told him over the talkback that it wasn't sounding quite right.

"Maybe we should try another room, Micky," I said. "For the ambience."

So, long extension leads were found and the microphone was set up downstairs in reception. Another "take" ensued, with a slightly confused receptionist looking on.

"Nah, still not quite right, Micky," I said. "What about trying it out in the street?"

So there's Micky Waller on the pavement on Lansdowne Road in Holland Park, headphones on, bashing a tambourine in front of a microphone while pedestrians step around him and the traffic goes by. He never caught on until we called him back in and he found us rolling on the floor with laughter.

After the Jeff Beck Group, Micky had joined a band called Steamhammer, which I had been to see at the Marquee, and I had been really impressed by that group's guitarists, Martin Pugh and Martin

Quittenton, so I got them in to play on the album. It was a tight little unit, all in all.

That first record took a week and a half to make, partly in the studio at Lansdowne Road and partly at Olympic Studios in Barnes, in southwest London. Lansdowne Road wasn't the most sumptuous of recording facilities. In fact, it was a bit dull and shabby. But it had been good enough for Lonnie Donegan in years gone by, so it was good enough for me. When we were recording, I liked to be in the sound room with the band, walking around with a microphone in hand, so that I could look them in the eye, interact with them—perform with them, basically. I think it slightly startled the engineer, who was more used to having the singer isolated behind screens, or in an entirely separate vocal booth. I remember hearing how Frank Sinatra had once been parked by an engineer behind a screen in a recording studio and he had made them take it down. In order to sing, he needed to feel the sound of the orchestra hit him in the chest. I guess this was my own version of that.

I was at liberty to choose the material that I wanted to record. I went straight for some old favorites: "Man of Constant Sorrow," the traditional folk song from that first Bob Dylan album that I had been fixated on in 1962, and Ewan MacColl's "Dirty Old Town." I think I wanted to show that, despite the recent heavier tendencies witnessed in the Jeff Beck Group, I was still a folkie at heart. Those were songs I had been singing for years. At the same time, I chose to cover the Stones' "Street Fighting Man." I say "chose"—it was entirely an accident. Originally, we were starting to work up a version of Little Richard's "The Girl Can't Help It," but for no particular reason I started singing "Street Fighting Man" over the top of it, and we took it from there. In retrospect, though, there was a point to it. I loved that Stones song to bits, but it always frustrated me that you couldn't hear the words better. The lyrics are brilliant, but they get chewed up a bit in the noise. It was nice to do an arrangement of the song that brought the words to the front. And was sung by a proper singer. (Only joking.)

And then there was "Handbags and Gladrags," a song which was to become a real item for me. A year earlier, in 1968, when Immediate Records had decided to become the latest in the line of record companies to fail to have a hit single with me, they had packed me off to see Mike d'Abo, who was the singer with Manfred Mann and a very smart musician and composer. Mike had been to Harrow and Cambridge, so probably thought of me as some terrible kind of oik. He had already written "Handbags and Gladrags" by then, and I was obsessed with it. It had this fabulous, melancholy melody. Whenever I was round his house, near Marble Arch, I would ask him to play it for me. In fact, I think he got slightly fed up with me asking. The problem was, he had already promised the number to Chris Farlowe, another Immediate act, and so for the single I ended up getting fobbed off with a much less imposing ballad called "Little Miss Understood." During the ensuing recording for that Immediate release, Mike, who did the production, put my back up by asking me if I would mind clearing my throat to get rid of the frog in it. I had to say, "Oi, that isn't a frog. That's my *voice*." "Little Miss Understood," true to form, crashed and burned in a raging storm of indifference from the radio stations.

Anyway, I now got my chance to record "Handbags" and to do it the way I wanted, and Mike agreed to help. We transposed the song from G up to B flat to better suit the relative height of my range. I was determined that there should be woodwind on it because that was what I had always heard around the song in my head, so the night before the session Mike worked until four in the morning scoring some woodwind parts.

To the intense irritation of Mike, when I came to record the vocal I changed the big line at the end of the chorus. As Mike wrote it, the line was: "The handbags and the gladrags that your granddad had to sweat so you could buy."

I changed that to: "The handbags and the gladrags that your poor old granddad had to sweat to buy."

It was a little shift, but the sort of thing that would drive you nuts if you were the writer. I just liked the reference to "poor old granddad" and found it easier to sing that way.

And then there were my own songs—four of them: "Blind Prayer," "Cindy's Lament," "I Wouldn't Ever Change a Thing," and "An Old Raincoat Won't Ever Let You Down." I wasn't a conventional songwriter by any means, and I had an unconventional method of going about it. I had ideas for riffs and chord progressions in my head, and I would explain them to the band, get the band playing them in the studio, and shape the music that way. We would then record the band, and I would take the tape away to play it over and over until I had a melody and some lyrics.

But, Christ, I found writing lyrics so hard. I liked narrative in a song. The best aspect of the blues, the best aspect of Dylan, for me, in both cases, was the storytelling. But when it came to writing those stories for myself, I would rather have done almost anything else. Even the prospect of slamming my fingers repeatedly in a filing cabinet would have seemed marginally preferable to sitting down and coming up with some verses and a chorus.

The entire process is a mystery to me, in any case. When we wrote "Maggie May" and the song was in its formative stages, just a sequence of chords that needed some words and a melody to fit, I hadn't got a clue what the number was going to be about. I was just mouthing away and making noises, some of them words, in the spaces where the vocal was supposed to be. And suddenly "Wake up" snapped into my mind—not even "Wake up, Maggie," just "Wake up." And where that came from, or why, I have no idea. You just have to think, "Thank fuck," and allow yourself to set off after it, down the path to the rest of the story.

Most times I would have to drag myself, screaming, to the paper.

I would leave it until the last minute—the night before the session, or even the morning of the session, or even in the taxi on the way to the studio, and use the pressure of the deadline to squeeze it all out. And I would feel fantastically self-conscious about anything that I came up with and really reluctant to expose it to people: unavoidably, there's some part of yourself in there, so it's like opening up your diary. Actually, it's worse than that. It's like opening up your diary and singing from it. In a roomful of musicians. My lyrics often drew on experiences in my past. The experiences would frequently end up very altered by the process of writing the lyric but, nevertheless, personal experiences were often the basis of them. "Cindy's Lament," for instance, is about trying to impress a girl from a social class above your own: a big theme for me in my early romancing, right back to the days of trying to persuade girls that I lived in a posher house than I did. And because of that personal element, it could feel raw exposing what I had written to people that first time—a feeling that could haul me right back to being pulled out in front of the class at school and made to sing. And that embarrassment wasn't just in the early days: it lasted for years. When I have gone in to record the vocal on a new song, and reveal newly written lyrics for the first time, I have more often than not had the studio cleared of everyone except the engineer—the producer at a push. It's the only way I can get around the self-consciousness.

And then, even when it's gone OK, and the recording is finished and I've been happy with it—proud of it, even—there can come the private backlash, maybe weeks later, where I suddenly feel embarrassed all over again by what I've done, and turn on it and dismiss it. That has happened to me periodically in the past—and occasionally to the irritation of record companies who were just gearing themselves up to promote the album that I have since turned against. It happened to me with that first album: almost as soon as it was released, I was dismissing my own songs, privately, but also to journalists, as being not up to much, not good enough.

It was almost certainly defensiveness, a self-protective desire to get the criticism in preemptively, before someone else could. But let's be charitable: with the perspective of time, those songs were pretty good for starters. And that's true of the whole album. It's a hodgepodge of styles and a little casually executed in places. On the track "An Old Raincoat Won't Ever Let You Down," for instance, there was meant to be a double-tracked bass part all the way through, except that Ronnie Wood accidentally got rolling drunk after recording the first one, with the result that the second one never quite materialized. (Just the idea, of course, suggests that youthful craving for novelty: "I know: let's put two basses on it. It'll be great.") But it hangs together and it endures.

The album was released in America first, in October 1969, on the basis that I had an American following of sorts after the Jeff Beck Group tours. I wanted to call the record *Thin*, which just happened to be a word I liked throwing into conversation at the time, and also because I was expecting thin sales. But the American record company preferred to avoid all possibility of confusion and to tell it like it was. They called it *The Rod Stewart Album.* In order to humor me, the word "thin" appeared in small letters in the bottom left-hand corner of the first print run of the sleeve, where it has baffled discoverers ever since.

In the U.K., however, where the album came out in February 1970, just after my twenty-fifth birthday, I got to use the title *An Old Raincoat Won't Ever Let You Down*—a far better name, although the choice of photograph for the front cover, in which an elderly man in a mac appears to be menacing a small child in a park, probably wouldn't have got very far through the marketing meetings today. What can I say? I thought it was a beguiling image at the time.

I remember feeling relief when the sales in America passed 30,000—thinking, "It's OK—there's an audience for this." Sales there pretty quickly reached 100,000, which wasn't shoddy at all for a debut album. In the U.K., however, the album was what you call a "critical success," meaning that only critics liked it. And they, of course, hadn't had to buy it. Still, better a critical success than no success at all. The main thing was, the album had done enough to earn me the right to make another, and just six months later, in the summer of 1970, I went back into the studio and recorded *Gasoline Alley*.

This one took a fortnight, from start to finish—which, come the gloriously indulgent 1980s, would be about the amount of time you would spend sitting on a leather sofa drinking coffee while the engineer sorted out a bass-drum sound. Then again, I should point out that the financial arrangement for this second album was as follows. Mercury in America agreed to provide Lou Reizner in London with a $12,000 budget for the recording. What was left over, after the bills were settled for the musicians and the studio time, I could keep. Why would you linger, in those circumstances? Why would you linger if, in particular, you had your eye on a rather nice four-bedroom mock-Tudor house on a quiet street in Winchmore Hill? It's basic accountancy, surely. (In 1969 I finally had enough money to move out of my parents' place and buy a small house with a front porch, not too far away, in Ellington Road, in Muswell Hill. But I was soon looking to upgrade. I kept Ellington Road, though, and through the early 1970s rented it out to Long John Baldry, who became a familiar figure in the Muswell Hill area thanks to his habit of walking out to the post office in the company of his white pet goat, which he had on a lead.)

We recorded the second solo album at Morgan Studios in Willesden Green, northwest London, which was not only the first studio in London to get a 24-track Ampex tape machine but was also, much more important, the first studio in London to have its own downstairs bar—a potentially disastrous idea, you would have thought, from the point of view of getting any creative work done, but that inevitably warmed one to the place.

In fact, we were very disciplined and didn't let the bar distract us unduly. I was on a mission to get the album completed, and I worked hard at it. I got the title, *Gasoline Alley*, from something said to me by a girl backstage at San Francisco's Fillmore West after a Jeff Beck Group gig. I had been chatting her up and she suddenly announced, "I've got to get home, or else my mother will say, 'Where have you been—down Gasoline Alley?'" The expression stayed with me and triggered the song I wrote with Ronnie Wood, about setting out boldly on a journey and then regretting it and longing to be at home.

Again, I wanted a mix of styles. There was another Bob Dylan cover—"Only a Hobo"—because you can't have too many of those. For the violin on that track, I invited along a fiddle player who had come serenading around the tables one night at a restaurant in Beauchamp Place. There was another Stones cover, too—"It's All Over Now"—and one of Eddie Cochran's hits, "Cut Across Shorty." As with the first album, there were strands of folk, rock 'n' roll, soul, and blues, plucked from all sorts of different places and gently twisted together. And, as with the first album, there was a certain amount of making do. Ian McLagan didn't make it into the studio on the day we were scheduled to record "You're My Girl (I Don't Want to Discuss It)," so we simply went ahead and did it without him. But that was a demonstration of my haste as much as anything else.

It worked. The reviews were even better than for the first album. According to *Melody Maker*, "Rod's voice is an extraordinary tool, seemingly shot to pieces and at times barely seeming to exist, yet retaining a power and depth of communication with which few can compare." In *Rolling Stone*, meanwhile, I found myself hailed as "a supremely fine artist." That made me very proud. Not bad for a bloke with a frog in his throat.

Gasoline Alley very quickly sold 250,000 copies in America and went into the *Billboard* Top 30. That was a huge breakthrough. Britain, on the other hand, the land of my birth, still remained stoically immune to my charms. The album crawled into the U.K. album chart somewhere in the high sixties and crawled out again a week later.

Third time lucky, though. *Every Picture Tells a Story* was recorded in 1971. This time it really was just me producing—left entirely alone to get on with it. Whether that's because Lou Reizner had another wedding to go to, or because I was now considered competent, I'm not sure. But let's go with the latter.

By now, at the third time of asking, the band really knew each other's playing, and you could hear it in the recordings. There was the usual mix-up of styles. I wanted to record "Amazing Grace" and maybe use that as the title of the album, but Judy Collins beat me to it. We also did the now obligatory Dylan cover, "Tomorrow Is a Long Time"; Tim Hardin's "Reason to Believe"; a touch of gospel on "Seems Like a Long Time," which was originally a folk tune; Arthur "Big Boy" Crudup's "That's All Right," which had given Elvis a hit, although we did it country-style; and a version of the Temptations' "(I Know) I'm Losing You."

And then there were the three original songs: "Every Picture Tells a Story," "Mandolin Wind," and "Maggie May"—a loose recounting, as we noted earlier, of the loss of my virginity in a blink-and-you'll-miss-it encounter with an older woman at the Beaulieu Jazz Festival of 1961. And "Maggie May," of course, changed everything.

Good job I didn't throw it away, really—which looked like an option at one point. I co-wrote the song with the aforementioned Martin Quittenton, a gentle chap, very quiet and studious with a permanently furrowed brow (and a lovely girlfriend), who was about the most inventive acoustic guitarist I had come across at that point, and had a head full of chords like I had never imagined, let alone been able to get my fingers around in my own stilted strummings. Martin, who lived in Sussex, stayed over at my house during the recording sessions for the album, and we worked out the basic structure of "Maggie May" one evening in the sitting room.

The whole song was recorded in two takes—not including cymbals. When the Beatles finished "Please Please Me," George Martin allegedly clicked on the talkback and said, "Congratulations, boys, you've just recorded your first number one." What would I have said, had I spoken to the studio after finishing "Maggie May"? Probably, "Well, that's sort of OK, I suppose. Drink, anyone?"

I mean, nice-enough song, obviously. Good little tale. Nice mandolin part, played by Ray Jackson from the folk-rock group Lindisfarne—and you don't often hear mandolin on a pop song, but it was a texture I had always loved in folk music. I certainly didn't think it should be a single, though. Actually, I even wondered for a while about leaving it off the album. It didn't have a chorus. It just had these rambling verses. It didn't really have a hook. How could you hope to have a hit single with a song that was all verse and no chorus and no hook? And it went on a bit: it was more than five minutes long, for God's sake, which was pretty much operatic by the standards of the pop single. In the end, it got shoved on the B side of "Reason to Believe," which seemed to me the best place for it. "Reason to Believe" was much more like the kind of thing that might get on the radio.

And then, of course, what happens is that some DJ on an American radio station, allegedly in Cleveland, Ohio, plays "Maggie May" instead of "Reason to Believe." Either he preferred "Maggie May" or he simply had the single on the deck the wrong way up. It doesn't really matter. Within a matter of weeks, DJs everywhere, in the U.S. and the U.K. alike, were doing the same thing, forcing the record company to reclassify "Maggie" as the A side.

Maybe I should have known from listening to Bob Dylan that a song didn't have to have a catchy phrase in the middle to be popular: that there was room for a good old rambling song. Yet in a way that I didn't predict, something in the story of the lyric and the flow of the song and the feel of the arrangement—all these things bundled together—reached people. An awful lot of people. In October 1971, "Maggie May" went to number one on the U.K. charts. It did the same thing, at the same time, on the U.S. charts. And as a consequence of the curiosity sparked off by "Maggie May," *Every Picture Tells a Story* simultaneously went to the top of the album charts in both countries. To my own dizzy amazement, and not inconsiderable pride, I suddenly had the number one single and the number one album, at the same time, on both sides of the Atlantic. It was like all the planets aligning. Nobody had ever done that: not even Presley, not even the Beatles.

The album got dislodged eventually by John Lennon's *Imagine*. The following week, *Every Picture* upped and dislodged *Imagine* and was back at the top. The only album that outsold *Every Picture* in 1971 was *Bridge over Troubled Water*. The only single that outsold "Maggie May" was George Harrison's "My Sweet Lord."

And suddenly it was raining fame and money. How would I cope? I didn't know, but I couldn't wait to find out.

Two more albums for Mercury would follow those first three: *Never a Dull Moment* in 1972 and *Smiler* in 1974. Busy, busy times. Hectically busy. Impractically busy, you could even say. Especially when you factor in the other little detail, which is that, for the whole of this period, I was also in a band. Quite a good one.

CHAPTER 9

In which our hero throws in his lot with the damaged remnants of the Small Faces and is reluctantly made alert to the perils of trying to run two careers at once. With sundry meditations on graffiti, Ronnie Wood's hooter, and the wearing of velvet in hot rooms.

n 1969, with a solo record deal under my belt, a debut album recorded and about to be released, and individual success on both sides of the Atlantic a tantalizing possibility if I simply put in some dedicated hard graft, I once again confounded my advisers by running headlong for the comfort blanket of a band. Call me a bundle of insecurity, call me a mess of contradictions, or call me a plain old scaredy-cat—it's immaterial to me, because the band was the Faces; we were together for five years, and I wouldn't have missed it for the world.

On a good night, the Faces were something special. On a bad night, we were bloody awful. But with the Faces, being bloody awful could sometimes be even more special than being good. And the feeling between the five of us—me, Ronnie Wood, Ronnie Lane, Ian McLagan, and Kenney Jones—when we were onstage was hard to surpass. Outside of certain football teams, I don't think it would be possible to experience camaraderie like it. By the end, of course, bands being bands, we'd all be traveling in separate limos, staying in separate hotels, threatening to quit every five minutes and squabbling like cats in a sack. But while it worked—God, it was brilliant.

That said, I couldn't have joined a band that was less enchanted by the idea of having a lead singer—not just me, but any lead singer. When Steve Marriott walked out on the Small Faces in 1969 and went away to form Humble Pie, the rest of the band were left with a mistrust of front men that would last them for the rest of their days. They had been bowling along, making some of the most iconic pop music of the 1960s ("All or Nothing," "Itchycoo Park," "Tin Soldier," all of *The Autumn Stone* album, which Ronnie Wood and I listened to all the time), and then Marriott had pulled the plug on them. Lead vocalists (or LVs) were, in the sneering phrase used by the band, "Luncheon Vouchers." The automatic suspicion was that singers were on the make, permanently alert to the main chance and out for themselves; that if they invited another one to join them, he would come in, take over the band, and then walk out, leaving everyone else in the lurch. And given the way it eventually panned out with me, Ronnie Lane and Mac, in particular, would probably have felt their suspicion was triumphantly vindicated. Well, they took a view. But I will always argue that it wasn't like that.

The remains of the Small Faces were rehearsing in a studio in the basement of a warehouse at 47 Bermondsey Street that belonged to the Rolling Stones, who used the place principally as a storage facility. You would walk in and there would be all these boxed two-inch tapes and quarter-inch masters on the shelves with things like "Honky Tonk Women" and "Gimme Shelter" written on them. And we all loved the Stones, and thought there was no rhythm section like theirs in the world when they were on song, so you couldn't help but feel the hairs go up on your neck slightly at the sight of that. The Stones were very good to the Faces in those early days: they never charged us for the use of the room. They were mentors of sorts and there was a good spirit between the bands—at least until the Stones purloined Ronnie Wood, when relations were put on hold for a while.

I was at a party with Mick Jagger in 1974, when the rumors of Ronnie leaving the Faces were beginning to bubble.

> ME: Are you going to nick Woody from us?
>
> MICK: I would never do that. I would never break up the Faces.

Oh yes you would, Mick.

But that was at the end. At the beginning was this basement where Ronnie Lane, Mac, and Kenney were knocking around, trying to find a new direction. And then Ronnie Wood, at a loose end after the demise of the Jeff Beck Group, started going down there with his guitar to join in, and I went along with him a few times, just to have some drinks and stand around listening—mostly looking forward to the moment in the evening when we would all go to the King's Arms pub up the road. The landlord there thought we were "nice boys" on account of the fact that we drank pricy spirits—rum and Cokes, mostly—rather than cheaply nursing half a pint of beer all night. That's a landlord's definition of "nice" for you.

At the studio, I mostly stayed upstairs in the control room, keeping out of the way, listening. And I wasn't particularly impressed with what I heard—or certainly not at first. It all sounded a bit aimless to me. They seemed to have two original songs: "Shake, Shudder, Shiver," which was a swaggering blues number with a lyric by Ronnie Lane about how cold his flat was, and "Flying," a slow and brooding rock song built on descending chords. Ronnie would be doing the singing and he had a nice voice, but he was no Steve Marriott. And Mac would sing a bit too, but he wasn't even as good as Ronnie.

There was obviously a singer-shaped hole, but their notion was that they would carry on rehearsing for now and sort the vocals out later.

One night I was standing in the control room as usual and Kenney said, "Rod, why don't you come in and have a shout?" So I left the security of my spot upstairs and went down into the hot and slightly sweaty-smelling room with the band and picked up a microphone.

I said, "What shall we do?"

Ronnie said, "Bit of Muddy Waters?"

Everybody knew the *At Newport* album, so we blasted through "I Got My Brand on You" and "Hoochie Coochie Man" and then "I Feel So Good." And it was pretty clear that we sounded good to- gether. (Some rough tapes of those early rehearsals are on *Five Guys Walk into a Bar*, the Faces' box set, so you can judge for yourself.)

Even then, no immediate invitation to join the band was forth- coming. It took several sessions like this before anything happened. Kenney and Woody would have had me in the band like a shot, but they had to melt down the resistance of Ronnie and Mac, who were still nursing the bruises inflicted by Marriott—not wanting to invite in a front man and then end up playing backing band to him. I wasn't party to these sensitive intraband negotiations, obviously enough. But some kind of board meeting took place in my absence and the board decided in favor of my appointment. Thus, in October 1969, were born the Faces—who continued to be the Small Faces for a while, for continuity's sake, although the "Small" had to go because Ronnie and I took the average height up to the point where it no longer applied.

As rehearsals continued, I still had plenty of doubts. Was this a pop group? A blues band? What was it? Some nights I would leave Bermondsey with Woody and say, "We'd better phone Jeff Beck and see if he'll have us back." At the same time, I looked around that room and saw, unarguably, a decent bunch of lads to hang out with. Woody, of course, was virtually a brother as far as I was concerned and the perfect bandmate for me. Kenney Jones, the drummer, was a Stepney boy, very quiet, easygoing—altogether lovely. That said—and this might sound a bit rich coming from me—the amount of time he spent doing his hair would come to annoy me. He liked it turned under nicely at the bottom, and curlers were involved. He could be hours getting it right. He was as tough as a nut, though. One night Kenney poked himself in the eye with a drumstick and, in agony, fell off the back of the drum riser. Did it stop him? No. He just got back up, weathered the backache, and did the rest of the gig with the use of his remaining eye.

He was the third drummer I had seen by the age of twenty-five drop backwards off a stage. I was starting to wonder whether it was me.

As for Ronnie Lane, I adored him, odd fellow though he could be from time to time. He was a very creative guy, tender and poetic in many ways, but he was always absolutely straight up as well. If he didn't like something I was doing he would tell me and not beat around the bush. When he eventually up and left the band, Ronnie Wood and I talked about it and agreed that was probably the engine gone. The fact the band struggled on for another eighteen months doesn't mean we were wrong.

With Mac I always sensed there was an undercurrent, something that prevented us from relaxing entirely in each other's company. We would laugh at the same things, but I always felt there was a slight edge. I think Marriott's departure and the end of the Small Faces had hit him hardest of all, and he could be pretty sour and chippy. The key thing, though, was that the humor Ronnie and I had got off on in the Jeff Beck Group days—the peculiar mix of British 1950s radio comedy, dark sarcasm, and basic schoolboy inanity—turned out to be shared by Mac and Ronnie Lane and, to a lesser extent, when he wasn't curling his hair, by Kenney. Accordingly, a bond was forged. We were a brotherhood—very quickly and very surprisingly. Put simply, in the crudest terms, and as everyone in the business of rock 'n' roll knows, the rule is as follows: in bands there's always one cunt who no one gets on with. In the glory days of the Faces, this time-honored truth simply didn't apply. And that was so refreshing, it made us stick at it. We were having a good time, so why not?

Soon enough we were ready to try a few tentative gigs, including one at an American airbase in Cambridgeshire, where suited airmen and their wives sat around tables and looked on in stunned and deafened silence as we blundered our way through "Around the Plynth," a refashioned version of the number that Woody and I had written for Jeff Beck, "Shake, Shudder, Shiver," and "Three Button Hand Me Down," a song put together by Mac and me. Everyone was chipping in and we were all coming up with stuff in different combinations, which was very pleasing, even if the American air force didn't find it appropriate for dinner-dance purposes.

The Faces' manager—installed after Marriott left—was Billy Gaff, a short, mildly spoken, and plausible-seeming Irishman with a fast-receding hairline who had worked as a band booker for the Robert Stigwood Organisation. While he was there, in the mid-1960s, Stigwood invited him to be tour manager for Cream. Gaff said he didn't think he was qualified for the job, because he had no experience of going out on the road with a rock band and wouldn't have any of the necessary skills. At this, Stigwood paused and then replied, "Have you ever looked after children?"

The truth of this summary of the tour management experience would be brought home to Gaff on an almost daily basis during his years with the Faces.

Gaff managed to get the band a recording contract with Warner Bros., who didn't exactly have to beat off a thousand rival bidders for the privilege. Most people thought that Marriott's departure had dealt the Small Faces a terminal blow, and that my addition, particularly as I'd hardly been pulling up trees for the last decade, was unlikely to change anything. Still, Warner Bros., God bless them, were ready to lob in some money. Flush with their record company advances, the other members of the band all rushed out and bought sports cars. Ronnie bought a silver Mercedes 190SL, Kenney an MGA, Woody a red Jaguar, and Mac a Triumph TR6. I, of course, already had my Marcos, courtesy of my solo deal. So now we were all Flash Harrys with flash cars.

We pretty quickly recorded a debut album, *First Step*, which came out in 1970 and sounded exactly like that: a debut album pretty quickly recorded. The fact that there are two instrumentals among those ten tracks gives some indication of the extent to which it was a work in progress rather than a polished jewel. But then we got out on the road, and that's where it really started to come alive. It was almost instantly apparent that this was not a band built for dreary rehearsal rooms and tiresome studios. This was a band built for the stage.

We weren't, by any means, a musically accomplished outfit. We were sloppy and loose, which took the band naturally in the direction of good-time rock 'n' roll. But our sloppiness and our looseness—and, more important, our attitude towards it—turned out to be the thing that made us vulnerable and appealing and, in the end, entertaining. You wanted an entertainer to give the impression of being capable of a fuckup. Even today I love it when my band goes wrong: if someone drops a clanger, I stop everything and point it out and the audience adores it. There's nothing like a grade-A musical howler for warming the room up, and the Faces, as much as any group in history, understood this—understood the timeless community value of going for an E chord, missing, and playing an F sharp instead.

Similarly, clothes were very important to the Faces because we realized our musical qualities weren't, perhaps, up to much. We thought that if we could be Flash Harrys, people might be distracted by it. My own style of dress became more flamboyant as the Faces took off—far more glam, which was the emerging taste of the time. We all wore crêpes and satins, bright colors, exotic prints, scarves, sashes. And we all went in for overlayering. I look back now at photos of the Faces onstage, and for some shows we seemed to be answering a challenge to wear as much as it was humanly possible to wear at any one time. Totally impractical, of course. It could be steamingly hot in some of those getups. Carrying 200 pounds of velvet and satin around a stage for ninety minutes—that's man's work, let me tell you.

And just as we used clothes to mask our insecurity, so we used alcohol for the same purpose. The Faces were prodigious drinkers. Drink gave you the necessary courage to go slightly underrehearsed into that good night. Spirits and wine were especially helpful in this regard. If you could have bottled the energy the Faces had . . . actually, forget it, because the Mateus wine company had already done so. And even when the backstage tables had been exhausted of their bottles of Newcastle Brown and rum, or if supplies weren't otherwise freely available, we knew a method for getting smashed on a single twelve-ounce can of beer. Here is that method in full, developed, I believe, in a motel in Tucson, Arizona:

1. Fill a one-ounce shot glass with beer.
2. Down beer.
3. Wait exactly one minute.
4. Refill glass and repeat process.
5. Continue repeating process until can is empty.
6. Feel pissed.

Now, the alcohol ended up costing us dearly, certainly in terms of the recordings the band made. There were four studio albums in total—the aforementioned *First Step*; *Long Player* and *A Nod Is as Good as a Wink . . . to a Blind Horse*, both in 1971; and *Ooh La La* in 1973—none of which, to my mind, really did us justice or brought the energy of which we were capable onto a record. But what did we expect? Recording sessions with the Faces always started out in the pub. Quite often we were in the pub longer than we were in the studio.

You believed that nothing would get the creative process flowing like a round of rum and Cokes—except possibly another round of rum and Cokes. Especially if it wasn't your round. (I had perfected the art of getting to the bar door first and opening it to allow everyone else through, which will normally spare you from having to buy the first batch of drinks. Bending over in the car park to tie up your shoelace is another good money-saving device in this area.) Unfortunately, the rum-and-Coke theory of creativity turned out to be bollocks. Glyn Johns, as he had shown with the Stones, was a producer bordering on genius when it came to getting a band's sound down on tape, and he did his best with us. But there were too many people throwing in ideas at the same time. And nearly all those people had had too much rum and Coke.

On the stage, though—that was different. True, to be in the Faces, you needed to be able to perform while lying down, but that was nothing to do with drunkenness. Or not completely to do with drunkenness. It was because big old human pileups were a regular feature of the act—Woody falling on top of Ronnie, me lying on top of Woody, Mac coming off the piano to jump on top of all of us—and we used to feel it hadn't been a particularly good show if we didn't end up lying in a mound in the middle of the stage at the end of it.

We were the first band to kick footballs out into the audience— that was my idea, of course, and I'm proud to say I'm still doing it. (Good-quality match balls, too. None of your cheap plastic rubbish.) And we were the first band to have a bar onstage, with a waiter, in full livery, serving us. It saved the time and energy wasted hopping into the wings for refreshments. It also gave us somewhere to go during Kenney's interminable drum solos. We could sit there while Kenney blatted himself into oblivion. One of us would say, "Do you think we should be getting back on?" And another would say, "Let's just have one more."

It was such a different thing for the times. You have to remember how serious rock music was becoming at this time. The rise of the Faces pretty much paralleled the rise of progressive rock—with po-faced guitarists furrowing their brows over nine-minute solos on twin-neck guitars and keyboard players working mock-symphonies out of banks of synthesizers for hours on end. And let's not forget to factor in, too, what a grim place Britain was in the early 1970s—in a slump, economically hammered, riven by strikes, its streets stacked with uncleared litter, the land of the government-enforced power cut. Those were a brown and dingy few years, and the Faces, down-to-earth but not downcast, brightly attired and three sheets to the wind, couldn't help but look like a rainbow in the drabness.

Yet, ironically, it was a potentially austere, daringly naked setup that we had. Every band in the world at this time deployed at least two guitars. We only had one, played by Woody. And he did a fabulous job of it, too. But, again, just as in the Jeff Beck Group, the single guitar left plenty of space in which I could sing.

I also had a lot of space in which to move—less so, perhaps, at the Croydon Greyhound or the Trentham Gardens Ballroom in Stoke-on-Trent, which were the kind of venues where we spent a fair amount of our career in Britain, but certainly on the big American stages to which the Faces very quickly graduated. And suddenly the showman that had been slowly and awkwardly emerging for almost a decade came pouring out of me. Pretty soon I had developed a whole new repertoire of tricks with that trusty prop, the microphone stand— setting it up high so I would have to crane up into it, swinging it about like a military baton, trailing it behind me across the stage, flicking it up so that it was directly above my head, or sweeping it into my arms and forcing it downwards like a tango partner. And then I learned to throw it, lobbing it with increasing confidence and catching it (with any luck) on the way down. The fact that, in nearly five years with the Faces, I didn't remove either my own eye or anyone else's must be accounted some sort of miracle. One night in Detroit I overcooked the move, flung the microphone stand upwards, and never saw it again. It got stuck in the lighting rig, I guess. It may still be there.

Typically, we would troop on, Ronnie Lane would say something like, "Sorry we're late—Rod's hairdryer broke," and off we'd go, storming into Chuck Berry's "Memphis, Tennessee" more often than not, which, if played right, could slam an audience right in the tender parts. It was always a wonderful feeling to hear that song set off and to plow in after it.

A set list? Set lists were for wimps. Wimps and professionals. Better to just get out there and communicate the set by shouting the old Faces' battle cry: "What number are we doing?" All we knew was that at some stage we'd get around to playing "Cindy Incidentally," say, or "Sweet Lady Mary," or Big Bill Broonzy's "I Feel So Good," and that at some other stage we'd stick Ronnie Lane up on an orange box so he could sing the first verse of Paul McCartney's "Maybe I'm Amazed," a song we adored and were deeply jealous of. Why couldn't *we* have written that?

The gaps between numbers, meanwhile, could be preposterously long, and not just because the message had to get round about which song was coming next. If Woody wanted to change the tuning of his guitar, he wouldn't reach offstage for another instrument, he would stand there and detune the guitar he was wearing. That's where I finally learned the art of talking to an audience: in Faces shows, in those aching gaps of nothingness while Woody was shifting into an open E. That was where I learned to say something other than the traditional "Talk amongst yourselves." Long John Baldry had planted the seeds of it: he was always very good at filling in for a minute or two, or telling the history of a song before he sang it. But it was in the Faces that I properly began to convert his lessons into practice.

In March 1970 we left Britain for a 38-date tour of North America, coinciding with the release there of the *First Step* album, and starting in Toronto, Canada. Once again, as with the Jeff Beck Group, the feeling was that Britain would be tough to crack, but that America was wide open if you were prepared to work at it and put in the miles. There was felt to be an appetite there for blatant, punchy British rock 'n' roll. And once again, the feeling proved to be completely right. In Toronto, at the Varsity Arena, we opened for the MC5 and Canned Heat and held our own. The next day we were meant to fly down to Boston to do three nights as a support act at the Boston Tea Party, a 1,500-capacity adapted warehouse on Lansdowne Street, and at the time the city's most happening rock club. But fog around Boston meant our plane was canceled. Billy Gaff told us we would have to pull out of the first show, and instead he booked us onto the only flight we could get out of Toronto, which was bound for New York. We were all sitting there on the plane, feeling a bit glum about the lost show, when the voice of the captain came over the intercom. "We regret that, owing to fog in the New York area, this flight is diverting to Boston." Cue loud cheers. The fates seemed to be on our side.

Boston was freezing cold. Because Woody and I had been before, we had sensibly brought overcoats. The rest of the band, on their first proper trip to America, were shivering in their jackets. Up to now, my and Woody's tales of what to expect while touring America had been greeted by the others with slightly patronizing "Yeah, yeahs," but now it was all "You might have warned us."

That afternoon, during the soundcheck, Mac discovered that the different electrical voltage levels in America left his Hammond B3 organ almost (but not quite) a whole key out of tune. As a result, the rest of the band's E was almost Mac's F, and he had to spend the first show transposing the songs as he went along—but still only ending up almost in tune. It was an inconvenient and discordant start, but fortunately, Pete Buckland, the band's chief roadie, managed to sort it out for the second night.

Detroit, in particular, loved us. On that first visit we played two nights at the Eastown Theater, supporting Savoy Brown. Detroit kids were, by reputation, a tough crowd in a tough city, but they were a wild audience if they liked something, and loyal, too. They responded to the party aspect of the show, and when that first tour looped back into Detroit for three more nights at the Eastown, they came out in numbers to see us again. It would become a kind of home away from home for the Faces over the next five years, and a proving ground. It was also the place where David Ruffin of the Temptations, who loved us, would often join us to sing "(I Know) I'm Losing You," which was a big thrill for me, as a huge admirer of his.

But everywhere we went we were gathering fans. That first tour of America lasted ten weeks in all and properly brought the band together, both on and off the stage. Returning to England that summer was tough—down to earth with a bump. We went from acclaim in big, well-organized theaters in the States to relative indifference in places like Cooks Ferry Inn in Edmonton, London. Audiences in our homeland were far slower to warm to us. Many people clearly regarded us as drunken tarts and cockney oiks. Others were suspicious of us because they couldn't quite make out what our connection was with the Small Faces, whose chart hits in the sixties had left them with the image, as far as some people were concerned, of a "teeny-bop" act.

Accordingly, in June, at an outdoor show, staged in aid of the World Wildlife Fund at Dudley Zoo in the West Midlands, the Faces went on after the Edgar Broughton Band, who had gone down so well that within three numbers of our set starting we were getting jeered at and canned. It would have got much nastier if Robert Plant of Led Zeppelin hadn't been there. He saw we were in trouble and came out on the stage and sang "It's All Over Now" with me. Because Plant was a Midlander and a local hero, his appearance turned the audience and saved us.

A key part of beginning to win British audiences over was earning the admiration of John Peel, the Radio 1 DJ. In 1970, Peel had just started hosting *The Peel Sessions*, which would feature a band playing live in front of a small audience, assembled at the BBC's studios on Lower Regent Street in London. Peel loved the Faces, and he had us on the show in June. We recorded "You're My Girl," "Wicked Messenger," "Devotion," and "It's All Over Now," and Peel said all sorts of supportive things. It really helped to get us across to people and break down some resistance. This was the beginning of my long, friendly relationship with Peel, during the course of which I was a guest at his wedding and, as I recall, fell into a lengthy conversation with an elderly aunt of his from Wales. The Faces recorded many further Peel radio sessions, when we would cause him terrible quantities of stress by keeping him in the pub opposite the studios until the very last minute before the broadcast was due to start. He would get in a right old panic and sometimes there was even a BBC heavy sent in to try to heave us across the road. We always made it, though.

In October 1970, we returned to America for twenty-eight more dates. And when we reached Milwaukee, we were told that the remaining sixteen shows on the tour were already sold out—an amazing result. We celebrated by drinking the bar dry and then, in the middle of the night, by storming Billy Gaff's hotel bedroom, turning the bed over, removing all the lightbulbs, and flooding the bathroom. Gaff, by the way, was in the bed at the time.

Of course, hotel demolition was something for which the Faces very quickly became notorious. In our defense, I would point out that a lot of what we got up to in this area wasn't so much wanton destruction as creative alteration. The removal of furnishings from a room, say, would frequently be followed by the reassembling of said furnishings, in perfect working order, in another location, such as the corridor, a balcony, or the hotel garden. In our further defense, I would say that we were often extremely bored. In 1970, we spent a total of four months on the road in America, split over those two tours. Away from home for that length of time, it was inevitable that fingers would start to twitch. Somehow one found that nothing passed a dull afternoon in Pittsburgh quite so efficiently as stuffing a lift full of mattresses and sending it down to the lobby. Withdrawing the bolts holding bed frames together, so that the bed was a glorious slapstick moment waiting to happen, was also popular. The removal of the microphone from the mouthpiece of the telephone handset, to the shouty enragement of the next user, had its advocates too, me among them.

Paintings on hotel walls, of course, were very vulnerable to alteration. If there was a medieval scene, one of us might draw a jet on it, or perhaps a bicycle. Woody used to do a very good airplane on any kind of reproduction seventeenth-century sylvan scene hung above a hotel bed.

Or, of course, there was always the ever-popular cartoon male appendage, or knob. I was particularly fond of a drawn knob in those days, and would inscribe one upon almost anything, to order. As an artist, the early to mid-1970s were very much my "knob period." And you could always tell my work, because my knobs were always "after the occasion"—sloping downwards, with drips. That was my signature knob. Everybody else's went boldly upwards, but I preferred to create something a little more poignant. That would be my artistic sensitivity coming through, I guess.

Actually, now I come to think of it, the knob-drawing went on well after the Faces, and continued deep into the 1980s. In fact, I'm ashamed to admit, even now, confronted, as one sometimes is in the more genteel kind of household, with a visitor's book, I can still feel the instinctive urge to—as it were—produce my knob. At the raging peak of my knob-based graffiti mania, my knob was frequently turning up in people's passports—including, as a matter of fact, really embarrassingly recently, after a shared flight from Dublin to London, the passports of all three members of the boy band McFly. "What am I going to do?" people will say, in genuine panic, when they discover a phallus in Biro on the photo page of their government-issued international travel document. To which the most efficient answer is, as it always has been: turn it into a tree and say your three-year-old did it.

On top of the graffiti and the disruption, relations between the Faces and their hoteliers were not improved by our habit of inviting the entire audience back to our hotel after the show. I would issue the invitation from the stage, telling everyone where we were staying and what floor we were on. And sometimes we would have literally hundreds of people in the corridor—most of them behaving very respectfully, I should add. Kids would turn up with their own wine, and you could leave the door to your room unlocked and nothing would be missing in the morning. However, it can't be denied that, on some occasions, in the more advanced stages of these evenings, nudity in the swimming pool was a distinct possibility, and also, back up in the bedrooms, acts of a sexual nature. For a bloke to have long hair, to be a member of a rock band, and to be English was clearly a very powerful combination at this time for young American girls. None of us was especially loyal when we were on tour. But the way we looked at it, if we weren't on tour, we wouldn't be shagging about. A pretty feeble piece of logic, but there it was.

Incidentally, one time we were on tour with Deep Purple and I gave out the address of their hotel instead of ours. That didn't go down well.

Of course, none of these practices was very astute from a financial point of view. The band was continually having to fork over large amounts of money to appease the managers of damaged hotels and dissuade them from involving the police. Billy Gaff would to go to check out and it wouldn't be "Anything from the minibar last night, sir?" It would be "Here's your bill for the future cost of redecorating the ninth floor." In Cleveland one time, Gaff found his path to the exit blocked by an irate manager and the local police sheriff. It cost him $5,000 in cash to get away. It wasn't the only time.

This behavior eventually lost our touring outfit the use of the

Holiday Inn chain. After one bathroom flood too many, we were finally blacklisted and banned from all Holiday Inn establishments—the first rock group, as far as we were aware, to whom this had happened. To beat the ban, we started booking ourselves in as Fleetwood Mac. When that was rumbled, we used the name the Grateful Dead. There is always a way around these things.

hadn't touched cocaine before the Faces, but on tour with them in America it became freely available. We all rather liked it. Dope was smoked in the band, too, but not by me, because I was too scared of wrecking my voice. I would chew a bit, very rarely, just for a dare or to be sociable. But cocaine seemed like a better idea. And cocaine was best of all, we keenly felt, in pharmaceutical form.

The very good news about that type of cocaine, we happily discovered—quite apart from the almost immediate euphoria it induced—was that when you were on it you could still get an erection. On other, less pure kinds of nasty street cocaine, it was like rowing a boat with a piece of rope, as the old saying has it. But with the pharmaceutical stuff, there appeared to be no immediate downside. Mac had a fake carnation in the buttonhole of his stage jacket which he would sprinkle with cocaine before a show, thus enabling him to tip his nose and inhale a reviving draft of powder during the performance. If the rest of us wanted a tiny snort, just to keep our dander up, we would have to pop behind the amps. And this will probably sound peculiar, from a modern perspective, but it felt like a very innocent pleasure. It was almost a schoolboy thing—silly fun. A lot of the pleasure was bound up with the thrill of getting away with it, with being naughty. It didn't feel the way it later did, all shrouded with guilt and the feeling that you were part of the workings of some huge, monstrous, destructive industrial machine.

Mind you, the amusement slightly went out of the cocaine experience one morning in the spring of 1973. The previous night, the Faces had played a particularly storming gig at the Locarno Ballroom in Sunderland, watched by some of the players of Sunderland Football Club, who were still celebrating a victory over Arsenal the previous weekend in the semifinal of the FA Cup. (They would go on to win the cup that year, beating Leeds United against all the odds and becoming the nation's favorite team for about ten minutes.)

A lot of footballers seemed to like the Faces. There was a sense that—give or take a bit of drug use and some hotel demolition—we were part of the same culture. The atmosphere at a Faces gig in England was like a benign and optimistic version of the atmosphere at a football stadium: lots of shouting and cheering and chanting and the hoisting aloft of tartan scarves. Football and the Faces seemed to be on common ground.

Anyway, after the show, Billy Hughes, the Scotland international, asked Woody and me if we wanted to join the Sunderland lads for training the next morning. So we dragged ourselves out of bed and headed to the ground. And it was there, in a private moment, beside the pitch, ostensibly while watching what was going on, that Woody pushed his face towards me, with his head slightly tipped back, and said, "Here, have a look at this, would you?" And by adjusting the angle of my head and looking up his nose, I could make out a small ray of sunlight where, in the conventional way of things, it really shouldn't have been, passing through his septum.

It was time, clearly, to think again about the cocaine snorting we had been doing. One idea, clearly, would have been to stop taking cocaine. Another idea, though—and for some reason this seemed to appeal to us both more—was to find another way to take it that didn't involve the nose. So we started buying anticold capsules from the chemist's, separating the two halves of the capsules, replacing their contents with a pinch of cocaine, and then taking the capsules anally, where, of course, the human body being a wonderful thing, they would dissolve effortlessly into the system.

Bingo. We found that worked extremely efficiently. It was a double result because Woody's hooter was obviously flying the flag of surrender, and I was starting to worry that cocaine, taken nasally, was affecting my voice by drying it out. Now we could just adjourn to the bathroom and insert the required medication French-style, via the Harris.*

It was on one of those early Faces tours that I learned a small but important lesson about care with the press. Woody and I had been gifted Polaroid "instant print" cameras, which would slide the picture out immediately after you had taken it: a seeming miracle of technology in the predigital era. And, because it was Woody and me, we mostly used those cameras in our hotel rooms to take pictures of girls with nothing on. It would be hard to recount the amount of pleasure the pair of us got from doing that slightly smutty "rubbing on the picture" motion that you used to have to do to warm the paper and speed up the developing process.

During the tour I did an interview with a senior reporter at the *Sun*. He seemed like a trustworthy sort of bloke, so when he'd turned the tape machine off, I said, "Here, cop a look at these." And I produced from my pocket this rather thick stack of Polaroids of blondes, all properly catalogued, with dates and cities of origin neatly written on them. Of course, this private moment between journalist and singer ended up in the *Sun* under the headline "Rod the Polaroid Kid." I don't think I'd ever felt quite so mortified. I didn't dare to go home to my parents for a while, because I was worried about having to discuss the matter with my dad. Eventually, I faced the music and knew the indignity of my dad scornfully ignoring me for two whole hours.

---

* Cockney rhyming slang: Harris = 'arris = Aristotle = bottle and glass = arse

My dad rather frowned on the Faces altogether, though—even when we weren't photographing groupies and showing the results to journalists with national newspapers. He was pleased, for my sake, with the band's success, but as he didn't drink I don't think he thought too highly of the Faces' overt alcohol consumption and of the behavior arising. He certainly didn't approve of the hotel pranks. I know that because my brothers and I tried one out on him one night, in a terrible misreading of the mood.

This was in Edinburgh, where we had gone with my dad and uncles the night before a Scotland football match. The hotel we were staying in was being decorated, and in the night, pissed as farts, my brothers and I took some ladders and some planking, tiptoed into the room where my dad was sleeping, and set them up around his bed. Then my brother Don climbed up onto the plank suspended between the ladders and pretended to be painting the ceiling as we switched on the overhead light to wake up my dad. Far from finding this surreal tableau amusing, as intended, he was furious—angry enough to chase us all out and down the corridor. I never sought to involve him in that kind of business again.

The Faces' legend grew, even in England. We played the Weeley Festival in 1971, supporting Marc Bolan, and blew the poor chap away. The audience wouldn't let him play. And then, in September of that year, we appeared at an outdoor show at the Oval cricket ground, Kennington, in a concert for Bangladesh on a bill featuring the Who.

I was rarely in a position to drive myself to a gig, in my own car, but this time I could. Accordingly, I arrived that afternoon in a white Lamborghini, recently bought with the earnings from my solo albums, in my stage outfit: leopard-skin coat and matching trousers that I had bought for the occasion from the Granny Takes a Trip boutique on the King's Road. All of us musicians used to shop at the same place in those days, which worked out very well from the point of view of avoiding fashion clash disasters: the assistants would see you pick something off the rail and gently say, "Oh, Mick's got that one," or, "You probably don't want that, because Bowie's just been in and bought it."

Anyway, I remember swinging into the Oval car park behind the scenes, and climbing out of the Lambo, dressed as a leopard from head to toe, with my girlfriend, Dee Harrington, who was wearing a tiny skirt, legs up to her neck, and the two of us setting off for the dressing room, arm in arm. And right there, as we walked, I had this over-whelming sensation of having arrived—not just at the Oval, but at a certain point in life, and thinking to myself, "Bloody hell—you're quite the rock star, aren't you, son?"

One other thing about that Oval show: I did the gig, drinking on-stage, police everywhere; I came off, had another drink with the lads; and then I got in the Lamborghini and drove home, waved cheerfully on my way by the police officers at the gate. And nobody thought anything of it. "Cheerio, Mr. Stewart, sir. Safe home." Staggering. Very different times.

The downside of the Faces' casual approach was that, when it came to the business side, no one in the band had their eye on the ball. No one took control financially: it all seemed to be cash in shoeboxes and envelopes, and Billy Gaff telling us not to worry about it. There was no proper accounting, so far as I was aware: just the occasional tally of expenses on a napkin. And no one took control in terms of planning our lives, either, and ensuring we had enough time off. Tours would be thrust upon us, and we'd all complain and say we weren't doing them—only for Old Mother Gaff to say, "Well, I'm afraid you *are* doing it, because the deposits have already been sent."

And thanks to the money generated by the touring in America, we were all living extravagant lifestyles: all rushing off to buy houses and cars or, in Woody's case, rushing off to buy his dad a big color television set (which his dad promptly chained to the radiator so that no one could steal it). We were young and foolish and nobody bothered with the details because we were all rich beyond our dreams. It's only natural in your twenties, but no one was giving a thought to the fact that it could all go tits-up at some stage.

And lo and behold, it all went tits-up. The problems were political, and slow burning, and mostly arose as a result of the success I was having with my own records, which created all sorts of complicated tensions and anxieties. At first the balance between my life as a solo artist and my life in the Faces seemed blissfully simple. I had the band, in which I could be a lawless, knockabout rock 'n' roller. And I had the solo albums, on which I could do rock 'n' roll as well, but where I could also express my other passions: the folk and soul influences. And there didn't seem to be any conflict between these interests. On the contrary, they rubbed along together perfectly happily.

In 1971, when "Maggie May" came out and I had to go on *Top of the Pops* to promote it, the Faces came along for the laugh. Backstage beforehand, we tried—and failed—to break into the dressing room of Pan's People, the show's resident female dance troupe, and settled instead for a highly competitive game of football in a BBC corridor against Slade, the glam rock band, the Faces running out 2–0 winners. For the recording, everybody dressed to the nines, and John Peel, our DJ and champion, sat on a stool and very self-consciously pretended to play mandolin (an instrument on which he had less than no experience) while Ronnie, Woody, and I hopped off the back of the stage and kicked a football around, not unduly concerned about exposing the golden trade secret of *Top of the Pops*—that the bands on Britain's favorite music show were pantomiming. We would go further the following year, when "Angel" was on the charts and Ronnie Lane couldn't make it along, so we replaced him on the stage with a cardboard cutout. But the "Maggie May" appearance was truly an emblematic moment, both for me and for the Faces. It forged an image of us as anarchic, silly, rather lovable if we said so ourselves. At that innocent early point, you would have struggled to see how my success could have been anything but good for the Faces, nor how the Faces could have been anything but good for my success.

The waters grew muddier, though. Ronnie and Mac were clearly constantly asking themselves suspicious, vexed questions: What was I giving more time to? Where were my best energies going? Was the band my priority, or me? And all those nights spent playing "Maggie May" and "You Wear It Well"—was that to their advantage or solely mine? Clearly their female partners were joining in on these discussions, too, which was never going to lessen the intensity of the debate. It didn't help that sometimes, at airports, Warner Bros. would send a car for the Faces, and Mercury Records, with whom I had my solo deal, would send a car for me. Suddenly we were traveling in separate limos—very divisive. Or sometimes Warner would book the band regular hotel rooms and Mercury would book me a suite.

Of course, I could have refused the key and insisted on downgrading. But then . . . well, I wouldn't have had a suite, would I?

I have to say, these logistical details never seemed to come between me and Woody. In New York for a show at Madison Square Garden in February 1975, I found myself booked into the Sherry-Netherland, with Woody staying opposite, across Fifth Avenue, in the Plaza. And he called my room and said, "Which floor are you on?" I said I was on the fifteenth. He said, "Brilliant. I'm on the seventeenth. Let's see if we can see each other." We both looked out: nothing. I said, "Woody, I don't think this is going to work." He said, "Hold on." I looked out again, and there, leaning right out of the window, a mile above the street, was a distant, hairy figure, holding a lit newspaper as a beacon.

What niggled Mac and Ronnie most of all, though, was if there was any chance that they could be construed as my backing band. Now, that grievance I really did understand, although there was precious little I could do to control it. Promoters were under strict instruction, from the start, to bill the group on posters or marquees as "The Faces." But in America, even at the beginning, in 1970, I had an album out, *Gasoline Alley*, that had sold 250,000 copies, and whatever you want to say about American concert promoters, they aren't stupid. Consequently, we would turn up at venues, and there, in big letters, it would say, "Rod Stewart and the Faces." At which point, Mac and Ronnie would go nuts. Ronnie was so furious about it one time, he clunked Billy Gaff around the head with a bottle. Invariably, at theaters that had offended in this way, the dressing room would be royally trashed on the way out as an act of vengeance.

Bickering increasingly prevailed. I didn't particularly help the deteriorating atmosphere within the band when, in an interview, I described the Faces' third album, *Ooh La La*, as "a bloody mess." I guess that was me and my previously noted tendency to turn against things I had recently done, but it was not the most helpful thing you could hope to hear from a lead singer on the eve of an album's release—although a true enough reflection of my feelings. I did apologize to the guys, but Mac was clearly thinking, "Typical bloody singer."

Before long, I was being accused of keeping the best songs for myself—of holding back the juiciest material for my own solo albums, and offering up leftovers for the Faces' records. That was never the case, and logically it couldn't have been, because I didn't write songs all the time, like a proper songwriter—like a Ronnie Lane, indeed. I only wrote when I got into the studio, under near-emergency conditions, when there were recordings to be made and songs were needed. I wasn't continuously preparing a catalogue of finished items to thumb through and dip back into when I chose.

Near the end of his life, when he was ill with multiple sclerosis, Ronnie took to claiming that I had stolen the song "Mandolin Wind" from him. It was untrue. And, really, the proof of the untruth is the nature of Ronnie himself: he was hardly someone who would stand by, uncomplainingly, while someone purloined one of his songs and not even mention it until years afterwards. He would have fronted it up with me there and then.

Ronnie left in 1973. Nobody thought he was serious at first because "I'm leaving the band" was a group catchphrase: the stock Faces response to any disappointment or setback. If you got slightly rained on between the hotel porch and the limo, you would automatically say, "I'm leaving the band." It had about as much content as that other favorite Faces expression: "Bollocks, you cunt." But this time, before a show in Roanoke, Virginia, Ronnie meant it. I think he thought the rest of the band would go with him, leaving me isolated. Instead, the four of us called a band meeting and sat around trying to think whom we could bring in as a replacement—which I think we all knew was a doomed idea, given what Ronnie had brought to the group, but what else could we do?

My first thought was to ask Andy Fraser, who had been the bass player with Free, a band whose early albums I really respected and listened to a lot while we were on tour. Andy wasn't interested, so we then approached Tetsu Yamauchi, who had replaced Andy in Free and was a sweet Japanese guy who barely spoke English. Tetsu appeared to be going through some emotional difficulties at the time, but because he didn't speak English we never really found out what those emotional difficulties were. We did, however, notice that he was a man who could hold his drink. I remember seeing his breakfast go by on a tray in a hotel one morning: sausage, beans, fried egg, rasher of bacon, and two shots of whiskey. The drink did get the better of him occasionally, though. There was one gig, on his first tour with us, where Tetsu had to spend the show leaning against the bass stack at the back of the stage, with a roadie behind the cabinets reaching round to hold on to his legs and keep him upright.

That, I hardly need add, was during the band's long, slow decline. Mac was going off me big-time. Much as Ronnie had done, Mac thought I was permanently on the verge of leaving and destroying the band, and he seemed determined to feel resentful about it in advance. In fact the thing that triggered my exit was the long-expected decision of Woody to take a job with the Rolling Stones—the band, let's face it, that he was born to be in. That, for me, was the killer blow. To lose Ronnie was bad enough, but to lose Woody as well . . . The jig was well and truly up.

The Stones had courted Woody for ages, and their interest in him was no secret. I don't think anyone was surprised that eventually he couldn't resist, or blamed him for succumbing. How many guitarists wouldn't have wanted to join the Rolling Stones? But Woody found it hard to make a clean break. For a while he thought he could work for both bands and keep everyone happy, but that was never going to be practical. Woody finished a tour with the Stones, and then came out on the final Faces tour, which took place in the autumn of 1975. We had a big orchestra and a fancy Italian-style balustrade constructed on the stage set, to help with four numbers that I wanted us to play off my new *Atlantic Crossing* album—all my idea (and paid for by me, I might add), but the rest of the band, and especially Mac, clearly thought it sucked.

Mac wouldn't believe it, but right to the end, right until it became clear that Woody was off, I wanted to be in the Faces—wanted to continue to be part of it. I always had. I didn't want to strike out on my own. Striking out on my own wasn't really in my nature. If I could have been a member of the Faces for the rest of my life, I would have been happy. But the grim fact was, by 1975 the Faces were no longer really there to be a member of. People had been in my ear for ages, trying to erode my position, bit by bit, and I hadn't succumbed. Now Billy Gaff and the record company were at it again, saying, "You must be mad, this is over, get yourself a band, do the solo career, do what you want, it's time." And eventually, in December 1975, I conceded that it was.

So the Faces were gone—but never to be forgotten. Eleven years on, in July 1986, at the end of a show I did in the pelting rain at Wembley Stadium, on came Woody, Mac, and Kenney, and on came Ronnie, terribly frail now and with a cane, but smartly suited and happy and literally cheered on by the crowd, who, at the first glimpse of him, broke into a chorus of "We love you, Ronnie, we do." And Ronnie sat on a stool, and I gave the microphone stand a ceremonial fling into the sky, almost impaling myself in the process, and we all then roistered our way, in a near-perfect replica of the old disorder, through "(I Know) I'm Losing You," "Twisting the Night Away," and "Stay with Me."

There was a repeat performance in 1993, on the occasion of my receiving an Outstanding Contribution award (or "retirement gold clock" as one likes to think of it) at the Brits. Ronnie, bless him, who had just four years to live at that point, was too ill to come. But Woody, Kenney, Mac, and I did some rehearsing, and also some going to the pub on the Caledonian Road, and gave them "Stay with Me" and "Sweet Little Rock 'N' Roller."

And then, in April 2012, our shambling contribution to rock's history (along with that of the Small Faces) was honored with an induction into America's Rock and Roll Hall of Fame. I missed the ceremony in Cleveland—struck down with strep throat. But then I'm doomed when it comes to Hall of Fame events. I didn't make it to my own solo induction either, having been pinned back at home by the great LA earthquake of 1994. Typical: you get into the Hall of Fame and, the night before, the earth tries to open up and swallow you.

Still, I'm mindful of the last days before my dear old mum died in 1991, aged eighty-five, when I would go to see her and sometimes find her sleeping. The confusion was most certainly upon her in those last few years, and very often she would wake up and say, "Oh, hello, Roddy. How are the Faces doing?"

They're doing fine, Mum.

DIGRESSION

◠◡

In which our hero survives a gunfight, wears some soppy shoes in front of one of the world's hardest men, and uncovers an everlasting love for Celtic. And in which he receives a memorable visit at home.

I DON'T LIKE TO think how much traveling all over the world to watch Celtic and Scotland has cost me down the years. But I do know that, in 1978, it nearly cost me my life.

That was the summer of the World Cup in Argentina. For the second successive time, Scotland had qualified for the tournament and England hadn't—a detail which by no means diminished the emotional richness of the occasion for Scotland supporters. Having failed once again to make the squad, I was at least selected to compose and record Scotland's official World Cup song, "Ole Ola." I think everyone was expecting bagpipes, but instead I opted for a South American flavor and thereby ended up standing in a studio in Los Angeles and delivering the immortal line:

Ole ola, ole ola,
We're gonna bring that World Cup back from over tha.

The team set off for South America amid an unusually heady gale of optimism and hype. Ally MacLeod, Scotland's beloved manager, had outlandishly declared that, even if Scotland didn't win the World Cup, they would definitely come back with a medal. I couldn't wait. Scotland were going to play three matches in the opening stage of the tournament—against Peru,

Iran, and the mighty Holland—and I wasn't planning to miss a minute.

I flew down to Argentina with my pal Ewan Dawson, and we settled ourselves into the Four Seasons Hotel in Buenos Aires in anticipation of a week of high living and football. The night before Scotland's opening match, against Peru, the local record company people kindly offered to take us out for dinner, and, as it very much goes against the grain with me to decline any free meal offered by a record company, I accepted. The record company said, "We're going to take you to the most exclusive restaurant because we don't want any trouble with bandits." And Ewan and I thought, "Fair enough, neither do we."

That night, despite the undeniably high-end nature of the chosen restaurant, I couldn't help noticing that two security guards had been appointed to accompany us on the journey from the hotel to the dining room—the only time in my life that I have ever had a personal bodyguard looking after me. Still, all seemed to be perfectly in order until right at the end of a very delicious meal, as the dessert plates were being cleared, when the doors to the restaurant crashed open and in ran two men with guns.

Bandits, apparently.

Terrifying. We were told to remove our jewelry and leave it in front of us. I nervously, and reluctantly, unclasped a rather nice Porsche watch and dropped it on the tablecloth. However, someone must have hit an emergency alarm button, because before the bandits could collect their prize, the sound of a two-tone police siren was heard from the street. And at this point, it all kicked off properly. The bandits were inside, shooting out, and the police were outside, shooting in. And I, with my heart pounding, was suddenly under a table with a security guard on top of me, listening to the sounds of gunfire and splintering glass.

Eventually the room fell quiet and we crawled out from under the table, scared out of our wits. It was clear that the gunfight had adjourned to the street and had then ended. A policeman checked that we were all right, and then said, "We shot them. Do you want to see?"

Well, many would have declined. But my feeling was, how many times in your life are you invited to get a look at a pair of bandits who tried to have your watch away but are now dead in a gutter? So I went out for a peep. Strangely, what stays with me, though, isn't the sight of the bodies so much as their guns on the ground: old-fashioned, long-barreled things, like you might imagine Wyatt Earp carrying.

And then the bloke who owned the restaurant tried to charge the record company for the meal.

"Are you kidding?"

They didn't pay. And Ewan and I also had a bottle of brandy off him to help calm our shattered nerves.

Anyway, the following day Scotland got beaten 3–1 by Peru, despite taking the lead in the nineteenth minute with a goal from the brick-built Joe Jordan: a humiliating result after all the pretournament bragging, and one which instantly sent "Ole Ola" plummeting down the U.K. charts in the direction of oblivion. That evening someone from Warner Bros. called to say they wanted me out of Buenos Aires because it was too dangerous and their insurance didn't cover me for acts of banditry in restaurants, even posh ones. So home I went, meaning I wasn't there to see Archie Gemmill score arguably the greatest goal in World Cup history, against Holland, and bring Scotland to the brink of qualification for the next round, only for Johnny Rep to pull a second goal back and put Holland through at Scotland's expense. Bloody bandits.

Where did it come from, this Scottishness, this passionate sense of identity with a place and a people three hundred miles north of where I grew up, and somewhere I was never taken as a child? I always had trouble explaining it. People thought it was adopted or affected, and even disloyal. "You're a cockney, ain'tcha? Woss all this tartan nonsense?"

Obviously, my dad was Scottish. But he never foisted Scottishness upon us, and I never claimed to be Scottish. I grew up in England, after all, and my mum was English and I shared her English accent—an accent which often, in the 1960s, meant watching Scotland play England on the sloppy terraces of Hampden, in Glasgow, with a tartan bonnet on my head but my lips firmly sealed for fear of revealing myself to be one of the enemy. (Those Hampden terraces were sloppy, by the way, because they were made of compacted mud held up by railway sleepers and often flowing with the piss of overrefreshed supporters. I don't understand why it's obligatory to be mashed off your face when you go to watch Scotland play, but that's the way it has always been, since time immemorial.)

Scottishness was what I knew, though—not just from my dad, but also from his brothers, my uncles, who were around a lot. Their accents filled the house and seemed both perfectly natural and yet wonderfully exotic to me. Those voices made it clear that I had inherited a connection with something deep, romantic, and truly compelling, a spiritual home, and all I had to do was reach out for it and claim it. And from then on it was bagpipes and all things tartan as far as I was concerned.

And Scottish voices told the football legends I grew up with. Scotland matches were sacred to my dad and had been all his life. In 1928, on the historic day when Scotland's "Wembley

Wizards" beat England 5–1 in the home internationals, he had gone along to Wembley Stadium, ticketless, with my uncles, and had climbed in over the back wall (Wembley had no roof in those days). He then looked around for somewhere to watch the match from, and settled on a spare seat in the Royal Box, reserved for the king of Afghanistan, who for some reason had not turned up. That tale, so often repeated in my house, of my dad the Scot, in the home of English football, crashing the royal party and living like a king, took on an enormous resonance for me.

Consider also the events of July 30, 1966, when, in what remains historically the greatest moment of glory for English football, England beat Germany to lift the World Cup. Pretty much every household in England with access to a television set watched that climactic and still resonant moment in the nation's culture. But not the Stewart household. My dad switched off the television in extra time when it became apparent that England were going to win. Things like that have a formative effect.

So I was dedicated to the Scottish national side from very early on. But affiliation to a particular club came much later. I had an attachment to Manchester United in the 1970s—but that was because they had so many great Scottish players in that period, including Denis Law, who was my first professional football hero. It was in imitation of Law that I would take to the pitch myself in a shirt with the sleeves pulled right down and the cuffs grasped with the fingers. I still do it.

There was a Faces show at Manchester Free Trade Hall in 1973 during which Law, his United teammate Paddy Crerand, and Mike Summerbee of Manchester City came onstage and presented the band with a gold disc. Directly after that, Denis's agent invited me to watch United play Leeds at Old Trafford, a fractious match in which Denis received a serious kicking and Billy Bremner of Leeds got sent off. Denis was eventually substituted, at which point his agent nudged me and said, "Let's go and see him."

So, with the match still going on, we went down the back stairs and along the corridors to the United dressing room, tapped on the door, and walked in. And there was Denis, completely naked, chatting amicably to Bremner, who was smoking a cigarette. I was enormously excited about it all when I joined up with the band again later that day. "You'll never guess what I saw this afternoon: Denis Law's pump and tool bag."

When I did eventually click with a team, it was Celtic. And, again, it all came out of being in the Faces. Kenny Dalglish, Jimmy "Jinky" Johnstone, "Dixie" Deans, and George McCluskey—all Celtic players—came to a gig in Glasgow in 1975 and Kenny, who became a friend, said afterwards, "Do you want to come to training tomorrow?"

In those days, Celtic used to train at the stadium, so the next morning I drove out to Parkhead, in the tough East End of Glasgow, to watch. And there, beside the pitch, in a thick, zipped-up tracksuit, was the manager, Jock Stein—seemingly carved from granite, one of the most magnificent football managers who ever lived and a truly intimidating presence. As Kenny introduced me, and I nervously held out my hand, I noticed Stein looking with amused contempt at my feet. I was wearing a highly foppish pair of white shoes. Poor wardrobe choice for the occasion.

Still, once you had met Jock Stein, you were a Celtic supporter. And once you had seen Jinky Johnstone, you were a Celtic supporter forever. Jinky was the greatest player to wear the hooped* shirt, a wee man who ran big defenders ragged and

---

* Horizontally striped

put them on their backsides, and I consider myself privileged
to have known him. He could sing, as well. In 2004, Jimmy
recorded a version of Ewan MacColl's "Dirty Old Town"—
something he and I had in common. In 2006, two weeks before
motor neuron disease took his life at the age of sixty-one, I
dropped in to see Jimmy at his house outside Glasgow. We knew
how ill he was at that point, so my brothers, Bob and Don, and
my friends Big Al and Al the Tout waited outside in the car.
Jimmy's wife, Agnes, showed me through to the room where
Jimmy was laid out flat on a bed, cruelly reduced by his illness
at this point—and yet with the biggest smile on his face to see
me. He called straightaway for a bottle of champagne. And then
through the window he noticed the car.

"Who's out there?" he said.

I said, "My brothers and a couple of pals."

He said, "Well, what are they doing out there? Bring 'em in."

The life that was still in the man, even then. And I had spent
the morning complaining of a cold. Some people humble you
forever.

Music and touring dominated my life for the 1970s and
beyond, and I wasn't in a position to start going to watch Celtic
regularly until the late 1980s. Shortly after that, there nearly
wasn't a club to support. Celtic got into financial difficulties,
culminating in 1994 when the business was within five hours of
being liquidated. Enter, blessedly, Fergus McCann, a Scottish-
born Canadian entrepreneur, who injected money and built
a new ground on the site of the club's battered old home,
Parkhead. I was invited to make the ceremonial declaration at
the opening of the North Stand, and McCann gave me the honor
of a seat at Celtic Park for life—the very best kind of lifetime
award.

My attachment grew still firmer in the club's four years

under the management of Gordon Strachan. One of the great
gritty Scots players in his own time, Strach used to bring his
battered legs to play football on the pitch at my current home
at Epping in our over-forties games, and Penny and I became
good friends with him and his wife, Lesley. I inevitably became
very excited in 2005 when Strach told me he might be up for
the job of taking over Celtic after Martin O'Neill left. When
Strach came down to Epping for a match on the Sunday after his
appointment had been announced, he found me on my knees on
the path, bowing to him.

One morning in July 2005, Strach phoned me and said, "Is
your pitch ready?"

I said, "Well, it's cut. It may not be marked out. Why?"

Strach said, "I want to bring the lads down for training."

I said, "Which lads?"

He said, "Celtic, of course."

I almost fell over. They were playing Fulham in a preseason
friendly. All the local clubs were already using their own
facilities. The last time Celtic had been in London, they had
ended up using a municipal pitch for training, and found it
covered in dog shit.

Strach said, "I thought it might be a nice buzz for the lads to
come to your place."

A buzz for them? A bigger buzz for me, more likely.

The day before they came, the gardeners worked on the pitch
until after sundown, making it perfect. Next morning, two huge
luxury coaches came rolling through the gates and around the
drive and came to a halt with a hiss. One brought the players, the
other brought the coaching staff and the gear and the food which
they would later eat, sitting around the pool. Around *my* pool!

I watched them arrive from an upstairs window, hidden by
a curtain—watched them step off the bus, one by one: Aiden

McGeady, Bobo Baldé, Kenny Miller, Neil Lennon, Artur Boruc, Gary Caldwell . . . the players from my team, on my drive. I had gone all shaky, like a teenage girl with a crush. I didn't want to come out of the house, didn't even want to meet them.

It took my wife to get my act together. Once they had changed in my tiny dressing room (now relocated and enlarged) and gone down to the pitch, I followed them with Penny, who was heavily pregnant with Alastair, our firstborn. We shook some hands and stood on the touchline. The staff had put out cones and the players were playing a game of one-touch, at amazing speed, it seemed to me—and on my pitch, which had never looked so beautiful. Gordon had told the team there was to be no swearing, but something went wrong for McGeady, who shouted "Fuck!" then immediately turned to Penny: "Sorry, ma'am." Good as gold.

Who else in the world has had his favorite football team train in his garden? What kind of schoolboy dream is that?

Here's an old joke: A wife says to her husband, "Sometimes I think you love the Celtic more than you love me." The husband says, "Dear, I love the *Rangers* more than I love you." For how much longer, though, will cracks like that be funny, or even possible? Rangers, Celtic's fierce cross-city rivals, went into liquidation in 2012 and now play in Scotland's lowest professional league. I was trying to explain to my young son Alastair—who seems to have caught the Celtic bug from somewhere—that there wouldn't be any Old Firm derbies for the time being, and he was genuinely saddened. I feel for the Rangers fans, especially the young ones. But there is loss for supporters on both sides of the divide: a century and a quarter of fervent, life-enhancing rivalry thrown into jeopardy. And Scottish football in general is such a frail and impoverished thing by comparison with the

English version. At a match in 2008, I found myself sitting next
to the Dundee United chairman Eddie Thompson, a lovely man
who, sadly, has since passed away, and who once sent me a recipe,
written in his own hand, for the club's meat pies. I asked Eddie
how much his club hoped to profit by finishing fourth in the
league at the end of the season. He said, "One hundred and sixty-
five thousand pounds." Al the Tout immediately said, "That's
Frank Lampard's wages for a *week*."

All you can do, though, is fly the flag and keep it flying. If
I'm in England and Celtic are at home, we'll take the plane up:
me, Big Al, Al the Tout, and Ricky Simpson, if he's around.
We'll go to Rogano in the middle of Glasgow and order the
cod and chips. Then we'll drive out east to the ground, see the
streets grow busier the closer we get, see the green-and-white
hooped shirts thickening in number. And then we'll pass the big,
brooding bronze statue of Jock Stein holding the European Cup
and head inside. I sometimes think I would go for the singing
alone: the passionate, inventive, nonstop chanting of the Green
Brigade, those great terrace originals who create the songs
the rest of the world sings. My seat for life is in the directors'
box, with a brass plate bearing my name, next to one for Billy
Connolly. In front of me and just to the right sit Billy McNeill
and, alongside him, Bertie Auld—two of the legendary "Lisbon
Lions" side of 1967*—and to sit there, as a fan, and be in the
presence of the club's history in that way is an immense privilege
and makes me a very happy man.

I was a Lisbon Lion myself once, you know. OK, only in
a charity match in 1994. Still, what a thrill, to sit in a dressing
room alongside Billy McNeill and Ronnie Simpson and John

---

* The 1967 Celtic team that defeated Internazionale 2–1 for the European Cup at the
Estadio Nacional near Lisbon, Portugal

Clark and be told by Bertie Auld, in full Scots brogue, before we ran out, "Rod, ah want ma passes *crusp*." (Translation: "Rod, I want my passes delivered crisply.") Our opponents were a Celtic XI, and Lou Macari, with no love lost, kicked me right up in the air from behind. I still owe him for that.

Even when I can't go, I'm still watching. In January 2012, I had to fly from London to Jakarta for a show. But I was hardly going to miss the Scottish League Cup semifinal against Falkirk, was I? So I went online and found a Celtic Supporters Club, the SingTims, in Singapore, and I arranged to break the journey there. And thus I found myself, approaching midnight, packed into a tiny bar, the best part of 7,000 miles from Glasgow, surrounded by Scots, all wearing their hooped shirts, and all shouting and singing at the television set, the picture on which kept freezing because it was being streamed from the Internet.

Celtic, incidentally, won 3–1, with two goals from Anthony Stokes and a penalty by the captain, Scott Brown. Not that we saw any of them. The television chose those moments to freeze.

It's all-consuming and, by any logical analysis, mad, and it has the power to change my mood, for better and worse, and I spend too much time thinking about it and I attach far too much importance to it. But what can you do? It's football. One time, at four a.m. in Vancouver, Canada, I was heading to a bar where I knew I would be able to watch the broadcast of a lunchtime kickoff, and the sun was just coming up, and I saw this bloke on his bicycle, with his cycle clips on, in his hooped Celtic shirt, pedaling determinedly through the empty streets, on his way to the game. And I thought, "Me and you both, pal."

Come on, you bhoys in green.

CHAPTER 10

In which our hero commences an affair with a wing commander's daughter, acquires a stupidly large house, and falls into fellowship with Elton John.

n July 1971, the record company throws a party for the Faces at a nightclub called Bumbles in Los Angeles. It's the usual scene: loud music, a foaming ocean of free drink, a number of record company types in various stages of nervousness and inebriation, and a horde of women in luscious night attire who are here with the sole aim of flinging themselves at the band, which they duly do with cheerful immodesty.

In these circumstances, I am learning, it is impossible, as a member of the group, to maintain a position in the middle of the room. You can start out there and cling on to the carpet with your toes as hard as you like, but you will eventually be forced outwards by the waves of people coming at you, until you are backed up against the wall, literally peeling people—mostly women—off yourself. That said, on this occasion I can hardly be accused of hiding from the attention: I have chosen for the night a white velvet suit bright enough to light up an ice hockey arena.

The girl I eventually notice, however, through the throng, is not flinging herself at me, nor pressing me up against the furniture while barking into my ear a startlingly frank proposal regarding the rest of the evening. On the contrary, she is sitting at a table to one side, in a blue-and-white dress and a pair of clogs. And she is observing the scene, including my suit, with an air of detached bemusement. I introduce myself—and the introduction is necessary because Dee Harrington from England is here with a friend and is no particular fan of the Faces, or indeed of rock music in general, and has very little idea who I am. She prefers soul music, as it turns out, but then soul is a passion of mine, too, so that's a point of connection straightaway. When Aretha Franklin's "Spanish Harlem" comes on, I ask her to dance. Then we sit down and talk some more. And then we leave the club and live together for four years.

Instant mutual attraction. Immediate comfort in another person's company. It's hard to unpack the chemistry of these things, but there it was, plain enough. Dee was twenty-one years old, a well-brought-up southern counties English girl, the daughter of a Royal Air Force pilot—Wing Commander Harrington, no less. She had been a secretary at a record company in London and was in LA looking for work and not quite finding it. And she was attractive in that appealing way that seems not to know exactly *how* attractive. A few days before I met her she had been sitting in reception at a photography studio, waiting for a friend of hers who was a model to come out, and a photographer had walked past and offered her a *Playboy* shoot on the spot. She had a plan to save some money, maybe move on to Japan. She ended up with me instead.

The urge to be alone, just the two of us—that was instant, too. We left the party and walked and talked, not really knowing where we were. A police car pulled up and checked us over at one point—were we all right? Nobody really walked around like this in LA. We were fine; never better. Eventually we found Sunset Boulevard and the Whisky a Go Go club, but we couldn't get in because Dee didn't look twenty-one and had nothing with her to prove that she was. So we walked back to the Beverly Hills Hotel, where the band was billeted, and Dee said she couldn't stay, because that just wasn't the kind of thing she did—just hook up with some rock singer in a nightclub and go back to his room . . . but maybe she could if we just slept. So we did.

But not before I had produced from my bag, for her approval, the model I carried with me of a Lamborghini Miura. "This is the car I've got back in England," I said. Am I the only person to have attempted to seduce a woman with a *toy* sports car? She said, "Oh yeah, I've been in one of those." She hadn't, though. She was just determined not to seem even slightly impressed.

The next day she came to see the Faces in Long Beach, traveling in the limo with me and through the back door and up to the side of the stage just before the show, so that when the lights went on she saw the crowd for the first time, this sea of people, and realized something about the scale of this thing. And backstage afterwards we got separated—at opposite ends of a long, packed corridor, me semaphoring madly to security to bring her through the press of groupies and hangers-on. Her second glimpse of the madness, which she never liked, or wanted any part of, although for a long time that didn't matter because our relationship took place in total and blissful isolation from it.

Back in London, I rang her and arranged a date at a pub in Lancaster Gate, where I pulled up outside in the yellow Lamborghini, to demonstrate that I hadn't made it all up. (And I think she secretly rather liked it: the two-seater aspect of it, the fact it went fast and that everybody looked at it. And why not? We were young and that kind of thing was compelling.) Within three months I had proposed to her, in a hotel in New York, slightly surprising her with the speed of the offer, and also perhaps the "squareness" of it, because getting hitched wasn't exactly a hip thing to be doing in those days—at least, she certainly didn't think so. (And, indeed, we never did get around to the wedding bit—just drifted along in a state of engagement.) And within three months of that, we would be shacked up in a rambling mansion in the English countryside.

Quite suddenly, and for the first time in my life, I had a lot of money coming in—an awful lot of money, to the point where my accountant was telling me to spend more. Specifically, he was telling me that it might be a smart idea to get rid of £100,000 or so on a property of some kind, to avoid having to pay the same sum in tax.

Well, if he absolutely insisted . . .

Except that, in 1971, finding a property that was worth as much as £100,000, and which wasn't Buckingham Palace or the Houses of Parliament, was quite a challenge. As close as I could get to the target was £89,000: the price on a stucco-faced Georgian mansion named Cranbourne Court, near one of the Queen's other places at Windsor, in the countryside not far west of London. Apparently Bob Hope had lived in this house at one time, which I rather liked the thought of, and also, while it was the home of an antiques dealer, Sophia Loren used to drop by on browsing expeditions.

Its owner, Lord Bethell, however, was an English aristocrat fallen on hard times. As he showed Dee and me around the property one afternoon, Dee nudged me and pointed out quietly that his trousers had worn so thin that you could make out his striped underpants through the material. If His Lordship had any dark feelings about flogging off the family heritage to some nouveau riche, long-haired rock star and his blond bird, he didn't share them. He was probably simply relieved that he had found a buyer.

So, on January 1, 1972, just six months after first meeting, Dee and

I moved out of my four-bedroom mock-Tudor house in Winchmore Hill and into a gigantic country pile with stone eagles on the pillars at the gateway, a sweeping drive through rhododendron bushes masking about seventeen acres of assorted gardens and paddocks, and an entrance hall with a forty-foot ceiling and a giant staircase climbing out of it. I was very proud when I first showed it all to my mum, but she looked worried more than anything else.

"Ooh, Roddy, how much did all *this* cost?"

"You don't wanna know, Mum."

But then, I don't think she or my dad ever really got their heads around how much money I was earning. In fact, many years later I would ask my mum what she wanted for Christmas.

"Go on," I said. "Let me treat you to something."

After a lot of thought, she said she wanted a new bread bin.

The problem wasn't going to be paying for Cranbourne Court— the problem was going to be filling it. When it was unpacked, the furniture from the old house took up less than one room in the new one, which left thirty-five more rooms in need of furnishing. Decorating the house was to become the project of the next two and a half years, the main thing to which Dee and I devoted our time.

We found a chandelier the size of a Morris Minor to hang in the hall. We hunted down leather Chesterfields and velvet sofas in antiques shops on the King's Road. We bought eight tall wicker butterfly-backed chairs to go around the dining table. My brother Bob, who was a carpenter, came to help sort a few things out and was still there two years later.

We set aside two of the bedrooms for my model railroad, knocking a pair of holes in the partition wall so that the lines could run from room to room. The coach house was pulled down to make room for a tennis court. I decorated the billiard room with pictures of Denis Law. I had an indoor swimming pool added on, converted the dingy old staff kitchen into something a bit more welcoming, and stuck in a Wurlitzer jukebox so we could listen to music while we ate. I made sure Aretha's "Spanish Harlem" was on there. It was our theme song.

The kitchen was where we hung out mostly. Dee cooked for us, standing at the counter, frequently in a tartan miniskirt, working up some extremely serious brunches: sausage, bacon, black pudding, beans, and mushrooms. Or on Sunday mornings, while I was up in north London playing football and dropping in on my parents, she would make a Sunday roast, and start serving up when she heard the sound of the Lamborghini's engine as I came off the roundabout at the bottom of the drive.

We had a cat called Pussy Galore, two collie dogs, an Alsatian (Carlo, named in honor of the house's Sophia Loren connection, after Loren's husband, Carlo Ponti), and a lorikeet, who liked Dee but hated me with a passion—mostly, perhaps, because when I got fed up with its screeching, I would shove its cage in the larder, turn out the light, and shut the door. Outside there were four bulls, specifically employed to keep the grass down, and a stable block with three horses, Cheval, Cara Mia, and Spotty, who later produced Little Spotty.

Dee (and definitely not I) rode the horses, I had my trains, and we seemed to be sharing a kind of domestic heaven into which the world could not intrude; a blissful place to return to, a refuge we had created from the tomfoolery outside. We threw one proper party the whole time we were there—the night, aforementioned, when Gary Glitter's wig floated off in the swimming pool. (I believe it was my brother-in-law who pushed him in, but frankly, in those days, if you wanted to push Gary Glitter in a pool you had to join the queue. Gary, incidentally, joined up with the Faces on tour at one point, as a support act in Paris, and got some of the worst dog's abuse I have ever seen from an audience. Beer cans were bouncing off his chest. But he carried on regardless. Whatever else you want to say about him, he was a trouper.)

Otherwise we just had people to dinner or for Sunday lunch. John Peel, the Radio 1 DJ, came over one day and Dee served him the full roast with trimmings, which he might have greeted more enthusiastically if he hadn't been a vegetarian. An artichoke was hastily boiled. It may have been the most miserable lunch he ever ate, but he was very polite about it.

Drugs, meanwhile, were banned. They had no place in this country idyll. Dee had no interest in them and I was more than a little paranoid about the police coming in and turning the place over, which seemed to be happening with increasing frequency to poor old Keith Richards. So I implemented a "leave-them-at-the-door policy." If you turned up with drugs, you were politely but firmly requested to return them to your car for safekeeping.

But mostly it was just the two of us anyway. With each other's undivided attention, we could talk for hours about anything on the planet. Dee called it the "mansion in the sky" because it was invisible from the road and nobody knew we were there. And we were very much in love and somehow, in this opulent and madly extravagant setting, very down-to-earth, ordinary at heart, and almost bohemian in the way we lived, slopping about in sweaters with holes in the elbows, shoes with old bits of ribbon for laces, and a pair of Afghan coats that the dogs liked to pull on, and sharing a solitary pair of pajamas—her the top, me the bottoms. The old-fashioned English phrases that I liked to use made her laugh: "Well, I'll go to the bottom of our stairs" (as an expression of surprise); "You're up and down like a pair of trousers, you are" (when someone can't sit still). Sometimes we just ran around the place like children, shouting and playing hide-and-seek, the house being the perfect venue for that game, apart from the risk of hiding and never being found. No diamonds, no glamour. Our idea of a night out was to walk down to the local pub, the Crispin, in our slippers: mine granddad-style tartan numbers, hers with pink pom-poms and a wedge heel.

Cute, wholesome, and not destined to last.

The madness, of course, went on in other places. This was a period of extraordinary professional success for me. The years that I was with Dee, from 1971 to 1975, with the success of the *Every Picture Tells a Story* album, and the big hits with "Maggie May" and "You Wear It Well," and then the *Smiler* album, were the years of my breakthrough as a singer—my arrival at a whole new level of fame. "Maggie May" was a hit just three months after Dee and I met. After all those years on the periphery, I was suddenly a star and the center of a lot of attention. I wanted to enjoy it. It would have seemed a bit perverse not to. It was what I had been working for.

The nightclub Tramp had opened on Jermyn Street, just below Piccadilly in London. It was set in a gorgeous room—like something off an ocean liner—clad with sumptuous wooden paneling and hung with chandeliers. And, most important of all, it was in the building's basement, which is where a nightclub always ought to be, in my considered opinion. (Going upstairs into a nightclub just feels wrong to me. History is littered with the corpses of clubs that closed because they didn't take the precaution of locating themselves in a cellar, as God intended.)

Tramp's cachet was that it attracted the famous: musicians, footballers, actors and actresses. In those early years, for instance, the chances of running into George Best were extremely high. Indeed, there was a period when he seemed to be as much a part of the place as the wood paneling. We always had time for each other, and also for the waiters, who were mostly Italian and Spanish and wanted to talk about football. The Faces had a couple of parties down there, and it became a port of call for me and remained so for many years.

Meanwhile, the house Elton John shared with John Reid was just a conveniently short drive from Cranbourne Court, and the parties there were long and legendary. Elton and I had known each other, on and off, since the Long John Baldry days. Bluesology, Elton's first proper band, played the blues clubs that I frequented in the early 1960s, and Long John joined and became their vocalist after the demise of Steampacket. But it was in the early 1970s that Elton and I drew especially close; the best of mates for a while. Just as Long John had christened me "Phyllis," he had christened Elton "Sharon," and that's what we were to each other: Phyllis and Sharon. Or just "dear."

"Hello, dear. How are you, dear? Really, dear?"

I loved his sense of humor, loved the fact that he was the kind of bloke who could see the comedy value in driving thirty times around the roundabout that surrounds the Marble Arch monument in the middle of London. (Sounds bloody stupid now, I suppose, but it was funny at the time.) We had football in common, obviously. And I respected his opinions about music. He had a proper understanding of blues and soul, and if he liked something I had done, it meant a lot to me, coming from him. I quietly envied the way that gigantic-selling popular melodies seemed to come to him in such a constant flow.

I also had to be in awe of the fact that, whether it was drink or cocaine, he could see me right under the table every time. One night at his house, we were applying ourselves to the medicinal powders and it got to six in the morning, at which point I tendered a short letter of resignation ("Fuck it, I surrender") and went upstairs to find a bed to sleep in. Four hours later, Elton woke me by thumping on the door.

"Come on, dear. We've got a football match to go to."

I looked, and felt, as if I had been run over from a number of different directions by a number of different traction engines. Elton, by contrast, standing in the doorway, was bright of cheek and white of smile, immaculate in a morning suit with a jaunty top hat and holding a gold-tipped walking cane. A night like we had just been through would take me weeks to get over. On Elton it would barely register, and he would be ready four hours later to watch Watford play Shef-field Wednesday.

But then I was always something of an amateur in this particu-lar arena, and, in truth, not especially concerned to be anything else. When it came to the consumption of drugs, I like to think I took a fairly gentlemanly approach. If it was something to brighten the eve-ning, then fine. But I was never some mad, rampant oblivion-seeker. Total loss of control didn't really appeal to me. "Social use" would be the technical term, I suppose—though with the proviso that, during certain periods, I was doing a lot of socializing.

Of course, the Faces drank heavily and proudly, and indeed made an occupation out of it. But even in that context I wasn't in the habit of taking it to the point where I was legless or facedown and comatose. As for drugs, anything that had to be smoked was out of the question because I wanted to protect my voice. And any enthusiasm I might have grown to have for anything psychedelic was terminated by the fate of my aforementioned friend Clive Amore, who, in the sixties, was the first among my group of friends to take acid—and then, in the belief that he could fly, threw himself naked from a top floor window and died. That stuff struck me as a bad idea from then on.

Also, to be perfectly frank, on any given night out, I was likely to be far more interested in chatting to women than I was in getting smashed, and after a certain point those interests become mutually exclusive. And I was permanently concerned about being in sound enough condition to play a game of football on a Sunday. Football may have saved me from a lot of excess, in this sense. All in all, con-sume as I did, I was a mere dabbler, relatively speaking, in a scene which included one or two major Olympians.

Some people have the brass-built constitution for the consumption of stimulants in thunderous quantities, and I—perhaps to my long-term advantage—possibly didn't. A case in point would be the night in Tramp, around 1977, when I unwisely volunteered for a session of excess with Keith Moon, the Who's famously unstable drummer. Moon always was dangerous—not in the way that you felt bodily threatened, because he was quite short and stubby and not physically intimidating. It was more the sense he gave off that he could erupt at any time and you wouldn't know why, or in which direction the smoke was going to carry.

Moon was a notorious presence at Tramp, and had been since the time he went on the dance floor completely naked. On this particular occasion, with his clothes in place, he abruptly declared to the assembled company, "Right, I'm staying up until the pubs reopen at eleven in the morning, and anyone who doesn't is a fucking wanker."

Something competitive in me was triggered. Instead of walking away then and there from this thrown-down gauntlet, I foolishly decided to pick it up. Cocaine and alcohol were duly abused in reckless quantities, at a succession of locations, including, unless I am mistaken, (a) Ronnie Wood's house, (b) a party somewhere in the West End of London to which none of us had been invited, and (c) Moon's strange, modern white house in Chertsey, with its five pyramid-shaped roofs, where there was a bar decorated with enormous and slightly disturbing paintings of cartoon superheroes. It was here, eventually, under pictures of Thor and the Incredible Hulk, that dawn broke and I realized my race was run.

"I can't do this, Keith," I whispered, and began to creep away home.

He absolutely killed me.

"You fucking ponce, Stewart. Come back here and finish what you started."

Moon, of course, was to pay the steepest price for his appetites, dying in 1978 from an overdose of sedatives. Indeed, "you fucking ponce" must have been pretty much the last words he ever said to me. I strongly suspect that Elton, too, would have been dead by now if he hadn't eventually taken the decision to give it all up. There is a limit, surely, to how much abuse a single man's constitution can take—even Elton John's.

I knew I couldn't compete with Elton in that area, but in music we had a proper rivalry going on for a while. We vamped it up for all it was worth, and made a joke out of it, but it definitely grew from a little seed of genuine competitiveness—wanting to outdo each other in sales and success. And it's still like that: we both had albums out at the same time in 2011 and there was considerable chafing (on my part) and gloating (on his) that Elton's reached number three in the chart while mine reached number four. (It's my contention—admittedly not supported by any statistical evidence *so far*—that a few hundred sales were somehow "found" somewhere.) Also we both have residencies at Caesars Palace in Las Vegas and, again, there's a bit of jostling over who sells more tickets. (Answer: I do, whatever Elton may tell his audiences from the stage.)

From time to time this rivalry has driven Elton to pull off some beautifully organized stunts. In 1985 I had a bunch of massive footballs, the size of blimps, tethered above Earls Court to mark the fact that I was doing concerts there. Elton hired a sniper to shoot them down with an air rifle. Or like the time the banner for my *Blondes Have More Fun* tour, outside the same venue, was matched by one that Elton put up on an opposite building, which read, "But Brunettes Make More Money."

The competitive spirit reached a height one night in a hotel in Paris when the pair of us managed to sustain a coke-enhanced dialogue until ten the following morning. The sole topic of this august debate: which of us had the most money in his bank account. The people who were with us had drifted away to bed and come down again for breakfast, only to find us still locked in the same discussion. Result of the debate: inconclusive, as (children be warned) cocaine-fueled debates very often are.

There is no more generous person on this earth, though, than

Elton—just incredibly generous. I have watches he has given me for birthdays: lavish, thickly jeweled pieces engraved "From Elt." He gave my first wife, Alana, with whom he remained good friends after she and I separated, a Steinway piano. Those don't come cheap.

And then there was the Christmas where I thought long and hard about the present I was going to give him. That's always a tough one: What do you get the man who has bought himself everything? Eventually, though, after a bit of scouring around the shops, I lit upon the solution: a novelty portable fridge. Brilliant. You plugged it in and pressed a button and its door opened automatically, and it lit up and a bottle rose out of it in a cloud of vapor. It seemed to me to offer the required "wow" factor. And it cost me about £300, which I thought was enough.

Elton's present to me that year: a Rembrandt.

A drawing—*The Adoration of the Shepherds.*

A fucking Rembrandt! I felt pretty small—although not as small as Elton presumably wanted me to feel when he later referred tartly to my present as "an ice bucket." It was not an ice bucket. It was a novelty portable fridge.

Anyway, I played it a bit better on his fiftieth birthday in 1997. I bought him a full-size, sit-under hairdryer like the ones you see in women's hair salons. Two years later, he marked my marriage to Rachel with a £10 voucher from Boots.* On the card he wrote, "Get yourself something nice for the house."

We traveled together a bit, too, or sought each other out when we were abroad. The band Queen rented a house in Bel Air, Los Angeles, for a while, and Elton and I spent a long evening there with Freddie Mercury, a sweet and funny man whom I really adored, discussing the possibility of the three of us forming a supergroup. The name we had in mind was Nose, Teeth & Hair, a tribute to each of

---

* A pharmacy chain in the U.K.

our most remarked-upon physical attributes. The general idea was that we could appear dressed like the Beverley Sisters. Somehow this project never came to anything, which is contemporary music's deep and abiding loss.

In 1985, Elton and I were even together on a short holiday in Africa, a wildlife safari, driving out into the bush to spot the fabled "big five": the elephant, the rhino, the buffalo, the lion, and the leopard. The best time to do this, of course, is at an unearthly hour of the morning, which was never my best time of day back then. But there would be Elton, rattling away at the tent flap: "Come on, dear." We shared a Land Rover and appointed ourselves "poopologists": experts in the detection of animals by their poop. In the evening, back at the camp, we dressed up regally in bowties and dark jackets for dinner round the fire.

Even on safari, Elton insisted on bringing his diamonds with him. He had a black box with various pieces of Cartier jewelry in it, worth God only knows how much, entrusted to his assistant Bob—a bit like the way the U.S. president has someone with him with a briefcase containing the nuclear codes. One night in Africa, as we were having dinner, members of the party decided to sneak this precious box away from Bob and hide it, just to get a reaction. But Elton is a very difficult person to faze. Bob began to panic, but Elton simply said, "Don't worry, darling, it's only the daytime stuff."

In addition to Elton's house, the other key center of amusement during these Cranbourne Court days was Ronnie Wood's place, the Wick, at Richmond, a Georgian mansion which he had bought off the actor Sir John Mills. Set up on a hill and with huge bay windows out the back overlooking the Thames, the Wick was widely agreed to offer one of the most beautiful vistas in England, if not the whole of Europe—and Ronnie Wood ends up in it. Funny old world.

The three-story house had an oval dining and drawing room, carved woodwork, and amazing fireplaces. Ronnie plumbed a recording studio into the basement, inherited a snooker table along with the deeds to the property, and acquired a parrot, which he had taught to say "Fuck off," but in terms of other domestic essentials, such as, say, a dining table, the house always seemed to me to be a bit on the light side. Mostly it appeared to function as a giant, multiroom wardrobe for Ronnie's stage costumes, which were hanging up against most of the available surfaces, and also as a cupboard for his guitars.

It was a good gathering place, though, somewhere you might drop in at the end of the evening, where there always seemed to be a crowd, mostly hanging out downstairs in the recording studio, jamming, or listening to other people jamming, or helping out Woody on a project of his. Down there you might run into Pete Townshend or Keith Richards, who lived in the cottage at the bottom of Woody's garden for a while, even though he had houses of his own, or, very occasionally, Paul McCartney. I still vividly recall the sensation of leaving that studio at the end of a night and going upstairs to discover that it had got light without my noticing—always a slightly poignant downer of a moment. And it was in that studio one evening that Mick Jagger—speaking, I assume, for and on behalf of Bianca—made a tentative inquiry about the possibility of a little light partner-swapping with Dee and myself. Well, I suppose it's always nice to be asked, and comforting to know that you are in someone's thoughts, but the answer had to be no. Partner-swapping wasn't my scene, and it certainly wasn't Dee's.

Actually, the Wick in its entirety wasn't Dee's scene. It tended to be full of people taking all kinds of things and talking all kinds of bollocks—which is fine if you're partaking, but she wasn't, and I think she found it dark and slightly intimidating. While we were there, I would sometimes look across at her and she would have the expression of a woman who was hoping the floor would open up and swallow her. It just wasn't how she was interested in spending her time.

Also, as my working life got busier and more complicated and required greater amounts of organization, the privacy of Cranbourne

Court began to be eroded—much to Dee's distress and disappointment. The pressure started to make itself felt; there were more deci-
sions to make, and more people directly involved in the running of
my life. One person who was around a lot, and who Dee really had
reservations about, was the perfectly named Tony Toon, who was my
assistant and publicist during those years. Tony wore a battered cor-
duroy jacket and shabby trousers and resembled a down-at-heel Fleet
Street hack. He was thin and substantially bald, and there was hardly
ever a time when he wasn't sucking on a cigarette, with his fingers held
daintily aloft. We called him Fag-Ash Lil. He was mincing, waspish,
scurrilous, incorrigible. He had this running joke where, at the end of
every meal, in every restaurant, he would tell the waiter, "Bring me a
large amaretto and a big butch man." He did this unfailingly. Others
would come to find the joke, and his presence, irksome, but I enjoyed
having him around. He made things fun.

He also made things up. You could say there are, roughly, two
types of publicist. There's the kind who sees it as their job to keep
their client out of the papers, to throw the press off the scent when
necessary, and to limit any damage which arises. And then there's the
kind who thinks the role is about getting their client in the papers
as frequently as possible, wafting the press as much scent as they can
take. Tony was very much of the second school—with the additional
kick that he was ready to get me in the papers irrespective of whether I
wanted to be there or not, and irrespective of whether the story might
be annoying or even harmful to me or people close to me. And if he
saw the chance to spin a tale from a few tiny threads of fact, then he
would happily seize it.

So, for instance, I would bump into Bianca Jagger in a hotel in
New York and have a brief and mildly flirtatious encounter in the
lobby, and a couple of days later a story would appear in one of the
papers that the two of us were on the verge of moving in with each
other.

Perhaps the classic Toon fabrication was the story of the thwarted love affair I supposedly had with the daughter of President Gerald Ford. Now, it was true that Susan Ford came to see the Faces play in Washington in 1975. She would have been eighteen at the time, glamorous, with long blond hair. It was also true that she came backstage afterwards, surrounded by an army of security men.

But from those meager details, Tony created a saga worth a week of newspaper headlines, in which our eyes had met across a crowded room, we had fallen hopelessly and permanently in love, Susan had invited me to an intimate dinner at the White House, but fog had prevented me flying in from New York, leading me to send fifty red roses by way of apology . . .

Another of Tony's tricks was the fabrication of meetings in restaurants. He would tell me that, for example, Mick Jagger had rung up, asking to go to dinner with me. And I would say, "Fine." And then he would ring Jagger and tell him that Rod Stewart wanted to have dinner with him. And Jagger would say, "Oh, OK, then." And thus this coming-together would be arranged, with both of us assuming it was at the other's request, and Tony would accompany us and get a free meal, while also having some gossip to offer the press.

I was constantly saying to him about one thing or another, "But how did they find out about this?" To which he would reply, "I don't know, dear. It wasn't me, dear. I'll find out for you, dear."

The tabloid guys must have loved Tony Toon. He was a gift to their trade. But for Dee, he was a less welcome presence. Needless to say, Tony's willingness to shop stories of my dalliances, invented and otherwise, hardly endeared him to her as a force for good within our relationship. She associated him, naturally enough, and in the broadest possible sense, with exposure. To her, he represented much of the madness that our life at Cranbourne Court had been carefully constructed to exclude.

Waiting on a luggage
trolley at Los Angeles
International Airport,
1975. Trying desperately
to look sensible.

Obviously taken after a Faces show. Everybody looking three sheets to the wind. What a band!

Left: The launch of the *Ooh La La* album at Tramp nightclub, with the obvious decoration of the can-can girls. *Right:* Old pals. *Opposite:* Woody and me discussing stage movements for the next song. Santa Barbara, California, early seventies.

Above: Trying to get into my car amid frenzied fans in Glasgow, with the help of Elton's manager John Reid. *Below:* In a girlie blouse, studying Sam.

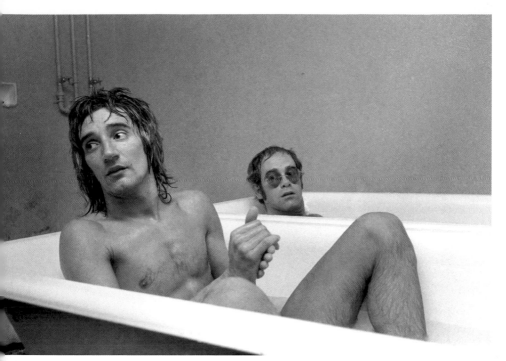

hyllis and Sharon, *not* in the same bath, therefore avoiding any hanky-panky. Football training at Vatford, 1974.

eddie Mercury and me in wide jackets, looking bashful. Freddie appears to be touching my knee.

Right: Me and Dee Harrington going on holiday, looking rather drab!

Below: Cutting the lawn at the glorious Cranbourne Court, with my Lamborghini Miura in the background, 1973. Life is good.

Opposite: Britt and me, circa 1976. Well, you just gotta laugh at this.

Is this Ruby Stewart or Rod Stewart?

Of course, I was a rock singer when Dee met me. Her first glimpses of me, remember, were behind the scenes with the Faces. She knew very well what the scene around rock bands was like, and she understood that the chances of me remaining faithful to her while I was out on tour were remote. But in the beginning, touring was a separate world and Cranbourne Court was our reality. It was a barrier against the madness of the rock world. Increasingly, though, the rock world was climbing over the barriers and coming into our lives and into our house. Without doubt the explosion of my fame after "Maggie May," and the extent to which it made me a piece of public property, created some deep fractures in our relationship. I don't think fame changed *me* very much; I think I remained pretty down-to-earth—maybe even quite remarkably so, in the context. But fame definitely changed the world around me. The adoration that suddenly starts coming at you from all angles, and from total strangers, can be very pleasant when you're the object of it but enormously troubling and unsettling for the person you're with. When we were out together, people would have no qualms about talking to me as if Dee wasn't there. Women would openly flirt with me right in front of her. We would try to go to the theater together and end up running out halfway through because people were saying, "Ooh, look—there's Rod Stewart." Jealousy, resentment, anxiety: these things definitely entered the relationship at that point and had a corrosive effect.

Our life was all about me and my schedule. We had this country idyll, and then all of a sudden helicopters were continually landing on its grass to spin me off to places: promotional trips, recording, touring. I had a band and a solo career at this point, remember, so I really was furiously busy. A lot of the time, when I was away, Dee was left alone, rattling around in that enormous house. And she was approaching her mid-twenties and beginning to think, "Well, what about me? What am I doing with *my* life?" She sometimes said she wanted to get a job, but I really didn't want her to. I told her that people would say, "You know that man who owns the big white house? He sends his girl out to work. How mean must he be?"

These tensions burrowed their way into the relationship and began to pick it apart. The joy of it began to be lost for both of us. There was a huge and growing ocean between us, and the relationship really needed to end, but neither of us could end it. By 1974, we were arguing with increasing frequency—and with increasing frequency those arguments were ending with Dee walking out in anger and frustration and going back to her parents. I would then be contrite and want her back, but—always pitifully afraid of confrontation—I would get my mate Micky Waller, from the Jeff Beck Group days, to phone her up and say, "If Rod rings, will you talk to him?" And if it turned out the worst had blown over, I would be straight on the phone, quietly asking her out to lunch at the pub in High Wycombe, and then pleading with her to return. And then the cycle would start again.

During one of those separations—a six-week one, this time—I went to a football awards ceremony and met the actress Joanna Lumley. This was before the television series *The New Avengers* made her name—and lest anyone wish to add her to the "long line of blondes" with which my name has been continually associated, let the record state that, at this period in her life, she had black hair.

She was also very well educated and altogether rather posh: I remember her referring at one point to "the family tapestries," and wondering if she meant the carpets, until it eventually dawned that she didn't. She was, therefore, not the first person you would have imagined consenting to hang out with someone who could easily have been mistaken for a rock 'n' roll urchin. But I've always enjoyed a challenge, and there seemed to be a bit of a spark between us; and if this was going to come down to class, I was always able to wheel out what I thought was an extremely upmarket line: "Would you like to come and spend the weekend with me in Spain on my boat?"

It was true, I had a boat: a thumping great seventy-foot-long, Dutch-built number with a steel hull, which I christened *The Gay Intruder*. At first it was docked on the Thames at Richmond and I decided that the nice thing to do, for its maiden voyage, would be to take my mum up the river one Sunday. I asked Cyril, my driver, if he thought he could handle a boat. "Of course I can," he said. "I was in the navy."

So we board, and set off smoothly up the river under Cyril's highly competent captaincy, and there really couldn't be a nicer way to spend a warm afternoon with one's mother than gently floating on the water, drinking wine.

"OK, Cyril," I say. "We should probably turn around and go back now." The boat is long and the river relatively narrow at this point, but Cyril is a veteran, so he expertly brings the boat's prow around through ninety degrees. Then he backs up and there's a horrible grinding sound and the noise of splintering wood as the back end of my gin palace takes out a small flotilla of prettily painted rowing boats, moored beside the bank.

After this escapade I decided the best place for the boat was down in Spain, and I had it sailed to Puerto Banús. There, a trustworthy Scottish bloke who happened to be living in the town was engaged to keep an eye on it, in my absence, and have it ready for use when necessary—such as, for instance, on any weekend when I might show up intending to impress Joanna Lumley.

A car delivered us to the harbor, where, dressed lightly in linens for a weekend afloat, I walked my companion the final yards to our awaiting vessel, pointing it out in the distance, among the many shiny, expensive yachts tied to the jetties. And then, finally, we were alongside and my companion got her first sight on board.

It looked as though someone had taken a bin from outside the back of a restaurant and upended it across the deck. The boat was ankle-deep in discarded food and rubbish. Every surface was grimy. My trusty Scottish ship-minder was asleep in a hammock beside a slew of empty beer cans. Five mates of his were dotted around the deck, similarly unconscious and stretched out to dry in the sun.

I proceeded to wake the boat-sitter by shouting at him and calling him a torrent of names, the full list of which is now lost in the mists of time, though I feel sure that at least one of them was "wanker." I then walked my companion crisply back around the harbor and we checked into a hotel. Fortunately, she seemed to find it funny, although I did notice that our relationship ended quite soon after.

My relationship with Dee reached its terminal crisis where it began: in Los Angeles, during a tour with the Faces. This was 1975. Dee had flown in from London to meet me that afternoon and was tired and said she was going to bed. I told Dee I had a meeting, which I did. What I didn't mention was that the meeting was at the Troubadour nightclub with Britt Ekland.

And then the awful thing: midway through the evening, Dee decides she feels better and goes out in search of company. The next thing I know, she walks in through the door of the Troubadour, with an innocent, anticipatory look on her face which suddenly changes to one of immense hurt.

There was no big scene. Dee turned around, walked out of the club, flew back to London, and moved out of Cranbourne Court, this time for good.

It was the right thing for both of us. But what a way to bring it about. How not to leave your lover.

CHAPTER 11

*In which our hero leaves Britain for Los Angeles under false
pretenses and moves in with a Bond girl, which works out well
until it doesn't. Of his struggles to settle in a land that doesn't
particularly understand football. And in which further most excellent
recordings are made, which you can still buy if you haven't already.*

Britt Ekland broadened my outlook on just about everything.
We were together for a little over two years, and deeply
wrapped up in each other for most of that time. It all went a
bit frosty at the end—and I suppose the clue there is that she tried to
sue me for $12.5 million. But these things happen and, as the old ex-
pression has it, if you're not at the fair, you can't win a coconut. I still
think of the experience as a wonderful love affair and an education
that I was fortunate to have.

Britt came to see the Faces at the Forum in Los Angeles in February 1975. A year earlier, she had made her iconic appearance as a Bond
girl in *The Man with the Golden Gun*, and was widely agreed to be one
of the most beautiful women in the world. She wasn't the first person

you would have expected to find knocking about in a rock group's dressing room, yet the backstage scene at some of those later Faces gigs did get extraordinarily starry. Steve McQueen came to see us when we played the Hollywood Bowl. Dustin Hoffman, too, turned out to be quite a Faces fan. In Britt's case, her friend Joan Collins brought her. Joan was married to Ron Kass, a record executive at Warner Bros., the Faces' record label, so that was the connection. Ron and Joan then hosted a dinner, in rather more refined circumstances, at the Luau restaurant in Beverly Hills. And it was there that Britt and I sat next to each other and talked.

She was thirty-two—two years older than me, but, as was straightaway apparent, whole decades more worldly. She had been married to Peter Sellers, the actor, and after that she had had a relationship with Lou Adler, who owned a record company and who produced the great Carole King album *Tapestry*. Britt had two children: a daughter, Victoria, with Sellers, and a son, Nikolaj, with Adler. Victoria was ten at this time, and Nikolaj was two. Her relationship with Adler had ended after he admitted to an affair. As Britt later put it in the book she wrote, "Rod came into my life six weeks after I parted from Lou and I rose back into the sky like a gull whose oil-soaked wings had been cleansed by a detergent."

So what does that make me? Fairy Liquid, I guess. I've been called worse.

Of course, you'll be asking, "But what did you see in the blond, full-lipped Swedish film star and internationally recognized 'Bond girl'?" She was, of course, staggeringly beautiful. In public she could come across as slightly grand and actressy, but a lot of that was self-consciousness in the face of the attention that she always got. In private, you couldn't have met a more genuine and down-to-earth person— always pitching in at other people's houses, helping with the cooking, doing the washing up. She was very house-proud altogether, in fact. It was a surprise to people who didn't know her when she answered the door in Marigolds.* The boys in the band loved her—she would make them eggy bread when they dropped in—and my family adored her as well. We spent the Christmas of 1976 at my brother Don's house in Cambridgeshire, Britt and I in the single bed in the spare room, twelve of us rammed around the table in the dining room for Christmas dinner. My mum got confused and called her "Dee" once or twice, but Britt couldn't have cared less.

We were very intimate, very quickly. The night of that first dinner, we went on to a party at Cher's house, but we were so absorbed with each other that we didn't talk to anyone else. I think we went out for dinner again the night afterwards and then, later in that week, we had our date at the Troubadour where Dee came in and discovered us. By that point I knew I was falling in love. Britt was drop-dead gorgeous, a beauty without compare, although less tall than I tended to like them. And she seemed exotic and a thousand times more cultured than me. Also—I have to admit this component of it—she was famous, a big, big star at the time. I had never been out with a famous woman. There was something very exciting about that aspect of it. I guess I was starstruck.

In the early heat of our relationship, we spent a lot of time having sex in the Malibu beach house that Lou Adler owned. During enforced spells of separation, Britt would send me love notes and letters in packages which also often contained a pair of her knickers. My word, how e-mail has changed things.

We weren't apart that often, though—not at the start. In those days, pre-music-video and pre-MTV, you spent a lot of time hopping from country to country, and from television station to television station, touting your wares. And Britt largely put her career on hold and came with me on those trips, which made it a lot more fun. We turned it into an international adventure.

---

* U.K. brand of rubber gloves, used for washing dishes and cleaning

I called her Poopy and she called me Soddy—which was sweet in private, although, like many aspects of our relationship, it became public knowledge and set a few people's teeth on edge. And during one interview she came out with that line about us being the new Richard Burton and Elizabeth Taylor, and I cringed and wanted to die, knowing perfectly well that no one would even consider the possibility that she might have been joking.

The papers were all over us. The mixture of British rock star and Swedish film actress seemed to be some kind of recipe for tabloid delirium. They couldn't get enough. But even that could be quite exciting for us at times, especially when we were devising ways to give them the slip. To avoid detection, we booked into hotels and restaurants as Mr. and Mrs. Cockforth. The idea that we liked the attention and went after it a bit . . . well, there's some truth in that as well.

When she was in Rhodesia, as it then was called, doing some filming, she urged me to write her a romantic letter. So I sent her a telegram which said, "Tired of pulling me plonker. Please come home. Love, Soddy." It was, though, a genuinely romantic time. We took a cruise on the QE2, which was something I had long fantasized about doing, and packed lots of 1930s outfits to wear. One of the items was an authentic straw boater that Britt had bought me at Harold's Place, an antique clothing store in Beverly Hills. That's the boater I'm wearing on the sleeve of *A Night on the Town*, and I really wish I wasn't. But we'll come to that. Let's just say for now that maybe I would have looked less of a ponce if I had worn another gift Britt gave me: a lionskin rug, complete with the stuffed head and a full set of dentures. We spread it on the floor of the flat that we rented in Beauchamp Place in London and tripped over it continually thereafter.

She knew about paintings and antiques. She could put a name and a date to things. I thought I knew about paintings and antiques, too, prided myself that I already had an eye, but I didn't really. It was Britt who taught me to look. She introduced me to lamps and vases by

Émile Gallé, these fabulous late-nineteenth-century art nouveau constructions in engraved colored glass, which we decided to start collecting. We would set off together on lamp-hunting trips to Paris, armed with thousands of francs in cash. We spent hours in markets, haggling with sellers. At least Britt, who spoke French beautifully, haggled. I stood off to one side, saying helpful things like, "You want *how* much? I could buy a new one for that." It didn't always help to be famous when you were looking for bargains. You could drive up the asking price just by coming through the door. Sometimes the best thing to do was to leave and send someone else back later.

She started me on the therapeutic benefit of professional massage, something I had been squeamish and terribly British about before then. ("What? You let a stranger touch your naked body—and you don't end up having sex with them?") And, a little more controversially, she started putting makeup on my face. Quite a lot of makeup. Thick black rings around the eyes. I looked a complete tart. This did not go unnoticed by the other members of the Faces. The band began greeting Britt's arrival with the shout of "Avon calling!"

She got a far rougher ride from Faces fans, who thought she was turning my head. Because her arrival coincided with the band's death throes, it was only too easy to paint her as the Yoko Ono at the scene of the crime. This couldn't have been more wrong. Britt did nothing to break up the Faces. We were doing a perfectly good job of that ourselves, thank you very much, and had been doing so since well before she arrived.

I also got a bit of a working-over in this period. The double whammy of film-star girlfriend and my eventual emigration to Los Angeles seemed to piss a lot of people off—not really among the general public, who, I think, didn't really give a monkey's, but certainly in the British press, where it was widely alleged, in a sneering manner, that "Rod's gone all Hollywood."

This used to irritate me something rotten. For the previous four years I had been living in a mansion in Windsor that was on the scale of a public library, with a fleet of cars in the garage and a kitchen the size of a basketball court, and nobody had really gone off at me for betraying my roots. So I had to think that a lot of this flak was arising from pure small-minded prejudice about Hollywood. I resented the assumption. Just because I had gone *to* Hollywood, it didn't automatically follow that I had gone "all Hollywood."

And just because I was wearing a lot of makeup . . . and posing in a straw boater with a champagne glass . . .

All right. I may have lost the thread a couple of times in that period.

But fuck it: I was the son of a north London plumber for whom life hadn't necessarily earmarked a spell of splendor in the California sunshine alongside a Swedish film star, and bugger me if I wasn't going to have some fun and worry about forgiving myself for it later, if ever.

That Christmas, Britt and I went to a party in Beverly Hills thrown by Cubby Broccoli, the producer of the Bond movies. It had been something like eighty degrees during the day, but the house and the lawn around it were thick with artificial snow and the trees hung with lights and baubles. It seemed incredible to me that I was there at all, let alone on the arm of one of the world's most beautiful women. It was a black-tie do, and I really remember, as I got out of the car and walked through this fake but fabulous scene with Britt beside me, feeling that this was probably one of those moments in my life when it would be a good idea to pinch myself.

By then, I was a resident of Los Angeles. In April 1975, when my relationship with Britt was just getting going, I left England and became a tax exile. This didn't go down particularly well with the British press, who thought I was betraying the land of my birth. It didn't go down especially well with Elton John, either. Round at his place one evening, I told him I was thinking of quitting Britain, and he called me a traitor and put on Elgar's "Pomp and Circumstance Marches" at a volume so high that we couldn't talk over it.

However, hear my plea: the particular rate of tax from which I was exiling myself was 83 percent. You can surely imagine how much it was paining me to have that much gouged out of my earnings on an annual basis. And it wasn't just me. Joe Cocker was on my flight out of Heathrow, headed the same way, and Eric Clapton was on the next one out. In fact, people from all walks of life seemed to be abandoning Britain for places where life cost less. The "brain drain," they were calling it—though not in my case, necessarily.

However, I still maintain that Billy Gaff, my manager, slightly bamboozled me into the move. At the very least, I was a little confused about the details.

Gaff—who was an Irishman and didn't care much for England in the first place—flew to LA in advance and found a three-bedroom house on Doheny Drive. The idea was that Tony Toon and I would join him out there. I thought I would give it a go for a couple of weeks and see how it panned out. And if I didn't get on with it, then never mind. I could always fly home again.

Maybe I should have listened a bit more closely. When I arrived at Doheny Drive and set my bags down in the bedroom (I got the master suite, obviously), Gaff explained to me that I couldn't go back to England for a year. I would be able to return there eventually, he said, for a set number of nights in any tax year, but not until I had served a full twelve-month period of absence.

My heart sank. A whole year away from Britain? Not even to visit? But what about the British things I loved: football, roast dinners, decent cups of tea, crap weather? What about my family?

That first year was tough. I felt like a tourist—couldn't see myself adapting, was just observing everything from a distance and waiting to go home at the end of it. Sometimes when it rained—which wasn't often—I would run out and stand in it until I was soaked, just to remind myself properly what wet weather felt like. I missed my parents and my siblings. Being with Britt helped. Gradually the sunshine helped. Being in LA helped. LA can be a great place to live, and I grew to love it eventually. I still do.

In the summer of 1975, I bought a house for $750,000 on Carolwood Drive in the Holmby Hills. The place had fallen into disrepair; most of its twenty rooms were clogged with bugs and there was a family of wild cats living under the terrace that had to be solemnly evicted. But it clearly had the potential to be a fabulous home—less grand than Cranbourne Court in Windsor, but dreamier. Britt moved in with me in August and we threw ourselves headlong into doing the place up, a project which took several months. Needless to say, art nouveau glass featured prominently. In the dressing room, the wardrobes had art deco glass doors. We had a set of leather sofas, backed with elephant tusks, nests of silver tables, and a pair of life-size ornamental pelicans—not exactly understated, but I thought it was fabulous, like a dream palace. I installed Tony Toon in the guesthouse in the garden. Britt, who seemed to share Dee's resistance to Tony's charms, insisted he could only come into the main house when he was invited, but he would occasionally plod into the kitchen in the morning, smoking a cigarette, fix himself a cup of tea, and plod out again.

And nearly every day the sun shone. Exile was beginning to have its advantages.

Because Britt's young children were often with us, we tended to stay at home a lot and enjoy the house. But if we did go out at night, it would very often be to Le Dôme restaurant. Le Dôme was established by Eddie Kerkhofs, a Belgian restaurateur who became a close friend. Eddie figured that if you could get celebrities eating in your restaurant regularly you were halfway to making it look like a happening destination. So he devised a start-up scheme wherein anyone who put up a $3,000 stake would be credited with $5,000 of food at the restaurant. He offered this deal to me, Elton John, Dudley Moore, Olivia Newton-John, various members of Pink Floyd, and all sorts, and soon he had quite a scene on his hands.

At the time, Le Dôme was one of the only places in LA that stayed open late—until one or two in the morning. And often, even after that, Eddie would be prepared to switch off the lights at the front and allow a lock-in for anyone who wasn't ready to go home. The premises were also handily equipped with a back exit to the car park, so that anyone leaving the worse for wear, or with someone they ought not to have been leaving with, could do so in relative privacy.

Inevitably, given the clientele and its tastes, the downstairs bathroom at Le Dôme rapidly became a sort of romper room for the ingestion of mood-enhancing substances and, occasionally, sexual dalliances—between-course intercourse, as it were. As a measure of how hard-core that facility could get, note only this: Elton John preferred to use the disabled bathroom upstairs because he found the one downstairs too rock 'n' roll for him. Even after one of its periodic redecorations, it never seemed to lose the faint odor of cocaine. And yet, for a long time, the bathroom was staffed by a gentleman called Gil, who, despite the debauchery raging around him (or perhaps because of it), would sit quietly in the corner, reading the Bible, and then silently offer you a towel on your way out. It was hard not to feel slightly judged.

One night I had a big table at Le Dôme for members of the Exiles (my football team, of whom more later), and Dudley Moore tried to get my attention across a crowded room by lobbing a pork chop at me. The most almighty food fight ensued, possibly the worst I have ever been in: a blizzard of meatballs and mixed vegetables. The scene appalled even the normally equable Eddie. He had a fit and banned us both on the spot. We were soon back, though.

God, I loved my job in those days—and continue to love it. Who wouldn't? A rock star: what a thing to be. But, particularly, what a thing to be in the mid-1970s. I was so fortunate in the timing of it— to serve my apprenticeship in the 1960s and to break through in the 1970s, when everything in this area was new and surprising and when you seemed to be on a largely unbeaten path. I loved the romance of it; I loved the excess of it. I was in a state of permanent wonderment about it: that someone from a pretty basic and humble background could suddenly find his life going "whoosh"—taking off in this quite extraordinary, completely transformative way. I don't think that state of wonderment has ever left me. It's always there, just below the surface of everything I do.

In the two years that I was with Britt, I made two of my most successful albums—as her lawyer would eventually point out in no uncertain terms. Billy Gaff had secured me a new solo recording deal with Warner Bros., and it was time for a shift of gear and a fresh approach. In 1974 I began preparing the *Atlantic Crossing* album, first in Los Angeles and then down at Muscle Shoals Sound Studios in Alabama, under the guidance of the legendary producer Tom Dowd.

The first shock about Muscle Shoals was how primitive it was. It was an absolutely tiny room, with egg boxes on the wall for soundproofing. There was nothing fancy about it at all.

The second shock was the Muscle Shoals session players. With the exception of Al Jackson, the drummer, they were all white. I thought I had ended up in the wrong studio. How could the rhythm unit on so many classic soul records not be black?

Tom Dowd was fifty and came, of course, with this monumental reputation. He produced Ray Charles's "What'd I Say?"; he did Otis Redding; he did Aretha Franklin; he did Dusty Springfield; he did Eric Clapton's best work. You were expecting somebody with a huge amount of gravitas, someone a bit frightening, possibly. But Tom was such a great old hand; a delicate touch, so gentle. He had a presence about him, but it was such a warm and quiet, twinkly-eyed presence, not authoritarian at all, just fatherly, in the nicest way. He would blend right in and let us get on with it. His attitude was: when it's going well and things are bubbling in the room, leave it alone. He would sit back and smoke his pipe and read the paper. And we would check back with him. "What do you think of that, Tom?" And he would listen and chew on the pipe and say, "Yeah, going well."

Because of his work, I had great respect for him. If he was doing nothing, I respected that. If he was talking to me about what I should do—which he only ever did in a very loving way—I definitely respected that. There was never any shouting, bad vibes, or anger. If he was frustrated, he never showed it. Other producers want to put their mark all over things, ladle on their so-called "signature sounds." Sometimes the ego of the producer is as big as the artist's, and that's not a recipe for fun. Tom was different, and you thought, "Christ, now I know why all those great people wanted to work with him. Not only does he know what he's doing, he's so *easy*."

For the first time, really, I was in a studio and properly relaxed. We had a lock-in at Muscle Shoals, meaning we could come and go as we pleased, and no budget constraints, so there was a lot of sitting around and telling stories. Tom talked about Otis Redding writing "Dock of the Bay" on a guitar that Steve Cropper had tuned to an open E. If you tune a guitar that way, you can play "Dock of the Bay" using only one finger, and that's how Otis did it. And he talked about the tussles he used to have with Otis about Sam & Dave, the R&B vocal duo, when both those acts were rivals on Stax, with Otis saying, "You've got to do something, Tommy, you've got to do something. It's getting hard to follow them on." Otis sounded great. He saw no shame in being commercially successful—in being an entertainer. I drew as much as I could from his example.

The first time we finished a track, Tom stood up and said, "Right, time to go out on the balcony." I was a bit confused. "It's the balcony test," he said. "They've all done it. Aretha's done it, Otis has done it . . ." And the idea was, you would go outside and listen to the track from the balcony, through the door. Then you would hear whether it genuinely had a groove. In the studio, turned up loud, pretty much everything sounds great. You need to get some distance from it to see if it genuinely works. Later Tom introduced me to the car test, another Muscle Shoals tactic: running a couple of wires out to a car in the car park and playing the track through its tinny speakers. If a track could survive that and still seem to be grooving, you knew you were on to something.

Did I miss Ronnie Wood and Micky Waller and my old muckers off the five Mercury albums? Well, Woody was on tour with the Stones when *Atlantic Crossing* was being prepared, so he wouldn't have been able to play any part in it anyway. I missed their company, of course. But at the same time, Tom had listened to the Faces and had suggested to me that they weren't musically flexible enough for what he was after; so here I was, singing with the legendary R&B instrumentalists, the MGs: with Al Jackson, "Duck" Dunn, Steve Cropper, and (on a track that didn't make it onto the album, a cover of the Bee Gees' "To Love Somebody") with Booker T. This, you could say, had its consolations. It was the realization of a dream.

The one dark shadow cast over these sessions was that Alabama was a dry state. Steve, Duck, and I had a bottle of rum back at the Holiday Inn, where we were staying, but we were having to eke it out very carefully, day by day, and there was no alcohol available at all on the morning when Tom phoned me up at ten and told me to come and sing "Sailing." I panicked. I'd never sung anything in a studio without having a drink—let alone a big old anthem. And I'd never sung anything, anywhere, that early in the morning. Got it in six or seven takes, though. "Sailing," which was written by Gavin Sutherland, was another huge song for me: a hit twice in the U.K., first in 1975, and then a year later when it was revived as the theme tune for a BBC documentary series about life in the navy. I, of course, as with "Maggie May," argued vehemently against releasing it as the album's first single. I wanted "Three Time Loser" instead. And once more I was proved amusingly wrong, and happy to admit it.

After my experience with Tom, I was in a fever to record again. Even while promoting *Atlantic Crossing* I was carrying bits of paper in my pockets with possible song titles scribbled on them for the next album. In early 1976, we were back together in the studio, in Los Angeles this time, making *A Night on the Town*, which yielded the cover image I so hated: the photograph of me in the straw boater, holding the crystal champagne glass. People blamed Britt for that, but they were wrong. Britt might have been responsible for buying me the hat, and I've no doubt, when I wore it, she said what she always said: "You look luverly, darklink." But she wasn't responsible for me posing in it like a ponce for an album cover, and approving it all the way down the line. At any point, I could have said, "You know what? This is the worst album cover I've ever seen. Let's do something else." But I didn't. I don't know how I got through that and came out the other end. I cringe now every time someone offers me that album cover to sign. I turn it over to the mock Renoir painting on the other side, which has at least got a splash of humor about it.

Still, I would say in my defense that I regretted it pretty quickly. When we toured the album, I insisted that the artwork on the advertising posters and on all the backstage passes for the band and crew feature a picture of a fist coming through a straw boater. It was an expression of disgust at what I'd allowed to happen; an attempt to say, "I didn't mean it, honest. I'm still in here somewhere."

Good album, though, embarrassing sleeve notwithstanding. And this despite the fact that my voice had decided to pack up during the LA sessions. I had been trying to sing and there was nothing there: the edge had gone right out of it. Very alarming. We wondered whether it was something to do with the LA smog, which would have been a nice comeuppance for my exile. "Rod's gone all Hollywood—and Hollywood's done his voice in." The sessions were moved from Cherokee Studios in Hollywood to Caribou Ranch in Colorado. Elton had recorded there, and the Beach Boys, and it was a beautiful rural setting, in a converted barn, high in the Rockies—too high, in fact: 7,000 feet above sea level. It felt airless to me and, if anything, my voice was worse. By now I was beginning to get desperate. But Tom kept calm and we moved again, this time to Miami, where finally my voice reappeared. This was by no means the last of the struggles that would go on between me and my throat.

"The Killing of Georgie (Parts I and II)" is on the album, probably the most ambitious song I have ever written in terms of narrative construction, and certainly one of the longest. The verses for it were coming to me in the middle of the night for what seemed like days on end. Every night I would have to get up and write another one down. I started to wonder whether maybe I wasn't writing a song at all, but a novel. It appeared to reach a conclusion eventually, though, and was just about short enough for a single. There were people at Warner Bros. who were medieval enough to fear that a pro-gay message would alienate my heterosexual following. Stuff 'em, I felt. It's one of the songs that I'm proudest of. (And was a big hit, so no one particularly got alienated.)

There's also the Cat Stevens song "The First Cut Is the Deepest," which was actually held over from the *Atlantic Crossing* sessions, and has been enormously good to me down the years. And there's "Tonight's the Night (Gonna Be Alright)," the tale of a slightly raunchy seduction in possibly virginal circumstances, at which a number of radio stations nervously balked—again, with no lasting damage from a commercial point of view—and where Britt does some rather exciting talking in French over the outro. She was as nervous as a kitten in the studio, but a little pinch of cocaine helped.

Tom Dowd worshipped her, by the way. Everybody did. Everybody except me.

New home, new record label, new music; same old problem with commitment. I was still very far from wanting to settle down. I was with Britt, yet I always had my eye on other women. Terrible. And eventually I started wandering off, as was my wont. I had a fling with the actress Susan George—to whom Britt had introduced me, so that was especially shameless. We had been to see Queen in concert and gone out for dinner in LA afterwards, and Britt had seen that Susan was on her own and invited her to our table. I talked to her for the rest of the evening, while Britt talked to Freddie Mercury. Eventually Britt drove home alone and left me and Susan still talking.

And I had another, and longer, affair with the actress Liz Treadwell, who was blond, tall, very beautiful, bright and witty, and whom I liked enormously. And that one blew up in my face spectacularly.

Britt thought she and I were heading for marriage. We had Victoria and Nikolaj, her children, whom I adored, around us, and it was like a ready-made family. And we had decorated the house at Carolwood Drive, building ourselves this very wonderful nest. Yet it was sad because I knew all along, deep down, that I wasn't going to marry her, that I wasn't anywhere near wanting to settle. And when that became apparent, it really hurt her. She must have felt so deceived.

Which I suppose serves to illustrate that you can be with one of the most beautiful women in the world and still behave like an arse. Not only that, but you can be with one of the most beautiful women in the world and still be unhappy.

As with Dee, the way I handled the breakup was less than gentlemanly. In the summer of 1977, Britt took the children off to Sweden for a holiday in the beach house she owned there, which used to belong to her grandfather. I flew to New York with Gaff for a meeting with Elton John to discuss some totally barking idea Elton had for a film. After the dinner, we adjourned to a nightclub where I met up with Liz. Our exit from the club was recorded for posterity by a photographer from the *New York Post* and commemorated on the following day's front page. This, I quickly realized, was unlikely to pan out well.

On her return from holiday, Britt went to a party in Hollywood thrown by the film producer Allan Carr. I didn't go, because I was working in the studio. At the party, Britt ran into George Hamilton, a former lover of hers, who asked anxiously after the state of her relationship with me—and after the state of mine with Liz Treadwell. It was the first Britt knew of it. She confronted me in the garden at Carolwood and I admitted that I had been unfaithful to her. Britt got her coat, and all other items belonging to her.

I have never separated from a woman the way I should have done. I have always been a coward in that department—an absolute coward. I was intent on avoiding the confrontation, because I just didn't know how to handle it, didn't know how to say I was no longer in love, that I was restless, feeling trapped, and that I wanted to end it. It was about not wanting to hurt Britt—and yet, of course, I *was* hurting her in the long run. And that was to become typical, I'm afraid. I just drifted off to another woman: just started disappearing and not coming home, only to find Britt waiting up and asking, "Where have you been?"— stuff that you see in the movies. And inevitably you get found out sooner or later, and that causes such tears and ugliness and shouting and heartbreak. Why didn't I learn my lesson? I didn't, and it went on that way for a long time.

"Palimony" was a bit of a buzzword at the time. A couple of years earlier, Lee Marvin's girlfriend Michelle Triola had attempted to sue him for half the money he had earned during the years that they were living together: the original "palimony" case. Triola was unsuccessful, the judge deciding that she had no rights to Marvin's property in the absence of a formal marriage. But that didn't stop other people having a bash, and Britt duly took some legal advice from smart lawyers in LA and waded in with a claim for the tidy old sum of $12.5 million.

What a withering moment that was. I was coming out the door of a recording studio and suddenly there was a bloke in a dark suit pressing an envelope into my hand. You're served, pal. That was something else that I thought only happened in movies. When I saw what was being asked for in the envelope, I was not best pleased. I thought it was greedy of Britt and plain unfair. I also thought it was wildly out of character. Billy Gaff, who was very close to Britt and remains so today, went to Miami, where she was filming a television program, and persuaded her, thankfully, to drop the lawyers. We settled privately.

A week after Britt and I separated, I slipped on a flower lobbed by a fan onto the stage of the Cow Palace in San Francisco, fell arse over tit, and smacked my face on the drum riser, breaking a tooth and requiring seven stitches. It seemed like a comment from the gods, although let the record show that I was drunk.

It also seemed a bit rich. Twenty years of competitive football without a serious facial injury beyond the knock, at the age of twenty-six, that slightly offset my nose. And then I go and get well and truly clattered by a flower. Funny old game, football.

DIGRESSION

In which our hero finds himself spurned by punk rockers.

IN 1977, JOHNNY ROTTEN called me an old fart. Not to my face: on a British television show. I was thirty-two—not that old, really. And not really a fart either, to my mind, although people will always be entitled to a view. The point was, in London, punk rock had arrived in a storm of spit, and I seemed to be one of the people getting spat at. For a new, young, angry generation, I was suddenly representative of a breed of musicians who were rich, out of touch, complacent, and (perhaps worst of all) given to singing ballads. The decision had been taken to give my gilded cage a good old rattling and it all turned a bit confrontational, at least in Britain. Ranged aggressively against the old guard, and looking to sweep them away, were the likes of the Sex Pistols and the Clash, who sang, "No Elvis, Beatles, or the Rolling Stones in 1977." And no me either, apparently.

I didn't help myself when I gave an interview to *New Musical Express* into which I dropped a line that would follow me around for a while: "There are no fucking safety pins falling off me." Which sounded reactionary and sneering—and was almost certainly intended to do so. But it was also true. While punks were dressing in ripped T-shirts and bondage trousers patched with beer towels, you would have found me in my Rudolf Nureyev phase: harem pants, silk slippers, silver clips around the ankles, bit of a sash going on at the waist. Looking back, I can see how that would have got right up the nose of a young whippersnapper with an electric guitar and some attitude.

Comfy, though—I'll say that much for it. Every man should have a brief Rudolf Nureyev phase, if the option is there.

But there was a sense, too, of betrayal. Apparently the Sex Pistols had been big fans of the Faces. They used to play "Three Button Hand Me Down" when they were rehearsing, a song written by this old fart and Ian McLagan. The Pistols liked the connection the band had with its audience, the sense that a show was a big party and that everyone was in it together—not like the Stones, say, who from very early on were a remote act who kept their audience at a distance. You might have felt you loved the Stones, but you never felt you knew them. And then the Pistols resented what happened to the Faces in the end and the way that I went on from there to become a star. John Peel, the DJ, had the same difficulty. He came out and said he was disappointed when I became a celebrity. He felt he had lost me to fame—our paths stopped crossing after I moved to LA—and that I had lost myself to fame, too.

But it gets bigger. It grows in ways that you aren't always in control of. The shows get larger—and, as everyone tells you, that's a sign that you're getting it *right*. And, as the shows get larger, it's a constant battle to maintain that connection with the audience, a battle which I've fought pretty well, I would say, by and large. I think my audience *does* feel it knows me, and I think my audience is right.

But it's also a battle to stop the scale of your success messing with your head. Every successful person in music loses that battle from time to time. I lost it in the mid-1970s, the photograph of me in the boater on the sleeve of *A Night on the Town* being a prime piece of evidence. But it even got to the Faces in the end. The Faces may have larked about like a bunch of blokes from the pub, but, trust me, the bickering that eventually went on in that band about limos and hotel rooms would probably have shamed the Eagles. If the promoter didn't provide Ian McLagan with a Steinway-built piano, as specified in the contractual agreement, Mac would wait until the show was finished and demolish the piano that had been provided. Does that sound like any down-to-earth bloke in the pub that you know?

So, in a sense, punk gave people like me and Elton what we deserved: a kick in the pants. A kick in the harem pants, in my case. I'm not saying I learned anything from punk, musically. I gained very little from what I saw and heard. I liked the attitude, the "just get up and do it" approach. It was very like the Faces in a way. But the music? Less so. The music I loved was still the music I had always loved: soul, rhythm and blues, folk, with a bit of rock 'n' roll thrown in for good measure. At the same time, punk was a little reminder, a reality check. Suddenly there was a pocket of resistance. Suddenly there was a challenge: a very public and very loud one.

I took a policy decision. I didn't go away and hide. In June 1977, I had a double-A-sided single out: "I Don't Want to Talk About It" along with "The First Cut Is the Deepest." Two ballads, if you please. The single went to number one in Britain for the whole of June 1977. And the single it held in the number two spot was "God Save the Queen" by the Sex Pistols. Touché.

Malcolm McLaren, of course, the Sex Pistols' manager, claimed skulduggery and dark fixings behind the scenes. It was the year of the Queen's Silver Jubilee, and McLaren's theory was that the authorities simply couldn't allow an antimonarchist song to be number one while the rest of the nation was celebrating twenty-five years of the Queen's reign. Certainly the BBC refused to play the Pistols' record, although whether that hindered its commercial performance or helped it, we shall never know. (There's nothing like a ban for igniting a bit of extra interest, as I discovered with "Tonight's the Night"). In any case, some thirty years later, Richard Branson, who had been the boss of Virgin Records, the Pistols' label, told a television program that the battle between the singles had been a fair fight, with nothing untoward, so I'm claiming a clean victory.

What was abundantly clear at the time, though, was that even in the brave new dawn of punk, an old fart could still have hits with the right songs. What I had to do was believe he could carry on having them. Joe Smith, the great head of Warner Bros., told me when I signed my solo deal with that record company, "If you can last ten years in this business, you'll last forever." Maybe. All I know is, that was nearly forty years ago now, and I've seen a lot of people come and go.

Of course, time tends to change us all. There was a Faces reunion tour in 2010, with Mick Hucknall of Simply Red on vocals (I was busy and couldn't take part), and the bassist was Glen Matlock, formerly of the Sex Pistols. Woody told me about it on the phone. "Glen's a bit broad in the beam these days," Woody said. "And he likes to wear a cravat."

So there we are.

CHAPTER 12

In which are exposed the workings and motives of the Sex Police, circa 1976–86. Plus some embarrassment in Arrivals at Heathrow and the perils of going onstage with a lamppost.

The night when I opened the door to my hotel suite and found a bass player stark naked and gaffer-taped to the bed was . . . well, it was pretty typical of the sort of things that used to happen on tour with the band in the 1970s and 1980s. I simply gave Charlie Harrison a nod, went to the adjoining bedroom, and got into bed, knowing that the situation would doubtless resolve itself eventually, and thankful at least that no live chickens were involved this time.

Charlie was just another victim of the Sex Police. And the thing about the Sex Police was, they could strike at any time. Who were the Sex Police? They were a loose affiliation of band members and tour crew, first assembled under the leadership of the tour manager, Pete "Gruppenführer" Buckland. Their founding intention was to stamp out sex on the road—to identify, within the touring party, the likely practitioners of sex, locate the places in which sex might take place, and prevent sex from happening. And there was a lot of sex on tour, what with one thing and another, so they were quite busy. Their remit quickly expanded, too, to include the arranging of pranks on the road in general. And let's be clear: just because you were a member of the Sex Police—and I confess that I was—it didn't mean that you couldn't be a victim of the Sex Police. Even the Sex Police feared the knock on the door from the Sex Police.

Not that the Sex Police would necessarily knock. To say they were exceptionally well organized is to put it mildly. The Sex Police had tool kits, walkie-talkies, cameras, and, best of all, skeleton keys, meaning that they could be on the scene (your hotel room, for instance) before you or (sometimes worse) after you. They had screwdrivers for the removal of door hinges. (You and your date for the night would go to push your key into the lock and the door would simply fall into the room.) They had lengths of nylon rope for suspending people's luggage down the hotel's outside wall from their window. (Difficult to find your suitcase in this circumstance. And equally difficult, once you had found it, ten stories below, to reel that suitcase back in.) Eventually, they had uniforms: a white boiler suit, with "Sex Police" written on the reverse and bearing, on its chest, the Sex Police insignia: two penises rampant and the Latin motto *cruella sed justa*, "harsh but fair." And they had chickens.

I believe the first recorded use of live chickens by the Sex Police was in a hotel in Dallas in 1985, and I was its victim. I was in a suite, filming an interview with the late, great Dick Clark, the legendary host of *American Bandstand*. The conversation was coming to an end when the door burst open, there was a chorused shout from the corridor of "Room service!" and, for one surreal moment, the room became a blizzard of feathers and chicken shit. Clark, a consummate pro, seemed to find the whole thing rather amusing.

I was possibly fortunate it was only chickens. Sheep had been considered but had proved impossible to source at short notice. Ducks, similarly. It was the Sex Police's lasting regret that a plan to fill someone's hotel bathroom with ducks never quite came off, though it got quite far down the line.

Chickens, though, were easier to procure. Accordingly, in Newfoundland, Canada, the Sex Police removed every item of furniture from the room of one of the crew, locked it all in an adjacent room (all standard procedure), and, for the final flourish, left two chickens behind. The crew member returned to the room with a girl that he had picked up—and spent a couple of hours there regardless, which would seem remarkable, except that behaving as if nothing had happened, as if everything was proceeding as normal, was absolutely critical. If you reacted, you were only inviting more and worse treatment.

Which is why, when I pulled my boots on at the end of a long-haul British Airways flight between Los Angeles and London on December 22, 1977, and felt the crunch of peanuts, coupled with a slightly gooey sensation, most likely attributable (experience told me) to strawberry jam, I didn't withdraw my feet at once, as instinct might have told me to. I finished doing up the boots and strolled off the plane and into Heathrow Airport, as naturally as a man can when his footwear has been filled with assorted airplane catering items.

Or maybe I was just too drunk to notice. Apparently I was still holding a glass of cognac and singing Jolson's "Mammy" when I reached the baggage collection area. But even then, surely, the realization was dawning on me that this time we had gone too far. Certainly the sight of Jim Cregan, my guitarist, his curly hair full of ash and cigarette butts and his face smeared with what seemed, upon closer inspection, to be honey, would have been a decent clue. And the laughing was definitely about to stop because Jimmy Horowitz, from the management team, was shortly to be arrested in the airport's precincts for public drunkenness. (Fine: £25 by the order of Uxbridge

Magistrates Court.) Behind us lay a British Airways first-class cabin liberally redecorated with mustard. And ahead of us lay a rightful bashing in the press for our disgraceful behavior. I don't know what came over us.

Actually, I do: cognac.

Still, as *The Daily Telegraph* reported: "Mr Horowitz admitted that some of the group had taken a ride on the luggage conveyor belt, but he said that Rod Stewart was too drunk to get on and just lay in a corner under some luggage." So, at least one of us maintained some decorum. Shortly after that, the border official opened Horowitz's passport and two slices of bacon fell out. A sorry episode, all in all, and one for which I apologized fulsomely in due course to British Airways. I would like to say we learned a lesson here, and were chastened, and got a grip on ourselves from this point forward. But we didn't.

It will be obvious from the above that touring behavior didn't become restrained after the Faces. On the contrary, when I set out on the road in 1976 for the first time as a "solo artist," it was as if the notoriety of the Faces was out there as a precedent. I think the word going around musicians was that if you joined Rod Stewart's band, you'd better get used to the bevvy and act daft. So it was as if the Faces were a benchmark to be surpassed. Looking back, I think that very often we managed it, posting new records for on-the-road stupidity by a touring rock group.

For the first post-Faces touring band, I wanted three guitarists. At the time, people sneered and said, "It's taken him three guitarists to replace Ronnie Wood," but it wasn't about that. I wanted three guitarists for the thickness of the sound, and for the dynamic between them, and also (I don't mind admitting) because I thought it would look good. I had seen it work for Fleetwood Mac.

So, on guitar there was Jim Cregan. Jim played that lovely, fluid acoustic guitar solo on Steve Harley and Cockney Rebel's "Make Me Smile (Come Up and See Me)." We christened him "the Somerset

Segovia." And also on guitar there was Gary Grainger. Gary had been in the band Strider, which had supported the Faces. He was there to provide a bit of raunch. And also on guitar there was Billy Peek. I had seen Billy on television in America, playing with Chuck Berry's band, and he sounded great. I rang Tom Dowd up and said, "We've got to get him." This was during the recording of *A Night on the Town*. I figured that if his rock 'n' roll playing was good enough for Chuck Berry, it was probably good enough for me.

Phil Chen, the bass player, was someone I had asked to consider joining the Faces after Ronnie Lane had left, but he had had another commitment at the time. The keyboard player was John Jarvis, a classically trained American who had played on *A Night on the Town* and was a proper musician. And the drummer was Carmine Appice, who had been in the rock band Vanilla Fudge. Carmine was American, but I talked to him about playing in a British style, rather than an American style. American rock 'n' roll drumming is right smack on the beat. I wanted a British feel, which is slightly looser, where you sit in just behind the beat. It's more relaxed. Of course, if it gets too relaxed, it all goes tits-up fairly quickly, as we discovered in the Faces on more than one occasion. So it's about going for a flow and a looseness, but still holding it together. It's what the Stones do so well.

I wanted us to take a relaxed approach in general, if at all possible. The word was, in those days, that Jackson Browne was doing virtually concert-length soundchecks. Then, afterwards, his band would be hauled back to listen to a tape of the entire show and everyone would have their errors and sins of omission pointed out to them. This wasn't the way I saw it going. Our soundchecks tended to be as short as possible. Fifteen minutes would have been strenuous. And there were definitely no postmortems. It mattered that the show was good, of course, and anyone who wasn't cutting it on the night found themselves moved along very quickly. But it was meant to be rock 'n' roll, after all. My attitude was that if it wasn't fun and entertaining for us, it wasn't likely to be fun and entertaining for anybody else.

At six, the evening before the first show of the tour, everyone had to come out in their stage gear for a formal presentation of the outfits. This was never less than hilarious. I encouraged everyone to go in for flamboyance and color. This wouldn't always work. People would step into the room and say, "What do you think?" And there would be cries of "Fucking hell! I'm not going onstage with you looking like that!" Phil Chen would have some good little outfits, but Jim and Kevin would make some truly awe-inspiring mistakes and Carmine, the drummer, was probably the worst of the lot: terrible snakeskin-look shirts and silver waistcoats and leather jerkins. Billy, meanwhile, was a bit short and dumpy and we never knew quite what to do with him, in terms of stage presentation. So we used to dress him up as a Frenchman and leave it at that.

I had cloaks made for the band: big velvet cloaks with their initials on them. The roadies had to stand there as the band came offstage after the show and swaddle them on their way to the limousines. And some of them didn't even sweat. What a waste of money.

Pranks not only took place offstage, they were popular during shows as well: another hangover from the days of the Faces. The show was in no way sacrosanct, and if you could think of a good way to send it up, that was fine. For instance, Carmine would take a drum solo (they were still obligatory in those days), which would end with him standing on his stool, sticks aloft. This was the cue for his drum roadie, at the back of the stage, to bash the giant gong suspended behind Carmine's kit (giant gongs, too, were obligatory at this time), thus bringing the solo to a resonant conclusion. The rest of the band was backstage at this point, remember, so it was the work of moments to snatch the beater off the roadie, leaving Carmine stood on his stool, waiting for the gong that never came.

Alternatively, because the microphone for the gong was generally placed to the rear of it, out of view of the audience, you could very easily replace the noise of the gong with the slightly more mocking sound of a toy hooter or a bicycle bell or, better still, a fart, if one could be mustered. (Farting into microphones became an increasing preoccupation of my touring bands as the 1980s wore on. Sound engineers learned to leave the microphones turned down until the last possible minute at the start of shows to prevent auditoriums abruptly filling with the vastly amplified sound of breaking wind.)

Sometimes slapstick didn't need to be created. Sometimes it just happened anyway. To create a moment of theater, we had a lamppost up in the rafters that used to be lowered down in darkness just before I sang "The Killing of Georgie." One night I got right underneath it by mistake, becoming one of a very small number of rock artists who have been flattened mid-show by a ten-foot pole. (Just bruises, thank you for asking.)

The band evolved: Robin Le Mesurier arrived on guitar, Kevin Savigar on keyboards—people who came to be close friends of mine in the ensuing years. The pranking evolved, too. In November 1984, the tour for the *Camouflage* album moved to Tokyo, Japan, where certain members of the band and crew discovered the sport of "ledge walking": the passage from one person's hotel room to another using only the windowsills. At heights of anything up to twenty-five floors, this game took a lot of nerve. Or a lot of drink. Or a lot of drink in tandem with a lot of nerve. Either way, although I could readily see the comedy value in appearing unannounced at someone's window on the twenty-fifth floor of a Tokyo high-rise and tapping to come in, I wasn't persuaded to join in. We all have our limits, and ledge-walking was mine.

As everyone knows, there's a lot of dead time to fill on tour with a rock band, and you are fighting the evil grip of boredom all the way.

1. If I balance this tray on my head, how many things will it be possible to place on it before the whole thing collapses?
2. If I put on this plastic cover that came with the dry cleaning, will it look like a straitjacket?
3. What would it be like if I wrapped myself entirely in cling film?
4. Will this headboard fit in that lift?
5. Where can one get ducks?

These are the kinds of questions which enter the mind of the touring rock musician and won't go away until they have been answered. And it might seem a slightly bizarre thing to say about an organization dedicated to releasing live chickens in hotel suites, but I think the Sex Police stopped us going mad.

[Answers to the above questions: (1) a fruit bowl containing fruit; a water jug; three miniature bottles of wine; two paperback books; a toiletry bag; and a pair of trousers, usually. (2) Yes. (3) You will look like a packet of uncooked chicken breast, but it will feel quite cozy. (4) Yes, if you push it hard enough. (5) Like I say, we never found out.]

CHAPTER 13

In which our hero, not heeding the advice of his father, marries, settles down, and has children. With various incidental reflections concerning buttocks, disco, Tony Curtis, and the wearing of spandex trousering.

Never mind Joe Smith of Warner Bros. and his theory about lasting ten years in the music business. An equally pressing question for me in 1977 was, could I last ten months with just one woman? In November, separated from Britt and Liz Treadwell, I started dating Bebe Buell, a former *Playboy* centerfold who had recently finished an affair with Todd Rundgren, the American rock musician. Things might have gone better with Bebe if I hadn't brought her to London for a week and then, while we were there, grown rather distracted by Marcy Hanson. At this point, I was technically two-timing a *Playboy* model with another *Playboy* model.

Was marriage particularly on my agenda at this point? I think we can fairly strongly infer that it wasn't.

But then I met Alana.

We first set eyes on each other in spring 1978 at a party given for my road crew at the Playboy Club in Los Angeles, a lushly carpeted institution where the drinks were served by girls in one-piece velvet bunny suits. (And that's how extravagant the music industry was in those days, by the way: even the roadies got a party at the Playboy Club.) Soon after that, I met her properly at a far nobbier gathering organized by the superagent Irving "Swifty" Lazar above Ma Maison restaurant. Alana Hamilton was tall, long-legged, and (I expect you can guess where this is going) blond, with the most fantastic smile; a Southern belle with edge in a beautiful long, tightly fitting white dress. We spoke about music, as I recall, and she told me straight out and laughing that she was a country and western fan, which put me in my place, but there was a real electric charge between us straight-away—that sense you have that something very exciting could happen in the right circumstances. She was there with a date, so our encounter was short and sweet, but I knew that I wanted to see her again.

My usual procedure in these situations was to get Tony Toon to ring up and inquire tentatively about the possibility of a date. This didn't impress Alana one little bit. She told Tony that if I wanted a date with her, I would have to call her myself. So I steeled myself and did so.

Alana consulted her clearly very busy social diary and said, "I'm going to a dinner at Robert Stigwood's. Do you want to come with me?" Stigwood was the imposingly successful theater and film producer who also worked as a manager of groups like Cream and the Bee Gees. I said, "Sounds good." It was during the course of that evening that Alana and I began to get to know each other.

She was thirty-three, the same age as me, but her origins made my humble background look almost regal by comparison. She had grown up in Nacogdoches, Texas, in real rural hardship, living in a remote house without electricity. She became an air hostess on a Texan airline (with a uniform of a fringed jacket and Stetson) and then made it onto the books of the Ford Modeling Agency in New York. After that she came to Hollywood, hoping to make it as an actress, and met and married George Hamilton, the film and TV actor. Alana and George had separated three years earlier, in 1975. They had a son, Ashley, who was four at this time. During their marriage, she had exploded onto the Hollywood social scene and now seemed to know absolutely everyone who was anyone and to be popular with them all.

At the end of the dinner, Alana said, "Let's go over to Tina Sinatra's house," and I said, "Fine by me." Tina, Frank's daughter, was Alana's best friend and her home was a kind of small temple to contemporary design, full of glass and Lucite. Some salsa music went on and Alana and I danced together flirtatiously on the white marble floor—kind of in jest but kind of for real, shoes clicking, bell-bottoms flapping—and I knew right there that she had a hold on me.

However, our next date didn't go so well. It was at a party, and I became annoyed because I thought Alana was spending too much time working the room and not enough time with me. A few days of haughty silence passed. But in that time, I found I was still thinking about her a lot. She had seemed so smart, so funny, so vivacious. So eventually I called her and asked her out to dinner again, and she turned up, looking wildly sexy, and told me that she had spent that time thinking about me, too. And from that night on we were inseparable.

We didn't move in together for the first eight months of our relationship. I continued to live at Carolwood Drive, where I had lived with Britt, and Alana had her own house in Beverly Hills. Yet there was probably only one night in that first year when we weren't together. And there were very few nights in that time when we didn't go out. More than any woman I had ever met, Alana knew how to have fun. Nightclubs, parties, dinners . . . we absolutely hit the town—went all out in the energetic pursuit of pleasure. One night in bed Alana handed me a little capsule and said, "Try this." It was a popper: a little container of amyl nitrite. The idea was that you cracked it and inhaled the contents at the moment of orgasm to intensify the pleasure. I had never done that before. Of course, it's not the cleverest thing to do to your cardiovascular system, but we didn't seem to care about the risks. Seeking ways to intensify the pleasure was what we were all about in that heady first rush of our time together. It was almost like a competition between us: who could do the most, drink the most, party the most, dance the most, fuck the most. And it made us both extremely happy.

Meanwhile, during the day, when I could get my battered head together, I was recording the music that became *Blondes Have More Fun*. As usual in this period, I had gone into the studio with nothing in the way of finished songs. The drill was, the band would set up on day one and we would start bashing away until something took shape. Inevitably, things we were listening to were always informing what we came up with. I would often say, "Can we do something along the lines of this?" It's a good way of getting the doors open. And at this specific time, in 1978, I had been listening to records by Chic, where the bass guitar is the driving force and almost the main provider of the melody. I had also been listening a lot to "Native New Yorker" by Odyssey, a track I loved. And then there was the Stones' "Miss You": a rock band's take on disco, a blend that really appealed to me. And so the question was "Can we come up with something along the lines of that?" And what emerged was a song called "Da Ya Think I'm Sexy?"

Probably nothing I have written has been as commercially successful. And certainly nothing I have written has caused me more ambivalent feelings. Ask me now, and I'll tell you I love the song to bits and that I'm fiercely proud of it. And yet, what was that thing Jeff Beck said about "Hi Ho Silver Lining"? "It was a pink toilet seat hung around my neck for the rest of my life." There was a time, early in the song's life, when I wondered whether "Da Ya Think I'm Sexy?" was going to be my "Hi Ho Silver Lining." The difference was that Jeff had to be coaxed into wearing his pink toilet seat, much against his will. I, on the other hand, had actually been the driving force in the creation of my pink toilet seat—had painted it myself, if you like— and had then very deliberately and perfectly cheerfully put my head right through it.

You never really have a clue about how a song is going to be received or the journey it's going to take. But what was quickly clear when "Da Ya Think I'm Sexy?" came out was that an awful lot of people liked it. It sold more than two million copies in America, half a million in Britain, and was a hit all over the world, including some places I'd never heard of, and some other places where it was news to me that they even had electricity. It was the fastest-selling single that Warner had ever had, until Madonna came along six years later with "Like a Virgin." So how could I not be proud? If you're a songwriter, you spend your entire working life dreaming of the moment when something you have written heads out into the world and triggers a response as broadly favorable as that.

And yet, in the same moment, I appeared to have alienated a portion of the people who up until then had felt close to me. Some of the fans from the *Gasoline Alley* days, in particular, felt truly let down. Some regarded disco as the bitter enemy, and wondered what I was doing, consorting with the other side. Music was strewn with battle lines in those days, in ways that (God be praised) it no longer is. In the late 1970s, there was soul and there was heavy metal and there was punk, and so on—with their followers all in their separate trenches with bayonets drawn. And you couldn't hoist yourself out of, say, the rock trench and make a sprint for the soul trench, even just to say hello, without serious risk of getting your head blown off.

Well, I had always mixed things up, right from the beginning, on all my albums—taken a bit of rhythm and blues, a bit of folk, a

standard, some rock 'n' roll, and hoped that the voice bound it all together. And, in a solo campaign lasting almost a decade, I had only
sustained very light wounding as a result of these tactics. But disco
was clearly regarded in some places as a dash too far. Cue heavy ar-
tillery fire—and especially from music critics who wrote off "Da Ya
Think I'm Sexy?" as a big old lump of cheese and the work of a terrible show-off, to boot.

What could I say? I got tired of pointing out that the lyric was
written in the third person—"She sits alone, waiting for suggestions /
He's so nervous, avoiding all the questions" and so on—and that when
it opens up into the first person in the chorus, you're meant to be hearing the unspoken thoughts of the bloke and the girl in the song, who
are aching to get each other's clothes off but don't quite know how
to broach the topic ("If you want my body, and you think I'm sexy,"
etc.). It wasn't *me* asking every Tom, Dick, and Harriet in the world
if they thought *I* was sexy. There was a story being told here. But that
rather tended to get brushed aside. And I didn't get much help from
my management and the marketing people, whose campaign for this
single had me stretched out in full spandex-clad glory beneath the slo-
gan "Da Ya Think I'm Sexy?" Heaven knows how a lot of my male
fans must have been feeling at this point. Possibly like putting my old
albums out of sight at the back of their wardrobes for a while.

Just to complicate matters, the Brazilian musician Jorge Ben Jor
eventually pointed out the similarity of the melody in the chorus to a
song of his from 1972 called "Taj Mahal." Bang to rights, too. I held
my hand up straightaway. Not that I had stood in the studio and said,
"Here, I know, we'll use that tune from 'Taj Mahal' as the chorus and
be done with it. The writer lives in Brazil, so he'll never find out." But
I had been to the Carnival in Rio earlier in 1978, with Elton and Freddie Mercury, where two significant things had happened: first, I had
developed a brief and hopeless crush on a lesbian Brazilian film star
who wouldn't let me anywhere near her; and second, I had heard Jorge

Ben Jor's "Taj Mahal" being given heavy rotation all over the place. It had been rereleased that year, and clearly the melody had lodged itself in my memory and then resurfaced when I was trying to find a line to fit the chords. Unconscious plagiarism, plain and simple. I handed over the royalties, again wondering whether "Da Ya Think I'm Sexy?" was partly cursed.

Now, the synth hook at the start of the song: that I *did* whip, very deliberately, from the strings on Bobby Womack's "(If You Want My Love) Put Something Down on It." But the rules are that you can lift a line from an arrangement—as distinct from a melody line—without infringing copyright. So you can't touch me for that.

I took the song out of the live show for a while at the beginning of the 2000s, feeling tired of it, but people who had bought tickets complained, and I felt I was selling them short by not doing it. And then when I put it back on the set list I realized that I was enjoying singing it again anyway. So it's back in the show now—late on, as a rule, where it tends to turn into a bit of a romp. It seems to evoke a whole era for people—the late-1970s disco period—and to connect them with their pasts, and you have to be grateful, as a songwriter, to have something as potent as that in your locker.

Also, I make no apologies for the bum-wiggling in the video, though this, too, attracted some flak at the time. I don't know why: it was nothing new for me. Since I had first properly discovered my confidence as a front man, in the Faces, I had been a major proponent of the bum wiggle, firmly believing the arse to be an important part of the rock 'n' roll stage performer's armory and a powerfully communicative tool, if harnessed appropriately. Plus I just happen to dance that way.

I'm prepared to admit, however, that the black spandex trousers—worn, for the purposes of this video, with a billowing silk blouson—gave the buttocks a prominence that they hadn't enjoyed in earlier, looser outfits. The same went for the leopard-print versions, in similar material, that I took a shine to in this period. But we're talking about a difference in fashion here, and the cut of the clothes, rather than a wholesale change in my approach to buttock work. Different trousers, yes; but same wiggling arse. That's my contention, anyway.

One final point about that video for "Da Ya Think I'm Sexy?": you may notice that, in the performance sections, when the band is on a stage, miming to the track, I quite often spin away from the camera and face the back. That was to hide the fact that I kept forgetting the lyric. You would have seen a lot less of my arse if I could only have remembered the bloody words.

The British leg of the tour for the *Blondes Have More Fun* album opened in Manchester in December 1978. Still keen to spend as little time apart as possible, Alana and I rented a house in Chester Square in London to use as a base, and brought Ashley over with us. I hadn't played in England for two years, and I didn't know what to expect. The U.K. press had been less than enthusiastic about the album. Did anybody care anymore? Would anybody turn up? It's something I live with constantly: the terror of the empty seat, the all-too-visible sign that you're on the fade, that the decline is under way. I once read how Al Jolson, one of my childhood heroes, was completely paranoid about the sight of empty seats, and I have definitely caught his fear.

No problem this time, though. The tartan hordes were still rampant, rushing the front of the stalls as usual, completely ignoring the seating plan. The tour seemed to build and build through to five nights at Olympia at the end of December, and the atmosphere of those shows and the atmosphere of Christmas seemed to combine to create a delirium like I had never known. And, more than once, when I started into "I Don't Want to Talk About It" and heard the words come back at me from the audience, heard the audience take the song out of my hands completely and charge off with it as they usually did, I got choked up and couldn't have sung along with them if I had wanted to.

༄

At the start of 1979, Alana said she thought she was coming down with flu. She wasn't, though. She was pregnant.

We had talked about children. I knew I wanted them. I had loved living with Britt's children, Victoria and Nikolaj. I loved Alana's son, Ashley. I loved being around kids. I came from a big family and I wanted a big family. I couldn't see how children were anything other than a good thing.

But did I want them now, in 1979—like, in less than nine months' time?

The reality of it threw me for a loop. I panicked, and in my panic I turned cool on Alana and we had a couple of really bad months. I got cold feet and behaved badly. On tour in Australia in February 1979, I had a fling with Belinda Green, the Australian model and former Miss World. I was on the other side of the globe, and in those days, when news traveled slowly and with difficulty, I genuinely expected to get away with it. A big feature in *The Sydney Morning Herald*, with a photograph, meant that I didn't. Word got back to Alana, who, understandably, was fantastically upset.

I felt about as popular as the lookout at Pearl Harbor. However, I managed to persuade myself, and her, that this transgression had been a final fling, just the terror of impending responsibility forcing me astray. And when Alana flew out to join the tour in Japan, we patched things up. And in the process of patching things up, we remembered that we were still in love and we decided to get married. There was no big romantic proposal, no going down on bended knee. Just a decision between the two of us that this was the right way. In the hotel, I wanted to pass the news to my parents back in London, but I was so afraid of telling them. I knew they wouldn't approve. I got my secretary, Gail Williams, to break it to them first, and then I took the receiver and spoke to them, slightly cringing and very nervous, perched on the end of a twin hotel bed. It was an awkward conversation. My mum did her best to sound pleased. (It was much later that she shared with the press her agreement with my dad's view that I "should have married a nice Scots girl.") My dad just came right out and said, "You're not old enough."

Ridiculous, of course: I was thirty-four, for heaven's sake.

We were married in April, although not before I had experienced a further couple of bouts of cold feet. In advance of the actual wedding, on the day when we were due to go together to pick up our marriage license, I disappeared off to a car showroom to look into buying a car—the sign, perhaps, of a certain lack of commitment on my part to the project. Clearly, the bachelor in me wasn't going to go under without a fight. I didn't bolt, though. On the day of the wedding, the bride wore cream and so did the groom—although Alana's was an off-the-shoulder number and mine was a suit, with a pink tie. We held the ceremony very privately among the glass and marble at Tina Sinatra's house. Tina was the maid of honor and Billy Gaff was my best man. And then we drove down to L'Ermitage, a French restaurant on La Cienega Boulevard, for the reception. Nobody had been told that the party was for our wedding. We said it was simply to celebrate the start of the American leg of my tour. We even kept the arrangements secret from Tony Toon because we realized that letting Toon in on the secret would have been like posting the plan on a billboard on the Sunset Strip. Nevertheless, people seemed to have twigged the real reason for the occasion: the pavement outside the restaurant was jammed with photographers, which tipped off most of the guests, too. We didn't care. A great party ensued. The plan had been to spend our wedding night at the Hotel Bel-Air, but the press would probably have followed us all the way in and up to the room, so we went back to Carolwood instead, and we were profoundly happy.

Marriage worked like the click of a switch. It wiped away all the doubts, cleared away all the fear. My transgression in Australia was forgotten. I became a husband: in love with Alana, in love with the role, in love with the whole idea. I was touring America, but I was flying home every night so that I could be with her. Why wouldn't I be happy? We were a newly wedded husband and wife, with a child on the way—a boy, of course. Roderick Christian Stewart. We had the name ready because, even though we chose not to find out the sex beforehand, we absolutely knew it was going to be a boy.

In August the baby came, arriving at the blissful end of a three-and-a-half-hour labor, during which Alana unleashed her inner Texan to a degree that even I had never witnessed. Language poured forth from her that I didn't know existed, even in Texas. And out came not Roderick Christian, but Kimberly Alana. And there is, of course, nothing like it. And there was, of course, nothing like her. I held her before Alana did. The doctor gave her to me and I was absolutely in love with her from the second I laid eyes on her. Our Kimberly.

So now we were parents and, at the same time, Hollywood hosts on a major scale. These were heady days. Alana's connections had taken me, blinking rather wildly, into a social world that I had never thought I would be a part of. We had a ballroom built onto one end of Carolwood, with an upper gallery all around it, and we would throw the most amazing parties—elaborately formal affairs, with tables set for dinner, and drapery, and dance bands, and guests instructed to dress smartly. It was our *Great Gatsby* period. On the guest list would be people like Barbra Streisand, Warren Beatty, Dustin Hoffman, Jack Nicholson, Anjelica Huston, Albert Finney, Linda Evans, Joan and Jackie Collins, Ryan O'Neal and Farrah Fawcett, with whom Alana was very close . . . it just went on and on. People say, "What were all those guys *like*?" Well, they all seemed great to me, but of course I saw them only when they were drunk or stoned and having a fabulous time, and when I was the same. I never saw them the morning after.

This was when I was introduced to serious cocaine—proper,

extremely high-quality stuff. It was considered so chic at the time, not least among show-business types, to whom its use was pretty much confined. The idea wasn't to snort line after line and then see in the dawn, goggle-eyed and gasping. You were using it more like snuff, to pep the evening along—just a little puff of this pillowy white powder off the back of your hand. And then maybe another little puff. And perhaps another . . . But no headaches afterwards, miraculously, and no nosebleeds—and no sense for me, slightly deluding myself, that something so pure could possibly be damaging my voice. Just a rather wonderful sense of well-being and overall enhancement. Some magical evenings ensued. Late one night, after dinner when everyone else had gone home, Tony Curtis ended up in the sitting room teaching me how to do the jive with a chair—skipping it up onto one leg, twirling it around. On another evening, similarly at the end of an evening when the guests had departed, I watched my great friend Jim Cregan, the guitarist in my band, playing flamenco and dancing with Liza Minnelli. Which would have been plausible if Jim could actually play flamenco. All in all, life appeared to have taken on the quality of an extraordinary dream.

To mark our first wedding anniversary, in April 1980, Alana and I had a sit-down dinner in the ballroom for a hundred guests, catered by Chasen's—caviar, Château d'Yquem wine, the works—the room all beautifully draped and dressed. Elton flew in for it, and David and Dani Janssen were there, and Gregory and Veronique Peck, and David Niven, Jr., and Jacqueline Bisset, and Johnny Carson, and Billy Wilder, and Tita and Sammy Cahn. A swing band set up on the gallery, and nobody below knew they were there until after the dinner when they launched into some Glenn Miller and everybody got up and danced. Freddie de Cordova, the producer of *The Tonight Show*, rose and said it was the best party he had ever been to in Hollywood.

Gregory and Veronique Peck, incidentally, were our next-door neighbors, and you couldn't have asked for nicer ones. They never once complained about the noise of my band rehearsing in the garage. Indeed, I went over and apologized to them about it one time, and they said, "Oh, no. We like to sit out on the terrace and listen." They cut a hole in their fence so that I could go through and use their tennis court whenever I fancied it.

Gregory came to see me in concert once, too, at the Forum in Los Angeles in 1979. He brought Fred Astaire with him, and when they took their seats the house lights were up and the whole place rose for them. I was so proud that I had an audience who would do that. They both came backstage afterwards and Astaire said, "Now, tell me, who does your choreography?" I had to say, "Well . . . you know . . . I just sort of make it up as I go along." Which, of course, he would have worked out for himself. But it was very charming of him to ask.

So, life was, in so many ways, extraordinary. And very quickly Alana was pregnant again. Kim was only about four months old when it happened. Alana didn't know it was possible to conceive while you were breastfeeding. And when the baby came, we were in Malibu, somewhat inconveniently. When I was on tour, back at the start of 1978, Alana had found us a beautiful beach house on a relatively deserted stretch of sand, with 270 feet of beach frontage and only a handful of neighboring properties. It looked like a miniature version of the Sydney Opera House, a big clamshell, and as soon as I had seen the photographs that Alana sent, I wanted it. We had great times at that weekend house in those early years. Alana used to say it was the only place she ever saw me properly relax. I can be restless. I need to be moving or doing things. But there I felt happy, for once, to be still, to have tea with the kids outside, sitting in the sand. It was a family place, when so much of the rest of our lives was filled with other people and moving around.

Anyway, it was in the beach house that weekend in September 1980 that Alana went into labor that second time, which sent us chasing into central Los Angeles from Malibu up the freeway, with Alana in serious danger, it occurred to me, not merely of having the baby in the car, but also of ruining the upholstery. With these two thoughts in mind, my foot was flat to the floor, and before long the lights of a police car were flashing in my rearview mirror. I pulled over and, without thinking, and even as Alana was shouting, "No! No! Don't do that!" I jumped out of the driver's seat and ran back towards the police car—which is, of course, the last thing you should do when pulled over by traffic cops, unless you want to give them the wrong impression. A police car door duly opened and a cop climbed out with his gun pointing straight at me. I was shouting, "My wife's having a baby!" The cop seemed to recognize me—or at least he lowered his gun and came towards the car, looking in at Alana, who was now shouting, "I've got to get to the hospital! I've got to get to the hospital!"

The cop said, "We'll call you an ambulance, ma'am." Alana, really now feeling that the baby was emerging, screamed, "There isn't fucking time! Get me to the fucking hospital or I'll fucking drive there myself!" At this, the cops seemed to decide she was not to be reasoned with and provided us with a police escort, lights flashing, all the way to Cedars-Sinai.

As we entered the maternity ward, Alana was asked to pause and fill out some paperwork. To which she replied, "Are you fucking insane? I'm about to drop this baby on the floor." Again, the maternal Texan had kicked in. Less than a quarter of an hour later we had a boy, and, as with Kimberly, as I held him I was absolutely in love with him from the moment I laid eyes on him. Our Sean.

So now we had two wonderful children, and a fabulous social life, and wealth and happiness, and so much to be grateful for, however you looked at it . . . and yet somehow it all began to go wrong.

DIGRESSION

Matters most serious, in which our hero
confesses to a disturbing addiction.

YOU UNDERSTAND HOW THESE things work. It's well
understood. You know the dangers, but you think you'll just
have a little dabble, just to find out what it feels like. And the
warning signs are all out there but you ignore them, because you
think you're different. You think you're the one in a million:
the stronger kind of person who can control it. The next thing
you know, your so-called little dabble has turned into a raging,
all-consuming habit, and you're spending hours on the phone to
a dealer, like he's your best friend.

But that's art collecting. It can get hold of a person. It can
take over your life and, more particularly, your walls. And I
speak as someone with intimate experience of fixing himself
up with late-nineteenth-century paintings. Many, many late-
nineteeth-century paintings.

I've always loved Pre-Raphaelite pictures, ever since I was a
kid: the romance of them, their color, the classical drapery, the
high drama and emotion. As a boy, they spoke to many of my
most obsessive interests: knights in shining armor, damsels in
distress, and, of course, tits. When I was busking in London, in
my late teens, I would often set up in Trafalgar Square, outside
the National Gallery, and when it rained I would drift in and
wander round looking at the Pre-Raphs and the Victorians. My
absolute favorite painting, though, was in the Tate: *The Lady
of Shalott* by John William Waterhouse. The girl in the boat,
with the pale face and the long red hair and the open-mouthed

expression and the detail of the embroidery and the river and the reeds—I absolutely loved it. Quite often I would take girls to the Tate just to see that one picture. It made a change from going to a coffee bar or to the cinema. And, of course, it alerted them to my thoughtfulness and sensitivity and range of interests as a human being, which has rarely been known to decrease a man's chances of copping a feel later on.

Britt Ekland, as I mentioned, introduced me properly to art nouveau, but it was while I was with Alana (who also had a very good eye) that I felt confident enough to make the move upfield from posters to paintings. The first painting I bought (my first "acquisition," as we like to call them in the art world) was by a completely unknown Victorian artist and is called *The Kiss*: two lovers snatching a quick snog in a fleeting moment on a country path. I got it for £12 off a Romanian bloke in a little shop in Ladbroke Grove in the late 1970s. It's not particularly big—about three feet tall and two feet wide in a gilt frame—and it's nothing special altogether, but I just liked the atmosphere of it, and that was the beginning of it all.

My first really serious purchase was steered my way by Alana, who knew someone in Beverly Hills who was selling (of all things) a John William Waterhouse. It's *Isabella and the Pot of Basil*, from the Keats poem. It cost me £30,000 in 1981, which felt like an absurd amount of money to be spending on an oil painting, yet I hesitate to think what it could be worth now—possibly as much as £1 million. Not that I'm thinking of selling it. When I stood in front of a Waterhouse as a slightly damp teenage busker, I didn't particularly imagine I would ever have one of my own hanging in the bedroom. It's a beautiful picture, first and foremost, but for me it also symbolizes a bit of a journey.

I've only been had twice, which is not bad going in the circumstances. I bought off an interior designer something that

I thought was an original Guillaume Seignac, but it turned out to be a copy. That was just me being naïve and getting a little overexcited. Still, I like the painting, and even as a copy it's probably worth a couple of bob. I also found a painting of the Princes in the Tower which I thought was a William-Adolphe Bouguereau. I thought to myself, "This is a complete steal." But it wasn't a Bouguereau at all. Happily, I did manage to acquire some original Bouguereaus eventually. I've got a large one in the passage. And, as anyone who collects late-nineteenth-century art will tell you, there's nothing like a large one in the passage.

Right from the late 1970s, I started doing the auctions. That scene really is addictive. The tension you feel when the picture you want is coming up is pretty intense. And you have to be careful because your ego can cause you all sorts of problems in the bidding process. I remember trying to outbid Gianni Versace once, which risked getting foolishly expensive until I came to my senses and pulled out, feeling somewhat bruised. Having a famous face can work both ways in that situation. Sometimes it goes in your favor because you frighten people off. Other times you'll get someone who wants to show the room he has more money than you, and then you'll get into an almighty and altogether unnecessary battle. On the whole it's probably best for me not to be there, and I tend to let my wonderful assistant Sarah do the bidding for me, or bid on the phone. What you need is an auctioneer in a major house or two who brings the hammer down quick when he knows it's you on the other end of the line. Not that I have ever found one who would stoop so low as to do so, you understand.

My arch-enemy in this arena is His Lordship, Sir Andrew Lloyd Webber. He has a truly spectacular collection of Pre-Raphs and is very hard to compete with. I've gone up against him at auction for a couple of things, and the bastard has always won. But he's a far broader collector than me. He doesn't stick to Victorian art, he has modern stuff as well, and he makes it all work. I couldn't put a piece of modern art on the wall, because I don't understand it and it just wouldn't look right. But he manages it. He invited us over to see his paintings once and we had a singsong around the piano that was most remarkable for a pissed rendition of "All I Want Is a Room Somewhere" from *My Fair Lady* by my dear wife, Penny—a stand-out moment in the history of musical theater.

I move pictures on when I'm tired of them and when enough time has passed for their value to have risen. That can be as much as fifteen years or more. It's not like the stock market: you need to be patient. And you need to love what you're buying, too. There's no satisfaction in getting your hands on it otherwise. I never shop for the sake of it. I'll buy because I need something for a particular wall in a particular position. I get the catalogues from the dealers and go through them, looking for something that might work. If I'm interested, I'll speak to Sotheby's and they'll send over an inspection report and give me photographs from different angles.

They put an ultraviolet lamp behind the picture so you can see where the canvas has been torn and touched up through the years. If it's had too many tears and too many touch-ups, I probably won't buy it. I've been caught out a couple of times, buying without seeing the painting in the flesh, as it were. Sometimes the colors in the catalogue reproductions are far richer than they are when you are actually standing in front of the painting, and when you get it, it just doesn't have the bounce that you thought it had. Then I'll set it aside and try to resell it. In general, when you look around, you can tell the expensive ones: they glow and jump off the wall at you.

No doubt when I die, my kids are going to say, "What the fuck are we going to do with all this stuff?" and then flog it as a job lot on eBay. However, all of them have, at some time in their lives, gone round the house counting the tits, or counting the swords, so there's definitely been an educational value there. Not long ago, my son Alastair was looking at a painting of St. Sebastian, martyred, with arrows sticking out of him, which hangs on the wall outside the kitchen in the house in Los Angeles, and he asked me what was going on there and why that man was naked and shot through like that, and it was very satisfying to be able to explain to the little chap the whole story—that it was because he had missed a penalty.

Sometimes, if I can't sleep, I count how many paintings I've got. I go from house to house and room to room. "One, two, three, eight in the hallway—don't forget that one in the loo." They have to be oils and they've got to be framed or they don't count. No drawings or sketches. Normally, by the time I get up to about 130, I'm ready to go off.

CHAPTER 14

In which our hero receives an unexpected visit, falls out with his wife on a London Routemaster bus, and tries to fool Rupert Murdoch, with only partial success.

One afternoon in late October 1982, the bell rang at the gate of the house on Carolwood Drive. I was out in the studio, working on tracks for what would become the *Body Wishes* album. Alana, who was at home looking after Kimberly, then three years old, and Sean, who had just turned two, answered the intercom.

A male voice said, "Is Rod there? There's someone here who wants to meet him."

Outside stood a man with a camera around his neck, a middle-aged woman, and an eighteen-year-old girl. The man was a photo-journalist from the *Sunday People* newspaper in London, the woman was called Evelyn Thubron, and the eighteen-year-old was the girl that I had given up for adoption in 1963—my daughter Sarah.

Her arrival was not entirely a surprise. There had been a couple of calls from the British press in the preceding months which had made it clear that someone was following up leads around the story of my adopted child. I had told Alana about those calls. She already knew about what had happened all those years ago. I had told Britt about that passage of my life, too, when we were together. The fact that I had had a child when I was eighteen and given her up for adoption wasn't something that I hid from any woman I was close to.

Still, the reality of Sarah's arrival, and the manner of it, was a shock to Alana. Sarah had turned eighteen near the end of 1981 and her adoptive parents, Brigadier Gerald Thubron and his wife, Evelyn, who had raised her in the East Sussex countryside, had disclosed to her that I was her birth father. And now, nearly a year later, here were Evelyn and Sarah on the doorstep—with a journalist. To an astonished Alana, the scene looked uncomfortably like an ambush. She told them I wasn't at home and then called me at the studio.

"Rod, the press were just outside the house with your daughter."

I was utterly confounded. It's impossible to account for the mixture of feelings that ran through me at that point, though fear was chief among them. But I also felt affronted. Why had she come with the press? Suspecting, like Alana, that some kind of trap was about to be sprung, I called Barry Tyerman, my unflappable and clear-minded lawyer. Barry took the situation over. He got through to the journalist and spoke to Evelyn, the adoptive mother, and explained that I was ready to meet Sarah, but absolutely not in the presence of a reporter. A meeting was set for the following afternoon at the Record Plant studios.

The next day I waited nervously in an empty back room. What would she look like? How would I feel when I saw her? How would she feel when she saw me? How would she be towards me? These questions circled in my mind. And then, finally, in came Sarah, moving very tentatively, smartly but plainly dressed: a girl so clearly mine that it was like looking in a mirror. And yet I didn't know her. Mine, yet not mine. I would have liked to have hugged her—I would have liked our relationship to have started off like that. But the situation seemed so contrived and strange, and the room so crowded (her adoptive mother and Barry were both present), that behaving naturally was impossible for both of us.

She stood, at first, slightly side on to me and was wary. We sat down on a sofa and I leaned in towards her as much as I could, trying to be paternal. I gave her some albums, which must have made her feel I was treating her like a fan, but I didn't know what else to do. I was sweating and shaking. I said, "I hope you understand why this happened." I also asked her if she saw Susannah, her birth mother, at all and she said she didn't. I said, "You know, I have a family now. It would be very difficult for me to make you a part of that—if that's even what you're looking for." She shook her head and said that wasn't why she was there. She had a family, after all: sweet, lovely, caring parents. She said she just wanted to make a connection.

In those circumstances, though, making a connection was hard. The meeting very soon broke up. Afterwards I felt drained and awful. And then I felt angry: angry that Sarah and her adoptive mother had allowed the press to manipulate them, and angry with the press for the manipulation. It should have been a warm, private reunion and it ended up being cold and somehow public. The *Sunday People* may have been excluded from the meeting, but it still had its field day, publishing a spread full of bullshit on "Rod's Love Child." Evelyn and Sarah both wrote me long, apologetic letters afterwards. I think they genuinely didn't know how it would look from my end and were naïve about how the tabloid press works. But it was a badly marred beginning and Sarah and I would have to start again.

Alana offered me loyal support over Sarah's reemergence in my life, but the general picture by 1982 was that our marriage was showing some irreparable cracks. The main bones of contention were the amount of time I spent working, football, and my friends.

I loved Alana's friends, and regarded them very quickly as friends of my own. The circles that Alana moved in, and the LA high life that she was able to show me, were hugely attractive to me, and I threw myself into that world and the fun I could have there. But I was still, at heart, a north London bloke who wanted to knock about with his football pals and the guys from the band. These chaps were far less glamorous than the people with whom Alana was used to socializing, and she preferred not to have them in the house if she could help it. And if they did show up, or if I brought them back, she would often freeze them out. I think she saw them as a corrupting influence, encouraging me to stay out late and drink—and she definitely had a point. But when I told her that our life revolved around her friends, but not mine, she would say that she found my friends less interesting than her friends. Then I would call her a snob—which was perhaps unfair, although Alana could definitely be choosy. She was the first person I ever met who, when people invited us to places, felt no compunction about asking, "Who else is going to be there?"

There couldn't have been a clearer demonstration of the social divide beginning to open up between us than an incident after a show at the LA Forum in December 1981. I played four nights there that year, and for the last of them I hired a London Routemaster bus to take my friends and family to the show. It wasn't quite your typical London bus: it was fitted with a bar downstairs, ensuring that everyone arrived at the venue smashed. I then decided to join everyone for the journey home afterwards. Alana couldn't see where the fun would be in traveling on a rickety old bus surrounded by my mates, and wanted us to take the limo. I thought she should be with me. Our argument continued on the bus, where eventually I suggested that she could always get off. Which Alana promptly did, despite the fact that we were somewhere in Inglewood at the time, miles from home, in the middle of the night. Police eventually rescued her from a phone booth, and my brother Don drove down to the police station to collect her and bring her home, weeping all the way.

The point was, though, in this period in our marriage there was less going out and partying altogether—and this was another source of friction. About six weeks after Kimberly was born, Alana came down with mononucleosis, and in the busy first year of Kim's life she never really had the chance to get over it properly. Then, shortly after Sean was born, she contracted Epstein-Barr virus, which can make you constantly tired and listless. I was less sympathetic than I might have been. I was full of energy and I wanted her to keep up with me. She was whacked out and, in any case, now wanted to spend her time at home with the children.

So, typically, I would go off to play football with the Exiles on a Sunday. And then maybe the team would have a bit of a drink after- wards, and by the time I got back it would be mid afternoon, the lunch would be dried up in the oven, and Alana would be steaming with fury. And then there would be two whole days when we wouldn't speak. She couldn't see why I wanted these outlets, and I couldn't see what had become of the fun-loving girl I had met who loved to stay up and party. Well, obviously what had become of her was that she was now the mother of three small children, two of them mine. But I simply wasn't ready to think about it maturely.

I began referring to Alana as "the War Office." Sessions in the Cock 'n Bull pub would often end with me standing up and saying, "Right, time to don the tin helmet and head home." The guys in the band, meanwhile, knew Alana as "And Then the Wife Showed Up." They grew used to feeling slightly chilly when she walked in. We would be having fun larking around . . . And Then the Wife Showed Up.

It didn't help that we were both stubborn and headstrong and we didn't have the first clue how to compromise or talk about things.

Instead we would become angry and silent. It never got violent, except on one occasion, in a hotel room in Cannes, when Alana, in a fury, threw a telephone receiver at me. Alas, it was on a curly elasticated lead, and it returned like a boomerang and clonked her on the forehead.

One morning, we awoke to find the words "Alana Piranha" daubed in black paint on the outside wall of our house—an eerie moment for both of us. We never found out who did it, or why. A perception had grown in certain quarters, though, that Alana was behind the sacking of two people who worked for me. That wasn't true. Two people who had been with me a long time, and who were close to me, did get fired in this period, but there were good reasons for it and they had nothing to do with Alana.

It was farewell, first of all, to Tony Toon, my personal assistant and self-styled publicist, but not because Alana loathed him (although she did). Tony went as the result of a poor piece of judgment on his part. During a stay in Hawaii, we found ourselves in an overbooked hotel. Alana and I had Sean and Kimberly in a room with us, and we asked Toon to share an adjoining twin room with Ashley, who was then seven. Toon, of course, couldn't resist pulling some bloke in the bar that evening and taking him back to the room. I fired Toon in the morning.

Toon's revenge was absolutely inspired. He fed the press a story in which, as a consequence of an evening spent orally servicing a gang of sailors in a gay bar in San Diego, I had been required to check into a hospital emergency room to have my stomach pumped. With minor variations (the quantity of the extracted fluid tends to fluctuate: seven pints, three ounces, half a quart; it's a relatively open field), this story has stayed with me ever since. Say what you like about Tony Toon— and God rest his soul—but he was good at his job.

For the record, then (and just to put it simply and clearly for posterity's sake): I believe I was in the Hotel Cipriani in Venice on the night of the alleged incident. I have never orally pleasured even a solitary sailor, let alone a ship's worth in one evening. And I have never had my stomach pumped, either of naval-issue semen or of any other kind of semen. Nor of anything else, for that matter. Again, it's all about clearing these things up and moving forward.

Also gone from the team was Billy Gaff, my manager of nearly thirteen years, since I joined the Faces. Our dispute erupted in 1982 on a private plane shuttling the band across the American Midwest in the later stages of the *Tonight I'm Yours* tour. I asked Gaff—clad, as I recall, in the big white fur coat he favored at this time—for a small advance for Robin Le Mesurier, one of the guitarists, and Gaff refused, saying there was no money available. This, to say the least, surprised me, given that we had been on the road, and earning money (or so I thought), for nearly three months. It made me very concerned about where the money had gone and how things were being organized. Gaff had a habit of going off like a rocket when questioned on absolutely anything—and this he now did. Accordingly, Gaff and I spent the rest of the flight shouting at each other, and at the next opportunity the man who was supposed to be my manager took off for Paris and stopped answering phone calls. I took the view that this wasn't ideal. So on March 3, 1982, I sent him a telegram which said, "You are obviously avoiding me. Am very dissatisfied with our relationship as it stands and consider it terminated as of today. Rod."

In order for me to get shot of Gaff formally, there needed to be a hearing before the Labor Commission. When this came around, Alana was magnificent. Despite the difficulties in our relationship, she came right to my side. On the morning of the hearing, she turned up in a black dress and a black hat with a veil, like a widow seeking justice for her freshly murdered husband—all very dramatic. Gaff, by contrast, arrived late, looking disheveled. The commissioner listened to the separate testimonies in which my side pointed out that Gaff was in violation of California law by acting as manager, record label, and music publisher all at the same time—a whole pot of conflict-ing interests. (I had really taken my eye off the ball in allowing that little situation to arise, and I cursed myself for doing so.) The com-missioner suggested that Gaff and I should probably try to sort it out between us, and a settlement was negotiated quickly enough. Gaff had good reason to settle, because he could have ended up liable to pay back the commissions he had earned over the previous years, which would have been a tidy old sum. He gave up his rights in my record-ings and publishing and in a batch of concert recordings and television programs, and I gave up my 30 percent share of Riva Records, the company Gaff had started in 1975 and which had been my label in the U.K. I felt relieved to be separated from him.

I now needed a new manager, and, again, Alana did the right thing by me, suggesting that I talk to Arnold Stiefel. He wasn't actu-ally from the music business, but was a young, high-powered movie agent at William Morris, where he represented some of Alana's fa-mous friends, among others. Arnold came to the house for a meeting and explained that while he knew fuck all about the music industry, he was confident he could apply the same strategic approach to my ca-reer as he was currently doing most successfully for actors, directors, and screenwriters. Actually, that rather appealed to me. Did I want a traditional rock manager? Most of them struck me as humorless bul-lies or shysters. So Arnold and I agreed to give it a go, and he went away to extract himself from William Morris, and, while he was at it, find out what things like "A&R," "road crew tour buses," and "All Access Passes" were all about. It turned out to be exactly the right move for both of us. Thirty glorious years later, we're still together.

The cracks in the marriage, however, were getting wider. In the summer of 1982 we all went to Spain for a holiday and to watch Scot-land take part in the World Cup. My dad, my brothers, my brother-in-law, and I would set off for the games and, invariably, arrive back at the house very late, the worse for wear. Alana and I ended up having a screaming argument about this in front of my dad, who got very upset on my behalf. His position was "Doesn't she understand? This is the World Cup. Why can't the men have this one day to do what they want to do?"

Of course, it was more than just one day: it was three—one for each of the group-stage matches. But you take his point. Also, could I just say that this was the World Cup at which, for fifteen dizzying minutes, Scotland led the mighty Brazil. Final score: 4–1 to Brazil. Even so, it stands to reason that the summer of 1982 was an uncommonly festive time for the Stewart family. Not that I could ever communicate this to Alana.

Another burden on the relationship was Alana's increasing interest in things psychic and spiritual. This was an area she had been drawn to all along, but the early 1980s really were a high tide for this kind of thing in California, and her attraction to it became quite pronounced for a while. She took to buying "wishing candles" from the House of Hermetic store in Los Angeles. The idea was that you made your desires somehow become reality by stating them as fact, or writing them on slips of paper and placing them under these candles. I wasn't sure about the science of this. If she could have drummed up a couple of results for the Scottish team, I might have been able to come on board. But in the absence of that . . . not really.

She also took herself off to various self-discovery meetings at which you might whack a leather bag with a broom handle while shouting about how much you hated your father. Numerology became a concern of hers, too. Alana had a close friend called Linda who claimed to be psychic, and Alana liked to consult Linda over the flight numbers of planes that we were traveling on, and the numbers of hotel rooms that we were booked into, just to check that they were OK, that we weren't somehow flirting with cosmological disaster by checking into suite 342, say, rather than suite 343. Personally, I thought this stuff was as close to bonkers as made no difference, but it's whatever works for you, I guess. What was definitely true was that it was evidence of a further lack of common ground between me and Alana.

I n the late summer of 1983 I went to a preview screening of a film called *Portfolio*, a docudrama set in the fashion world, featuring models from the Elite agency. As moments in movie history go, it wasn't exactly *Citizen Kane*, but a face on the screen took my breath away. I really wanted to meet her. To get the date, my people told the model's people that I had written a song for her, which was a downright lie. But it got me into a restaurant with Kelly Emberg.

Before the date could happen, though, at the beginning of September, I was invited for a week of partying and a football match at Elton's house in Windsor, England. I enjoyed staying at Elton's. You had to be prepared to move an awful lot of priceless Victorian dolls off your bed before you could get into it, but you were always made to feel very comfortable. The scene during this week was extremely lively but also—it possibly goes without saying—a touch gay. Accordingly, I had arranged for Kara Meyers, a beautiful and charming American model of my acquaintance, to fly in and keep me company in Windsor.

I had met Kara on tour in June 1983 as the result of an extraordinary coincidence. We were playing in Berlin, and on the day of the show I had gone to sit in a café, opposite which a fashion shoot was taking place. I spotted her, and thought she looked lovely; she was busy and didn't see me at all. I didn't think anything more of it. Later, I was onstage and I went to pull someone out of the crowd to sing "Hot Legs" with me—and there, right in the crush at the front, was Kara, the very same model I had spotted. So up she came, and, overcoming some initial reluctance, danced and gave it some serious "I love you, honey!" into the microphone on cue.

When the song finished, I made sure she was taken to the side of the stage and invited her to dinner, where I learned that she was a former squeeze of Prince Albert of Monaco. We spent a very sweet, and entirely chaste, night together. I saw her again a fortnight later, when the tour moved on to Paris, where she was living at the time. Then, when she moved back to live in New York, I continued to see her, on and off, for a couple of years.

However, the story of our return flight at the end of that weekend of pleasure chez Elton is pretty typical of the farcical situations that I seemed unerringly to get myself into in those days.

We were due to fly out to New York on the Concorde. Kara was originally booked on a flight departing a couple of hours earlier, but I got it changed so that I could spend a couple more hours in bed with her in Windsor and then, with any luck, another night in New York. Of course, as Arnold, my manager, who was traveling out of London with me, patiently pointed out, I couldn't exactly stomp through Heathrow Airport with a tall blond model in tow without being likely to excite the interest of the press and, shortly thereafter, my wife. So it was arranged that we would travel independently to the airport and that Kara would be seated away from me on the aircraft.

All goes well. Kara and I get through the airport without appearing to be any kind of item, despite the fact that, in a planeload of mostly suited businessmen, Kara is wearing a black leather jacket, a tiny red leather skirt, and red patent-leather high heels. Still, we take our seats on the plane, innocently separated by three rows, and I feel I can relax. Kara and I can leave the plane and no one will ever know.

However, as we wait for the plane to pull away from the gate, I notice that Arnold has turned a shade of gray normally seen only on people who have been dead for some time. He says, "Don't look around now, but have you seen who Kara is seated next to?"

I look round. Kara is sitting next to Rupert Murdoch.

Brilliant. My secret date and Concorde stowaway is chatting cheerfully to the man who owns practically every tabloid newspaper in the Western world. I wonder, briefly, about making a run for it, but

Arnold has begun to calm down. "It's fine," he says. "The doors of the plane are about to close. Even if Murdoch catches on, he can't get to a phone before we land." (Remember that this was in the days before mobile phones and phones on planes.)

At this point the captain makes an announcement: there is a small problem with the plane, so if everyone would be kind enough to return briefly to the lounge . . .

Back in the lounge, fearing that Rupert Murdoch is even now pumping coins into a phone box, Arnold makes some countertactical phone calls of his own. The ideal ploy would be to get a plausible "Rod Stewart girlfriend" figure to be on standby to meet me at JFK, throwing the press completely off the scent and enabling Kara to exit unnoticed. But it's the middle of the night in New York. The best Arnold can come up with is Sandy Harmon, who happens to be a beautiful woman but who also happens to be short, dark-haired, middle-aged, and Jewish.

I say, "Sandy? Sandy Harmon?"

Arnold says, "Throw yourself into it. Act it. It'll be fine."

At JFK, the swarm of photographers is so thick that there are police sawhorses in place to control the crowd. Arnold's decoy duly performs her meet-and-greet, but the photographers have spotted Kara, their intended prey, and they pour after her out of the airport.

I have a limo waiting. Kara makes it into a taxi and joins us, as instructed, at the Mayfair Regent Hotel. She is pretty sure she hasn't been followed. A short while later, I look down from the window of my room. Parked by the pavement opposite the hotel on Sixty-third Street is a flatbed truck, loaded with paparazzi.

And, of course, I have a date. I shamelessly inform Kara that I have to leave for a business meeting and tell her to make herself comfortable in my absence. I then escape from the hotel through the service doors at the back of the building and arrive, embarrassingly late, for my first dinner with Kelly Emberg, with whom I immediately fall in love.

The following afternoon, when I get out of the car at Carolwood, Alana, who has seen the newspaper pictures of "Rod's mystery JFK blonde," is standing on the drive looking thunderous.

The breakup was slow and torturous and dotted with doomed attempts at reconciliation. We went back and forth: again, my terrible problem with finality. We decided to live apart for a while, to see if it would help. But, of course, I was now starting to see Kelly Emberg without Alana knowing, so the experiment was inevitably flawed. I moved out of Carolwood and rented a house in Beverly Hills but I was rattling around inside the place and feeling miserable. So I moved in with Jim Cregan, who was living in a small house in the Hollywood Hills, just off Sunset Boulevard, and was also recently separated from his wife. It was nice to have someone to take a cup of tea to in the morning—although, as I always grudgingly said, as I set the mug down beside the bed, "I bet Elvis wouldn't have done this." I was there for five months. In the afternoons I would pick the kids up from school, take them back to Carolwood and play with them in the pool, and then leave again, feeling wretched: the routine of the separated dad.

Parties continued at Carolwood to which I wasn't invited. Malcolm, my assistant, would say, "They're in there, drinking your wine." I would drive past and see all these cars parked up outside and think: "These people are having fun in my house." But deep down I didn't mind. After all, if Alana found someone else, maybe that would magically solve everything. Jack Nicholson seemed to be on the scene and I had hopes for him and Alana—and, indeed, they did get together for a while, but only later. One afternoon I was coming out of the house after dropping in to see the kids, and there was John McEnroe about to pull into the drive. He caught sight of me and drove off again, and I wanted to run after him up the street and shout, "No, no, come back, it's fine. You've got nothing to fear from *me*."

Then one day Alana called me from New York, after a dinner with friends, and said, "Who is Kelly Emberg?"

I said something about her being someone I occasionally ran into. Alana said, "You need to tell me the truth." We agreed to have dinner at Carolwood, and I told her that I had feelings for Kelly but that I didn't want to break up our marriage and lose her and our children. Alana told me that I would have to figure it out.

On it went, for weeks on end, with me knowing that I wanted out, but then going back to see the kids and feeling torn and miserable and being totally indecisive and frustrating Alana immensely. In December 1983 we made a last attempt to mend things. We rented a house we had used before on Old Church Street in Chelsea, and attempted to have the perfect London Christmas, which was, perhaps, always going to be a bad idea. I flew out from LA in advance with the kids. Alana, who was in the middle of filming a role she had in a TV series called *Masquerade*, arrived on Christmas morning. But the mood between us was flat and wouldn't rise. When I went to visit my parents, I didn't take Alana with me. Later, the conversation got around to Kelly and I confessed that I was still thinking about her. Alana packed her things, and the kids' things, and left.

That Christmas in London was the penultimate straw. The last straw was not long afterwards, in early 1984, when Alana discovered that the party I was taking to Hawaii for a short break in order to work on some music also included Kelly. Alana filed for divorce that day.

It was March 1987 before the divorce was finalized. Under its terms, I bought Alana and the children a house in Brentwood and got Carolwood back. What had my dad said about being too young to marry at thirty-four? It turned out he had a point. It turned out that Alana, too, had a point when she accused me of failing to grow up. It would be a little while yet.

DIGRESSION

෴

*In which our hero helps bring "soccer" to his adopted land, loses
a few balls in the ocean, and investigates the wisdom of combining
Mudslides and vitamin shots within a sporting fitness regime.*

I HAVE ASSOCIATED FOOTBALL with home since childhood, when the football teams my dad ran were all through our
lives and all around our house. It's like the song says: wherever
I wash my strip—that's my home. Inevitably, then, part of
growing to feel completely at home in LA when I moved there
was finding a football team to play on. I joined a bunch of
expat Brits who played a pick-up game every Thursday night
on a patch of ground which used to be a fire station in Beverly
Hills. These guys were electricians, carpenters, salesmen: blokes
trying to work their ticket in America. No stars here—apart
from me, I guess, for whom no exceptions were made and for
whom no quarter was given. We'd play for a couple of hours
and then adjourn to the Cock 'n Bull pub on the Sunset Strip
for refreshment. And here were sown the seeds of what duly
became, in 1978, the legendary Los Angeles Exiles football
team, who were to enjoy their most fruitful period under the
stewardship of the equally legendary Lionel Conway, possibly
the most competitive man on God's earth.

We toyed with becoming the Hamilton Academical
All Stars, in honor of the obscure Scottish league side, and
consideration was also given to the name Cocaine All Stars, but,
wisely, we settled for the Exiles. We moved to a pitch in Malibu,
but got fed up with the ball running away down a cliff. We then
found a field at Manhattan Beach. I managed to persuade Puma

to give us some free shirts because, as is widely accepted, you can't be a proper team without the matching shirts. And soon we found a place in the Pacific Soccer League. Training on Thursday nights, games on Sunday mornings: back in the old routine and happy as could be.

At the beginning of the 1985–86 season it was politely suggested to Lionel, a music publisher by day, that his best playing days were behind him and that he should concentrate on management. Concentrate he did. From here on, Lionel's assistant in the office was solemnly told that all calls relating to football should be given priority over calls about music publishing. Simultaneously, a revolutionary approach to recruitment was put in place. Lionel had noticed that the British expats weren't an entirely reliable source of playing staff: one week they would be there, and the next they wouldn't because they had been clobbered by immigration.

So Lionel began scouting for squad reinforcements among a more stable talent pool: the indigenous students at UCLA. Some of these guys were on the college soccer team and playing at national student level, and some of them would eventually graduate to Major League Soccer, but Lionel would entice them by the simple measure of paying them. Out of his own pocket, I should add. Appearance fees, win bonuses, goal bonuses— whatever it took. There was one season when Lionel estimated that he had sunk $30,000 into wages for the Exiles.

The Exiles duly prospered, reaching the semifinal of a U.S. national cup competition in New York. I was unable to play because of a concert in Atlanta the previous night, but I flew up the coast the following morning, arriving near half-time, with the score level at 1–1 and everything to play for against a side of rather frighteningly focused expat Greeks. Unfortunately, I had brought with me, to share the big-match excitement from a seat on the bench, two strippers of my acquaintance from the fabled Atlanta Gold Club, a popular postshow haunt for me and the band in those times. Despite being off work, neither of these women had chosen to wear much—and certainly not much in the way of skirts. Fatally distracted, the Exiles fell 4–1 behind and had two men sent off, bringing the glorious cup run to an end. I still blame myself.

God, could we take ourselves seriously, though. I had heard about these vitamin injections: B$_{12}$ shots. They were supposed to do marvelous things for energy levels. So I arranged for a doctor to come up, prematch, and administer them to the entire squad. This produced a memorable scene: the team lined up, shorts around ankles, as the doctor moved from one backside to the next with his syringes. Did it make a difference? Not one little bit. But you have to experiment with these things if there's any chance that they could yield that vital extra 1 percent.

That said, fitness tended to take a backseat after games. Victory and defeat alike were toasted in high style, and several squad members down the years ended up with DUIs on their records as a result of the imbibing they did after Exiles games. The team's favored postmatch cocktail was the Mudslide: vodka, coffee liqueur, and Baileys. We would get them lined up on the bar, but no one was allowed to touch them until the drinks had been blessed with the singing of the official Mudslide anthem: "Mudslides, mudslides . . ." sung to the tune of "Amazing Grace." And any excuse for an awards dinner was eagerly taken—black tie for preference, and nearly always at my place on Carolwood Drive, with trophies, speeches, the works.

The Exiles were extreme, laddish, deluded, obsessed to the point of madness, and, as far as I was concerned, along with the sunshine, one of the best things about living in LA.

The other big asset I owed to Lionel—and, again, it played

no small part in my eventual complete assimilation into America—was access to English football on television. Lionel had one of the first satellite television systems, involving a ridiculous nine-foot-wide dish parked in his garden. This vast plate of metal looked as though it ought to be contacting Mars but was actually just beaming football games from England. It was supposed to be for bars, but somehow Lionel had wangled it for his home use, and I got him to wangle it for me, as well. The signal, I think, was being bounced from London to Ireland, from Ireland to Canada, and from Canada to Los Angeles, and on one out of three matches the chain would break somewhere on the journey and the picture would go down, leaving Lionel and me ringing each other up in frustration. "Have you got it?" "No. Have you?"

These days there is more English football on American television than there is on English television. When I arrived in the country, there was nothing. An early method of keeping in touch during the big games involved ringing my dad in London. He would then carefully position the phone receiver next to a radio broadcasting the commentary. This, of course, resulted in alarmingly high phone bills. However, the bills were so alarmingly high that I would sometimes be able to ring the phone company and say, "I think this must be an error. There's an entry on here for an international call lasting more than an hour and a half . . ." And the phone company would agree that it did indeed seem most unlikely, and deduct the charge.

The absence of football bit deepest in the first months of 1975 when, in order to qualify as a tax exile, I was obliged to spend twelve months outside the United Kingdom and was not even allowed a fleeting visit. Accordingly, I may be one of a very small number of people who have flown 5,000 miles from Los

Angeles to Ireland specifically in order to watch Scotland on telly. It was for the annual Home Championship game: England v. Scotland at Wembley. No way was I going to miss it. I invited the family in England to join me in a Dublin hotel and turned the occasion into a reunion party. Final score: 5–1 to England. Quite a long way to go for a pasting, I guess. Indeed, if you break it down, I had traveled 1,000 miles per England goal. Ah, well. It was good to see my family.

Fortunately, by the time Scotland got round to exacting their revenge, beating England 2–1 at Wembley, it was the summer of 1977 and I was free to travel to Britain again. That precious victory over the Auld Enemy on their own turf caused thousands of Scotland fans to pour over the advertising hoardings onto the pitch after the game. The scenes would become notorious when a fan called Alex Torrance was filmed climbing onto one of the goalposts and briefly sitting astride it before it snapped, duly triggering a serious debate in the media about whether this was perfectly acceptable elation or outright football hooliganism. My own feeling was that it was elation, but then I speak as someone who was on the Wembley pitch at the time.

I said to my dad, as everybody ran forward on the final whistle, "I'm going on." He said, "No, you're not." Too late. At the edge of the pitch a policeman stopped me. I lifted the hat I was wearing and showed my face a bit more. The policeman looked a little more closely and said, "Oh, it's you. On you go then, I suppose." And on I ran.

Great to feel the fabled turf beneath one's feet, although, to be honest, once you were on there, there wasn't a lot to do, really, except bounce around a bit with some blokes who were possibly even more pissed than you were. However, mid-bounce, I suddenly found myself grabbed and hoisted upwards, and the next thing I knew I was on somebody's shoulders, being carried aloft in triumph. So touching.

Back in the stands, I looked to see what the time was and found only a naked wrist where my Cartier watch had been. Mugged! Not long after, though, a kind gentleman in Edinburgh got in touch to say that he thought he had my watch. As indeed he had. The watch was returned in full working order and nothing further was said about the matter. That's the brilliance of Scottish football fans; the best in the world, by common consent. Even when they're dishonest, it's not for long.

Other fans that day didn't get off so lightly. Charges were pressed against a number of supporters who had torn up patches of the Wembley turf to take home as souvenirs. But in the marvelous words of one of those grass thieves, who defended himself in court: "Yous haven't got a team, so yous dinnae need a pitch."

I continued to play for the Exiles as often as I could right through the early 1990s, until age caught up with me and I was obliged to seek a team in an older league. And in all those years of service, I don't remember once being made a target on account of who I was, or getting clattered by an opponent just for the hell of it. Indeed, the only time that ever happened to me was back in dear old Blighty, on the pitches at Highgate Woods, circa 1971, just as I was beginning to get famous. A guy came crashing into me at a corner, gave my nose an almighty clunk with his elbow, left me facedown in the mud, and said, "Why don't you stick to fucking singing?" In football, this is what is known as "letting the opponent know you're there." My dad, less than sympathetic, and perhaps not entirely up on the latest medical breakthroughs, suggested brown paper and vinegar for the wound. That was when my nose acquired the distinguished shape it so nobly retains today.

Fully forty years later, in 2011, a surgeon offered to straighten the hooter. He reckoned he could insert two fingers into the nostrils and crack it back into place, rectifying the damage. "But it might change your voice," he added.

Somehow I found it in myself to say, "Thanks, but no thanks."

CHAPTER 15

In which our hero falls heavily for a supermodel, buys another house, and meditates on the effects and advantages of big hair; and of matters variously frivolous and disturbing.

So, in September 1983, after a busy day of failed subterfuge involving a model in a leather jacket, Rupert Murdoch, and a mildly delayed flight on the Concorde, I eventually headed out for a dinner in New York, arranged under slightly false pretenses, with Kelly Emberg.

The date was for 8:30. As time wore on, Kelly was lying on her bed in her apartment in Greenwich Village, with her dress on, thinking of giving up and going to sleep.

Finally, at around ten, I call up from the lobby. When she steps out of the elevator I perform a running jump and arrive at her feet on my knees. She says, "Who do you think you are—Rod Stewart?" And in that moment I realize that I am already pretty hooked on Kelly Emberg.

We go to Christos Steak House, one of those old, traditional, former

Mafia haunts, with bloodred leather booths and pictures of Lana Turner on the walls. She is a twenty-four-year-old supermodel and I am a thirty-eight-year-old singer, and she only really knows roughly what I look like from one of her sister's albums—has a vague prior impression of sticky-up hair and a big nose. She is the face of a hundred magazine covers from *Vogue* to *Cosmopolitan*, not to mention a veteran of that great annual work of sporting literature, the *Sports Illustrated Swimsuit Edition*. She poses for a living, and yet she is so natural and sweet and just about the least affected person I have met in my life. Texan, as it happens, like Alana. I seem to have developed a thing for Texans.

At one point the conversation threatens to get bogged down slightly when I move on to that famous first-date-clinching topic, writer's block. Always wows 'em. Or maybe not. What can I say? I was really beginning to suffer with it at that time and it was in my mind a lot. I would taunt myself with questions: Why weren't songs coming? Where was the material? When was the last time I had written anything good? I used to beat myself up about it all the time.

Still, Kelly doesn't seem too put off. She certainly doesn't start looking around the room distractedly while I'm talking about it. Nor does she begin yawning loudly, humming, or making animal shapes out of her napkin.

After dinner, we drive back to her apartment and I walk her to the elevator. I say, "Can't I come up?" And she says, "No, you can't." And I say, "I just thought maybe I could." And she says, "No, you can't." So I plead with her to let me see her tomorrow. But she says she is busy. She's going to Pennsylvania, where she is in the middle of doing up a house and someone is coming to give her an estimate for some work. And I say, "Please—don't go. Cancel it. I'll call you." And she laughs and gets into the elevator.

And then I drive back to the Mayfair Regent and a hotel suite containing a slumbering Kara Meyers.

Dear Lord. Who did I think I was? Rod Stewart?

ᦝᦝ

The following morning, Kelly waited until eleven, gave me up as a hopeless case, and caught a bus to Pennsylvania. I didn't call until one and, in any case, I had a wife to fly home to in Los Angeles and a photograph inside the *New York Post* to discuss. (It mostly showed Kara Meyers's very long legs disappearing into a taxi, but the evidence was substantially incriminating.)

Nevertheless, I was intent. I called again the next day. Kelly told me she was going to Dallas to do a catalogue shoot. I told her I would be there. She laughed and said, "I'm not holding my breath." I flew there for no other reason at all and checked into the Mansion on Turtle Creek Hotel. She was in the Best Western. I rang her and said, "Come and stay over here. It's nicer." She said, "I'm not staying in your room." I said, "I'll get you a room of your own."

I booked her a room and left in it a bouquet of flowers the size of a hedge, and a note: "For the fabulous one." And when I knew she had moved her stuff across from the Best Western, I knocked on the door and got ready so that when she opened it I was down on my knees on the threshold, offering in my outstretched hands a toilet roll and saying, "For you."

Even in Dallas we ended up having dinner and fun and nothing else. I had to court her. She had a boyfriend and she took a lot of persuading to leave him. Over the next weeks, I called her constantly. I would find out where she was working and turn up there and surprise her. I went to photographers' studios and blagged my way in. I gate-crashed the shoot for a Maybelline commercial and sat at the back trying to distract her. And then I would persuade her to come out to lunch or dinner, or just walk around with her, saying stupid stuff. "You see this crack in the pavement? We may never have this moment with it again."

I was head over heels. She was so together. She took flights—*on her own*. I never did this. There was always an assistant with me. Never a bodyguard, because I have never felt I needed one of those, but always someone alongside me. And sometimes she would go to the cinema by herself. Again, I couldn't have imagined doing that. She had this fabulous way of talking on a laugh, she was always up, she was as sentimental as anything; she was clearly someone who didn't have a bad bone in her body. At dinner one time, even before we had consummated the relationship, I told her, "I think I'm going to marry you." She said, "Are you crazy? That's completely nuts." But I really thought it.

Eventually we were an item. For two years, our relationship was long-distance, split between New York and LA. Kelly had her career and she had her apartment in Manhattan, and she was too smart and organized to set it all aside casually. But even in that period, the longest we went without seeing each other was ten days. In New York we would go to the theater and hang out with her model friends, Kim Alexis and Christie Brinkley. Which was no particular hardship, I have to say. And then, on weekends in LA, she would come to watch me play football and go out with the boys afterwards and we would drink Mudslides until we were cross-eyed. She never had any problem being around my friends, nor with any of the raucousness and stupidity that would frequently break out. The boys in the band adored her, welcoming her warmly to the Under the Table Supper Club (a formal dining society in which, at various points in the evening, everyone would slide under the table and hide from the waiter). The band also had a bit of a thing at this time for dining in restaurants trouserless—and occasionally, it must be admitted, underwearless—with nudity concealed from the waiter and other diners by the tablecloth. And Kelly seemed perfectly comfortable with that, too. Nothing fazed her.

This was the 1980s, the era of big hair. It was simply in the air at that time: the circumference of your hairdo expanded by at least four inches in about 1982 and stayed that way for three or four years, whether you wanted it to or not. It was something to do with the economy, probably. Anyway, my hair had certainly never been bigger than it was in 1983. Kelly, too, when I first saw her on the screen in *Portfolio*, had truly massive hair. She didn't always wear it that way, though. And when she didn't, I would spend a lot of time teasing it and fluffing it, trying to make it bigger. It seemed to me just wrong to be living in the 1980s and not trying to maximize the bigness of your hair.

We began spending a lot of time together in England. I hadn't owned a house there since I had sold Cranbourne Court, the giant country pile where I had lived with Dee Harrington until the mid-1970s. I had kept that house for a little while after I moved to America, and members of my family had gone to live there and look after it. But it was way too big—possibly even dangerously big. One day my sister Mary went up in the attic and accidentally knocked the ladder down behind her. And, my parents being pretty deaf by then and the house being so huge, Mary couldn't attract anybody's attention and was stranded up there for hours. It could have been the last we ever saw of her.

This was the period when my dad had access to my former driver, Big Cyril, and to my six-door, tinted-windowed Rolls-Royce, which had once belonged to Andrew Loog Oldham, the former manager and producer of the Rolling Stones. Dad would depart from Cranbourne Court in his suit, tie, and carpet slippers and, driven by Big Cyril, head for the betting shop in Ascot. Or at least that's what he did until the day he landed a really stinky bet, copping several thousand pounds on a tiny stake, and was quietly advised by the management (who now suspected him of being some kind of insider) that they no longer wished for his business. If Dad couldn't use the bookie's in Ascot, then Cranbourne Court really had lost its purpose.

In 1986, though, in the pages of *Country Life* magazine, I found the Wood House, a lovely late-nineteenth-century English manor house in the countryside not far north of London. It stood in what had once been the vast estate belonging to Copped Hall, now derelict and away on the horizon, a huge mansion and a former hospital for wounded army officers. This part of Essex had been Winston Churchill's constituency when he was an MP, and the legend was that he had stayed at the Wood House and that during the Second World War he had stood at its upstairs windows and watched German bombing raids on London, back when I was a newborn and Adolf Hitler was at the end of his tether, trying and failing to kill me.

The place had rolling lawns and a lake and a paddock for horses and a large amount of privacy and, crucially, a flattish area off to one side, which my trained eye immediately told me would lend itself to a long-imagined and deeply personal project of mine: the creation of a full-size football pitch. I bought it and we moved in, and I still remember the first meal Kelly and I ate in this newly acquired home, sitting in the bay window of a gorgeous, broad, wood-paneled room, with just a few items of furniture in boxes and wrappings around us, plus the snooker table that the owners had left behind, and, ahead of us, the exciting and romantic (if slightly expensive) prospect of making this place our own.

So, if everything was so perfect and so well set up, why did I end up floating off and fooling around with another woman? The woman was Kelly LeBrock, the film actress. It was nothing serious, just a fling. She invited me to a film premiere and I, by way of return, invited her to join me on a boating trip to Catalina Island, whereupon a certain amount of alcohol was imbibed and relations of an intimate nature ensued. We decided afterwards that the outing had been such a success that we really ought to repeat it. And she was a lovely woman, a rose raised in England, and very fastidious about intimate cleanliness, as I recall. As soon as anything got going in that direction, one would be packed straight off to the showers, quicker than in a boarding school after games. But it was all conducted lightly, in the spirit of seizing the day and other things—altogether typical of the dalliances I used to have. When it came to beautiful women, I was a tireless seeker after experiences. "Miss Inbetweens" was the phrase I had for them. And

Miss Inbetweens would arise because the opportunity came very easily to me, and because the opportunity looked like fun, and because in those days I simply didn't know how to resist. And also because I thought I could get away with it.

I'm not trying to cover myself in excuses here, but this was Kelly LeBrock. She was the star of the movie *The Woman in Red*. And what was *The Woman in Red* about if not the complete irresistibility of Kelly LeBrock? If, in the mid-1980s, you could have found me a solitary heterosexual man of sound mind, married, attached, or single, who would have declined the opportunity to spend some time on a boat with Kelly LeBrock if he thought he could get away with it, I would have . . . well, I would have looked that person right in the eye and shaken him firmly by the hand because he was obviously a better man than me.

It turned out that I couldn't get away with it, though. Kelly found out about Kelly. Kelly Emberg and I were eating at the Ivy in LA. Kelly LeBrock, whom I had not seen for some time, was at another table. Kelly LeBrock, daringly, perhaps even provocatively, sent the waiter over with a message. (Remember: this was an era long before the invention of texting.) On the scrap of paper, she had written, "I miss you." And Kelly (Emberg) read it.

Short of being found actually in flagrante (which, astonishingly, never happened to me: I wonder what odds you could have got on that), I could hardly have been caught more red-handed. And let me tell you, if you haven't been there, after a handwritten note revealing your affair has been dropped onto a table in front of your girlfriend, then take it from me that it's very difficult to find something appropriate and calming to say. You can't really sit there and say, "Trust me, in a few years' time we'll look back and laugh about this." Nor can you very well fold the piece of paper back up again, drop it on your empty plate, and say, "Well. Anyway. Coffee?" I simply started up the usual train of utterly see-through denials and protestations of innocence, which continued as we left.

The first Mrs. Stewart, the delightful Ms. Alana Hamilton, on the day of our nuptials, 1979.

Stealing the show. Kim and Sean onstage with me at Madison Square Garden, 1982.

Above: Alana, with someone who's been let out for the day! *Below:* Video shoot for "Tonight I'm Yours." What would me mum think?

old band. All the lads are jolly.

new band. Never trust a man who says, "I've never taken my trousers off in public."

The notorious Sex Police. My dear friend Jim Cregan (next to me, who later became Penny's and my best man), Robin Le Mesurier, and Malcolm Cullimore, my loyal personal assistant (far right), planning a raid on someone's hotel room. *Inset:* Let's leave this one to the imagination. Mexico, in the eighties.

For some unknown reason, I left my Lamborghini parked inside the studio for nine days while we recorded. Don't ask why.

The delectable Kelly
...nberg, giving me a
...le breast time.
...hat a girl!

...: My gorgeous Ruby, age four. *Right:* A gullible Arnold Stiefel, signing a management contract,
...3. You don't know what you're letting yourself in for, mate.

Me with two of Scotland's football icons: the late, great Tommy Burns of Celtic, and Sir Walter Smith of Glasgow Rangers. No great divide here! *Inset:* Getting the pitch ready at home in Epping.

Being held aloft by jubilant Scottish fans after we had defeated the Auld Enemy 2–1 at Wembley, 1

The Fram guys celebrate winning the league at our Beverly Hills home.

The Vagabonds on my glorious pitch in Essex, which has seen the likes of Celtic, Liverpool, and Newcastle train upon its sumptuous surface. My good friend Alan Sewell, aka "Honest," director of football, is in the back row, far right. *Inset:* My mate Lionel Conway, founder of the Exiles FC.

The male section of the Stewart clan head off to Glasgow to see Scotland play England, on a private jet in the seventies. The good old days.

Mum and Dad at my house in Spain in the mid-eighties. Mum looks like she has seen a shilling on the floor and is distracted. If it wasn't for them, who knows?

Brothers Bob and Don, sister Mary and me celebrating Mum and Dad's millionth wedding anniversary.

The worst of it was that, a year or so before this happened, Kelly E. had been offered a part in a John Hughes movie—had accepted it and gone through the whole rehearsal process, right up to the point of shooting the thing, only to be taken off the picture because another actress had suddenly become available. The film was called *Weird Science* and the actress who replaced Kelly was called . . . Kelly LeBrock. Kelly E. was not the sort of person to carry a grudge; in fact, she was the precise opposite of that sort of person. But I don't suppose her feelings about my secret affair were especially improved by the coincidence.

Kelly went back to New York, extremely betrayed, confused, and upset. I realized I had been an idiot to risk losing her and began calling her and pleading with her, trying to charm her into coming back. She stopped taking my calls, which drove me even more insane. I was on the phone to her assistant in tears at least a couple of times. Eventually I got to speak to her again, and I told her that I had been a fool and that I was serious about her and that nothing like that would happen again, and that we should go to Spain that weekend and make everything better. She was meant to be doing a photo shoot for Tom Ford, but I persuaded her to drop it and come to Spain with me. While we were there we patched things up. And we decided we would have a baby, which would pull us together like we were supposed to be.

The conception may even have happened there and then, in sunny Spain. At any rate, towards the end of 1986, Kelly was pregnant. Pregnant with a girl. We both knew as much. Well, we didn't know it. But we both said it. Kelly wanted to call her Ruby. I had a small problem with that. In cockney rhyming slang, the ancient vernacular of my home city, a "ruby" is a curry: Ruby Murray—curry. So you might say, "Shall we eat in tonight, or shall we go out for a ruby?" As I explained this to Kelly, I could see from the blank expression on her face that the confusion was unlikely to arise in America. Nor in many other places, really. And it was, I had to agree, a very pretty name. I set my objection aside. Ruby it was.

We went to tell Kelly's parents. There I was, going down to Texas to inform some Texans I had never met that I was having a child out of wedlock with their daughter. I figured I would be lucky to get away without being shot or lynched, or possibly both at the same time. In fact, they were nice, understanding people. Kelly's father was a giant, but gentle with it, fortunately. Her mother was more formidable—and had an amazing singing voice, as it turned out. Some years later we were in the Ritz hotel in New York for the New Year, and she got up and sang and the hotel offered her a contract for a residency, on the spot. She declined it. Anyway, at that first meeting, I turned on the charm. There was talk of marriage, which seemed to settle a few nerves. And I meant it.

On June 17, 1987, at six in the morning, Kelly went into labor and we rushed in a panic to Cedars-Sinai hospital only to be told that the baby wasn't going to arrive for at least another twelve hours. I was in the middle of shooting a video, so we agreed that I might as well go away and get on with it during this intermission and then come back to the hospital in the evening for the main event. At the video shoot, a few glasses were quaffed to celebrate the baby in advance, so I was in somewhat enthusiastic spirits when I returned to the hospital that evening. I had dutifully gone with Kelly to what seemed to me like several hundred birthing classes—done the breathing exercises, watched the videos, bought the prematernity T-shirt, you name it—so I considered myself amply prepared for the important events that were about to unfold. However, as I moved confidently towards the bed, a member of the medical staff put a firm hand on my shoulder and said, "Stand back, Mr. Stewart. We'll take over from here." Cost me hundreds of dollars, those classes.

And out came the lovely Ruby—with a broken clavicle, poor thing. And a conehead like you've never seen. Although maybe you *have* seen it because a member of the honorable fellowship of British press photographers managed to get into the hospital and photograph our newborn infant in her cot. Welcome to the world, Ruby.

Early the next morning, ecstatic, underslept, and slightly hung-over, I rang Jim Cregan and bestowed upon him his first sacred duty as Ruby's future godfather: to come down to the hospital with some bacon sandwiches because we were starving. Jim has yet completely to forgive me for making him walk through the corridors of one of Los Angeles's most famously Jewish institutions smelling strongly of fried pork.

As the 1980s began, I faced musical challenges on a number of fronts. As far as music critics were concerned, I was about as welcome as a hole in a parachute. "Da Ya Think I'm Sexy?" and the surrounding hoopla had convinced the music writers that I had been led astray forever by the glitter of the disco ball and the Hollywood lifestyle and was irredeemable. It was only a pop record, of course, but if you had picked up a music paper at this time you would have thought I had opened a chemicals factory that was poisoning the water supply in a deprived area of the world.

I think I can put my hand up to a bit of a loss of focus at that time—say 1979 to 1981. I'm not entirely sure what the root causes were, but I suspect that too many late nights, too much partying, too much booze, and a few too many dabs of recreational cocaine might have had something to do with it. Certainly the unignorable sign that things were awry was that although I had always been a bit of a stickler for punctuality in the workplace (and remain so today), in those turn-of-the-decade years, sessions were commonly booked for two in the afternoon and if I was there by five the band felt unusually blessed. It all went a bit fuzzy at the edges for a while, and when I eventually snapped to, a certain amount of slippage had taken place.

How would I have rationalized this behavior to myself at the time? I think I would have felt that, as a rock star, I had an awful lot of drinking, shagging, and general carrying-on to get done. And there are only so many hours in the day. If other aspects of the rock-star role—such as songwriting or rehearsing, say—were put to one side for a little while, then that was only inevitable, given the constraints of time that all of us face in our working lives.

And, incidentally, I never thought in this period that the "being a rock star" aspect of being a rock star was beside the point, or even something I needed to apologize for. On the contrary, it seemed to me (a) where an awful lot of the fun was, and (b) exactly what one had signed up for in the first place. That was the deal, surely. If I hadn't considered the drinking/shagging/carrying-on to be at least a part of my terms of employment—and if I hadn't done my best to hold my end up as nobly as possible in those areas—I would have felt I was letting down the union.

Still, was this slightly loose approach to my business as a singer and recording artist reflected in any of my output as the 1970s blurred into the 1980s? Please do draw your own conclusions. (The relevant albums are available in the foyer after this performance for anyone who wants to conduct a critical reevaluation.) All I can report is that "Passion," on the *Foolish Behaviour* album, has the distinction of being my mum's least favorite song of any that I wrote. In other words, it was a song not even a mother could love. And this was an area in which she tended to be pretty loyal.

Indeed, late in her life I took her to the Wimbledon Theatre to see a performance by Max Bygraves, whom she adored. Max very kindly came to meet her in her box before the show, and said, "Elsie, is there any particular song you would like me to sing for you tonight?" And my mum said, "Can you do 'Sailing'?"

Exit Max Bygraves, looking a little crestfallen.

Foolish Behaviour was recorded (like a fair bit of my stuff) at the

Record Plant in Los Angeles, where, very typically for the period, we had a lock-in and a seemingly limitless budget from the record company. That's not always a recipe for creativity. Immediately, you're thinking, "What's the hurry? It's not my money that's being spent here." But, of course, it *is* your money in the end, because the record company is going to spoil the fun by deducting it from your royalties. Nevertheless, you don't really think about that very hard at the time. Instead, you think, "Brilliant, a studio to play around in for as long as we need. Let's spend fourteen days programming the drum machine." My recollection is that we were in there, recording *Foolish Behaviour*, for many years on end—although, to be honest, with the lapsing of time, I could be running a few albums together here. However, I do recall how there were doors at the back of the Record Plant for loading the gear into the studio, and that I grew very preoccupied, in a very coke-sozzled sort of way, with wondering whether I could get my Lamborghini through them. And happy days, because it turned out that I could. The car remained parked in the studio for about a week, as I recall, until I needed it to go home. We kind of recorded around it.

The fact was, I had been releasing solo albums at the rate of one a year for just over a decade. *Foolish Behaviour* was my tenth studio album, not including the four that I made with the Faces, an output that would have most of today's young Johnnies on their backs and gasping for mercy. It's not really surprising that the demand of getting a new album out annually, while being on the road for six months in the interim, was starting to tell and that a few threadbare patches were in evidence around the elbows.

I mentioned earlier my fear of the empty seat. On tour in 1981 and 1982, I was seeing a few of them. In America, I could always pull good crowds on the coasts. But in the 1970s I had grown used to filling venues across the middle of the country, too, and now those audiences seemed to be on the wane. So this needed addressing. If you lose the middle like that, you're in trouble, because then the whole idea of doing a national arena tour becomes unsustainable and you have to go back to theaters—no big productions, no huge stage sets, no massive lighting rigs. And then, perhaps, it's good-bye planes and hello tour buses. Could I have seen myself clambering back on a tour bus at this point in my career? Well, I'm sure I would have done it if I'd had to. But let's just say I'd rather not have had to, if the option were there.

And I loved arena shows. I loved the scale of them, the theatricality of them, the atmosphere at them, the pure show business of them. It was very fashionable at this time, among my peers, to deride stadiums and sports halls as places for rock music, to say they lacked intimacy and were emotionless and had no soul. My argument was the opposite of that. I reckoned that, if they felt cold and soulless, it was because you weren't doing them right—weren't using the theatricality, weren't working hard enough to engage the audience and set the place properly on fire. I would have been gutted not to have been able to play arenas.

From September 1983 I was under new management and ready to roll up my sleeves. Quite literally: the rolled-up, or at any rate pushed-back, jacket sleeve was a big look at this time. Arnold, my new manager, worked up a strategy to try to point my recording career in the right direction; and, to get the touring side back on track, he brought in Randy Phillips, who was previously a music promoter at Stanford University and later the chief executive of AEG Live.

One of Arnold's first moves was to enter into the lengthy period of diplomacy with Jeff Beck's manager that ultimately brokered Jeff's appearance—as mentioned in that earlier chapter—on the track "Infatuation" from the *Camouflage* album, which came out in 1984, and then subsequently on the tour. Those negotiations were only slightly less complicated than developing a peace plan for the Middle East. Jeff, as we know, didn't stick out the tour. But with "Infatuation" I had a bona fide rock hit and a fairly emphatic statement, for anyone who needed one, that my so-called "disco era" was over. *Camouflage* also contained a cover of Jeff Fortgang's "Some Guys Have All the Luck," which I had heard Robert Palmer do, and fancied a stab at, throwing in a little hook from Clarence "Frogman" Henry's "Ain't Got No Home" for good measure, just to keep rhythm and blues fans on their toes. Even if the song hadn't been good, I probably would have had to record it, just so that headline writers could use the title in stories about me.

The rhythm now became two years between albums, rather than one, which seemed a little less reckless and altogether more amenable. So two years separated *Camouflage* from *Every Beat of My Heart* in 1986 (or *The Rod Stewart Album* as it was imaginatively known in America). And the touring recovered. *Every Beat of My Heart* triggered the biggest tour of Europe I had ever done. And then *Out of Order* followed in 1988. I had sat back and left the production of records to others for a little while—mostly laziness on my part, if I'm being honest. Plus those guys were getting paid a lot of money, so why not let them get on with it? But for *Out of Order* I felt rejuvenated enough to get involved in that aspect of the process again. I co-produced it with Andy Taylor and Bernard Edwards. Bernard, of course, was a hero of mine, having been a member of Chic. Andy had been the guitarist in Duran Duran and, more recently, the Power Station. He and I wrote some good stuff together for that album. Actually, we wrote some good stuff apart, too. I remember shuffling off for weekly football practice one Wednesday night, and when I got back a couple of hours later, he had written the music for what became "Lost in You." I added the lyrics.

The producers changed, but otherwise the usual rules applied. The band and I continued to arrive at the studio, at the beginning of an album, completely songless, and worked material up by bouncing ideas off each other in the sound room. And we continued to commence our recording sessions with a statutory stint in the bar next door. Indeed, the Entourage, the bar beside the Record Plant in its former location on West Third Street, became known as Studio E, and we were in there so much that Chris Stone, the owner of the studio, eventually arranged to run a direct phone line between the control room and the bar. Chris then went one step further and constructed a pub for us inside the Record Plant itself, complete with bar stools, a pub piano, and a dartboard. It was called the Dog and Clit. A snifter or two, and then one would adjourn to the control room.

This could easily look, from the outside, like shoddy or even unprofessional behavior. But let me tell you, some of the best work of those days was done in the pub beforehand. Sometimes we would be able to compose entire songs in there, simply by discussing them. "Why don't you do this . . . and then I'll do that . . . and then we'll have a kind of whatsit underneath it . . ." "Forever Young," which was one of the most successful songs I recorded in this period, was composed almost entirely in the Dog and Clit. I had taken the title from the Dylan song, which I wanted to rework, and Jim Cregan, Kevin Savigar, and I talked it all out and then went in the studio and recorded it.

And even then I almost dumped the song before it could get to the album. We were going through the tracks and discussing overdubs, and we got to "Forever Young" and I said, "I'm not happy with this song. Let's bin it." A bit like with "Maggie May," I wasn't sure that it had a strong-enough hook. And suddenly, the engineer, a guy called Steve MacMillan, who had worked in dutiful silence throughout the entire project and had never offered an opinion on anything, ever, piped up and said, "I wouldn't get rid of that if I were you. It's the best song you've got."

A momentary silence fell while we all gaped in amazement at the fact that Steve had actually said something. And then we listened to the track again and realized he was right. I got nominated for a Grammy for the vocal performance on that recording, and it went on to enjoy virtual anthem status in America. Some things you can plan; other things are down to serendipity.

In all, *Out of Order* gave me four big single hits in America and marked, you could say, the completion of something of a turnaround for me in the U.S. In addition, the single "My Heart Can't Tell You No" off that album was a Top 10 hit in the U.K., which was comforting because I seemed to have been getting into a bit of a bat-and-ball situation vis-à-vis the country that raised me. The stuff that worked for American audiences—the harder, rockier stuff—seemed to struggle a bit in Britain; and the stuff that worked for British audiences—the more pop-oriented things like "Sailing," "Baby Jane," "I Don't Want to Talk About It"—seemed to do less well in America. It was something about which Arnold and I had an earnest meeting in London with Rob Dickins, the executive who ran Warner Bros. in the U.K.

I had known Rob for many years. Indeed, as a fledgling record company type, he had once come backstage at *Top of the Pops* when the Faces were on the show. Whereupon I had, allegedly, turned to Ronnie Wood and said, "Who's this cunt?" Tip for young musicians: be polite to people on the way up. One day they may turn out to be the head of your record company.

Rob had a habit of saying what he thought and only later, if at all, wondering whether he might have offended anyone. This has its plentiful downsides, although in an industry crammed full of people telling you what they think you want to hear, it could also be quite revealing. Anyway, on this occasion, Rob's opening remark was "Why did you let Paul Young steal your audience?"

That really pissed me off. Paul Young? For fuck's sake. I mean, nice chap and good voice and everything, but . . .

Rob's argument was that while I was busy in the 1980s making American-produced rock records, I had vacated my rightful role: interpreting songs, taking material and making it my own. And Young—with singles like "Wherever I Lay My Hat" and "Every Time You Go Away"—had moved in. Rob said, "People want to hear you sing great songs."

Pretty truculent by this stage, I simply said, "Well, find me a great song, then."

And then I went away to sulk for a couple of weeks. Paul Young! Fucking hell!

Still, the good thing that came out of this conversation was that in mid-1989 Dickins visited me in Epping, clutching a cassette and a ghetto blaster. He said, "I want you to listen to this," and he played me a song. When it finished he said, "Don't say anything." And then he played it through again. When it finished the second time, he again said, "Don't say anything." And then he played it a third time. By then I was wishing I had written it. And I was bursting to sing it.

The song was Tom Waits's "Downtown Train." It had a melody that connected emotionally and a lyric that absolutely ached with yearning. My son Sean, who was eight at this time, had come into the room during the third playing of the song and said afterwards, "Why was that guy singing so bad?" Which made the point very clearly, really: here was a great, great song, but sung by someone whose voice was always going to be an acquired taste, therefore hindering the song's chance of being a hit. (I love Tom Waits's voice, but it's not for everyone.) I recorded "Downtown Train" with the hugely talented Trevor Horn and, even though the album had technically closed, it was inserted at the very last minute, following some expert lobbying of Warner Bros. in America by Arnold, as a new track for the *Storyteller* compilation—the box set retrospective of my humble career (and still available from all reputable stockists). It gave me a hit—Top 10 in the U.K. and number three in *Billboard*—and it got me on the cover of *Rolling Stone* again. But, more important than any of that, it reminded a few people who I was and what I could do—a few people who, maybe, used to know but had forgotten, or maybe who had chosen to forget and turned away. And it reminded me, too.

Pretty much every aspect of the business I'm in has, at some time or other, and for however short a period, seemed slightly irksome to me. Songwriting, recording, producing, making videos, doing promotion: there have been phases when each of those has, for whatever reason, failed to gladden my heart or come to seem a bit of a chore. That's bound to be the case with any job: you go on and off things, blow a bit hot and cold in certain areas.

Performing, though—never.

Since I had got past the initial nerves and self-consciousness of my rock band apprenticeship in the 1960s, and finally come out from behind the amplifiers, I don't think there had been a single occasion when the thought of getting up and singing in front of an audience, with the band thundering away behind me, hasn't filled me with pure, unadulterated enthusiasm. Accordingly, whatever else was happening to my commitment levels and concentration in the 1980s, my attitude to touring was unwavering. I turned forty in 1985, but, perhaps subconsciously in defiance of that, I was flinging myself into performing with more abandon than ever before, storming about stages like an idiot. I'm often tempted to think it's playing so much football that has turned my knees into the noble ruins currently to be found separating my thighs from my shins, but, looking back at recordings of me throwing myself around in the 1980s, I realize that a lot of the damage has been done by gratuitous knee-sliding across the stages of the world's enormodomes.

Let me stress, too, that my enthusiasm for performing has never had to be artificially stimulated. Between the end of the show and the encores, the crew would have a little reviving sniff of something available for me at the rear of the stage, which, combined with the heady release at the end of a successful night, would send me back onto the stage in a state of enormously enjoyable euphoria. It was like a reward: "Well done. Have a little line." But before a show, I have never needed to take anything to get me up. The prospect of getting out in front of an audience will do that on its own.

Fueling up with cocaine mid-show did seem to be a fairly standard practice among the musicians in my band in this era, although Patrick "Boiler" Logue did his best to complicate the process. A little background, if I may: Boiler had originally joined the crew in the mid-1970s as a guitar technician, in which capacity he quickly revealed himself to be a master of not just guitar management, but unexpected nudity in public places. Guitarists would step into the wings to switch instruments and find their next guitar being held out to them by a completely naked Boiler. And few who witnessed it will ever forget the sight of Boiler emerging from the gents' in a Tokyo cocktail lounge and being given a naked piggyback by Peter Mackay, the tour manager, for the entertainment of the band, who were the only people in the bar when Boiler went into the bathroom but who, as he realized too late, had been subsequently joined by a large party of Japanese businessmen.

When he moved up to stage manager, Boiler's domain inevitably expanded, enabling him to practice nudity more widely across the backstage area and also to put into operation such time-honored pranks as placing peanuts in harmonicas, filling accordions with talcum powder, and taping together the undersides of organ keys so that if one key was depressed, every single note sounded.

But where Boiler really excelled was in devising ways to come between the band members and their drugs. He more than once placed cling film over the lines of cocaine set out offstage for the brass section, so that when they hopped off for a reviving snort they found themselves repeatedly sniffing in frustration at immovable powder. And, classically, in order to test the desperation for a break-time fix of one particular band member, whom we choose not to name and shame (but was actually Carmine Rojas, the bass player), Boiler laid the cocaine out very neatly along the most intimate part of his own anatomy, and then stood waiting in the wings, naked, with the said intimate part extended between thumb and forefinger. A brief standoff ensued, as the musician, between numbers, weighed up the pros and cons, but, as it happened, Carmine was indeed very desperate for his pick-me-up.

The shows in the 1980s got louder and wilder and bigger. On the tour for the *Camouflage* album in January 1985, we headlined at the inaugural Rock in Rio festival in Rio de Janeiro in front of an audience of 200,000 people. You don't often see those sorts of crowds down the Fisherman's Arms in Purley, let me tell you. Rock in Rio was altogether one of the most beautifully organized and extravagantly wild festivals I have ever played at. We had flown in fearing chaos, but we couldn't have been more wrong—at least, not in the way the event was run. A series of giant banners were flying from the buildings on the waterfront: "Welcome, Rod Stewart," "Welcome, Queen." The festival took place in a vast clearing that had been cut into the rain forest. They had three separate stages on train tracks with a points system—which was always going to appeal to me, I guess, given my interest in railways—and these stages were simply shunted off, redressed, and shunted back out again, like clockwork. And the noise that came at you when you walked out in front of that 200,000-strong crowd—just this wave of sound that was almost like a wind: a complete thrill. It sent the hairs up on the back of my neck and on my arms and probably in other places that I didn't have time to check.

Offstage, the hotels were all full of musicians for a week, and scenes of madness inevitably abounded. Queen headlined on the Friday night (I headlined on the Saturday), and Freddie Mercury was to be found wandering about wearing a pair of anatomically correct female breasts. Cocaine was available at roughly fourpence a bucket. The only dark mark on the whole occasion was that, after our second performance, back at the hotel we took on the Go-Go's, Belinda Carlisle's all-girl rock group, in a coke-snorting competition. This was a tactical error which someone, surely, should have been in a position to warn us about. Those girls could snort the lacquer off a table. We lost, heavily.

When the morning came, we thought it would be fun to enjoy the small remaining amount of cocaine down on the beach. Before we did so, I proposed a relay swimming race out to a pile of wood, visible in the middle distance, bobbing on the water. Arnold, my manager, got off to a quick start and reached the target soonest. But he swam back even quicker. It wasn't a pile of wood. In Rio, we discovered, they released the sewage into the water at around 5:45 A.M. From afar came the sound of screaming band members.

Still, at least we had that last line of cocaine to look forward to. It had been entrusted to Tony Brock, the drummer. "Break it out, Tony," we said. Tony reached into the pocket of his shorts—the wet shorts he had just swum in—and produced a small dripping package which had once been our cocaine. Chins hit the floor.

In the other performing landmark of this period, in July 1986, I made my first appearance at Wembley Stadium. Football fans will know what that meant to me. I had dreamed of playing there as a professional and had invaded its pitch as a drunk and euphoric spectator, but now I got to stand at one end of it and look out across 66,000 people with their arms in the air in the pelting rain, and, even allowing for Scotland's momentous victory over the English in 1977, that felt like the best thing that had happened to me in that ground. Or a close second, anyway.

Something else that was lovely about that gig at Wembley: backstage as my special guest, and at the party afterwards, was Sarah, the daughter I had given up for adoption. She had got back in touch with me in 1985, and we met in London for tea, privately, and were able to talk properly and openly, and the terrible awkwardness of that initial meeting in the recording studio in Los Angeles was set aside and we began again. Both of us knew it could never be an ordinary father-daughter relationship. I hadn't brought her up, I hadn't changed her nappy, taken her to school, done homework with her, played sports with her. I wasn't around when she brought her first boyfriend home. Those fatherly bonds aren't there and, try as you might, you can't conjure them from the air. But we have our own bond, which grew still stronger in 2007 after the death of Evelyn, her adoptive mother. And backstage that night in 1986, it felt special to be able to introduce her to people, saying, "This is my eldest daughter."

It was all very well, me being enthusiastic about touring, but the major worry I faced, as the 1980s wore on, was whether my voice continued to share my enthusiasm. Going out on the road for at least six months of every year was my idea of a life well lived, but it was clearly beginning to take its toll on my vocal cords—sensitive enough little things in the first place. And if they rebelled, I genuinely was going to be fucked. But what could I do? The band played so loudly. We kind of prided ourselves on it. The volume at which we played was a badge of honor. And I think this, too, in a way, was the legacy of "Da Ya Think I'm Sexy?" It was like: "We'll show 'em. We're no disco pussies. We're a rock 'n' roll band. A loud, kick-ass rock 'n' roll band." Night after night I was forcing my voice to compete with that volume, and by the end of the show I had very commonly blown my throat out. The next day, I would walk around feeling as though I had been gargling barbed wire. Then it would get to 6:00 P.M., two hours before the next show, and I would realize that I simply didn't have a voice to sing with.

The solution was not a particularly healthy one: I started taking steroids. Prednisone tablets, to be precise. I took them intermittently at first, but by the time the 1980s ended I would be well on my way to developing an addiction to them.

Steroids make you hungry, they keep you awake, they cause your cheeks to bloat . . . but they make you sing like a bird. Good old steroids, then. Except not. Much worse was to come of this in due course.

Meanwhile, my relationship with Kelly played out to its end in a kind of doomed slow motion. The firmness of purpose I seemed to have found on our trip to Spain and the commitment to her that I had declared soon dissolved. While Kelly was pregnant, I began seeing another model. This, clearly, was the behavior of an arsehole. The affair was purely about sex and heading nowhere at all. But I couldn't stop slipping away to see her. Horrible, horrible behavior. She rang the house one day and Kelly, who was then eight months pregnant, answered it. I heard her say, "Couldn't you at least wait until I've had this baby?" Apparently the model said to her, "I'm obviously giving him something you're not." It was all really unpleasant, a mortifying testament to how cock-happy I was in those days. The shame of what I did to Kelly there still haunts me now, to the point where I was reluctant to mention it here.

I think Kelly thought she might have the baby and leave me immediately, but the birth of Ruby in 1987 brought us together again and we did, in fact, have many happy and contented times in the first years of her life. After my divorce from Alana, I was able to return to the house at Carolwood, and Kelly and I divided our time between there and the house in Epping. My family loved Kelly, Kelly loved England, we had a beautiful daughter, and we were blessed materially with everything that we could possibly have wanted.

Yet, for all that, the little demon was at work in my head saying, "Don't settle, don't get tied." Anxiety, the shadow of my previous, mistimed and failed, marriage, the knowledge deep down that again it wasn't right for me and that I wouldn't make it last . . . to Kelly's increasing exasperation and uncertainty, these things made me shy away from marriage.

Unlike, strangely enough, my dear friend Elton John. In 1984, Elton rang me and said, "I've got married, dear. To a woman." To which the only possible response was "What the fuck?" Elton gave an interview to *Rolling Stone* in the 1970s in which he referred to the fact that he might be bisexual, but it was common knowledge among the people around him that he was gay.

He said, "I just thought it was the right thing to do, dear."

I said, "What are you going to do when you have sex?"

He said, "Oh, I'll just tie a couple of lolly sticks around it."

For me, there was no such imaginative willingness to compromise. I seemed to be hell-bent on going down in history as the Last of the Great Philanderers. Kelly found a note in my bag, left there on tour by a one-night stand, saying, "I will never forget the night we had." In circumstances like that, the patience of even the saintliest of women will diminish. Kelly's emotions were always close to the surface, but the bright, unquenchably cheerful girl from the beginning of our relationship was now frequently unhappy, confused, and tearful. Tearful in lifts, tearful in hotel lobbies, tearful in cars and on planes. I had never seen anyone shed so many tears. Eventually, at the start of the summer of 1990, Kelly decided she had done enough crying and left me, taking Ruby with her.

It was another godawful mess. And if I could make a godawful mess of a relationship with someone as genuine as Kelly, then surely the message was clear now, even to me. I wasn't meant to be with anyone permanently. I was a bachelor and always would be. Safer for everyone that way.

A few weeks after Kelly had left, Arnold got a call from Pepsi, wondering if I would be interested in doing a commercial. This wasn't a line of work that especially interested me, although down the years there had been many offers. A company in Holland, for instance, was very keen to have me endorse their condoms. And this was in the days when people could hardly bring themselves to say the word "condom." I can't think for the life of me what they thought the "synergy" between me and their product was. Still, nice to be asked, obviously, though I turned that one down.

I also turned down Cadbury's, who wanted me to advertise

chocolate in the U.K. In the U.S., however, Pampers offered the tidy sum of $2 million to use a blast of "Forever Young" in a commercial for nappies—and that I did accept. But they didn't ask me to appear. They used pictures of cute animals instead, which was probably smart. I look terrible in nappies.

But this Pepsi one was tempting. First, I wouldn't have to sing a jingle, or try to make the word "Pepsi" sound soulful, or anything potentially embarrassing like that. I wouldn't even have to be seen drinking the product and looking delighted. Instead, the idea was for me to record a proper song with Tina Turner: "It Takes Two," the Marvin Gaye and Tammi Terrell Motown number. Then Pepsi would shoot a video of Tina and me performing it, and clips from the video would be used in the commercial. And, likely as not, Tina and I would get a hit single out of it and be able to use the unedited video as promotion.

All of which was very persuasive—although not nearly as persuasive as the clinching part of Pepsi's offer, which was that the video could be shot in the location of our choice. I think they thought I would say Burbank, or maybe, at a push, Anaheim—somewhere conveniently near to them, anyway. In fact, discussions with management took place along the following lines:

> ME: Where do we fancy?
> ARNOLD: Somewhere by the sea?
> ME: In Europe would be nice.
> ARNOLD: What's more beguiling than Cannes at this time of year?

And so it was that, at the beginning of August 1990, I joined Arnold at the Carlton Hotel in Cannes with Don Archell, my on-the-road assistant, and, along for the ride, my great pal of long standing, Ricky Simpson, a very successful hotelier and fellow Celtic supporter.

I was given the penthouse suite, which was monumental. The bathroom had a domed ceiling, much like St. Paul's cathedral—except, of course, with a far better power shower. Furthermore, if you left your pants or socks on the floor, they would magically disappear and then return, clean, in paper and cardboard packaging like presents from the great dry cleaner in the sky. Ricky and I skipped about like schoolboys. We had clearly landed in the bachelor pad to end all bachelor pads. And, accordingly, it appeared to me that it would have been remiss not to use those lavishly appointed facilities in pursuit of the bachelor purposes for which they were so clearly intended.

There duly followed the ten-day period of excess which has gone down in history as the "long hot summer." (Well, that's how Ricky and I took to referring to it.)

Phone calls were made, flights were reserved, cars were booked, and in they came: old flames, new flames, old flings, new flings, women amenable to the prospect of a night in Cannes with a first-class return thrown in. I went through the little black book, as it were, and took my pick. As soon as Arnold got wind of these plans he packed his bags and decamped in horror to the safety of the Hôtel du Cap. Probably wise—although, in my defense, it was all accomplished in a very polished and professional manner. The arrangements had the precision and rigor of a military operation. Don Archell would drive the outgoing girl to Nice Airport, drop her at Departures, then head round to Arrivals to collect the incoming replacement. I reckon the logistics for the 2012 Olympic Games were only marginally more complex than those involved in the smooth running of the "long hot summer."

We did venture from the suite occasionally. I had the video to film, of course—although that was just Tina and me romping around on a stage in a club full of beautiful people, so it wasn't the most taxing of film roles. Tina invited us to see her sing at the Sporting Club in Monte Carlo, too. I liked Tina. We had forged a bond in December 1981 when she had appeared onstage with me at the Los Angeles

Forum, a gig that was shown on closed-circuit television in cinemas around the world and, as a result, was seen by an audience of 60 million people. It had helped refire her career, because of course she became a huge star again in the subsequent years. Obviously, she has that wonderful, brash, larger-than-life bravado, and that huge, concrete-cracking voice, but she turned out to be touchingly timid in the studio. When we recorded "It Takes Two," we got to the end of the song and I was trying to get a call-and-response thing going between us for the fade-out, but it proved really difficult. You'd think she would eat that kind of thing up, but she was very shy about ad-libbing.

Anyway, the afternoon before Tina's show, Ricky and I hit the shops and treated ourselves to new shirts, new suits, new ties, and new shoes, and promptly stepped out of the hotel that evening believing ourselves to look the business. Delivered by limo to Monte Carlo, we announced ourselves proudly at the door as guests of Ms. Turner. Whereupon the doorman said, "Sorry, sir: I'm afraid you are inappropriately dressed." I said, "Really? We thought we looked rather fine." The doorman said, "I'm afraid the rule is black tie." We sheepishly headed off to a restaurant.

Mostly, though, the "long hot summer" trip was Jack the Lad writ large—a slice of rich hedonism. So rich, in fact, that I ended up sickening myself. What's that Woody Allen quote? "Sex without love is an empty experience—but as empty experiences go, it's one of the best." That's undeniably true, let me tell you, from a position of some expertise in this area. Yet in a quiet moment, between the comings and goings, I found myself thinking, "You're a forty-five-year-old man and you're flying in shags. Is this what you now amount to? Is that all you've got?"

I returned to Los Angeles feeling subdued. I felt even more subdued when I learned that Kelly had been seen out and about with someone. That sent a real pang of jealousy through me and caused me to panic. In that terrible way of not wanting something until you can't have it, it brought her loss right home to me. I thought, "Shit, what have I let go?"

I decided to propose to her. That was the obvious solution. It had been the obvious solution all along, only I had been too foolish to see it. But if it was going to work, I was going to need to win her round. I was going to need a big romantic gesture—something she would find charming and irresistible, something that would remind Kelly why she liked me in the first place and would bring her round.

Somebody told me that, on the Sunday of the Labor Day weekend, Kelly was going to be taking a boat trip with her new beau to Catalina, off the California coast. A plan hatched in my brain. I knew, from going to Catalina myself, that little prop planes often buzzed above the beaches, trailing advertisements. What if Kelly were to look up from the deck of her boat and see my marriage proposal written in the sky? Could it get any more sweetly romantic than that?

I got the number of a company that could organize a plane and a banner for me for early Sunday afternoon, which I figured would be the best time to be sure of catching Kelly's attention. I told them I wanted the banner to say: "Kelly—will you marry me? R.S." That would do it, wouldn't it?

Feeling far happier with this plan in place, I went back to the business of my week, which happened to include a night out with Sylvester Stallone, whom I had got to know well and with whom, incidentally, I almost once shared the big screen. (I was asked to appear in the 1981 football movie *Escape to Victory*, but I was touring and couldn't do it. How different the history of cinema could have been.) On the Saturday, as I recall, Sly and I met for dinner and then went on to an LA nightclub called the Roxbury.

And across the floor of the Roxbury, I caught sight of a woman whose face I knew really well. And I couldn't believe she was there, because I had been staring at that face and wondering about that face ever since I had first seen it in a television commercial. And here was that vision from the screen made real. I had to introduce myself to her. And then I had to convene a small party back at my place so that I could invite her along with her friend and get to talk to her properly.

And she did come and we did talk, and when she and her friend went home at the end of the night it seemed blazingly apparent to me that this was the person to whom I wanted to dedicate the rest of my life.

Love at first sight? I don't know. Love at the end of the first evening? Definitely.

I awoke the next morning glowing with excitement. In the midst of the euphoria of it all, it was at least ten minutes before I remembered, with a cold feeling abruptly passing across my kidneys, that I had arranged an airborne marriage proposal for that lunchtime.

No problem. I'll cancel it. I call the advertising company. The phone rings and rings. I hang up and try again. Same thing. Nobody there. It's Sunday. On Labor Day weekend. Everybody has packed up and gone.

This is awkward. I have hired a plane to carry a banner saying "Marry me." I can't very well hire a second plane saying, "Sorry—scratch that. RS." What am I going to do? Pray for a hurricane? Get out there on a boat with a large gun and shoot the fucker down?

No. What I'm going to do is spend Sunday wincing in anticipation and with my fingers crossed.

And what do you know? Come Sunday, my grand, absurd, and doomed marriage proposal went up, fluttered across the sky, and came down again, entirely unseen by its intended recipient. Truly, there is a God.

And just as well for Kelly, who, as it must surely be clear by now, deserved someone far better than me.

DIGRESSION

৶৶

A brief digression in the course of which our hero, among other things, steals a car, has an affair with a performance artiste, and gets into a fight in a bar, but only finds out about it later.

IN THE NOW-FAMOUS WORDS of Kelly Emberg, "Who do you think you are—Rod Stewart?"

Yes, I did think that and continue to do so. But I'm not the only one. It turns out that quite a lot of people think they're me. Or, if they don't actually think it, they are happy to pretend to be me. You would be surprised about some of the places I show up. And you would be equally surprised about some of the things I get up to when I'm there. *I* certainly am.

For instance, in the summer of 2012, Arnold got a call from a journalist on the *Chattanooga Times Free Press* asking him for some clarifying detail on a number of sightings of me over a twelve-hour period in the Chattanooga area, where I had been happily signing autographs, chatting in a hotel lift, and posing for photographs with local well-wishers. Arnold had to concede that it was, indeed, a bit of a scoop for the paper, given that I was in the countryside just outside London at the time.

The article duly ran, under the headline "Rod Stewart Lookalike Dupes Chattanooga." Quite right, too. "Rod Stewart Signs Autograph in Chattanooga": not much of a story. "Bloke Passing Himself Off as Rod Stewart Signs Autograph in Chattanooga": that's a story. Apparently, people were convinced in particular by the "white Capezio shoes." Twenty-five years ago, maybe. "I shook his hand, I bought him another beer," said the owner of a café. So he did. And, at the same time, so he didn't.

It seems that it's not too hard to convince people that you are Rod Stewart. Get the hair and the nose right, and you're well on the way. There were perhaps a few early stirrings of this kind of thing way back in the days of Steampacket, in the mid-1960s, at the start of my career, when Brian Auger would go around a club at showtime, rounding up the band, and would regularly come up behind me in the bar and tap me on the shoulder and say, "Come on, Rod, we've got to go on," only to find it wasn't me at all, but some bloke with my haircut.

So I don't suppose I should have been too surprised, many years later, when a sheriff rang Arnold from somewhere in a back bayou of Louisiana and solemnly announced, "Sir, I'm sorry to inform you, but we are holding your client in a cell following a drunken brawl in a bar." Arnold empathized, saying, "That's appalling. But also surprising. Because he's sitting right across from me in my office."

And then there was the Rod Stewart who was so convincing in and around Manhattan that he pulled the wool over the eyes of Jann Wenner, the esteemed creator and publisher of *Rolling Stone*, and certainly a man who knew me well.

In 1985, Jann called Arnold and said, "I am totally insulted. My wife and I were just coming out of the Plaza Hotel, and standing right in front of us was Rod Stewart. And I said, 'Hello, Rod,' and he completely froze me out and walked off. I don't understand. Have I offended him?"

Arnold's explanation of my actual whereabouts at the moment of this supposed callous insult—California—failed to satisfy Jann.

"Arnold, come on. I know Rod Stewart's face when I see it."

In the end, to convince him that I was indeed a long way from the Plaza Hotel, Arnold eventually got Jann to call me at the studio in Burbank where I was recording, and I was able to set his mind at ease.

This seems to have been the same highly plausible guy, incidentally, who almost managed to land himself a Ferrari in New York by pretending that he was me. He had driven it out of the showroom before someone thought to run one final check. The impostor was picked up eventually by the police after committing a traffic violation. Apparently, his English accent was perfect. Hats off to him for nerve, though. Using your resemblance to a well-known singer to knock off a supercar is taking the notion of a tribute act to a whole new level.

And let's not forget the cabaret singer and performance artiste who called Arnold to see if he would be coming to the concert of her song stylings for which engraved invitations had been sent out under my name. Arnold was, naturally, keen to learn a little more. The singer/artiste lowered her voice slightly and told Arnold that she thought he ought to know that, for the last five months, she had been having a series of secret and passionate liaisons with his client in her New York apartment, for which I would fly in very much on the QT.

Arnold asked, "What does he look like?"

"Rod Stewart, of course," said the singer/artiste, slightly impatiently.

"So, how tall is Rod Stewart?" inquired Arnold.

She said, "He's five foot eight."

Arnold said, "Well, he seems to be losing three of his best inches on the plane ride over, because the last time I looked, my client was five foot eleven."

The singer/artiste was still adamant. "But he sings to me. He serenades me in bed."

Arnold said, "What does he sing?"

She replied, "He hums the theme from the film *Romeo and Juliet*."

And with that single detail the guy was busted. When it comes to humming during moments of intimacy in the boudoir, I'm much more of a Beethoven's Fifth man, myself.

Get it right next time.

CHAPTER 16

In which our hero loves, loses, and gets his heart broken.
With incidental thoughts on sore throats, drinking deeply
from the back of Ronnie Wood's car, and amusing an
audience the size of Switzerland on a beach in Brazil.

first set eyes on Rachel Hunter in a commercial she made for a fitness video, *Sports Illustrated's Super Shape-Up*. The advertisement was being heavily rotated on U.S. television in the summer of 1990, and if it's possible to become addicted to a two-minute infomercial with a synth-driven backing track, then I was an addict. Life had to stop whenever it came on. The ad also starred Elle Macpherson and Cheryl Tiegs, but the one who caught my attention was the girl in the metallic Lycra with the gorgeous shock of curls who preached the virtues of "body-sculpting," which, the voice-over suggested, was a good way to "tighten up those frustrating areas that won't go away." I thought I had seen a goddess.

I was watching this commercial one day, for the umpteenth time, suffused with a romantic, heart-struck glow and musing wistfully on the wonders of love and all its glories, when Malcolm, my assistant, came and stood beside me. When the ad had finished, and Rachel Hunter had promised "eight weeks to a better body," Malcolm made the following glittering utterance: "I'd rather be in that than the army."

Extraordinary to think that from these unpromising stirrings grew a romance that redefined the term "whirlwind," an eight-year marriage and a separation that left me as emotionally broken as I have ever been.

Coming across Rachel in the Roxbury Club that Saturday night was a sensational fluke: my video dream made flesh. I had that weird, double-take feeling: "It's *her*. Off the telly." I could hardly just let the moment go. So, smoothing my jacket, checking the knot on my tie, and gathering all the immense quantities of suavity in my possession, I went across to her and . . . did the naffest thing I could possibly have done at this moment, which was to mime one of her area-tightening exercises from the video.

What was I playing at? Why didn't I just calm down and use my usual icebreaker in these circumstances? I had long ago discovered that if you wanted to open a conversation with a woman in a club, you simply had to go up to her and say, in your best cockney accent, in a tone of genuine curiosity, "Hello, darlin'—what you got in that hand-bag?" Or you could try the slightly more colorful variation, "Hello, darlin'—what you got in that basket?" It worked for me every time—and never better, indeed, than when the woman in question hadn't actually got a handbag/basket.

On this occasion, though, reason deserted me and I mimed. When I had finished miming, Rachel attempted a sympathetic smile as a cold wind whistled and a ball of tumbleweed blew through the club. But at least she didn't turn away. She was with a girlfriend. I told them I was having a little gathering at my place at the end of the evening, if they fancied coming along, and I gave them the address on Carolwood Drive, hoping but hardly expecting to see them.

And I nearly didn't see them. Her friend drove up and down, failing to find the house. She was about to give up when they spotted it. A few of my friends had come back from the Roxbury for a few more drinks, including my pal Ricky Simpson and Teri Copley, the television actress and *Playboy* model, with whom I had spent the evening chatting warmly but whom I now, rather shamefully, dropped like a hot brick. Coming through the front door, Rachel tripped and went sliding across the slippery hall floor—her grand entrance. So now at least we had both embarrassed ourselves.

There was a connection straightaway. She was extremely beautiful, it goes without saying, but there was something very no-nonsense about her as well. It was there in her New Zealand accent, but also in her face, which was at once very open and yet, you felt, not the face of someone who was likely to be taken for a fool. She was smart—as far removed as could be from the stereotype of the flaky model. And she already had money and fame, so she had no need to attach herself to somebody to achieve those things. That was a relief for me, because in my position that suspicion was always there: Does this person really like me, the way they seem to, or does this person just like the stuff that surrounds me?

And there was a naïveté about her, too—but why wouldn't there have been? She was just shy of her twenty-first birthday. I was forty-five. There were nearly twenty-five years between us—but that calculation is irrelevant, much though people on the outside of our relationship liked to get hung up on it. It wasn't that she was too young *for me*. She was, quite simply, too young: too young to get married, too young to become caught up in another person's life, which is what happened. Christ, she had barely lived. But I didn't see it. I just sailed on.

That evening at Carolwood, I believe that alcohol was consumed—

certainly by me—and that dancing of a largely ridiculous nature took place. I believe that I showed Rachel around the house. I believe that in particular I showed her the dogs, the three Border collies I had at this time, who lived outside and whom she was keen to see. I believe that, in a moment of high spirits, the pair of us ended up chasing through the house, pursued by the dogs. I never used to let the dogs into the nice bits of the house, because they destroyed things. That evening, I clearly didn't care. I really *must* have been in love.

She flew back to New York the morning after our first date. I sent two dozen red roses to her agency. Then I flew to New York, on no pretext at all, so that I could see her again. I called her up and invited her to dinner. We met at the Peninsula Hotel in Los Angeles, where I had taken a room. She wore a stunning white dress. I held doors open, escorted her into the restaurant, helped her with her seat, as a proper gentleman should. Over dinner, we didn't so much talk as gabble, covering a lot of ground in a big hurry. We were falling very fast.

But not that fast. Later that night, back at the hotel, Rachel came to bed in a T-shirt down to her ankles—a T-shirt that said, "Not tonight, thank you" as efficiently as if she had come clanking out of the bathroom in a deep-sea diving outfit. A bit of a shame, of course. But a good sign, I knew. A sign that maybe we were at the beginning of something serious.

I don't know about eight weeks to a better body, but we were five weeks to an engagement and three months to a wedding—startling even some of my closest friends, who knew and loved Rachel and saw how deeply I had fallen for her, but clearly thought we should go more slowly and were quite willing to say so. But love won't listen to objections. I thought they were wrong and I was right, as simple as that.

The morning after our first date, I said, "Let's go steady." She said, "OK, then." She had a modeling job at the end of that week in Fort Lauderdale. I flew down on the Thursday to be with her. Sunday was September 9: Rachel's birthday. We made a plan to go back to New

York and celebrate lavishly—both her big day and our new relationship. And maybe (if I was lucky) have sex, which we hadn't got around to yet. Not that I was desperate or anything.

The celebrations didn't happen. Late in the afternoon of Rachel's birthday, I got a call in New York from my sister Mary. She said, "Roddy, Dad's died."

I had spoken to him on the phone that lunchtime, New York time. We had talked about the Scottish and English football results. And apparently, not long after that, he said he felt tired and went upstairs to bed and was gone. He was eighty-six.

I don't need to say how much his death crushed me. I wept, and Rachel held me. And it was an extraordinary situation all around because here I was, full of new love and now in mourning. I think one refers to this as "mixed emotions." But Rachel was amazing, full of comfort and support. Suddenly it wasn't me who was the senior half of the relationship, it was her. She took control and helped me through.

We flew back to London for the funeral—me, Rachel, and Ricky Simpson, who knew my dad well. Rachel stayed behind in Epping while I went to the service. She had never met him, of course—and that was a huge additional sadness to me, that Dad hadn't seen me with the person with whom I thought I would be happy and settled for life, that he hadn't finally seen me come good and make a go of it. But Rachel also didn't come to the funeral because we knew how much the press would have made a distraction out of her being there.

As it was, the day was about Dad. There was a funeral procession to Highgate Cemetery. My brothers and sister and I organized a floral tribute in the shape of a football pitch. Gordon Strachan and Kenny Dalglish and a host of other footballers sent flowers and the respects of Scottish football. A Highland piper led the hearse and people stood still in the streets, as if all of Highgate had stopped to watch Bob Stewart set off down Muswell Hill Broadway for the last time.

We worried most of all about how my mum would be after this.

She was finding the world to be a very confusing place by then. But in fact she was fine. She seemed to assume, for the most part, that Dad had just popped up to the bookie's.

Is there a bookie's in heaven? I'll know where to find Dad if there is.

My dad's death may have had the effect of speeding things up even further between Rachel and me. After the funeral, we flew back from London to New York, I helped Rachel pack up her apartment, and then we flew back to Los Angeles and she moved into Carolwood so that we could live together.

Almost immediately, though, she had a modeling commitment to fulfill: another shoot for *Sports Illustrated* with Elle Macpherson, in Puerto Rico. The job meant she would be away for three weeks while I was recording in LA. It was an agonizing prospect for both of us. But work was work. Still, there was always the phone. We were virtually never off it for those weeks. I guess that was really the period when we found out about each other properly, talking for hours—about our lives, our families, stupid stuff and serious stuff, nothing and everything. Rachel's phone bill at the end of the three-week trip was $10,000.

When Rachel's job had finished, I took a Learjet down to Puerto Rico to collect her, and then we took the plane on to Nassau in the Bahamas, where I had chartered a boat for the weekend. The plane hit some turbulence on the way, but we agreed that we were so happy that if we fell out of the sky and died, right there and then, we wouldn't care.

That night, on the boat, our relationship was consummated. As a gentleman, I must insist upon my right to draw a gauzy veil over those proceedings. I can tell you, though, that as dawn's rosy fingers began to illuminate our lovers' bower, both of us found our attention drawn to an unsettling sight: a long brown stain, midway down the bed sheet. There was, for both of us, a period of flustered self-examination: "Surely I haven't . . . surely we didn't . . ."

Closer investigation revealed the mark to be the remains of a complimentary chocolate, left on the pillow but brushed aside unseen in the haste of our passion.

Back in Los Angeles, I proposed to Rachel during a picnic in a park. And on December 15, 1990, a little over three months since I had mimed to her at the Roxbury nightclub, we were married. The service was at the Presbyterian Church in Beverly Hills. My brother Don was best man. The ushers were mostly my football mates from the Exiles, and I got them to wear sunglasses and carry white canes, so that, as they showed the guests to their seats, they would be performing an impression of the blind leading the blind. When Rachel arrived at the altar she performed the wonderfully romantic gesture of giving me a thick, thumb-and-forefinger pinch on the bum. As we left the chapel, kilted pipers played "Scotland the Brave."

And afterwards, the guests were invited to what the embossed invitations explicitly declared to be a "piss-up" in the Four Seasons Hotel. On the seating plan for the reception, the tables were given names of football teams. The wedding feast was roast New Zealand lamb with mint sauce, roast potatoes, and sprouts. The cake was in the shape of the Houses of Parliament with a three-foot-tall Big Ben and a kiwi fruit on the roof. Long John Baldry came, and Ian McLagan. Ronnie Wood couldn't make it, unfortunately, because he was recuperating after his latest car crash. (Woody's ability to wipe cars the length of walls is almost without equal in the Western world.) And when it was time for the groom's speech, I stood up and told the room, with feeling: "I'm as happy as a dog with two dicks."

Unbeknown to me, my sister Mary had sat at the table that day and confided in the person sitting next to her: "That girl will break his heart one day." Not just yet, though. In concert at Wembley Stadium on June 15, 1991, I proudly told the crowd that I had been married to Rachel for six months. "What's that?" said my mum, from her wheelchair. Someone repeated what I had said. My mum thought about it for a moment, and then asked, "Does Rachel know this?"

I think she did. Rachel had a favorite saying in those days: "The past is the past. The future is what we've got together."

A lso attending my wedding to Rachel was Rob Dickins, the head of Warner Bros. in England, who had hooked me up with the song "Downtown Train." I told him to bring some more songs with him when he came. I figured that if he was coming all this way to drink my wine and eat my roast lamb and sprouts, I might as well get something out of it.

A couple of days before the ceremony, Rob was in a car with Arnold and he put on a tape—though only after a lengthy and apologetic preamble which sounded like it didn't bode all that well. He said to Arnold, "I'm worried that you'll think I'm taking the piss." The song he was about to play, Rob explained, was one that he had been sitting on for about seven years. Its writers, Marc Jordan and John Capek, wanted him to push it to me, but he had never had the nerve. The song sounded so like me, Rob reckoned, that I would think it was a parody.

Arnold listened to it once and called me from the car.

"We have to get together immediately. Rob just played me a song that I know is a worldwide hit for you."

I had the wedding rehearsal to do, and after that I went to Arnold's house.

Rob was still sounding less than confident. "Don't hate me for this," he said.

Arnold said, "Stop with all the disclaimers and play it. It's a total fucking smash."

The song was "Rhythm of My Heart" and I absolutely adored it. Parody, my arse. It was a big old anthemic lump of Scotland complete with skirling bagpipes, a timeless tale of a warrior far from home— and so clever, the way it took "Bonnie Banks o'Loch Lomond" ('Ye'll take the high road and I'll take the low road," etc.) and made something new out of it. (Connoisseurs of traditional Scottish song will cotton on at once to the matching rhythms of the lyrics, "On the bonnie, bonnie banks of Loch Lomond" becoming "Where the ocean meets the sky I'll be sailing.")

I recorded the song with Trevor Horn and made it the opening track and first single off my next album, *Vagabond Heart*, which came out in March 1991. (There was a quiet tribute to my dad in that title, originated by my brother Don: Dad's old football team was called the Vagabonds.) The recording is remarkable for involving almost certainly the motliest choir of backing vocalists ever assembled under my banner, including Arnold; Lionel Conway, the fabled manager of the Exiles; and Garry Cook, another former Exile and the future chief executive of Manchester City F.C. Even despite this impediment, the song went to number three in the U.K. charts and to number five in America. The single was also a monster in Germany—the biggest hit I had ever had there, staying on the chart for about forty weeks. All in all, everything was set fair for the massive, yearlong *Vagabond* tour, which set off after it. Yet trouble awaited.

What I remember most vividly is being in the kitchen at 507 Archway Road and talking to my mum. In fact, I was onstage in front of several thousand people in Sheffield. But that's hallucinations for you. You never know where you are with them.

The date was June 5, 1991, deep into the European leg of the *Vagabond* tour, and I was about to pay a grisly price for trying to keep my career on the road by taking steroids.

As the 1980s wore into the 1990s, I had been facing an increasing struggle with my voice. The pounding my throat was taking over six- and seven-month tours, straining to be heard above one of the most inconsiderately loud bands in show business, was beginning to piss it off and it had started to react accordingly. Some nights I was a pale and scratchy imitation of myself. Sometimes I was trimming two or three numbers out of the set in order to get to the other end—which I hated doing, because it felt like short-changing people. Other nights, I had nothing there to sing with at all and shows had to be wiped out completely. And that I hated most of all.

There's no such thing as a good cancellation. But the worst cancellation is one where the audience is already in the house. That just feels like an unpardonable waste of people's time. Imagine the embarrassment of canceling dinner with someone who is already at the restaurant. Then imagine multiplying that embarrassment by 12,000. Or more. I canceled at the Toronto SkyDome with the audience already in, and it proved to be a very successful way to piss off 25,000 people in one go. And it happened at an 18,000-capacity outdoor arena in Berlin, where bottles duly flew from the hands of disgruntled customers and the riot police had to be called. The crew, working at the sound desk out in the middle of the arena, had to take the precaution of removing their tour laminates to avoid getting a recriminatory thumping. Mortifying times.

Germany seemed to cop the worst of it, for some reason. We canceled the same velodrome in Cologne five times during this period. On one of those occasions, we tried to loop back and do a rearranged show in a gymnasium just outside the city, by way of compensation. This, we thought, would at least show willingness and reduce some disappointment. The tour had crossed to England, as scheduled, and then planes were chartered out of Luton to fly the gear back over to Germany again and set it all up in the second venue—and then, again, I had no voice and we canceled. The people of Cologne must have begun to think it was personal. I would like to state here that it genuinely wasn't.

It got to the point at the beginning of the 1990s where I was virtually uninsurable. Lloyd's of London had paid out so many times on shows that didn't happen that they simply weren't going to take the risk anymore. And if they didn't insure me, the cost of canceling a show was going to come right out of my pocket: the trucks, the crew, the buses, the flights. A stadium rock 'n' roll show is not an inexpensive venture. Steroids, as prescribed by a doctor, seemed more and more attractive.

Very quickly my voice problems became a psychological condition as well as a physical one. We singers are paranoid about our voices on the best of days—worried about the temperature in rooms, worried about air-conditioning, worried about pollen and humidity levels. I would start anticipating the problem even before it arose. In the afternoon of a show, I'd feel a little tickle at the back of my throat and think, "Fuck, what's that?" And then I would take a steroid just in case. It reached the stage where I was almost as dependent on the steroids mentally as I was physically.

By the time the *Vagabond* tour rolled out, in Aberdeen in March 1991, I had graduated from prednisone tablets to a cocktail of drugs in a syringe which I would take with me to inject before a show— normally in my hand. The cocktail was a mix of an antibiotic, a steroid, and vitamin B. It would bring down any inflammation—or, at any rate, numb the effect of any inflammation. My throat could feel like I had removed its lining and used it to scour frying pans, but the cocktail would get me up and out there.

Of course, all this was at some cost to my mood. Steroids mess with your temper. I grew aggressive and impatient—quick to snap at people when things didn't go smoothly. Some might have thought it was just typical diva behavior, and up to a point they might have been right. But it definitely had a new steroidal edge.

Also, I began to fatten up. Steroids will do that for you, too, and not just because you're so steamingly hungry all the time: you retain fluids and your cheeks go all hamsterlike on you. There comes an alarming moment when you look in the mirror and the line of your jaw has gone. Inevitably there were comments in the press about how I was putting on weight. Some expert observers attributed it to middle-age spread, others to the contentment of newly married life. Both were wrong, but I could hardly come out and explain what was happening. It would have been career suicide. "Don't worry, everyone—keep buying the tickets. I'll probably be there because these steroids work great!"

And then came Sheffield and the night of the hallucinations. Five hours before the show, my throat was painful and my voice almost nonexistent. I injected the steroid cocktail. Three hours before the show, there was almost no improvement. I was in a state of desperation: now even the cocktail didn't seem to be working. I took cortisone tablets on top of the cocktail. Cortisone should really only have been taken on a full stomach. My stomach was empty. While I was onstage my stomach lining ruptured and I spent the show quietly bleeding internally.

I closed my eyes to sing, and when I opened them it wasn't Sheffield anymore, it was the old kitchen in my birthplace at Archway Road and my mum was over by the sink. I closed my eyes again, and suddenly the Sheffield audience swung back—but the Sheffield audience seen through a goldfish bowl. The room seemed to be folding in on me. I was clinging on to the microphone stand to prevent my legs giving way underneath me. I clung on and sang.

I don't really remember getting offstage. The next thing I knew, I was bundled up in the limo and heading away from the confused audience in the arena, and the insurance company's doctor was tending to me. This doctor's specialty was actually proctology—a fact which incensed an increasingly concerned Rachel when she found out about it. "What the fuck is an arse doctor doing looking after my husband's fucking throat?" As we drove through the night back to Essex, the "arse doctor" administered a blood transfusion in the back of the car.

The following morning I felt much better, but I was told that I needed another transfusion. At the clinic, it was recommended that I remain on a bed for twelve hours while the fluid went into my system, but I decided I could lie around with a tube in my arm just as well at home, so, still under the supervision of the "arse doctor," I was driven back to Epping, attached to the necessary plasma pack.

At home I discovered, to my intense amusement, that I could support the plasma pack on the tip of a pool cue. I walked around the house like this for a while, until the joke wore thin. Actually, it had never worn that thick on Rachel in particular. But I thought it was funny.

When it got to lunchtime, I sat in the kitchen while Rachel cooked steaks (highly recommended as sustenance while having a blood transfusion at home). Much to Rachel's consternation, the "arse doctor" announced that he was going to pop out for an hour and get himself something to eat at the pub.

"But what do I do if there's an air bubble?" asked Rachel, pointing to the tube in my arm.

As he left, the doctor smiled and said, "Trust me, there's not going to be an air bubble."

Rachel returned to the steaks—but rather more distractedly now, convinced in her mind that at any second, on her watch, I would die. Lo and behold, exactly as she feared, no sooner had the doctor's car pulled away than Rachel was confronted by a nightmare vision: the sight of an air bubble departing the plasma pack and setting off down the tube in the direction of her husband's arm.

There was no air bubble, I am as good as 100 percent sure of that. But Rachel had convinced herself that there was. And, having convinced herself, she had no option, really, but to take the necessary drastic action. I am thus in the fairly unusual position of being able to report that, when someone, screaming loudly, grabs hold of a plastic tube that is attached to you by a needle and a plaster, and unsentimentally rips it right out of your arm, it hurts like a bastard.

The quickly resummoned proctologist returned to a scene of carnage: blood from the plasma pack all over the floor, a woman in a state of tearful panic, and, worst of all, overcooked steaks, uneaten, in a pan. Me? I was actually laughing hysterically. After the stinging pain had died down, I seemed to find the whole thing fantastically funny. But that could have been light-headedness, as a result of the blood loss.

In the longer term, it was clear that a blood transfusion alone—even successfully administered, in an appropriate location, with a compliant patient and no paranoid wife pulling the tube out—wasn't going to save my career as a performer. And neither were steroids. Fortunately for me, technology intervened.

Even before the nasty debacle in Sheffield, Lars Brogaard, who has been the sound engineer on my live shows for many years, had talked to me about getting hold of some in-ear monitors. Nowadays these little waxy earpieces are a completely familiar sight in the ears of popular entertainers all over the world. In 1991, though, the idea of feeding the onstage sound back to the performer through an earpiece was entirely new. We were all still using a system which had been in place practically since Roman times: a line of speaker wedges along the front of the stage, directing a mix of the sound back at you so that, with any luck, you could hear what was going on and join in. But the mix was always a bugger to get right and the system was inherently loud and very often I was singing to make myself heard above the racket and doing myself a mischief.

Lars promised me that in-ear monitors could make all the

difference, and I agreed to give them a try. Near the end of April 1991, Lars and I flew back between dates in Germany to go to a specialist on Harley Street in London and have some impressions made of my ears. A few days later we had a set of perfectly tailored earpieces to attach to a receiver which could go in my back pocket and through which a mix could be played that (a) might not blow my head off, and (b) might not cause me to blow my voice out.

The problem was that the tour was under way, so there was no time to rehearse with them. Eventually I agreed to shove the plugs in my ears experimentally near the end of a show in Munich. But it felt all wrong to me—like I had just dropped to the bottom of a swimming pool—and I took them out almost immediately. Gradually, though, I weaned myself onto them. The effect was transformative. It smoothed the whole process out. I wasn't having to push my voice uphill like a boulder anymore. For the next tour, we switched the whole band over to them.

The system also had the advantage of getting rid of all those ugly lumps of speaker, excitingly opening up the lip of the stage as an area for further prancing about: an exciting expansion of the workplace. And stage sets immediately looked a lot prettier with all that unwanted furniture out of the way.

Thus my voice managed to recover and the cancellations tapered off. It's no exaggeration to say that I owe my career to the invention of the in-ear monitor. Without it, I would have been finished as a live performer twenty years ago—probably after one final, tragic gig in a three-quarters-empty sports hall in Cologne, babbling incoherently to a vision of my mum in her kitchen.

In the eight years that I was with Rachel, I was entirely faithful to her. This was unprecedented for me and, given my form, I don't think you would have found too many people prepared to put money on that outcome at the beginning. Yet it wasn't difficult. It wasn't even conscious. I had no desire to wander. Rachel was everything I wanted and I went from Lord of the Philanderers to devoted husband over-night. But maybe that was the point: I just needed to find the right person. And that person, I fully believed, was Rachel. As I felt confident enough to announce to the press, very early on in the relationship: "I've put my last banana in the fruit bowl."

I was so happy, I even went riding. Rachel loved horses. I barely knew one end from the other, but I agreed to ride with her one day. And, of course, I wasn't just going to jump up there in a pair of jeans and a T-shirt. I needed to dress the part. Accordingly, I emerged from the house that fine morning in jodhpurs, well-shined boots, a fancy waistcoat, and an immaculate red jacket. As I stiffly guided my horse down a lane in Epping Forest, a photographer emerged from a bush and started snapping. The embarrassment of it. And also the annoyance. I went into full "Git orf my land!" mode. "This is private property!" I shouted, although, in fact, it was a public right of way. Pictures duly ran in the papers, which made me nearly as regretful as I was in the wake of the fabled boater shot on the cover of *A Night on the Town*. Rachel, of course, found the whole incident hysterical.

My happiness only expanded with the birth of our daughter, the beautiful Renee, born at the Portland Hospital in London in June 1992. Again, I played an important role in the birthing process: mostly rushing about in a hospital gown saying, "It's all going to be fine." Rachel was only twenty-two; so young to be a mother. I have a photo of her leaving hospital with Renee in her arms and a look of pure terror on her face. For three weeks after, there were a lot of postnatal tears. We would go for walks around the lake in Epping, with Rachel saying, "What if I can't do it? And what if I'm a terrible mother? And what if she gets to twenty-one and she's a crack addict?"

I would tell her, "Rachel, it's fine. You're going to be a great mother. Of course you are." I was so right.

Just over two years later, we had a wonderful son, Liam, to add to our daughter, and now, when I toured, we went as a family, lifting our sleeping children in and out of arenas and onto planes, and carrying them gently through hotel lobbies.

What also made me happy was dining at home together. I loved us to dine formally, at eight, and to dress up for it. I loved it especially because when I was on the road, so much of my life was chaos, and this represented order. Rachel and I would go upstairs to our separate dressing rooms and then meet on the landing in our evening attire, pause to appreciate each other's outfit, and descend the stairs together.

I had no idea, until afterwards, when we talked about the reasons why it ended, how oppressive Rachel found this, how swallowed up she felt, how much she wished she could have been in her jeans, eating poached eggs on toast, like girls in their twenties do.

MTV had always been a good thing, as far as my career was concerned. On the world's first nonstop music channel's first day on air, August 1, 1981, "She Won't Dance with Me" was the third video to be played. (The first was "Video Killed the Radio Star" by the Buggles, and the second was Pat Benatar's "You Better Run.") What this meant was that, within fifteen minutes of the channel's launch, viewers had been subjected to the sight of me shaking my arse in the rough direction of Jim Cregan, and then bouncing and strutting like a loon around a headache-inducing black and white polka-dot set.

Eleven videos later, they played "Sailing," making me the first artist to be on MTV more than once. Nine videos later, "Da Ya Think I'm Sexy?" was called off the bench for a run-out; ten more videos after that, "Passion" got the nod; twelve more and it was "Ain't Love a Bitch" . . . and on it went. Sixteen videos on day one. As Mark Goodman, the MTV VJ, later so movingly put it: "We played Rod Stewart up the wazoo."

Furthermore, when MTV launched their inaugural Video Music Awards in 1984, Ronnie Wood and I were the opening act on the show, at Radio City Music Hall, and were then given the honor of presenting a lifetime achievement award to Quincy Jones. Alas, somewhere between our performance and the presentation, we imbibed a little freely in the greenroom, and returned to do the honors wearing a lampshade (me) and carrying an ironing board (Woody). I'm not sure that this was felt to have achieved the aimed-for solemnity.

But I had cause to be most grateful for the largesse of MTV in 1993 when the station invited me to do one of its *Unplugged* shows. This was the format which—counterintuitively for the original home of the wall-to-wall video—invited artists to play pared-down, acoustic-instrument-only sets in front of a small audience in a simple, unadorned studio. Eric Clapton and Paul McCartney had already appeared and released albums of their performances, and now it was my turn.

It was a nerve-wracking prospect. Quite apart from following Clapton and McCartney, there was a lot of pressure to get it right, and the format was very exposing: you make a mistake in that setting, and your mistake is going to get heard. Also, traditions of the show dictated that all musicians remain seated for the duration, an aspect I thought I was going to have trouble with. What? No running around? No slinging the microphone stand? No knee-slides? Over the course of a two-hour stage show, I commonly expect to lose in excess of four pounds in weight through sweat and exertion. A seat was going to feel like a straitjacket to me.

In January 1993, I convened a band at a studio in Los Angeles for three weeks of rehearsals. It was a bit of an old-school reunion, and also a merging of the troops: Ronnie Wood came and sat in; and Kevin Savigar and Jim "the Somerset Segovia" Cregan from the early solo bands were there, with Chuck Kentis, Jeff Golub, and Carmine

Rojas from the later lineups. The first thing to notice was how many of us, with the slow but inexorable march of time, now seemed to need glasses: me, Woody, Jim, Carmine . . . There were spectacles all over the stage.

Woody had arrived in a four-by-four, and his first move was to invite everyone out to the car park to have a look in its trunk. He flung open the lid, and inside was what basically amounted to a mobile pub: coolers containing beers, spirits, and fine wines from all corners of the globe. We were, Woody insisted, free to nip out and help ourselves at any point. So that set the tone for the rehearsals that followed.

And, of course, the trip from electric to acoustic was, for some of my old songs ("Every Picture Tells a Story," "Mandolin Wind," "Maggie May"), a short journey to travel; merely a journey back to their roots, in fact. It was apparent very quickly that the combination of these songs, in this format, with these musicians, was going to produce something special.

We recorded the show on February 5 at Universal Music Studios. The audience was so close—intimidatingly close, like a pub audience. And in the round, too, so there was absolutely no chance of escape. In the event, even confined to a seat, I still managed to kick my legs up and swivel about as much as possible and occasionally lean to one side to put Woody off. But between the monkeying around and the banter between numbers, the show seemed to gather a real momentum, and I found myself right back in these songs and connecting emotionally with them to a depth I hadn't experienced for years.

Indeed, the performance ended up totally taking me over. On the last day of rehearsal, literally the day before the show, to general, muttered alarm from the band, I had decided to throw in "Have I Told You Lately," the Van Morrison ballad which I had recorded in 1991 for *Vagabond Heart*. And when we got to the end of that song on the night, I found myself thinking of Rachel, and Renee, just shy of eight months old, and I made a cradling motion with my arms and found that I had moved myself to tears.

When I watched the show back afterwards, I realized that I had just delivered probably the best set of vocal performances of my career. And what was heartening for me about this experience was its demonstration that, if you stripped it all back, and took away the noise and the show business and the fooling around, this was what I had: a voice that could carry a song. And if the truth be known, as an artist, that was all I had been trying to prove about myself from the very beginning.

The recordings were released as *unplugged . . . and seated*, Arnold having deftly crossed the diplomatic minefield surrounding MTV's *Unplugged* branding in order to secure the use of the lowercase lettering and the addition of the reference to my out-of-character containment in the chair. I hadn't had an album do so well in America since *Blondes Have More Fun* in 1978. We toured the show through 1993 and on into 1994, and then, on New Year's Eve that year, it was back to Rio de Janeiro for a one-off show.

No Go-Go's this time and no swimming in sewage-infested waters. No audience of 200,000, either. This time there were 3.5 million people there.

That night held the Guinness World Record for the largest audience attending a concert. The scale of it was unfeasibly huge. When the crew went to check the sound system—big clumps of PA speakers distributed every hundred yards or so along the shoreline—they had to use a taxi.

And before the show? I had the shits. Not out of fear, though. I had the shits because of something I had eaten. We were supposed to go on at midnight, and at 10:30 P.M. I still couldn't get out of bed. A doctor gave me a shot—and then I really *did* have the shits. But it seemed to clear everything out and it gave me enough energy to do the show. Alas, I can tell you very little about the experience of standing up in

front of that many people and being the center of that much attention, because I felt so groggy. But at least I didn't cancel. Canceling on
3.5 million people is not something you really want to countenance.
And at least it wasn't my voice this time.

The morning after, however, I was taken in a dirigible above the
site so that I could see the area that we had played to. It seemed to
stretch on forever, along the bay and right around the horseshoe, an
endless strip of sand where the scaffolding and staging was now being
dismantled and where some of the local populace appeared to have
done a good job already of making off with the woodwork. I'm quite
glad I saw the full expanse of it the day after, rather than the afternoon
before. I might not have gone on at all.

That following day, I got into serious trouble when the paparazzi
snapped me drinking a can of Coca-Cola. Nothing scandalous about
that, of course. Except that the event had been sponsored by Pepsi.

Incidentally, the Rolling Stones have also played to a lot of people
on Copacabana Beach (although nowhere near as many as I did), and
Ronnie Wood says, in his book: "Rod Stewart holds the all-time
record for a concert crowd on Copacabana Beach but he played there
on New Year's Eve and it's tradition that everybody celebrates New
Year's Eve on the beach, so no disrespect to Rod—people would have
been there anyway. We (the Rolling Stones) claim the record for the
most people ever on the beach who came to see a concert."

To which I have only one thing to say.

Bollocks.

had plans. I had already sold the house on Carolwood Drive and
arranged for the building of a brand-new mansion in Beverly Park.
Now I planned to move house in England, too. The Wood House in
Epping meant a lot to me, but it's a listed building, meaning you can't
go knocking it around, and I had always had my eye out for something

bigger that I could adapt. In 1998 I made an offer for Stargroves, a beautiful country mansion in Hampshire, England. Mick Jagger used to own it and it now belonged to Frank Williams, who ran the Williams Formula One team. Williams wanted to sell and we agreed on a price. Then I began to look into selling the Wood House. David and Victoria Beckham were after a place near London and seemed keen to take it off me. Meanwhile, I contacted interior designers and landscape gardeners and began to discuss plans for what I was going to do with Stargroves. I was buzzing with enthusiasm. Few things make me happier than a building project.

And then it came, right out of the blue. One day I was showing Rachel pictures of some furniture that I had ordered. And I noticed that she wasn't looking at them. She was looking at me. And she said, very quietly, "I don't think I'm going to be around."

I didn't know what she meant. She had to repeat it. "I don't think I'm going to be around."

And then it all spilled out: that she was unhappy, that she had been unhappy for a while—maybe for as much as a whole year; that she had been trying and trying to conceal her unhappiness, but that she couldn't anymore and that she was going to leave me.

It was like getting cracked across the back of the head with a cricket bat. I had no inkling this was coming. Not a solitary clue. When I thought back over the previous weeks, I remembered how I had been in Los Angeles, rehearsing with the band, and there had been possibly fewer phone calls from Rachel than there might normally have been. But it was a tiny detail, and I had just assumed she was busy with the kids. Otherwise, I could think of nothing I had missed that would make sense of this.

I asked her whether she had found someone else. She hadn't. She said it was all coming from inside her; that she was unhappy in her life. In fact, she didn't really feel like it *was* her life. She felt she had entered my world as an unformed twenty-one-year-old and been consumed by it, and that now she was merely trailing along in my wake all the time. She was worried that she had no identity of her own. She had reached twenty-nine and she could see thirty coming, and yet she felt she didn't even know who she was. She needed to go.

That conversation took days to digest. I was in a state of disbelief. The realization that I had been blithely forging on, obliviously making plans for the future, and not reading the feelings of the person I thought I was closest to, was crushing. I felt foolish and I alternated between retreating into myself in my embarrassment and reaching out to plead with her to change her mind.

When I realized there was no difference I could make, I began to extricate myself from the house purchase. I withdrew my offer for Stargroves. I canceled furniture orders and called off designers. People were very understanding, but it was a painful and humiliating process.

Rachel's decision to leave came at the end of 1998 but, clearly, going our separate ways at Christmas would have been particularly awful for the children, so we decided to be together through the holiday. In the interim, I had a run of British shows, including five nights at Earls Court, which were the most difficult performances I have ever done. I felt like I was singing with a weight on my chest. In London, especially, I had a fantasy that Rachel would appear at the show and everything would be all right. I kept looking over to the wings, thinking, "She'll come tonight." When she didn't, it cut me to ribbons.

For Christmas, we flew to the house in Palm Beach. News of our decision to separate had got into the papers by now. On the plane over, I found myself sitting near Jeffrey Archer, the novelist and former Conservative politician. "Rod," he said, "this is when you should start writing your book." And I did. I wrote a few things down, but I soon set it aside because I couldn't concentrate.

We said good-bye, quietly and painfully, and Rachel flew off to New Zealand with the kids to see her family. It was only when I was back in Los Angeles, on my own in the house we had shared, and realizing that our relationship was genuinely over, that the misery really came over me. It was like some kind of nineteenth-century romantic fever. For four months, I was beside myself. I lost twelve pounds in weight. I felt cold all the time. I took to lying on the sofa in the day, with a blanket over me and holding a hot water bottle against my chest. I knew then why they call it heartbroken: you can feel it in your heart.

I was distracted, almost to the point of madness. One week, I had Renee and Liam staying with me, and also Ruby, and I decided out of the blue to take them off somewhere. A family holiday, a week away. I thought this would jolt me back into life. I walked into the room and clapped my hands and said, "Right, we're going to Hawaii." I told them to pack a bag for themselves and hurried them out the door. It was insane. When we got to the other end, Renee and Ruby had packed seashells and Barbie dolls. None of them had packed anything to sleep in. I sat on the beach while they played, and tried to feel connected. After two days, I couldn't be still any longer and I gathered them up and brought them home again.

Friends rallied around, and Kim, my daughter, moved back into the house with me and that provided a real comfort. I went to a bookstore and left with a bag full of books off the self-help shelves and drew some consolation from one of them, *The Road Less Traveled* by M. Scott Peck, which talked about the importance of suffering in order to come out the other end stronger, and seemed inspiring to me in the midst of my misery.

However, other methods of pulling myself out of the depths descended into farce. I tried to take up yoga. A man came to the house to teach me the fundamentals. As I was attempting to master a beginner's-level "balancing table" position, I fell over into the fireplace. (Surely if God had meant us to do yoga, he would have put our heads behind our knees.)

And I tried therapy. This had never really appealed to me. Alana had convinced me to go with her for counseling a couple of times when our relationship was in trouble, but I hadn't seen any lasting results from it. For me, it was a bit like a Chinese meal: very filling at the time, but then an hour later you're hungry again. Of course, I'm British. We don't do therapy. We do strong cups of tea, a couple of ginger nuts, and a stiff upper lip.

But I was in extremis, so I went. Indeed, I tried three different therapists. Therapist No. 1 was a middle-aged woman, and what can I say? She came on to me. I'm sure there are one or two stern paragraphs advising against that kind of thing in the professional statutes for therapists. Anyway, in answer to your obvious question: no, I didn't respond to her interest. Instead I got out pretty sharpish and moved on to . . .

Therapist No. 2, who suggested that I get a cat. Now, that wasn't such a stupid idea, really. I'm more of a dog person, it's true, but a cat would, I suppose, have given me something to look after and could perhaps have made a handy hot-water-bottle substitute, if I'd got one that was tame enough. However, "get a cat" wasn't quite the heart-soothing, spirit-lifting advice I was hoping to hear at this time. And certainly not at $150 an hour.

And then there was Therapist No. 3. And he said, "Don't worry about it. You've seen one cunt, you've seen them all."

For Christ's sake. Put the kettle on and break out the ginger nuts.

And the guy who really helped me? Big Al. I was lying listlessly on the sofa in front of the television in the middle of the day, which is something I never do. The door opened and Alan Sewell, my old friend, the Ilford scrap dealer, came in like a ray of sunshine, unannounced and all the way from Essex, eleven hours away by plane, on his own—a man who absolutely hates traveling. I'll never forget that he did that for me. It was the beginning of getting over it.

I think of it now as eight amazing years spent with someone I deeply loved, albeit that it ended in delusion on my part. At the heart of those years was a girl who was too young, who hadn't grown up and eventually needed to spread her wings, only to find by then that everything was locked in tightly around her. And even though it ruined me for a while when she left, I knew how brave of her that was.

I knew something else: clearly I would *never* be happily married.

CHAPTER 17

In which our hero is obliged by cruel circumstances beyond his control to contemplate the end of his career and is consequently driven to reflect widely on life, death, destiny, and the meaning of everything. Sort of.

n May 2000, I went for a routine medical checkup at Cedars-Sinai hospital in Los Angeles. I expected to be in and out, as usual. After all, I was clearly as fit as a butcher's dog—working out every day, doing shows, still playing weekend football at the age of fifty-five. Following the various tests, I sat down in the waiting room and confidently waited to be dismissed.

The wait went on for a little while. And then a doctor called me back into his office and explained that a scan had revealed something they wanted to have a further look at—something on my thyroid gland. The following day I went back to the hospital and underwent a biopsy. Under a local anaesthetic, part of the affected area was removed using a needle and taken away for analysis. And the day after that I got a call at home, which I took standing up and which made my palms go cold. The results of the tests indicated that the "something" on my thyroid gland was a malignant growth: cancer.

That piece of news will really do it to you. When the initial numbness wore off, I felt fearful, vulnerable to a degree that I never had before. The only blessing was that measures were in train so quickly that I didn't have much time for those feelings to reign. Two days after the biopsy, I was driven back to Cedars-Sinai for an operation, checking into the hospital at 5:00 A.M. to escape notice and going under the name Billy Potts (the names of my two dogs, in fact) to narrow the chances of a leak to the press, who would probably not exactly shy away from the story of "Rock Star Rod" going into hospital for a "cancer op."

Before the operation I lay on a gurney in the room just outside the operating room, woozy from the premed, with my headphones on, singing along to a CD on a Walkman—Sam Cooke, my ever-reliable comfort in times of need. Outside, a nurse passed through the waiting room and nodded in the direction of the noise of my voice coming through the wall.

"He's actually not bad, is he?" she said.

Annie Challis, my managerial assistant, who had come along to the hospital to look after me, replied, "We're hoping he might take it up professionally one day."

The procedure took four hours and brought the surgeon's knife to within a fraction of an inch of my vocal cords. Any slip at that point and it really would have been "Good night, Vienna" as far as my career was concerned. But the operation was a complete success. When I came round, I was given the news that the surgeon had removed everything that needed to be removed. And, because all the bad stuff was out, no subsequent course of chemotherapy was needed—which, in turn, meant there was no risk that I would lose my hair. And let's face it: if we're ranking threats to the survival of my career, losing my hair would be second only to losing my voice.

That evening my ex-wife Rachel visited me in my hospital room, bringing our children, Renee and Liam, and Annie went out and brought us all lamb stew back from Le Dôme restaurant—which I was only able to pick at. But the atmosphere was celebratory. A frightening episode seemed to have passed.

In fact, the real alarm, from my point of view, was only now starting. In order for the surgeon to get to the tumor, it had been necessary to cut through the muscles in my throat. The muscles would mend. But, as it was explained to me in subsequent consultations, the muscle memory built up in them over years of singing would be gone. Those muscles wouldn't have a clue what they were doing for a while. They would need to relearn.

Naturally enough, I was keen to know: Would they manage it?

Give it three months of rest, the doctor said, and I could fully expect some kind of singing voice to return.

Phew.

Of course, it might not be the same voice . . .

Ah.

So, what if the voice I got back was a different voice? What if the voice I got back was the voice of—for example—a not very good singer? I didn't want any old voice back. I wanted *my* voice back.

Rest for three months was all the doctors could say, and see what happens.

Never mind the singing; it was several weeks before I could even talk in anything other than a scratchy whisper. My voice had always had a rasp to it. Now it was nothing *but* a rasp.

As for singing, three months went by and I still couldn't do it. Not a note. Four months, five months . . . nothing. I opened my mouth and all that came out was a thin, weak, sandpapery sound— colorless, without tone. These were some of the longest weeks of my life. I would wake up in the morning and think, "Well, maybe today there will be a difference I can notice." And then, heart-sinkingly, no change. Hadn't they said three months? Before long I was up to six and I still couldn't sing.

Was it time to reconcile myself to the idea that it was all over? And how would I go about doing that? "Ah, well, you've had a decent crack at it, mate. Sold a few records, made a bit of money, had your share of fun. Actually, more than your share. Look on the bright side: if they'd offered you all this when you started out, you would have bitten off their hands."

Yes, but no more singing, no more records, no more performing . . . How easy would it be to let all that go? And what would remain of me, in its absence? "Didn't you used to be Rod Stewart?" How easy would it be to have it all just . . . stop?

And not at the time of my choosing, either, but abruptly, miserably, as the result of some random cellular malfunction. No big farewell under a spotlight on a stage somewhere; just a shrug and a silent wave good-bye.

I once read something Sting said: that if it all ended for him tomorrow, if the music dried up and the money was gone and the fame evaporated, then he would be perfectly happy living in a one-bedroom flat again, the way he had done before he made it. I bet he bloody wouldn't, though. I know *I* bloody wouldn't.

What was I going to do with myself in the absence of singing? I was definitely going to need a job; I mentioned earlier my dad's recipe for a man's contentment: a job, a sport, and a hobby. I couldn't lack one of those ingredients and remain content. One day, in the midst of my misery, I stared out of the window and thought, "I know, if I can't be a singer, I'll be a landscape gardener." The designing, the vision, the planning, the standing there on the terrace and pointing: an Italianate fountain here, a statue of Hercules there, a stand of orange trees below . . . I could do that. R. Stewart & Sons, Landscape Gardeners.

But even as I was hatching this unlikely plan, part of me was sane enough to understand the following: that if you've been a singer in a rock 'n' roll band, there is very little that you can do afterwards that is likely to match it for job satisfaction. Singer in a rock 'n' roll band is, in my opinion, quite simply the best job in the world. It could only be a comedown after that—even if I turned out to be a very good land-scape gardener indeed.

When the sixth month passed, though, something clicked in my mind and I changed tactics. I had been waiting for my voice to come back, and it hadn't shown up. What about trying to force it to come back? And if I screwed it up for good in the process, well, what was the difference?

I contacted a guy called Nate Lamb. He was a cantor at a nearby synagogue, and I had been told that he knew everything there was to know about voices and making them stronger. Nate came round and he showed me some vocal exercises: him at the piano, me sat beside him, feeling self-conscious and worried. It was like a daily work-out for the voice—one that I still use today. He got me doing scales, runs, arpeggios. He forced me to make raspberry noises and humming sounds. He was determined, patient, and confident. He was exactly what I needed. Day after day, Nate came back, and day after day we did the same thing. I owe that guy one hell of a lot.

And then I went to stage two of my plan. Stage two was that I would phone up my band, get them up to the house, install them in the garage, and just fucking *sing*. And if the voice went, which it certainly was going to, I would do the same thing the next day, and the next day, and the day after that, until eventually it came back prop-erly, or didn't come back at all, whichever.

So the band came over—Chuck Kentis, the keyboard player; Carmine Rojas on bass; Paul Warren, the guitarist; Dave Palmer on drums—and we thought "Maggie May" would be as good a place as any to start. I managed the opening line, and then the voice disap-peared entirely. But never mind. We reconvened the following day.

And that time I could manage a pair of lines, and then the voice shut down again.

But the next day, it was half a verse. And soon after that, it was two verses.

And then, after a week or so, there was a whole song there, and then a pair of songs—and then half a set, and then eventually, weeks later, a full show. The patience and faith shown by those musicians and close friends of mine in this period was extraordinary. And my throat was no longer aching like a bastard afterwards and my voice was holding strong to the end, and I knew the overwhelming relief of feeling that I could go on from here and . . . well, as Annie said to the nurse, take up singing professionally, even.

We had put the story out that it was the removal of a benign vocal nodule, a common enough operation for singers. But the truth got out eventually and some of the papers started billing the episode as "Rod's fight with cancer."

There was no fight, of course; no battle, no brave struggle. I wish I could pretend there was, but that would be an insult to people who really have been ill, who really have fought and battled and struggled. In my case, the cancer was there, and then a couple of days later it was gone.

And, accordingly, I don't feel comfortable with drawing big conclusions from my so-called "brush with death," or seeing myself as a "cancer survivor," or claiming to be permanently changed by it. That stuff always seems a bit too neat to me, in any case.

It's true, though, that you can't face up to losing something without working out how much it matters to you—and also without realizing how fortunate you were in the first place. Rock 'n' roll is full of singers who got lucky and started putting it down to hard work. And of course there is hard work involved, but what you are working with, and trying to make the most of, is your amazing piece of luck in the first place, the quirk of fortune which means that, when you open your mouth, this particular sound comes out, rather than any other particular sound, and that this particular sound sells more than 200 million records and brings you fame all over the world and secures you a life more charmed than anyone has a right to dream of.

In those circumstances, to be the recipient of another quirk of fortune which meant that, when you got thyroid cancer, you were rid of it within a matter of days and free to carry on . . . well, lucky, lucky man. Lucky as fuck.

CHAPTER 18

Penny.

When Rachel left, the last thing I wanted to do was fall head over heels in love with a tall blond girl in her twenties. I knew where that could lead a man of my years, and it wasn't necessarily a happy place.

Within eight months I had fallen head over heels in love with a tall blond girl in her twenties.

But this time I needed to be sure. Last time, when I thought I was right, I was absolutely wrong, and I really didn't want to go through that again. I needed to take patient steps—assuming I was capable of doing that, which very little in my headlong romantic history thus far had suggested I was. I duly embarked upon something that I seemed to have been largely allergic to in my various love-related hurries down the years: a long courtship.

In the spring of 1999, four months after Rachel departed, and following the failed therapy and the swiftly aborted yoga, the misery of our separation began to lift. Through the clearing gloom I started dating again. I went out with Tracy Tweed, the Canadian model and actress, who was one of the funniest women I have ever met. I had some very enjoyable dates with Kimberley Conrad, who had recently separated from Hugh Hefner. And I went out for a while with Caprice Bourret, the American model. Poor Caprice was the victim of a sustained *Sound of Music*–style eviction campaign by certain of my children, who seemed to take against her, dropping pet mice in her lap and placing pictures of my ex-wife all around the house when they knew she was coming over. The relationship didn't take off.

All these affairs were great fun, and with beautiful women for whom I had the utmost respect. But none of them was quite the right thing at the time. I wanted to find someone to love and spend the rest of my life with.

On and off during those months, I occasionally found myself wondering about a beautiful, special woman I had met, extremely briefly, in London the previous December. Badly bruised by the end of my marriage, I had been drinking with friends at the Dorchester Hotel when a tall blond girl in her twenties had come over and asked for an autograph. She had been cajoled into doing this as a dare by her girlfriends, who were smirking on the other side of the room.

Her name was Penny Lancaster. She was twenty-seven. And yes, she was tall and blond, and with a drop-dead figure. (I later found out that she modeled underwear.) But what I was also attracted to was the real and obvious warmth she had about her, and the kindness in her face. I asked her what she did, and she told me she was a model and also a photography student at Barking College in Essex. I asked her if she would find it useful to photograph one of my shows and she seemed interested in that. I told her if she came to the door at Earls

Court on the Saturday night, I would make sure that there was a pass for her and she could snap away to her heart's content.

She came to the show and took pictures, but I didn't see her, beforehand or afterwards. Carmine Rojas, the bassist in the band, went out to the front to check that she was OK, and I knew that she had given him her phone number. Every now and again, over the next few months, I would ask Carmine to pass it on to me. But he always laughed and said, "Oh no—she's much too good for you, mate." Eventually, though, he relented and in early August 1999, nearly eight months after that first meeting, when I was back in England for a while, I called her.

I said, "I'm in town. Why don't we catch up over dinner with some friends of mine? Oh, and bring along the photos," I added.

We met at Neal's, a little restaurant in Loughton, not far from the Wood House. Penny, who was now twenty-eight, arrived in "pleather" trousers—quite edgy, but emphatically not a skirt—a top that carefully concealed all trace of cleavage, and a jacket covering her arms and shoulders. I was immediately struck by her fresh face and girlish demeanor. I had invited my friends Alan "Big Al" Sewell and his wife, Debbie. I think Penny was nervously anticipating music-industry people, and was enormously relieved to find herself at the table with a couple who were so comforting, down to earth, and hilarious to be around. It helped put her at ease.

At the start of the evening, I asked Penny if I could see the pictures she had taken, back in December, and she handed me a batch of prints. They were not the best concert photos I had ever seen. Penny had assumed she would be in the photographers' pit, right in front of the stage. But the crew had put her out on the sound desk in the middle of the hall, where, in the absence of a long telephoto lens, she had been reduced to taking pictures of a set of small figures jousting mistily in the distance. A lot of compensatory blowing up and cropping appeared to have gone on in the darkroom.

We put the photographs aside and ordered food and talked, and the evening went pretty smoothly right until the moment when Penny got up to use the bathroom and knocked two glasses of wine over on the adjacent table. This convinced her she had blown the date completely, but in fact it simply made the night feel even funnier and warmer.

As we walked out to the cars, I asked Penny if we could meet the next day. She said she would love to, much to my excitement, but that it was her granddad's birthday and she was taking him out to the Theydon Oak.

I said, "That's my pub."

Penny said, "What, you own it?"

I said, "No, it's where I go. I could see you there."

She said, "I'm sure my granddad would love to meet you."

I said, "Then I'll see you tomorrow."

The next day, not long after two in the afternoon, the intercom buzzed from the front gate.

A hesitant female voice said, "I'm looking for Rod?"

"Yeah, this is Rod."

"Er, it's Penny? You said you would meet me and my granddad?"

I was confused. I thought we had a date for the evening. I buzzed them in and went out onto the drive. Penny explained that her birthday treat for her grandad, Wally, was lunch, not supper. Furthermore, after the lunch had come and gone without any sign of me, Wally had stood up and said, firmly, "We'll go over there. We'll go over to Rod Stewart's house."

Penny had said, "We can't just . . . go over there."

And Wally had said, "He said he would come. And if he said he would come, we should hold him to his word."

I shook Wally's hand, apologized to him profusely for the misunderstanding, and then we had a long chat. In later days, when Penny and I were eventually together, Wally and I would slip off for a pint every now and again. He had been a fireman in the war, and people who have stories from that era have my ear straightaway. He once told me, "I've got to be honest with you. I don't think much of your music, but I like your taste in art."

He had a photo of himself, sat in the driver's seat of my Lamborghini, which he used to take to show people at the British Legion. The poor old boy was knocked down by a bus and killed on his way to pick up his pension at the age of ninety-five. He had that photo in his pocket that day and it went to his grave with him.

After that missed lunch, Penny and I saw each other a few times, but the relationship built very slowly and tentatively, over many months. At this point, Penny was engaged to someone with whom she had been in a relationship for ten years. She was always completely open with me about that. Recently, she said, things had not been going too well, but she was torn about letting this person go. I told her I would be there to talk to her, if she wanted me to, about her sadness over that breaking relationship and I explained that I had just been through a breakup of my own. The more we talked, the more I realized how altogether smitten I was with Penny—yet I was proceeding very cautiously, too, and wanting to get everything absolutely right. It was a long time before we kissed for the first time. This happened at the Wood House one afternoon, after tea. We talked about Pre-Raphaelite art, which Penny had been studying as part of her course. I showed her the paintings in the room we were sitting in, and then the ones in the corridor outside. The tour continued with the paintings on the stairs, and then slowly onwards until we were looking at the paintings in my bedroom. A laden silence fell. And then, on an overwhelmingly romantic impulse, I asked Penny if she would lie back across the bed. She hesitantly did so. Then I walked around until I was directly behind her, on the other side of the bed, put my hands on her shoulders, leaned forward, and kissed her, upside down. She reached up to my face and began to kiss me back. Then I stood up,

Clockwise from top:
• A very young and apprehensive Rachel Hunter prepares to become the second Mrs. Stewart, with a lot of goodwill from fans peering through the window. December 1990.
• Renee and Liam hanging with Dad at our house in Palm Beach.
• Rachel in a vain attempt to straighten out my dreadful posture.
• On a flight to Australia we had a bet who could keep their pacifier in the longest. How to keep your children quiet.
• "Your car's rubbish, Dad." Liam, age two.

Above and left:
A man should always have a hobby to be well rounded. Don't snigger. Building model railroads is a big love of my li*Inset:* Hard at work.

fearless, albeit delightful, manager Arnold Stiefel. What would I have done without him?

: The irresistible Clive Davis, a very clever fellow. *Right:* My dear friend Richard Perry, producer confidant, in a parental pose.

My beautiful girls: Ruby (now twenty-five), Kim (now thirty-three), and Renee (now twenty), c
the day Penny and I wed in Italy in 2007. What more can I say? *Inset:* Sarah Streeter, my firstborr

Celebrating my sixtieth on a chartered yacht around the Caribbean with family and friends. See
here having a laugh with brothers, sister, and Scottish mate Ricky Simpson.

Left: C'mon you bhoys in green! Glasgow's green and white. From left to right: Liam (now eighteen), Dad, Alastair (now seven), Aiden (now twenty months), Sean (now thirty-two).

Below left: Look closely. I had carved "RS loves PL" into a tree while on safari in Africa. I had fallen in love.

Below right: A naturally beautiful Penny Lancaster on tour with me for the first time. Life together was just beginning.

A miracle made possible by Penny, who managed to bring all of my children together, plus my granddaughter, Delilah, and took this lovely photo of them gathered around me. Pure love. Los Angeles, August 2012.

ft: A kilted Rod with my delicious Penny, in Monaco. *Right:* That wildly romantic day in Paris, ...en Penny accepted my offer of marriage. Both of us looking very dewy-eyed. The finest woman. ...rch 2005.

...: Revisiting Paris together, Penny pregnant with Alastair. She makes me happy. *Right:* Enjoying ...early sunrise with our boys in Palm Beach. I feel truly blessed.

Sharing an embrace of laughter and tears. Love and happiness personified. June 16, 2007.

took her hand, helped her to her feet, and said, "Come on." And with that the art-history tour resumed.

And that, dear reader, was the birth of the "upside-down kiss," which, to this day, Penny refers to as "the most romantic and seductive meeting of lips" she has ever known. Try it one day.

Penny was very quiet in those early days, perhaps a bit intimidated. I would quickly learn how she wasn't really shy at all. I would learn this in particular in late 2008, when I was invited to play at the sixtieth-birthday party of Prince Charles at Highgrove House and looked out from the stage to see Penny dancing to "Da Ya Think I'm Sexy?" with the Prince, our host. He asked her to dance in the hope of encouraging everyone else out onto the floor, which certainly worked. Afterwards, he asked her, "Where did you get your dance steps?" To which Penny replied, "My dad." In the same show, I looked out again—this time during "The Way You Look Tonight"—and saw that Penny had now been swept up by Prince William, who asked for, and got, her permission to "dip" her in a formal flourish at the end.

It was quite a relief to Penny to be invited back among royalty after what had happened a couple of years previously. I was playing at a special event at Windsor Castle to honor patrons of the Prince's Trust charity, for which Penny and I are ambassadors, and Penny was seated next to Prince Charles at dinner. When the waiters appeared at Penny's shoulder with the main course on a platter, the Prince was mid-anecdote. As she served herself, Penny continued to hold the Prince's eye, as she believed protocol demanded, missed her plate completely, and heaved a portion of meat onto the tablecloth between them. The Prince merely said, "Oh, don't worry—I do that all the time," and casually covered the mess with his napkin. What a bloke.

Anyway, it was one of the things I quickly grew to love about my adorable wife—that you never quite knew what she would do next, or when that little look of mischief would glow in her eyes, the naughty mixed with the nice. On tour in Australia eight years ago, we were driving back to the hotel on a really hot day, slightly woozy after a tour of some vineyards, and suddenly there was a stunning vista of endless fields with huge wheels of cut hay stacked up in them. This inspired Penny to leap from the car, jump over the fence, and start running, gradually shedding items of clothing as she went, right down to her underwear, before climbing a distant hay bale on the horizon and turning back to wave. That, in turn, caused me to jump from the car and set off after her, shouting wildly and joining her on the hay bale, where we embraced. By now two or three cars had pulled up behind ours, so the driver called us back. We ran, gathering Penny's clothes along the way, and flung ourselves into the backseat, laughing like fools.

On those nervous early dates, however, I was constantly reassuring her that it was OK if she talked. Quite early in the relationship we spent an evening at Ronnie Wood's house in Wimbledon. Woody is very friendly with Jimmy White, the snooker player, who was a big deal in the sport in his day, and a bit of a lad. Somewhere in the evening, White said, "I need a volunteer for a trick shot." Penny, thinking perhaps that this would be a good moment to come out of her shell and show herself to be game, said, "I'll do it."

For this trick, she had to lie on her back across Woody's snooker table, with the back of her head on the baize and a golf tee between her teeth. White put a red ball on the golf tee and declared that, from the other end of the table, he would hit a jump-shot with the white ball which would take the red ball off the tee and put it in the left-hand pocket beyond Penny's head.

I was looking at this and thinking, "You'd better get this right, pal."

Crack! The white ball leaped away from White's cue, missed the red ball, and smacked against Penny's jaw. From the sound of it, I was imagining broken teeth, though actually she was only bruised. White was profusely apologetic but I was furious. I said, "We're leaving." And we did, amid much frostiness.

Our devotion to each other grew over a series of romantic voyages abroad. Very early on, I whisked Penny away to the Bahamas for a holiday with a group of eight old friends of mine—potentially intimidating and alienating for her, but she fit right in. To surprise her on her arrival, I had a whole new wardrobe of Dolce & Gabbana clothes and shoes waiting for her in the guest room. Getting the right size shoes presented me with a problem, but I solved it brilliantly: by trying them on myself. If they were slightly too tight on me, I knew they would be perfect for Penny. And I was right.

We also went driving through Provence in the south of France in my convertible Lamborghini, just the two of us—a trip we would repeat several times over the years and that eventually inspired us to seek a place down there to which we could constantly return. It was Penny who flew to France several times on what turned into a four-year property-hunting mission and who eventually found us the perfect house in the hills above Nice, which we own and love to this day.

I went back to America in due course and invited Penny over, periodically, for short breaks together. In between, we had endless long-distance phone calls, sharing our inner thoughts and talking about anything and everything. She was finishing her photography course at Barking College. I would tell people, "My girlfriend's got her school holidays, so she's coming out." I loved the appalled reaction that this got. It must have been strange for Penny, though. One minute she was at college in Barking and the next she was flying down to Miami and getting driven across the tarmac to the Learjet where her pouting, posing boyfriend was waiting for the fifteen-minute flight up to his house in Palm Beach.

Our emerging relationship was difficult for both our families. My brothers and sisters were initially suspicious and worried about a repetition of my relationship with Rachel. Meanwhile, Penny's brother, Oliver, was clearly anxious about his sister consorting with a rock star. He would eventually come to know me as the fine, up-standing gentleman that I am, of course. But in the meantime, we decided the best way to remove some of these understandable familial tensions was to arrange for me to meet her dad, Graham. Graham is the same age as me, and a lawyer. Neither of us was quite sure what to wear for our dinner date. In the end, Graham came dressed like a rock star—denim and leather—and I came dressed like a lawyer, in a dark suit with a perfectly pressed shirt and a well-knotted tie. We hit it off straightaway, though, and ended up back at my house in Epping, drinking whiskey and listening to Sam Cooke records.

I knew of Penny's desire to have children. She was honest with me over how she felt about children and how much she hoped to have them. And I was honest with her about how, at this time, I felt I really couldn't have any more kids, or get married or move forward with anyone in a serious way. We both said we were having fun and it didn't matter; that we would just let this relationship take its course. But I knew I couldn't make her 100 percent happy for that reason.

Also, Penny had to make up her mind to leave a person that she had been with for a long time—a person with whom, perhaps, she could have stayed and started a family. She was once crying in my arms because she was in anguish about this decision, and I suggested that she go and sit down by the lake for a while and just try to clear her head. As she sat there, a swan rose up off the water and flew away, and, after it had passed, a solitary white feather floated down and landed beside her. Is it too fanciful to think that this was a sign? It was certainly a happy coincidence and an inspiring sight. Penny came back to me in the house, resolved and holding the feather. She still has it.

After Penny separated from her boyfriend, it would have been so easy for me to say "Move in with me." Again, though, with great restraint, we went slowly. Penny went home to live with her dad, not far from the house in Essex. The bed she was sleeping in there was the one she had had when she was eight. Her feet were hanging over the edge and the springs were gone. So I bought her a new bed, causing a small commotion in the neighborhood when the van from Harrod's turned up to deliver it. On reflection, this may have been the least romantic gift I have ever given a woman: a new single bed, to enable her to carry on living at her dad's house.

Eventually, I suggested that she move into the little guest cottage at the end of the drive in Epping—bringing her closer, but still not bringing her right in. But then there was a wonderful period of three weeks when Renee and Liam were staying over and the Wood House was being redecorated. So Penny, the kids, and I all lived in the guest cottage together for a while, sharing the two bedrooms very snugly. Renee and Liam would come into our bedroom in the morning and do trampolining on the bed. Penny took them down to Southend on the Essex coast, sugared them up good and proper, and let them see how Essex does the seaside: the beach, the deck chairs, Peter Pan's Playground. This clearly brought her enormous pleasure, but it made me ache to think she would never do things like that with her own children. Why couldn't this relationship have happened sooner?

But, of course, there was this overriding need to be sure—for both of us. We would be out on tour, walking hand in hand around towns and cities, and we'd find ourselves wanting to go into a church. There wouldn't be a service on, but something kept drawing us into churches, and we both felt compelled to sit there quietly for a little while and to pray. And it wasn't something we questioned one another on; it was just an urge. Something just drew us in. We'd be in New York, and on a mission to do something or go somewhere, but then we would pass a church and find ourselves saying, "Let's go in." And we'd sit at the back and bow our heads for a bit. We only opened up to each other about this after we had got married, but it turned out that, as we sat side by side at those times, we were both praying for us to find a way to be together in the future. Still, at this time we didn't discuss it. We would pray and then hold hands and leave.

In 2003, we went to Tanzania for New Year's. We had seen an advert on the television in which a couple wished each other a happy New Year in the middle of the African bush, and we thought, "That looks like the most romantic thing." And on that trip, I picked up a stone and scored into the trunk of a tree "RS loves PL." It was something I had never said to her, and even then she didn't know whether I was fooling around or being sincere, and I didn't clarify it for her.

And then came September 11, 2004, the third anniversary of the attack on the World Trade Center. We were at Wood House, sitting by the lake on one of those bright, clear English autumn afternoons. We were talking about what had happened those years ago and about the families destroyed that day and the children left behind. And after a while I said, "Let's make a baby."

She was overcome because she hadn't been expecting to hear that from me. But the realization that that was what I wanted for us both had been a long time coming, and I knew I meant it, as well as I knew anything. We tried immediately and, in fact, Penny got pregnant that Christmas, but she miscarried very quickly. Still, we resolved to keep trying.

In the meantime, I had another idea. In March 2005, Penny was nearing her thirty-third birthday. I told her, "I'm going to take you on a surprise trip—you, and your mum and dad. It's just for the day, but you'll need your passport. And dress smartly."

That morning, Penny and I met her parents at Stansted Airport. Peter Mackay, my tour manager, was along to look after us, and I had entrusted a small but important box to him for safekeeping, but not even he was told the purpose of the day. Penny wore a black pencil skirt and a white shirt, the teacherly/secretarial look of which I'm unashamedly fond. I couldn't believe that she hadn't read my purpose—and maybe secretly she had. She was obviously nervous, sensing that something was up.

As we were crossing the tarmac to the plane, I hung back slightly with Penny's dad, and above the whine of the engine I leaned into his ear and said, "Do I have your permission to ask your daughter to marry me?"

Graham's a tough man, but his legs almost went from under him. I had to hold him up for a moment. "Yes!" he said. "Yes, you do!"

Good job, because the rest of the day would have come off a bit damply if he had said no.

Graham somehow managed to sit on the secret all the way to our destination: Paris. He and Sally, Penny's mum, had never been there. We went to Fouquet's on the Champs-Élysées for coffee, but I couldn't relax at all. I kept looking at my watch. "Twelve thirty. Drink up. We need to be going." Chivvied along by me, we left Fouquet's and drove across to the Eiffel Tower. There we ascended in the lift to the Jules Verne restaurant on the tower's second platform, where Pete escorted us to the bar and left us.

I was in the middle of hastily ordering a round of vodka cocktails when a surge of panic rushed through me. The package in Pete's pocket! I chased out after him and just managed to head him off by the lifts, before he disappeared into Paris for an hour, which really would have cocked up everything. I tucked the box into the inside pocket of my jacket and headed back to the restaurant bar, where I proceeded to soak my jangling nerves in a vodka cocktail, followed immediately afterwards by another one.

And then, right there at the bar, I went down on one knee, held out the ring in its box, and asked Penny to marry me.

Penny had a minute of disbelief. Her hands went to her face and her eyes welled. In the background was the sound of Sally sobbing hysterically. This seemed to go on for some time. I had a dodgy right knee—an old footballing injury—and I wasn't sure how much longer I would be able to take this. Eventually I said, "Please say something, Penny, because me knee is killing me."

She gave me a sobbing yes. And at last I was able to stand up, relieve my knee, and become Penny's partner for life.

After lunch we drove back to the airport and flew home. Paris was our special place from that day on, a city we return to when we can to remind ourselves of that day. I couldn't believe how very much in love we were and how lucky this aging rock star had become. And that night we conceived Alastair, our beautiful son.

The baby came on November 27, 2005. Penny had loved being pregnant, and I loved it too. On our way into the Hospital of St. John and St. Elizabeth in St. John's Wood in London, we paused at the chapel beside the maternity ward to say our prayers. And then, after a long and emotional labor, with Penny sometimes in and sometimes out of the birthing pool (we had chosen to have a water birth), Alastair finally arrived—delivered onto the linoleum in the end, which, I couldn't help noticing, amid the euphoria of the moment, bore a very similar pattern to the floor at 507 Archway Road. As Penny recovered, I held Alastair and sang him "Flower of Scotland." And as we left the next morning, I told the nurses, "See you next year."

In June 2007, Penny and I were married in front of a hundred guests at a chapel decorated with white roses in the town of Santa Margherita on the Italian Riviera. There had to be some smoke and mirrors to prevent the press from inviting themselves. We set out for Italy from the south coast of France by boat, getting dropped off in two separate bays. It was like the D-day landings. The sense of subterfuge only added to the excitement.

And what an incredibly joyous weekend we had. The night before the ceremony, we threw a white-themed party in our hotel and, as ever, on countless key occasions in my life, it devolved into a singsong. Out came the old numbers: "Show Me the Way to Go Home," "Knees Up, Mother Brown," "On Mother Kelly's Doorstep," and, of course, "Get Me to the Church on Time." And my sister Mary was there, and my brothers, Bob and Don, with whom I have shared those songs all my life, and the party conga-danced its way out the hotel doors and onto the street—the way that parties conga-danced out the front door of 507 Archway Road all those years before, some things never changing.

At the service, unknown to me, Penny had arranged for her procession down the aisle to be accompanied by an Italian boys' choir singing "Fields of Athenry," the great Irish folk ballad adopted by Celtic supporters. I welled up and almost lost control completely. In honor of the Epping swan that rose up from the lake while Penny watched that day, there were swans' feathers in the flower displays, on the invitations, in the hanging decorations above the ballroom. And when, in the traditional order of things, the bride and groom led the way onto the dance floor, their choice of song was Etta James's "At Last."

And, yes, as a sixty-seven-year-old man now, I can regret that this relationship, this marriage, this family, didn't come sooner. But I know that's just greed talking and that the blessing, the relief, and the ever-renewing amazement of it for me is that those things came at all; that I am happier and more in love than I have ever been; that the journey ever reached this place, when I had given up hope that it would or could.

There's a photo from the wedding. It's taken after the service, and after the reception. The fireworks have just been let off on the jetty, the cake is about to be cut, and we're standing on a hill above the water. Penny has got her arms across her body and I'm standing behind her with my arms around her, holding her tightly, and what the expressions on our faces and the setting and, really, everything about the picture seem to say is: at last.

DIGRESSION

❧

*In which our hero meditates on the tribulations
and rewards of fatherhood.*

NOBODY CAN TEACH YOU to be a parent. It's something
that you learn as you go along, anxiously feeling your way
forward, failing in places, succeeding in others, making the
best of it that you can. Still, knowledgeable guidance is always
welcome, so permit me to present my personal Top 20 parenting
insights, a set of practical observations based on hands-on
experience with seven children and more than thirty years in
the fatherhood business, much of it in Los Angeles, a city which,
as everyone knows, presents its own special challenges in the
rearing of offspring.

1. Small children and an extensive collection of priceless
   Gallé lamps are not an ideal combination. I sold off many
   of my best specimens when the kids started coming along,
   because it seemed more prudent than trying to stick them
   back together.
2. Many of the pranks learned in years of touring and staying
   in hotels with rock bands turn out (perhaps unsurprisingly)
   to have applications within the context of family life at
   home. For example: positioning a bucket of water over the
   door to a child's bedroom.
3. Similarly, secretly removing all that room's lightbulbs to
   create confusion and frustration.
4. But watch out for the "cellophane over the loo seat in
   the bathroom" trick, conducted as direct revenge, at

the parent's expense, for the aforementioned lightbulb removal/bucket of water.

5. Should your one-year-old, while perched on her mother's hip, reach out and snatch the false teeth right out of her aged and confused grandmother's mouth, don't panic. Wrest the false teeth from the one-year-old's fingers, rinse the dentures quickly under the kitchen tap, and place them on the table. With any luck, it will all happen so fast that the grandmother in question will give the teeth on the table a quizzical look, as if to say "Aren't those mine?" and then throw them back in her mouth, and nothing more will be said about it.

6. When packing your child's lunch for school be sure to include, as well as the obvious sandwich and chocolate bar, random items such as a screwdriver, a piece of sandpaper, or a plastic figure from a railway set, just to keep them on their toes.

7. Covering yourself in a bed sheet and pretending to be a ghost is an absolutely fail-safe way to frighten children out of their wits, especially if you have access to a large, centuries-old house in the English countryside.

8. If your child finds your choice of a pale blue Lamborghini "*so Miami Vice*" and is vocal about their embarrassment at being seen in it, willingly concede to their demand to be dropped around the corner from school, out of sight, rather than directly at the gates. But then, after waiting a short while, follow them round to the entrance, hooting, waving, and calling "good-bye" loudly as they go in.

9. However, note that nothing embarrasses children quite so devastatingly as the sight, in a swimming pool setting, of their father in a Versace speedo.

10. Kids of all ages enjoy the "couch game," wherein everyone

sits in a line on the couch and, on the count of three, leans backwards as hard as they can to cause the couch to go over onto its back. Hours of fun. There are very few moods so dark that they cannot be lightened by a round or three of the couch game.

11. Equally good value: the "table game." The object of this is to shift a restaurant table, very gradually, inch by inch, during the course of a meal until, imperceptibly and to the confusion of the waiting staff, it has come to occupy a place in the middle of the room, or elsewhere. Especially amusing in al fresco city restaurants where, at some point, the table can be half on and half off the pavement, and eventually out in the traffic. And also amusing in St. Tropez, where the table can end up in the sea. Straight faces essential.

12. Books make a handy, obstructive covering for a child's bed, especially if stacked very neatly across the entire surface of that bed, three or four deep.

13. Even the most sluggish of teenagers can be roused for school in the morning if you position enough alarm clocks around their bedroom in enough hard-to-reach places.

14. Equally effective in this regard: a recording of bagpipes played loudly outside the teenager's door.

15. If your teenager persists in parking near the house in a spot where you don't want them to park, wrap that teenager's car key in thirty layers of cellophane in order to carry home the message.

16. If you are fed up with your offspring's chihuahua crapping in your garden, and that crap going uncleared, place the offending waste matter on a napkin under the driver's seat of your child's car and allow natural heat and humidity in the car's interior to create a memorable lesson in pet care.

17. The same waste matter placed on a napkin on the floor of the offspring's room will have a very similar effect in terms of reinforcing the message.
18. If you are fed up with your offspring's chihuahua in general, try drawing "666," the number of the beast, on its forehead in marker pen.
19. That homeless person, discovered early one morning by your housekeeper asleep on the sofa in the sitting room next to the kitchen, may not be a homeless person at all. It may be Munky, the guitarist from Korn, kipping over, having been a late-night guest of your offspring. Therefore, your housekeeper need not immediately call the police and report an intruder. (I was away when this happened, I'm glad to say.)
20. And while we're on the subject of being away: when Tommy Lee, a founding member of the metal band Mötley Crüe, and his pilot take it into their heads, while visiting your children, to try to land a helicopter in your back garden, you might want to be on tour, as I was, so that you miss the ensuing chaos and leave someone else to explain to the estate management and the fire department exactly what the fuck is going on.

My more than thirty years in parenting have left me not only with the extremely useful accumulated knowledge above, but also with a thing about Father's Day. It means far more to me to be remembered on that day than it does on Christmas Day or on my birthday. Father's Day is the one that can get overlooked. I actually get nervous about it beforehand, wondering whether this will be the year that one of my children forgets. And when they don't, and they get in touch and they send their love, it melts me away because that's all I want to hear.

Perhaps I need that reassurance because I am prone to feeling guilty, and one of the things I am prone to feeling guilty about is whether, as a father, I have been all that I could be. I have never been a bad father. On the contrary, I have always been a good father in the sense that my love for my children has been unwavering. But I was certainly, for significant periods of my older children's lives, an absent father. The nature of the job meant that I would be home for a month, and then gone for three. That was difficult for my children, and the fact that they didn't know life to be any different didn't make it easier. And then, periodically, I would make things even more complicated by starting another family. Each of my children knew they had my love, but my love was coming from such a distance a lot of the time. And I realized, too late, that this was ground I wouldn't make up and time I wouldn't get back. All you can do is try to mend it as best you can, which is what I'm doing now—trying to be more of a present father in their lives.

I'm so proud of them: Sarah, Kimberly, Sean, Ruby, Renee, Liam, Alastair, and Aiden, the last (I can confidently state) of my children. Aiden was a little while in the making. We tried for two years for a sibling for Alastair before specialists discovered that Penny had high levels of mercury in her body and recommended that we try in vitro fertilization. This route didn't prove entirely easy for us, either. We had three rounds of IVF in all, and it's physically very punishing for the woman, and heartbreaking for both of you when it doesn't work. Still, we kept on going and turned it into as much of an adventure as possible. I was offered the opportunity to provide my samples at the clinic, but I preferred to do so in the privacy of my own home. Then Penny and I would jump into the Ferrari and speed off to the clinic with the tube kept warm between Penny's

thighs. I was on tour in Moscow in the summer of 2010 when
Penny phoned to say she was finally pregnant, and we both
wept for joy. On February 16, 2011, our lovely boy arrived.
Six months after that, Kim gave birth to Delilah and made a
proud new father a proud new grandfather.

I love the fact that my children refer to one another as
brothers and sisters—not as half-brothers or half-sisters. There
are no half measures here. There's a real family gravity drawing
them close—a proper clannishness, the Stewart clan.

One of the battles I have had down the years—both with
their mothers and with my own conscience—is with the material
side of parenting, the question of what children should be given
and what they should have to go and earn. I cling so hard to the
working-class ethic that I came from—of coming from nowhere
and making something of yourself. But, of course, my own
kids don't come from nowhere; they started off on another level
of privilege altogether from where I started. It's about finding
the balance between enabling them and indulging them, and I
concede that I struggle with it, veering one way and then the
other.

But, through all that, I am fortunate that I still have a good
relationship with their mothers. When you've had children with
somebody, you share that for the rest of your life, over and
above the differences you may have had. Kim is raising Delilah
in the guest house of my home in Beverly Park, so Alana, as
grandmother, is often around, helping her out, babysitting,
pushing a stroller up the drive and out to the playground. Kelly,
who eventually got married and had two sons and now lives
in San Diego, became an interior designer, and I employed her
to design some of the rooms in Celtic House in Beverly Park.
We get along fine. Rachel and I never actually fell out, so our
friendship is still strong. Rachel had some disappointment in a

love affair following our marriage, and it's a sign of where our relationship is now that she came to me to talk about it.

In fact, relations between us all have been so stable that, in 2000, we felt close enough, at my suggestion, to hold a big family Christmas. It took place at Celtic House: Christmas dinner for all the children, Alana, Kelly, Rachel, and Penny, whom I had only been seeing for a few months and for whom this must have been a uniquely terrifying experience—thrust into a room with the three variously formidable mothers of her new partner's children, who had never been together in this way, and in the volatile circumstances of Christmas, too.

There was some competitive turkey cooking in the kitchen. It was generally agreed that Alana's turkey turned out best, while Rachel ruined hers by throwing at it every single herb she could find. Kelly did the roast potatoes and the sprouts. Penny, very cannily, stood back and let them get on with it. Everybody got along well enough and the children, of course, loved it. Was it the kind of Christmas the adults in the party would choose to have every year? Perhaps not. Have we done it again since? No. But I was able to look around the room during that afternoon and cast my eyes from one face to the next, and think to myself, "OK, maybe you wouldn't have sat down and planned it this way, and Lord knows there was enough grief and strife along the road. But in a profound and unshakable way, this family is a unit and it works." Twelve years later, I feel that even more strongly.

It's impossible for me to recount in full the immense joy I have had from my children, the mountains of love that I have received from them, and the pleasure I have had in watching them grow from little toddlers to strong young adults—and now doing it all again with Alastair and Aiden. It's a blessing. No record sales compare to that, nor ever will.

CHAPTER 19

In which our hero despairs of ever having a hit again and then promptly has a whole bunch of them. With musings upon personal reinvention, cottages in Scotland, and the wisdom of dancing cheek to cheek with a music-industry legend.

One night, I was having dinner with Arnold in Morton's on Melrose Avenue in Los Angeles, and, after we had ordered, I ran past him the idea I had for the next album.

I said, "I think I should do a record of standards."

Could it be that, at this exact moment, a crumb of bread roll went the wrong way down Arnold's throat? I couldn't be sure, but his face had gone very red and he seemed to be having trouble suppressing a fit of alarmed coughing.

I carried on, regardless. "Yes, a standards album—the wonderful American songs, Cole Porter, Irving Berlin, Rodgers and Hart. The songs I grew up with, the stuff I heard while sitting on my dad's knee."

I could see Arnold trying to compose his face as if I hadn't just announced a near-certain death wish.

In due course, he said, "Can I be absolutely honest with you?"

I said, "Of course."

Arnold said, "I think you should store that idea away for a decade or two."

And he was absolutely correct. The dinner I'm talking about took place in 1983. Arnold had only recently taken over as my manager. Of the tasks facing us both at that particular moment, probably the most pressing was fixing the collateral damage caused by the wild success of "Da Ya Think I'm Sexy?" and taking all necessary measures to realign people's mistaken impression of me as Mr. Disco Trousers. It's unlikely that this problem would have been best dealt with by releasing a version of "These Foolish Things," no matter how hot. So, instead, I went away under orders from Arnold to reconnect with my rock 'n' roll roots and made the *Camouflage* album.

Still, I mention this conversation in order to show how the urge to record those great American songs was always there, bubbling away. They had been a part of me since the warm tones of Ella Fitzgerald came flooding out of the radiogram at Archway Road. And finally, nineteen years later, the time did come.

Even then, it felt like a giant leap. A British rock singer with a fondness for football and a penchant for lobbing his microphone stand about, tackling the American popular classics? Quite apart from the possible charges of presumptuousness, I knew I would be entirely repositioning myself in many people's eyes, and throwing a lot of expectations up in the air. Yet it was a risk I felt inclined to take. The last album I had released—*Human*, in 2001—had sold poorly. Alarmingly poorly. It had seemed to go down about as well as a wart in a swimming pool. It had the worst opening week for sales of any album I had ever made. It was also the first album I had ever released to which I contributed absolutely no songs of my own. If those two facts were related to each other, I certainly didn't have the confidence to make the connection myself. Indeed, my assumption was that I was completely finished as a songwriter.

Why wouldn't I think that? The last really successful song I had written was "Forever Young" in 1988—since when almost fourteen years had passed. Songwriting has always been hard for me, but in the 1990s it seemed to become impossible—and for reasons that I couldn't explain, which only increased the frustration of it. I remember discussing the problem with the producer Trevor Horn. Trevor said, "Why don't you rent a cottage in Scotland and just go up there on your own with an acoustic guitar and see what happens?" He meant well, but I couldn't think of anything worse. The idea of being alone in a remote part of the country with an acoustic guitar was pretty much my definition of hell.

And when I did manage to write songs in that period, I suffered some knock-backs. I put some material forward to the record company which got dismissed as derivative and not up to muster. I was failing to get songs on my own albums, which was discouraging. I only had two of my own songs on *A Spanner in the Works*, the 1995 album, and *When We Were the New Boys*, which came out in 1998, contained just one song that I had a hand in: the title track. The rest were songs plucked out for me by the record company, who did their best. But I wasn't bringing anything to the table and I was beginning to think of myself as entirely a voice for hire: tell me what to sing, and I'll sing it. And on *Human*, it showed. All in all, it felt like a very good moment to try something different.

One night, I was out for dinner with the producer Richard Perry, a good friend of mine. Richard had produced some of the greatest pop tracks of all time: Carly Simon's "You're So Vain," Barbra Streisand's "Stoney End," albums by Harry Nilsson, the Temptations, Art Garfunkel, Tina Turner, and many others. Richard's home in West Hollywood sat just above Sunset Boulevard and was always known for what he christened "Perry's Pub"—a party room with a fully stocked bar. It was the scene of much late-night skulduggery through the 1970s and beyond, and a place you knew you could always fall into at the end of an evening for a full-blown knees-up with drink and music and dancing.

Over dinner, I mentioned to Richard my long-standing dream of a standards album. He loved Billie Holiday and Ella Fitzgerald as much as I did, and he really warmed to the notion. We started throwing titles of songs at each other: "Cheek to Cheek," "I've Got You Under My Skin," "September in the Rain" . . . I had to ask the waiter for a pen and some paper so I could write them down. One of us would mention a song, and I would start singing it to Richard, testing whether it would work. The other diners in the restaurant must have thought they were present at some wildly overcooked seduction scene—me singing "It Had to Be You" loudly at the man across the table.

We decided to record some demos. Richard hired some crack jazz-pop session musicians and we laid down five songs from our list in three or four hours. But I wasn't that thrilled with them. The approach was very conventional and I thought anybody could do it that way, and had done it that way. I wanted to make it different and open it up to more contemporary influences. So Richard started again, with some different musicians, this time in a little demo studio in the Valley, and built a set of backing tracks that were much more lush and synthesized and altogether more modern-sounding.

Eventually we had ten tracks in some shape or other, ready to show people—songs like "You Go to My Head," "Stormy Weather," and "I've Grown Accustomed to Her Face," the Lerner and Loewe song from *My Fair Lady*, a number I had already recorded back in 1974 for the *Smiler* album. We felt it was a strong set and were pretty excited about it.

The question was, would anybody else like it? Arnold promptly took the tracks to Val Azzoli, the co-chairman of Atlantic Records, part of Warner Bros., which was my label at the time, to see if he would be interested in releasing a Rod Stewart standards album. Azzoli shook his head and said, "No, certainly not."

Not selected by my own team: that was a bitter blow.

Arnold's next port of call was Mo and Michael Ostin and Lenny Waronker, with whom I had worked for a long time and very successfully at Warner Bros., but who were now at DreamWorks. Their reaction was like Azzoli's, only slightly worse. They said, "This is terrible. This will never sell. This is not good for Rod's career."

Blow number two.

Still, having done the decent thing and given the first listens to our closest and firmest associates in the business, Arnold now at least felt able to widen the net and take the record to the person he had always thought would be ideal: Clive Davis, the quintessential artist/music man, a legend in the industry and the former president of Columbia Records and Arista Records, who, in 2000, had founded the label J Records. Arnold flew to see him in New York and played the tracks to him in his office.

Clive listened carefully and said, "I love the concept, and I love some of the song choices, but I don't think the tracks sound right." Arnold thought he was about to be shown the door again. But something about the notion had clearly hooked Clive. After a while he said, "If Rod Stewart's willing to risk it, so am I. Let's do it. But it's a one-album deal." Some hours and lots of excited talk later, Arnold left Clive with a two-album deal in hand.

Clive thought the contemporary production was a mistake, so Richard and I made some more demos in which we took out the synthesizers and the programmed percussion and put in band instruments and strings. One afternoon in 2002, we took these versions to Clive in Bungalow 8A at the Beverly Hills Hotel, where he was staying. It turned into one of the most surreal business meetings I have ever attended. It was clear that the demos were closer to what Clive was hoping to hear, but he still wanted the songs to be more danceable. He said, "I don't want these low *movie* strings. I want it lilting, lilting—like Fred and Ginger, lilting, *lilting*." And as he spoke, this seventy-year-old music mogul stood up and began wafting his hands in front of him as if conducting an orchestra, and swaying from side to side. And Arnold and I stood up and began doing the same—conducting with our hands and weaving our shoulders, and then Richard stood up, and suddenly all four of us were Fred and Gingering around the room and saying, "Lilting, lilting . . ." Arnold and I were still dancing when we left, twisting and turning along the path, calling out, "Lilting, lilting . . ."

So, with that message received, we went back into the studio. Richard got to produce some of the songs, and the producer Phil Ramone, a very sweet man with an incredible track record encompassing everyone from Dylan to Sinatra, was brought in to provide additional "Fred and Gingerfication" on the others.

It was in this phase that I felt the project become extremely personal to me. I was playing this new material to Penny. After dinner, up at Perry's Pub, Richard and I would play tracks to her and gauge from her reaction if they were working. This was in the very early stages of my and Penny's relationship, when she was going back and forth to London to complete her college photography course and her suitcase always seemed to be packed and waiting by the door. And so many of the songs I was working on seemed to speak directly to our predicament: parting and reuniting, longing for each other from a distance, those first pangs of romance. "Ev'ry Time We Say Goodbye," "The Very Thought of You," "We'll Be Together Again," "The Nearness of You": these songs were a soundtrack to those first months of our courtship, almost as if they were designed to tell its story, which, in turn, caused me to form an even stronger bond with the material and an even greater desire to get it right.

Eventually, we had an album: *It Had to Be You . . . The Great*

American Songbook. Now all I needed to do was convince the public that Rod Stewart, hitherto known primarily as a rock star, was also a plausible singer of 32-bar ballads. I loved singing these songs as much as I loved singing anything. The internal rhymes, the unforced, conversational way in which the lyric rides the tune, the sheer amount of craft and polish in the construction—for a singer, this stuff is a gift.

But it was one thing to close your eyes in the privacy of a studio and deliver songs made famous by Billie Holiday and Ella Fitzgerald, and quite another to go and do it in front of other people. One of the most nervous times of my life was before the launch event for the album at the St. Regis Hotel in Los Angeles. It was set up as a swanky listening session, over cocktails and hors d'oeuvres, in a huge, lavishly decorated ballroom, with little round candlelit tables, for five hundred music-industry and show-business bigwigs. Clive was tireless in the promotion of this record—gave countless interviews, came on television with me to talk it up (which was great, because I hate doing that stuff myself), and generally treated the thing as if it were the second coming of the Beatles.

On this particular night, he went onto the stage and talked about the music with love and conviction and played some of the tracks. And then I came out and, as a surprise, sang four of the songs live. Round the back beforehand, I realized I was experiencing the kind of fear I hadn't known since I got up with the Jeff Beck Group at the Fillmore East in New York all those years ago and first sang the blues to Americans. I had the same sense that I was about to be *exposed.* I said to Arnold something that I had found myself telling him pretty frequently during the development of this project: "Management, if this all goes tits-up, then be it on your head." And then I breathed deeply, knocked back a cocktail, went out there, and gave them "They Can't Take That Away from Me," "The Way You Look Tonight," "These Foolish Things," and "You Go to My Head." Really, all I wanted to prove was that I wasn't there as an impostor, that I could treat the songs with reverence, just giving them voice and letting their truthfulness come out.

And it went well. Soon after, on a Saturday evening in New York, I taped for television an in-concert live performance of the songs at Sony Studios, and this bolstered my confidence even more. The show was rehearsed with a full orchestra, on a beautifully lit stage, in front of an audience of a couple of hundred people, with music stands with an "RS" logo on them: the works. I wore white tie and tails that night, and as I put them on in the dressing room, the trepidation was there again, but once I was out there I got over it by listening to the band and sinking into the songs, and gradually my shoulders went down and it began to flow.

The album went platinum in the U.K. and double platinum in the U.S., sold 5 million copies, and launched a series. To my amazement, a second volume, released the next year, 2003, entitled *As Time Goes By . . . The Great American Songbook 2*, was as successful as the first. And on it went. By the time this series wrapped, we'd clocked 22 million copies.

The clincher for me, though, was sometime after the fourth *Songbook* volume came out, when I got into a conversation in a café in Los Angeles with an American GI who had been part of the second wave of allied landings on Omaha Beach in Normandy in the Second World War. After we had talked about that for a while, this guy said, "By the way, you make those old songs sound brand-new." I couldn't have hoped for a better vote of confidence from a better source.

And I actually won a Grammy—Best Traditional Pop Vocal—for 2004's *Stardust: The Great American Songbook 3*. When I found out (I was on tour in Australia when the awards were announced), I knew for sure that the world truly was upside down. I had been nominated for one of the American music industry's prestigious awards no fewer than twelve times in my career, stretching back to 1980, and had never won one, and I had long since decided that it must have been something I had said.

The staggering and unlooked-for success of the *Songbook* series—and, more specifically, the fact that this staggering and unlooked-for success came when it did—was just fantastically empowering, unexpected, validating, and something for which I will always be grateful. In 2001, before it happened, I was thinking, "Well, it's been a good run, mate, but maybe it's time to admit that the party's over and get your coat."

And then, the next thing I know, it's 2010, I'm sixty-five years old, and I'm looking back over what was the most commercially successful decade of my entire life.

CONCLUSION

In which our hero meditates profoundly on his retirement
from everything, recounts a visit to Buckingham Palace
in unconventional neckwear, and rules out golf.

am under no illusions. I know that one day it will come to an end.
I know that eventually—and it may be sooner, rather than later—I
will reach a stage where getting out there and performing is simply
no longer possible. And I don't know how I'm going to feel about that.
It's been there all my life. I've given so much to it, and it's given so
much back to me. I worry about the hole it will leave.

I'm talking about playing football, obviously.

For now, though, I'm hanging in there. I play in an over-fifties
league for Fram, a team founded by expat Norwegians in Los Angeles, but now mostly featuring expat Brits. You'll find me up bright and
early on a Sunday morning and driving out to the coast to our home
ground, Framsen Field—surely the best pitch in the league for having
a good flat covering of grass and no potholes, bunkers, or exposed

sprinkler spikes, unlike some of the other death-pit places where we play. And we're all more beat up than we'll ever admit, but we simply don't care, because we're out there in the kit, playing. And I've still got my cuffs clamped in my palms like Denis Law, and, at sixty-seven, I'm still good for forty-five minutes, maybe even seventy if it comes to it, and still jogging over to deliver an utterly lethal in-swinging corner from the left-hand side when called upon.

And then, when the game's done, we'll all trudge—and often limp—back to the clapboard changing room, which is decked with British football memorabilia, scarves from Scotland and England, pictures of Charlie Cooke and George Best playing in California, and a photo of me, clipped from *Playboy*. And we'll sit around on the benches for a while—Ken and Trevor, who run the team, Freddie, Celtic John—and someone will open a box of beers and Tommy the Scot will get up and tell utterly disgusting jokes and there'll be banter and piss-taking, some of it at the expense of my rather lovely, soft brown Prada kit bag, and for that half an hour or so I'm as contented as a man can be.

But when I can't do that anymore, what then? I hate to think of it. Golf? My dad played it, but I don't think it's me. I'd enjoy the clothes, probably. There's a lot of golfing knitwear out there that I'd be quite excited about putting my head through. Plus-fours have a certain vintage appeal, too. But the game? I'm not so sure. I don't think I have the patience.

I did try it once. The film actor Sean Connery persuaded me to go out with him and give it a go. This was on a course in Spain one time in the 1980s. He taught me the grip and the stance. "Feet apart, Rod. Try to keep your shoulders level . . ."

I took a swing, caught the top of the ball, and watched it shoot, at roughly rabbit height, about twenty-five feet off to the right into a nearby clump of grass.

Sean was very patient. He said, "What you need to do is loosen your grip. You're choking down too tightly."

So I tried again, with looser hands. This time I missed the ball completely. It was still on the tee. The club, on the other hand, flew straight down the fairway, arcing through the air, a distance of many yards. That was it for me. Lesson over. I returned to the clubhouse.

Outside of football, I don't worry about aging so much. I look around at people I've worked with down the years and I think, relatively speaking, that I'm not doing too badly. Moisturizing is the key, ladies and gentlemen: plenty of Oil of Olay. But it's mostly luck, of course—luck and genes. My brother Don is still refereeing football matches, and he's in his eighties. But I do work at it—in the gym or out on the pitch every morning in the company of my highly learned personal trainer, Gary O'Connor, whose brief is, essentially, to enable me to become the world's oldest still-playing right back. And I'm sensible in my habits: the right food, a glass of wine or two with dinner, but no more.

And, of course, no drugs. Cocaine ended for me in the early 2000s, by which time I was hardly touching the stuff in any case—just the occasional small line to jolly along a night out in Epping, say. But even in those tiny quantities, I realized it was getting to my voice—drying out the membranes. And then Penny said, "Look, you're not getting any younger. You need to be taking better care of yourself. Also, when you do that stuff, you don't become fun: you become absorbed in one topic and it's usually football. So if that's going to happen, I'm not coming out." That was enough for me.

Do I regret those days when I took it? Well, I'm not denying that I had some fabulous times. But I'm not proud of it. And I was one of the lucky ones. I did it when it was new and fun and exciting. I did it on some extremely high-quality stuff. And I got in and got out unscathed. I never reached the stage where my life depended on me having to have cocaine—or anything else. Others weren't so lucky and suffered badly for it.

And here's something to confess: I've never bought any drugs in my life. Never bought my own cocaine. Wouldn't really know how to go about it, actually. How bad is that? It was just around. Someone in the band would always have some, so I would say to Boiler, the stage manager, "Go and see if any of the boys have got a little bit of movement," as we used to call it, or, "See if you can find me a little bit of shovel."

Didn't have to buy my own coke, can't buy a drink in my local pub in Essex, the Theydon Oak, even if I want to . . . life's been kind. (John and Sheila, the landlord and landlady at the Oak, have always looked after me very well.)

I worry about the end of my career far more than I worry about aging. There is no template for growing old as a rock star. There's no pattern out there that you can follow. We were the first to come this way, flaunting our youth as we did so, and we've got no choice but to be pioneers going out the other end, when youth has ceased to be an option. So we've got no choice but to make our own paths and try to do what suits us. What I'm hoping is that I'm going to have the judgment and the foresight to pack it in at the right time instead of hanging around for ages, playing smaller and smaller places. I've got a lot of pride holding me in check in that respect. But, at the same time, who knows how desperate one could be to keep it going, in some form—or any form? After all, the performing—it's who I am. It feels like what I was put down here to do. If I go a month without a concert, I get all jittery and miss it. And when that ends, it will be a huge lump out of my life.

The happy thing is, it shows no sign of ending. Business hasn't plateaued in quite a while—not since the early 1990s, when I really did think I was on my way to the wastepaper basket. But the success of the *Songbook* albums meant that people started coming out to the shows again. The tour I did in 2004, after the first of the *Songbook* albums, was one of my favorites of all time. It was titled "From Maggie May to *The Great American Songbook*," and we played a rock set, then a *Songbook* set, and then finished up with "Da Ya Think I'm Sexy?" and "Maggie May." Despite the signpost in the title, a few older listeners came expecting only to hear the standards. Now, that's a tour I would love to do one day. But on this occasion, when we came on and blasted into "Sweet Little Rock 'n' Roller," there were a few startled faces. They seemed to get into it, though. The band was in tuxes, the girls were in long dresses, I was in tails, and we were on this beautifully draped classical set designed by Ian Knight, an absolute genius in this area with whom I collaborated closely on sets for my tours from the mid-1980s onwards. Ian would build these wonderful HO-scale models of the sets, with little figures for the band—which I really related to, as a model railroader—and he came up with some glorious schemes, including an in-the-round set for the 2007 tour which had a 1,500-yard tartan curtain wrapped right around it. Ian died in 2010 and is much missed.

In August 2011, I was fortunate enough to be offered a two-year residency at the Colosseum at Caesars Palace in Las Vegas. My brother Don said, "You won't like that, Roddy—all those people eating their dinners and chatting while you're trying to sing." But, of course, that's old-school. In this case a residency means twenty-six nights a year in a 4,100-seat concert venue that is probably the best room I've ever played in: superb acoustics, and a lovely low stage, so you feel really close to the audience. And me and the tightest band I've had in all my years on the road turn out some roistering versions of the hits, and I kick a few footballs out at some point and go walk about among the floor seats if the fancy takes me. It's a party.

And on it goes. A little while back, Arnold and I sat down with my schedule for 2013 and, after we had blocked off the important dates (the Scottish Cup Final, the friendly international between England and Scotland at Wembley in August), we began to outline the touring—and we were putting in runs at the O$_2$ Arena in London,

Hampden Park in Scotland, Madison Square Garden in New York. After all this time, it's just remarkable. I feel extremely grateful.

I f I was staggered to get a Grammy in 2005, I was knocked to the ground to get a CBE in 2006. That's "Commander of the Most Excellent Order of the British Empire," to give it the full title, an honor awarded to British nationals who are deemed to have made an impact on their country. Penny and I were with Alastair in Palm Beach when the news of the award came through, and Arnold flew down and threw me a party with three cakes spelling out CBE. Then, in July 2007, just two weeks after our wedding, Penny and I went to Buckingham Palace for the official ceremony. If you're a working-class lad from north London, an invitation to be honored at the palace feels like the stuff of fantasy. Both Penny and I, as kids, had driven past the place, stood outside the railings, and sat on the ornamental lions of the Victoria Memorial. Buckingham Palace is part of your lore as a British kid. Now here we were, sweeping in through the gates, driving under the arch into the inner courtyard, walking up the red carpeted steps and going inside, exactly like we had seen people do on television. I wore a blazer with some white slacks, a white shirt with black stripes, and a skull-and-crossbones tie. I think I was meant to be in morning dress, but never mind—I looked very dashing. We were taken into an anteroom and offered a glass of wine, and then ushered carefully into line in the ceremonial room where a small orchestra was playing and where the atmosphere was formal yet light and jubilant at the same time. At the head of the line, Prince Charles congratulated me and handed me my medal on a silk ribbon in a velvet case.

I'm very proud of my CBE. I stick those letters on the end of my name whenever I can. Some people keep their medals packed away in their cases. Not me. Soon after I got it, I wore it to a café with four of my kids and got snapped by one of the papers, leaning across the table with the medal dangling beside a bottle of HP Sauce—surely the closest a CBE has ever been to a bottle of the legendary brown condiment. I like having my CBE where I can regularly see it. At the moment, it's hanging around the neck of a statue of Napoleon in my bathroom.

So there were the *Songbooks*, and there was the Grammy, and there was the CBE, and there was even the musical based around my songs: Ben Elton's *Tonight's the Night*, which ran at the Victoria Palace Theatre in London for a year from October 2003. Penny took a part in that show for the last three weeks of its run, as leader of the Hot Legs Dance Troupe, reprising the role she had played for fun in a one-off charity version of the show earlier in its life.

And the next thing I know I'm being asked to sing in front of Her Majesty the Queen. And I mean right in front of her. She was about ten feet away from me, on a small throne. What an extraordinary honor for a bloke from the Archway Road—and what an utterly nerve-shredding challenge. It seems the stroppy, faux-Marxist teenager who posed with a copy of the *Daily Worker* was a royalist in the end. This was in the summer of 2007 at St. James's Palace, during an evening on behalf of the Royal National Institute of Blind People. I sang "The Way You Look Tonight" and dedicated it to Penny, a fortnight before our wedding.

These wonderful new experiences and vindications kept coming in the 2000s. But there was still a shadow at the back of my mind, because the thing I knew was gone for good was songwriting. That was all over. It had always been difficult, and then it was so much easier not to bother. I convinced myself that I had made the best of the little bit of talent for songwriting that I had been given. I persuaded myself, indeed, that maybe it wasn't ever truly a gift that I had had. Don't get me wrong, I'm proud of the catalogue of songs I've written—of "Maggie May" and "You Wear It Well" and "Mandolin Wind" and

"Forever Young." But it was almost as if a person I didn't know used to write those songs.

And then, when I was least expecting it, I bumped into that person again.

Late in 2011, Jim Cregan came for Sunday lunch at the Wood House in Epping, and afterwards we went and sat in the White Room, and Jim got his guitar out and started strumming. He wanted to show me something he had written, and then he said, "Why don't we try and come up with something?" To be perfectly frank, I was rather looking forward to a Sunday-afternoon postlunch snooze. And Jim can be so serious when he picks up a guitar—like he's saying to you, "This is a very important part of my life." So the level of my enthusiasm for an impromptu writing session at this time was not high. Still, Jim strummed, and I hummed a bit of a melody over the top of what he was playing, and Jim was recording what we did on his iPhone. And after a very short while, I said, "Let's knock it on the head now, Jim," because I thought, "This is going nowhere."

And he took what we had done home, and he worked on the iPhone recording in his studio and replayed the guitar part and smartened it up a bit, and then he sent it back to me. And when I played it back, I found myself thinking, "Hang on, this is actually really good." And then the title "Brighton Beach" dropped into my head—from nowhere, as titles always used to, and for no reason I could put my finger on—and right then I started writing a lyric: about hobnobbing on the south coast of England as a kid and being a beatnik. And very quickly—much quicker than I was used to—I found myself with a finished song. Better than that: a good finished song, one I could feel proud of.

And that was it: I was away. Suddenly ideas for lyrics were piling up in my head. Next thing I knew, I had a song called "It's Over," about divorce and separation—something, as we may have discovered in these pages, that I know a bit about. And now I was getting up in the middle of the night to write things down, which has never happened to me: a song of advice for my children, a song of gratitude to my dad. I finished seven or eight songs very quickly and I still wasn't finished, and it became apparent that I might just have ten original songs to record—a wholly original album, and I've never done that. It's always been about five or six, and the rest cover versions.

I don't know why it happened. No one pushed me. It was clean out of the blue. It felt like another piece of the pure luck with which I have been blessed in my life. (And trust me, there is not a day goes by that I don't wake up and think how lucky I am.) But something clicked and I realized that I had things to write about again. A whole life's worth of topics, in fact. The book you've just read.

Taking those new songs into the studio in 2012 and beginning to shape them up for an album release in 2013, I fell back in love with the whole process. I was living and breathing it again. It was like a rebirth, a root right back to the beginning. In fact, I'm not sure I had this much enthusiasm when I made those first albums of mine in London, back in the early 1970s, as a kid with a rooster haircut, feeling his way forward by instinct and sheer nerve. But what is definitely true is that I haven't felt so confident about a new set of recordings, as a writer and as a producer, since *Gasoline Alley*.

Of course, the album will come out, and then we'll see. But whatever becomes of those recordings, hit or miss, is irrelevant, really, beside what I understand to be the true moral of this episode, which is that sometimes when you think you've finished, it turns out that you haven't.

Mind you, I'll be absolutely gutted if the album is anything less than an international sensation.

ACKNOWLEDGMENTS

To everyone I've known along the way. There isn't enough room between these pages to mention you all, but surely you know who you are, and moreover, the part we played in each other's lives. From the bottom of my heart, thank you.

And especially to Giles Smith, my wonderful editor and confidant. I couldn't have found a lovelier, more talented and tireless bloke to work with on the book. You've made remembering my life such a pleasure.

That's it from me, then. I'm off to put the kettle on and make a nice cup of tea. Bye.

DISCOGRAPHY

ROD STEWART: STUDIO ALBUMS

1969, *An Old Raincoat Won't Ever Let You Down* (Vertigo, U.K./ Mercury, U.S.)
1. *Street Fighting Man* (Mick Jagger, Keith Richards) 2. *Man of Constant Sorrow* (traditional, arranged by Rod Stewart) 3. *Blind Prayer* (Rod Stewart) 4. *Handbags and Gladrags* (Mike d'Abo) 5. *An Old Raincoat Won't Ever Let You Down* (Rod Stewart) 6. *I Wouldn't Ever Change a Thing* (Rod Stewart) 7. *Cindy's Lament* (Rod Stewart) 8. *Dirty Old Town* (Ewan MacColl)

1970, *Gasoline Alley* (Vertigo, U.K./Mercury, U.S.)
1. *Gasoline Alley* (Rod Stewart, Ronnie Wood) 2. *It's All Over Now* (Bobby Womack, Shirley Jean Womack) 3. *Only a Hobo* (Bob Dylan) 4. *My Way of Giving* (Ronnie Lane, Steve Marriott) 5. *Country Comfort* (Elton John, Bernie Taupin) 6. *Cut Across Shorty* (Wayne P. Walker, Marijohn Wilkin) 7. *Lady Day* (Rod Stewart) 8. *Jo's Lament* (Rod Stewart) 9. *You're My Girl (I Don't Want to Discuss It)* (Beth Beatty, Dick Cooper, Ernie Shelby)

1971, *Every Picture Tells a Story* (Mercury)
1. *Every Picture Tells a Story* (Rod Stewart, Ronnie Wood) 2. *Seems Like a Long Time* (Theodore Anderson) 3. *That's All Right* (Arthur Crudup) 4. *Amazing Grace* (traditional by John Newton, arranged by Rod Stewart) 5. *Tomorrow Is a Long Time* (Bob Dylan) 6. *Henry* (Martin Quittenton) 7. *Maggie May* (Martin Quittenton, Rod Stewart) 8. *Mandolin Wind* (Rod Stewart) 9. *(I Know) I'm Losing You* (Cornelius Grant, Eddie Holland, Norman Whitfield) 10. *Reason to Believe* (Tim Hardin)

1972, *Never a Dull Moment* (Mercury)
1. *True Blue* (Rod Stewart, Ronnie Wood) 2. *Lost Paraguayos* (Rod Stewart, Ronnie Wood) 3. *Mama You Been on My Mind* (Bob Dylan) 4. *Italian Girls* (Rod Stewart, Ronnie Wood) 5. *Angel* (Jimi Hendrix) 6. *Interludings* (Art Wood) 7. *You Wear It Well* (Martin Quittenton, Rod Stewart) 8. *I'd Rather Go Blind* (Billy Foster, Ellington Jordan) 9. *Twisting the Night Away* (Sam Cooke)

1974, *Smiler* (Mercury)
1. *Sweet Little Rock 'n' Roller* (Chuck Berry) 2. *Lochinvar* (Pete Sears) 3. *Farewell* (Martin Quittenton, Rod Stewart) 4. *Sailor* (Rod Stewart, Ronnie Wood) 5. *Bring It on Home to Me/You Send Me* (Sam Cooke) 6. *Let Me Be Your Car* (Elton John, Bernie Taupin) 7. *(You Make Me Feel Like a) Natural Man* (Gerry Goffin, Carole King, Jerry Wexler) 8. *Dixie Toot* (Rod Stewart, Ronnie Wood) 9. *Hard Road* (Harry Vanda, George Young) 10. *I've Grown Accustomed to Her Face* (Alan Jay Lerner, Frederick Loewe) 11. *Girl from the North Country* (Bob Dylan) 12. *Mine for Me* (Paul McCartney, Linda McCartney)

1975, *Atlantic Crossing* (Riva Records, U.K./Warner Bros., U.S.)
1. *Three Time Loser* (Rod Stewart) 2. *Alright for an Hour* (Jesse Ed Davis, Rod Stewart) 3. *All in the Name of Rock and Roll* (Rod Stewart) 4. *Drift Away* (Mentor Williams) 5. *Stone Cold Sober* (Steve Cropper, Rod Stewart) 6. *I Don't Want to Talk About It* (Danny Whitten) 7. *It's Not the Spotlight* (Gerry Goffin, Barry Goldberg) 8. *This Old Heart of Mine* (Lamont Dozier, Brian Holland, Edward Holland, Jr., Sylvia Moy) 9. *Still Love You* (Rod Stewart) 10. *Sailing* (Gavin Sutherland)

1976, *A Night on the Town* (Riva Records, U.K./Warner Bros., U.S.)
1. *Tonight's the Night (Gonna Be Alright)* (Rod Stewart) 2. *The First Cut Is the Deepest* (Cat Stevens) 3. *Fool for You* (Rod Stewart) 4. *The Killing of Georgie (Part I and II)* (Rod Stewart) 5. *The Balltrap* (Rod Stewart) 6. *Pretty Flamingo* (Mark Barkan) 7. *Big Bayou* (Floyd Gilbeau) 8. *The Wild Side of Life* (Arlie Carter, Wayne Walker) 9. *Trade Winds* (Ralph MacDonald, William Salter)

1977, *Foot Loose & Fancy Free* (Riva Records, U.K./Warner Bros., U.S.)

1. *Hot Legs* (Rod Stewart) 2. *You're Insane* (Phil Chen, Rod Stewart) 3. *You're in My Heart (The Final Acclaim)* (Rod Stewart) 4. *Born Loose* (Jim Cregan, Gary Grainger, Rod Stewart) 5. *You Keep Me Hangin' On* (Lamont Dozier, Brian Holland, Edward Holland, Jr.) 6. *(If Loving You Is Wrong) I Don't Want to Be Right* (Homer Banks, Carl Hampton, Raymond Jackson) 7. *You Got a Nerve* (Gary Grainger, Rod Stewart) 8. *I Was Only Joking* (Gary Grainger, Rod Stewart)

1978, *Blondes Have More Fun* (Riva Records, U.K./Warner Bros., U.S.)

1. *Da Ya Think I'm Sexy?* (Carmine Appice, Rod Stewart) 2. *Dirty Weekend* (Gary Grainger, Rod Stewart) 3. *Ain't Love a Bitch* (Jim Cregan, Rod Stewart) 4. *The Best Days of My Life* (Jim Cregan, Rod Stewart) 5. *Is That the Thanks I Get?* (Jim Cregan, Rod Stewart) 6. *Attractive Female Wanted* (Gary Grainger, Rod Stewart) 7. *Blondes (Have More Fun)* (Jim Cregan, Rod Stewart) 8. *Last Summer* (Jim Cregan, Rod Stewart) 9. *Standin' in the Shadows of Love* (Lamont Dozier, Brian Holland, Edward Holland, Jr.) 10. *Scarred and Scared* (Gary Grainger, Rod Stewart)

1980, *Foolish Behaviour* (Riva Records, U.K./Warner Bros., U.S.)

1. *Better Off Dead* (Carmine Appice, Phil Chen, Kevin Savigar, Rod Stewart) 2. *Passion* (Phil Chen, Jim Cregan, Gary Grainger, Kevin Savigar, Rod Stewart) 3. *Foolish Behaviour* (Phil Chen, Jim Cregan, Gary Grainger, Kevin Savigar, Rod Stewart) 4. *So Soon We Change* (Phil Chen, Jim Cregan, Gary Grainger, Kevin Savigar, Rod Stewart) 5. *Oh God, I Wish I Was Home Tonight* (Phil Chen, Jim Cregan, Gary Grainger, Kevin Savigar, Rod Stewart) 6. *Gi' Me Wings* (Phil Chen, Jim Cregan, Gary Grainger, Kevin Savigar, Rod Stewart) 7. *My Girl* (Carmine Appice, Phil Chen, Jim Cregan, Gary Grainger, Kevin Savigar, Rod Stewart) 8. *She Won't Dance with Me* (Jorge Ben, Rod Stewart) 9. *Somebody Special* (Phil Chen, Jim Cregan, Steve Harley, Kevin Savigar, Rod Stewart) 10. *Say It*

Ain't True (Phil Chen, Jim Cregan, Gary Grainger, Kevin Savigar, Rod Stewart) 11. *I Just Wanna Make Love to You* [live, bonus track] (Willie Dixon)

1981, *Tonight I'm Yours* (Warner Bros.)
1. *Tonight I'm Yours (Don't Hurt Me)* (Rod Stewart, Jim Cregan, Kevin Savigar) 2. *How Long* (Paul Carrack) 3. *Tora, Tora, Tora (Out with the Boys)* (Rod Stewart) 4. *Tear It Up* (Dorsey Burnette, Johnny Burnette) 5. *Only a Boy* (Jim Cregan, Kevin Savigar, Rod Stewart) 6. *Just Like a Woman* (Bob Dylan) 7. *Jealous* (Carmine Appice, Jay Davis, Danny Johnson, Rod Stewart) 8. *Sonny* (Jim Cregan, Kevin Savigar, Rod Stewart, Bernie Taupin) 9. *Young Turks* (Carmine Appice, Duane Hitchings, Kevin Savigar, Rod Stewart) 10. *Never Give Up on a Dream* (Jim Cregan, Rod Stewart, Bernie Taupin)

1983, *Body Wishes* (Warner Bros.)
1. *Dancin' Alone* (Robin LeMesurier, Rod Stewart) 2. *Baby Jane* (Jay Davis, Rod Stewart) 3. *Move Me* (Tony Brock, Jay Davis, Kevin Savigar, Rod Stewart, Wally Stocker) 4. *Body Wishes* (Jim Cregan, Robin LeMesurier, Kevin Savigar, Rod Stewart) 5. *Sweet Surrender* (Robin LeMesurier, Rod Stewart) 6. *What Am I Gonna Do (I'm So in Love with You)* (Tony Brock, Jay Davis, Rod Stewart) 7. *Ghetto Blaster* (Jim Cregan, Kevin Savigar, Rod Stewart) 8. *Ready Now* (Rod Stewart, Wally Stocker) 9. *Strangers Again* (Jim Cregan, Kevin Savigar, Rod Stewart) 10. *Satisfied* (Jim Cregan, Kevin Savigar, Rod Stewart, Bernie Taupin)

1984, *Camouflage* (Warner Bros.)
1. *Infatuation* (Duane Hitchings, Rowland Robinson, Rod Stewart) 2. *All Right Now* (Andy Fraser, Paul Rodgers) 3. *Some Guys Have All the Luck* (Jeff Fortang) 4. *Can We Still Be Friends* (Todd Rundgren) 5. *Bad for You* (Jim Cregan, Kevin Savigar, Rod Stewart) 6. *Heart Is on the Line* (Jay Davis, Rod Stewart) 7. *Camouflage* (Michael Omartian, Kevin Savigar, Rod Stewart) 8. *Trouble* (Michael Omartian, Rod Stewart)

1986, *Every Beat of My Heart* (Warner Bros.)

1. *Here to Eternity* (Kevin Savigar, Rod Stewart) 2. *Another Heartache* (Bryan Adams, Rod Stewart, Jim Vallance, Randy Wayne) 3. *A Night Like This* (Rod Stewart) 4. *Who's Gonna Take Me Home* (Jay Davis, Kevin Savigar, Rod Stewart) 5. *Red Hot in Black* (Jim Cregan, Kevin Savigar, Rod Stewart) 6. *Love Touch* (Gene Black, Mike Chapman, Holly Knight) 7. *In My Own Crazy Way* (Frankie Miller, Troy Seals, Eddie Setser, Rod Stewart) 8. *Every Beat of My Heart* (Kevin Savigar, Rod Stewart) 9. *Ten Days of Rain* (Tony Brock, Kevin Savigar, Rod Stewart) 10. *In My Life* (John Lennon, Paul McCartney)

1988, *Out of Order* (Warner Bros./WEA)

1. *Lost in You* (Rod Stewart, Andy Taylor) 2. *The Wild Horse* (Rod Stewart, Andy Taylor) 3. *Lethal Dose of Love* (Rod Stewart, Andy Taylor) 4. *Forever Young* (Jim Cregan, Bob Dylan, Kevin Savigar, Rod Stewart) 5. *My Heart Can't Tell You No* (Simon Climie, Dennis Morgan) 6. *Dynamite* (Rod Stewart, Andy Taylor) 7. *Nobody Knows You When You're Down and Out* (James Cox) 8. *Crazy About Her* (Jim Cregan, Duane Hitchings, Rod Stewart) 9. *Try a Little Tenderness* (Jimmy Campbell, Reginald Connelly, Harry M. Woods) 10. *When I Was Your Man* (Kevin Savigar, Rod Stewart) 11. *Almost Illegal* (Rod Stewart, Andy Taylor)

1991, *Vagabond Heart* (Warner Bros.)

1. *Rhythm of My Heart* (John Capek, Marc T. Jordan) 2. *Rebel Heart* (Jeff Golub, Chuck Kentis, Carmine Rojas, Rod Stewart) 3. *Broken Arrow* (Robbie Robertson) 4. *It Takes Two* [duet with Tina Turner] (Sylvia Moy, William "Mickey" Stevenson) 5. *When a Man's in Love* (Jeff Golub, Chuck Kentis, Carmine Rojas, Rod Stewart) 6. *You Are Everything* (Thom Bell, Linda Creed) 7. *The Motown Song* (Larry John McNally) 8. *Go Out Dancing* (Jeff Golub, Chuck Kentis, Rod Stewart) 9. *No Holding Back* (Jim Cregan, Kevin Savigar, Rod Stewart) 10. *Have I Told You Lately* (Van Morrison) 11. *Moment of Glory* (Jeff Golub, Chuck Kentis, Carmine Rojas, Rod Stewart) 12. *If Only* (Jim Cregan, Kevin Savigar, Rod Stewart)

1995, *A Spanner in the Works* (Warner Bros.)
1. *Windy Town* (Chris Rea) 2. *The Downtown Lights* (Paul Buchanan)
3. *Leave Virginia Alone* (Tom Petty) 4. *Sweetheart Like You* (Bob Dylan)
5. *This* (John Capek, Marc Jordan) 6. *Lady Luck* (Jeff Golub, Carmine
Rojas, Kevin Savigar, Rod Stewart) 7. *You're the Star* (Billy Livsey,
Graham Lyle, Frankie Miller) 8. *Muddy, Sam and Otis* (Kevin Savigar,
Rod Stewart) 9. *Hang On St. Christopher* (Tom Waits) 10. *Delicious*
(Robin LeMesurier, Rod Stewart, Andy Taylor) 11. *Soothe Me* (Sam
Cooke) 12. *Purple Heather* (traditional by Francis McPeake, arranged
by Rod Stewart)

1998, *When We Were the New Boys* (Warner Bros.)
1. *Cigarettes and Alcohol* (Noel Gallagher) 2. *Ooh La La* (Ronnie
Lane, Ronnie Wood) 3. *Rocks* (Bobby Gillespie, Andrew Innes,
Robert Young) 4. *Superstar* (Joseph McAlinden) 5. *Secret Heart* (Ron
Sexsmith) 6. *Hotel Chambermaid* (Graham Parker) 7. *Shelly My Love*
(Nick Lowe) 8. *When We Were the New Boys* (Kevin Savigar, Rod
Stewart) 9. *Weak* (Robbie France, Martin Kent, Richard Lewis)
10. *What Do You Want Me to Do?* (Mike Scott)

2001, *Human* (Atlantic)
1. *Human* (Karl Gordon, Connor Reeves) 2. *Smitten* (Macy Gray,
Arik Marshall, Jeremy Ruzuma, Dave Wilder) 3. *Don't Come Around
Here* (Paul Berry, Jackie Joyce, Mark Taylor, Kenny Thomas) 4. *Soul
on Soul* (John Capek, Marc Jordan) 5. *Loveless* (David Frank, Connor
Reeves) 6. *If I Had You* (Andrew Davis, Sergei Rachmaninoff)
7. *Charlie Parker Loves Me* (John Capek, Marc Jordan) 8. *It Was Love
That We Needed* (Curtis Mayfield) 9. *To Be with You* (Raul Malo)
10. *Run Back into Your Arms* (Brian Rawling, John Reid, Graham
Stack) 11. *I Can't Deny It* (Gregg Alexander, Rick Nowels) 12. *Peach*
[bonus track] (Prince)

2002, *It Had to Be You: The Great American Songbook* (J Records)
1. *You Go to My Head* (J. Fred Coots, Haven Gillespie) 2. *They Can't
Take That Away from Me* (George Gershwin, Ira Gershwin) 3. *The*

Way You Look Tonight (Dorothy Fields, Jerome Kern) 4. *It Had to Be You* (Isham Jones, Gus Kahn) 5. *That Old Feeling* (Lew Brown, Sammy Fain) 6. *These Foolish Things (Remind Me of You)* (Harry Link, Holt Marvell, Jack Strachey) 7. *The Very Thought of You* (Ray Noble) 8. *Moonglow* (Eddie DeLange, Will Hudson, Irving Mills) 9. *I'll Be Seeing You* (Sammy Fain, Irving Kahal) 10. *Ev'ry Time We Say Goodbye* (Cole Porter) 11. *The Nearness of You* (Hoagy Carmichael, Ned Washington) 12. *For All We Know* (J. Fred Coots, Sam M. Lewis) 13. *We'll Be Together Again* (Carl T. Fischer, Frankie Laine) 14. *That's All* (Alan Brandt, Bob Haymes)

2003, *As Time Goes By: The Great American Songbook 2* (J Records)
1. *Time After Time* (Sammy Cahn, Jule Styne) 2. *I'm in the Mood for Love* (Dorothy Fields, Jimmy McHugh) 3. *Don't Get Around Much Anymore* (Duke Ellington, Bob Russell) 4. *Bewitched, Bothered and Bewildered* [duet with Cher] (Lorenz Hart, Richard Rodgers) 5. *Till There Was You* (Meredith Willson) 6. *Until the Real Thing Comes Along* (Sammy Cahn, Saul Chaplin, L. E. Freeman, Mann Holiner, Alberta Nichols) 7. *Where or When* (Lorenz Hart, Richard Rodgers) 8. *Smile* (Charlie Chaplin, Geoffrey Claremont Parsons, John Phillips) 9. *My Heart Stood Still* (Lorenz Hart, Richard Rodgers) 10. *Someone to Watch Over Me* (George Gershwin, Ira Gershwin) 11. *As Time Goes By* [duet with Queen Latifah] (Herman Hupfeld) 12. *I Only Have Eyes for You* (Al Dubin, Harry Warren) 13. *Crazy She Calls Me* (Bob Russell, Carl Sigman) 14. *Our Love Is Here to Stay* (George Gershwin, Ira Gershwin) 15. *My Favourite Things* [bonus track for Japan and U.K. only] (Oscar Hammerstein II, Richard Rodgers)

2004, *Stardust: The Great American Songbook 3* (J Records)
1. *Embraceable You* (George Gershwin, Ira Gershwin) 2. *For Sentimental Reasons* (William Best, Deek Watson) 3. *Blue Moon* [featuring Eric Clapton] (Lorenz Hart, Richard Rodgers) 4. *What a Wonderful World* [featuring Stevie Wonder] (Bob Thiele, George David Weiss) 5. *Stardust* (Hoagy Carmichael, Mitchell Parish) 6. *Manhattan* [duet

with Bette Midler] (Lorenz Hart, Richard Rodgers) 7. *'S Wonderful* (George Gershwin, Ira Gershwin) 8. *Isn't It Romantic?* (Lorenz Hart, Richard Rodgers) 9. *I Can't Get Started* (Vernon Duke, Ira Gershwin) 10. *But Not for Me* (George Gershwin, Ira Gershwin) 11. *A Kiss to Build a Dream On* (Oscar Hammerstein II, Bert Kalmar, Harry Ruby) 12. *Baby, It's Cold Outside* [duet with Dolly Parton] (Frank Loesser) 13. *Night and Day* (Cole Porter) 14. *A Nightingale Sang in Berkeley Square* (Eric Maschwitz, Manning Sherwin)

2005, *Thanks for the Memory: The Great American Songbook, Volume IV* (J Records)
1. *I've Got a Crush on You* [duet with Diana Ross] (George Gershwin, Ira Gershwin) 2. *I Wish You Love* (Albert A. Beach, Léo Chauliac, Charles Trenet) 3. *You Send Me* [duet with Chaka Kahn] (Sam Cooke) 4. *Long Ago (and Far Away)* (Ira Gershwin, Jerome Kern) 5. *Makin' Whoopee* [duet with Elton John] (Walter Donaldson, Gus Kahn) 6. *My One and Only Love* [featuring Roy Hargrove] (Robert Mellin, Guy Wood) 7. *Taking a Chance on Love* (Vernon Duke, Ted Fetter, John Latouche) 8. *My Funny Valentine* (Lorenz Hart, Richard Rodgers) 9. *I've Got My Love to Keep Me Warm* (Irving Berlin) 10. *Nevertheless (I'm in Love with You)* [featuring Dave Koz] (Bert Kalmar, Harry Ruby) 11. *Blue Skies* (Irving Berlin) 12. *Let's Fall In Love* [featuring George Benson] (Harold Arlen, Ted Koehler) 13. *Thanks for the Memory* (Ralph Rainger, Leo Robin) 14. *Cheek to Cheek* [included on the Japan and U.K. versions only] (Irving Berlin) 15. *I've Grown Accustomed to Her Face* [included on the U.K. version only] (Alan Jay Lerner, Frederick Loewe)

2006, *Still the Same . . . Great Rock Classics of Our Time* (J Records)
1. *Have You Ever Seen the Rain?* (John Fogerty) 2. *Fooled Around and Fell in Love* (Elvin Bishop) 3. *I'll Stand by You* (Chrissie Hynde, Thomas Kelly, William Steinberg) 4. *Still the Same* (Bob Seger) 5. *It's a Heartache* (Ronnie Scott, Steve Wolfe) 6. *Day After Day* (Peter Ham) 7. *Missing You* (Mark Leonard, Charles Sandford, John

Waite) 8. *Father and Son* (Cat Stevens) 9. *The Best of My Love* (Glenn Frey, Don Henley, J. D. Souther) 10. *If Not for You* (Bob Dylan) 11. *Love Hurts* (Boudleaux Bryant) 12. *Everything I Own* (David Gates) 13. *Crazy Love* (Van Morrison) 14. *Lay Down Sally* [bonus track] (Eric Clapton, Marcy Levy, George Terry)

2009, *Soulbook* (J Records)
1. *It's the Same Old Song* (Lamont Dozier, Brian Holland, Edward Holland, Jr.) 2. *My Cherie Amour* [featuring Stevie Wonder] (Stevie Wonder) 3. *You Make Me Feel Brand New* [featuring Mary J. Blige] (Thom Bell, Linda Creed) 4. *(Your Love Keeps Lifting Me) Higher and Higher* (Gary Jackson, Raynard Miner, Carl Smith) 5. *Tracks of My Tears* [featuring Smokey Robinson] (Smokey Robinson) 6. *Let It Be Me* [featuring Jennifer Hudson] (Gilbert Bécaud) 7. *Rainy Night in Georgia* (Tony Joe White) 8. *What Becomes of the Broken Hearted* (Jimmy Ruffin) 9. *Love Train* (Kenny Gamble, Leon Huff) 10. *You've Really Got a Hold on Me* (Smokey Robinson) 11. *Wonderful World* (Lou Adler, Herb Alpert, Sam Cooke) 12. *If You Don't Know Me by Now* (Kenny Gamble, Leon Huff) 13. *Just My Imagination* (Barrett Strong, Norman Whitfield)

2010, *Fly Me to the Moon . . . The Great American Songbook Volume V* (J Records)
1. *That Old Black Magic* (Johnny Mercer) 2. *Beyond the Sea* (Jack Lawrence) 3. *I've Got You Under My Skin* (Cole Porter) 4. *What a Difference a Day Makes* (María Méndez Grever) 5. *I Get a Kick Out of You* (Cole Porter) 6. *I've Got the World on a String* (Ted Koehler) 7. *Love Me or Leave Me* (Gus Kahn) 8. *My Foolish Heart* (Ned Washington) 9. *September in the Rain* (Al Dubin, Harry Warren) 10. *Fly Me to the Moon* (Bart Howard) 11. *Sunny Side of the Street* (Dorothy Fields) 12. *Moon River* (Johnny Mercer)

ROD STEWART: LIVE ALBUMS

**1974, *Coast to Coast: Overture and Beginners* (Mercury, U.S./
Warner Bros., U.S.)**
1. *It's All Over Now* (Bobby Womack, Shirley Womack) 2. *Cut Across
Shorty* (Wayne Walker, Marijohn Wilkin) 3. *Too Bad* (Rod Stewart,
Ronnie Wood) / *Every Picture Tells a Story* (Rod Stewart, Ronnie
Wood) 4. *Angel* (Jimi Hendrix) 5. *Stay with Me* (Rod Stewart,
Ronnie Wood) 6. *I Wish It Would Rain* (Roger Penzabene, Barrett
Strong, Norman Whitfield) 7. *I'd Rather Go Blind* (Billy Foster,
Ellington Jordan) 8. *Borstal Boys* (Ian McLagan, Rod Stewart, Ronnie
Wood) /*Amazing Grace* (traditional, arranged by D. Throat) 9. *Jealous
Guy* (John Lennon)

1982, *Absolutely Live* (Warner Bros.)
SIDE A: 1. *The Stripper* (David Rose) 2. *Tonight I'm Yours* (Jim Cregan,
Kevin Savigar, Rod Stewart) 3. *Sweet Little Rock 'n' Roller* (Chuck
Berry) 4. *Hot Legs* (Gary Grainger, Rod Stewart) 5. *Tonight's the Night
(Gonna Be Alright)* (Rod Stewart) 6. *The Great Pretender* (Buck Ram)
SIDE B: 1. *Passion* (Phil Chen, Jim Cregan, Gary Grainger, Kevin
Savigar, Rod Stewart) 2. *She Won't Dance with Me /Little Queenie* (Ben
Jorge, Rod Stewart) 3. *You're in My Heart (The Final Acclaim)* (Rod
Stewart) 4. *Rock My Plimsoul* (Jeffery Rod)
SIDE C: 1. *Young Turks* (Rod Stewart) 2. *Guess I'll Always Love You*
(Tony Brock, Jim Cregan, Robin LeMesurier, Kevin Savigar, Rod
Stewart, Bernie Taupin) 3. *Gasoline Alley* (Rod Stewart, Ronnie
Wood) 4. *Maggie May* (Martin Quittenton, Rod Stewart) 5. *Tear It
Up* (Paul Burlison, Dorsey Burnette, Johnny Burnette)
SIDE D: 1. *Da Ya Think I'm Sexy?* (Carmine Appice, Rod Stewart)
2. *Sailing* (Gavin Sutherland) 3. *I Don't Want to Talk About It* (Danny
Whitten) 4. *Stay with Me* (Rod Stewart, Ronnie Wood)

1993, *unplugged . . . and seated* (Warner Bros.)
1. *Hot Legs* [studio version previously released on *Foot Loose & Fancy
Free*] (Gary Grainger, Rod Stewart) 2. *Tonight's the Night* [studio

version previously released on *A Night on the Town*] (Rod Stewart)
3. *Handbags and Gladrags* [studio version previously released on *An Old Raincoat Won't Ever Let You Down*] (Mike d'Abo) 4. *Cut Across Shorty* [studio version previously released on *Gasoline Alley*] (Wayne Walker, Marijohn Wilkin) 5. *Every Picture Tells a Story* [studio version previously released on *Every Picture Tells a Story*] (Rod Stewart, Ronnie Wood) 6. *Maggie May* [studio version previously released on *Every Picture Tells a Story*] (Martin Quittenton, Rod Stewart) 7. *Reason to Believe* [studio version previously released on *Every Picture Tells a Story*] (Tim Hardin) 8. *People Get Ready* [studio version previously released as a single with Jeff Beck] (Curtis Mayfield) 9. *Have I Told You Lately* [studio version previously released on *Vagabond Heart*] (Van Morrison) 10. *Tom Traubert's Blues (Waltzing Matilda)* [studio version previously released on *Lead Vocalist*] (Tom Waits) 11. *The First Cut Is the Deepest* [studio version previously released on *A Night on the Town*] (Cat Stevens) 12. *Mandolin Wind* [studio version previously released on *Every Picture Tells a Story*] (Rod Stewart) 13. *Highgate Shuffle* [previously unreleased] (arranged by Rod Stewart) 14. *Stay with Me* [studio version previously released on *A Nod Is as Good as a Wink . . . to a Blind Horse* by the Faces] (Rod Stewart, Ronnie Wood) 15. *Having a Party* [previously unreleased] (Sam Cooke) 16. *Gasoline Alley* [bonus track on the *unplugged . . . and seated Collector's Edition*; studio version previously released on *Gasoline Alley*] (Rod Stewart, Ronnie Wood) 17. *Forever Young* [bonus track on the *unplugged . . . and seated Collector's Edition*/studio version previously released on *Out of Order*] (Jim Cregan, Kevin Savigar, Rod Stewart)

THE FACES: STUDIO ALBUMS

1970, *First Step* (Warner Bros.)
1. *Wicked Messenger* (Bob Dylan) 2. *Devotion* (Ronnie Lane) 3. *Shake Shudder Shiver* (Ronnie Lane, Ronnie Wood) 4. *Stone* (Ronnie Lane) 5. *Around the Plynth* (Rod Stewart, Ronnie Wood) 6. *Flying* (Ronnie

Lane, Rod Stewart, Ronnie Wood) 7. *Pineapple and the Monkey* (Ronnie Wood) 8. *Nobody Knows* (Ronnie Lane, Ronnie Wood) 9. *Looking Out the Window* (Kenney Jones, Ian McLagan) 10. *Three Button Hand Me Down* (Ian McLagan, Rod Stewart)

1971, *Long Player* (Warner Bros.)
1. *Bad 'n' Ruin* (Ian McLagan, Rod Stewart) 2. *Tell Everyone* (Ronnie Lane) 3. *Sweet Lady Mary* (Ronnie Lane, Rod Stewart, Ronnie Wood) 4. *Richmond* (Ronnie Lane) 5. *Maybe I'm Amazed* (Paul McCartney) 6. *Had Me a Real Good Time* (Ronnie Lane, Rod Stewart, Ronnie Wood) 7. *On the Beach* (Ronnie Lane, Ronnie Wood) 8. *I Feel So Good* (Big Bill Broonzy) 9. *Jerusalem* (traditional, arranged by Ronnie Wood)

1971, *A Nod Is as Good as a Wink . . . to a Blind Horse* (Warner Bros.)
1. *Miss Judy's Farm* (Rod Stewart, Ronnie Wood) 2. *You're So Rude* (Ronnie Lane, Ian McLagan) 3. *Love Lives Here* (Ronnie Lane, Rod Stewart, Ronnie Wood) 4. *Last Orders Please* (Ronnie Lane) 5. *Stay with Me* (Rod Stewart, Ronnie Wood) 6. *Debris* (Ronnie Lane) 7. *Memphis, Tennessee* [incorrectly titled on original U.S. pressings of the album as simply *Memphis*] (Chuck Berry) 8. *Too Bad* (Rod Stewart, Ronnie Wood) 9. *That's All You Need* (Rod Stewart, Ronnie Wood)

1973, *Ooh La La* (Warner Bros.)
1. *Silicone Grown* (Rod Stewart, Ronnie Wood) 2. *Cindy Incidentally* (Ian McLagan, Rod Stewart, Ronnie Wood) 3. *Flags and Banners* (Ronnie Lane, Rod Stewart) 4. *My Fault* (Ian McLagan, Rod Stewart, Ronnie Wood) 5. *Borstal Boys* (Ian McLagan, Rod Stewart, Ronnie Wood) 6. *Fly in the Ointment* (Kenney Jones, Ronnie Lane, Ian McLagan, Ronnie Wood) 7. *If I'm on the Late Side* (Ronnie Lane, Rod Stewart) 8. *Glad and Sorry* (Ronnie Lane) 9. *Just Another Honky* (Ronnie Lane) 10. *Ooh La La* (Ronnie Lane, Ronnie Wood)

THE FACES: LIVE ALBUM

1974, *Coast to Coast: Overture and Beginners* (Mercury, US/Warner Bros., US)

1. *It's All Over Now* (Bobby Womack, Shirley Womack) 2. *Cut Across Shorty* (Wayne Walker, Marijohn Wilkin) 3. *Too Bad* (Rod Stewart, Ronnie Wood)/*Every Picture Tells a Story* (Rod Stewart, Ronnie Wood) 4. *Angel* (Jimi Hendrix) 5. *Stay with Me* (Rod Stewart, Ronnie Wood) 6. *I Wish It Would Rain* (Roger Penzabene, Barrett Strong, Norman Whitfield) 7. *I'd Rather Go Blind* (Billy Foster, Ellington Jordan) 8. *Borstal Boys* (Ian McLagan, Rod Stewart, Ronnie Wood)/*Amazing Grace* (traditional, arranged by D. Throat) 9. *Jealous Guy* (John Lennon)

ROD STEWART AND THE JEFF BECK GROUP

1968, *Truth* (Columbia)

1. *Shapes of Things* (Jim McCarty, Keith Relf, Paul Samwell Smith) 2. *Let Me Love You* (Rod Stewart) 3. *Morning Dew* (Bonnie Dobson, Tim Rose) 4. *You Shook Me* (Lenore Dixon) 5. *Ol' Man River* (Jerome Kern, Oscar Hammerstein II) 6. *Greensleeves* (traditional, arranged by Jeffrey Rod) 7. *Rock My Plimsoul* (Jeffrey Rod) 8. *Beck's Bolero* (Jimmy Page) 9. *Blues de Luxe* (Rod Stewart) 10. *I Ain't Superstitious* (Willie Dixon)

1969, *Beck-Ola* (Columbia)

1. *All Shook Up* (Otis Blackwell, Elvis Presley) 2. *Spanish Boots* (Jeff Beck, Rod Stewart, Ronnie Wood) 3. *Girl from Mill Valley* (Nicky Hopkins) 4. *Jailhouse Rock* (Jerry Leiber, Mike Stoller) 5. *Plynth (Water Down the Drain)* (Nicky Hopkins, Rod Stewart, Ronnie Wood) 6. *The Hangman's Knee* (Jeff Beck, Nicky Hopkins, Tony Newman, Rod Stewart, Ronnie Wood) 7. *Rice Pudding* (Jeff Beck, Nicky Hopkins, Tony Newman, Ronnie Wood)

ROD STEWART AND THE STEAMPACKET

1992, *The First Supergroup: Steampacket Featuring Rod Stewart* (Valley Media Inc.)
1. *Back at the Chicken Shack* (Jimmy Smith) 2. *The In-Crowd* (Billy Page) 3. *Baby Take Me* (Jo Armstead, Nickolas Ashford, Valerie Simpson) 4. *Can I Get a Witness* (Lamont Dozier, Brian Holland, Edward Holland, Jr.) 5. *Baby Baby* (unknown) 6. *Holy Smoke* (unknown) 7. *Cry Me a River* (Arthur Hamilton) 8. *Oh Baby Don't You Do It* (Lamont Dozier, Brian Holland, Edward Holland, Jr.) 9. *Lord Remember Me* (unknown)

Photography Credits

Pages ii–iii: Graphic based on a photograph by Penny Lancaster

All images in the photo inserts are courtesy of the author, with the following exceptions:

Insert 1 *Page 2:* Getty Images (above) / *Page 6:* Redferns (below, large) / *Page 7:* Getty Images/Michael Ochs Archives/Stringer (above); Ray Stevenson/Rex Features (below) / *Page 8:* Getty Images

Insert 2 *Page 1:* Redferns
Page 2: Getty Images (above); Alan Messer/RexUSA (below left); Redferns (below right) / *Page 3:* Redferns / *Page 4:* Richard Upper (below) / *Page 5:* Mirrorpix (above); SSPL via Getty Images (below) / *Page 7:* SSPL via Getty Images / *Page 8:* Redferns

Insert 3 *Page 1:* WireImage (above); Mirrorpix (below)
Page 2: SSPL via Getty Images (above); SSPL via Getty Images (below)
Page 3: Penny Lancaster (below)
Page 4: Courtesy of Jim Cregan (above and below)
Page 5: Getty Images (above); Courtesy of Annie Challis (below right)
Page 6: Mirrorpix (above); PA (below)

Insert 4 *Page 1:* WireImage (above); Courtesy of Annie Challis (left column) / *Page 2:* Steve Crise (above and below) / *Page 3:* Larry Busacca (below left); Penny Lancaster (below right) / *Page 7:* Getty Images (above left)

Every reasonable effort has been made to contact all copyright holders, but if there are any errors or omissions, we will insert the appropriate acknowledgment in subsequent printings of this book.

INDEX

Blind Prayer ❦ An Old Raincoat Won't Ever Let Yor
❦ Gasoline Alley ❦ Lady Day ❦ Jo's Lament ❦
Wind ❦ True Blue ❦ Lost Paraguayos ❦ Italian
Toot ❦ Three Time Loser ❦ Alright for an Hour ❦
Still Love You ❦ Tonight's the Night (Gonna Be Alr
❦ The Balltrap ❦ Hot Legs ❦ You're Insane ❦
Got a Nerve ❦ I Was Only Joking ❦ Da Ya Thin
Best Days of My Life ❦ Is That the Thanks I Get?
Last Summer ❦ Scarred and Scared ❦ Better Off
❦ Oh God, I Wish I Was Home Tonight ❦ Gi' Me
Special ❦ Say It Ain't True ❦ Tonight I'm Yours
Only a Boy ❦ Jealous ❦ Sonny ❦ Young Turks ❦
❦ Move Me ❦ Body Wishes ❦ Sweet Surrender ❦
Blaster ❦ Ready Now ❦ Strangers Again ❦ Sat
❦ Camouflage ❦ Trouble ❦ Here to Eternity ❦
Take Me Home ❦ Red Hot in Black ❦ In My Ow
❦ Lost in You ❦ The Wild Horse ❦ Lethal Dose
❦ When I Was Your Man ❦ Almost Illegal ❦ R
No Holding Back ❦ Moment of Glory ❦ If Only
We Were the New Boys ❦ Too Bad ❦ Stay with M
Guess I'll Always Love You ❦ Around the Plynth
❦ Sweet Lady Mary ❦ Had Me a Real Good Tim
Need ❦ Silicone Grown ❦ Cindy Incidentally ❦
Let Me Love You ❦ Blues de Luxe ❦ Spanish Boo